W9-AOG-899

Spanish Picaresque Fiction

Spanish Picaresque Fiction

A NEW LITERARY HISTORY

Peter N. Dunn

Cornell University Press

Ithaca and London

CARL A. RUDISILL LIBRARY
LENOIR-RHYNE COLLEGE

This book is published with the aid of grants from the Thomas and
Catharine McMahon Memorial Fund of Wesleyan University and
The Program for Cultural Cooperation between Spain's Ministry of Culture
and United States Universities.

Copyright © 1993 by Cornell University

All rights reserved. Except for brief quotations in a review, this book, or parts
thereof, must not be reproduced in any form without permission in writing
from the publisher. For information, address Cornell University Press,
Sage House, 512 East State Street, Ithaca, New York 14850.

First published 1993 by Cornell University Press.

International Standard Book Number 0-8014-2800-9
Library of Congress Catalog Card Number 92-36854
Printed in the United States of America
Librarians: Library of Congress cataloging information
appears on the last page of the book.

⊗ The paper in this book meets the minimum requirements
of the American National Standard for Information Sciences—
Permanence of Paper for Printed Library Materials, ANSI Z39.48-1984.

To the memory of
Nicholas (1957–1988)
Pamela (1929–1989)

who would have smiled to see it finished

Contents

Contents

Preface

Both picaresque novels and detective stories are defined by reference to a figure whose prototype exists in the real world at the time of writing. Each is mobile, and each is tricky; there the resemblance ends. The detective comes to the scene of events from outside, follows their development at the same time that we do, and attempts to uncover their cause. The picaro is the center of his world, creates himself, and is his own justification. We know what a detective is and does, but there is little agreement on who in the real world should properly be called a picaro, or on the relation between a fictional picaro and his world or between one novel and another.

There has been no lack of theorizing on the picaresque, but the enterprise has been frustrating: the stronger the theory, the fewer the works it is able to encompass. Why do picaros vary so greatly in their relationships with their world and with their own past selves? Why are theories that seek inclusiveness incoherent? This book grew out of a realization that the texts we read and the way we describe them are not consistent: that the way we have classified them has determined what we find in them.

My subtitle, *A New Literary History*, inevitably promises more than it can deliver, but it is intended to indicate both the book's scope and its limits. It does not pretend to give complete interpretations of any of the novels discussed in it. In the final analysis, the interpretations are controlled, as far as may be possible, by each author's desire to create a space for his own work. This space is more often than not a place of contention, so that reading the differences between novels and what is at stake in the differences is more important than balanced critical appraisal. I also try to envisage the publics and their expectations. These matters are conjectural, but the attempt must be made if we are to reach an understanding of the texts' past meaning; their significance for the present will lack depth and density without the historicizing effort.

Procedurally, this book is unusual, so a few words of guidance may be helpful. In the first chapter I examine the problems of current theories of the picaresque as well as those of genre theory generally. It is essential to do so if we are to understand the problems that underlie our reading of individual texts, and of history. I realize that in devoting close attention to difficulties created by the prevailing critical model, I am creating a negative impression. This may be the appropriate place, then, to redress the balance and to acknowledge my intellectual debt to those scholars who formulated the model and whose keen insight illuminated my understanding of individual works. If the theoretical model building of Claudio Guillén, Fernando Lázaro Carreter, and Francisco Rico had not been supported by fine scholarship and clarity of argument, there would be less need to point out how their theory runs counter to their best critical readings.

Most of the rest of Part One and the whole of Part Two are devoted to the three canonical works, *Lazarillo de Tormes*, *Guzmán de Alfarache*, and *La vida del buscón*. This choice was unavoidable, because every theory of the picaresque novel, every proposed generic model, stands or falls on the relationship it establishes among these founding texts. Chapter 2 presents structures, codes, traces in the principal novels not only of one another but of other kinds of literature, from Byzantine romance to oral anecdotes. An important aim of this chapter is to foreground neglected relationships and their consequences: to show how each novel, rather than helping to build a genre, disrupts our reading of its predecessor and directs us to types and discourses other than its own.

The early modern age in Europe is a critical moment in the history of consciousness, when the social base that structured identity was transformed, as Natalie Zemon Davis, Stephen Greenblatt, Timothy Reiss, and others have shown. The constitution of the self should be of crucial importance to the historical critic of picaresque fiction, whose canonical texts promote an urban realism within the mode of autobiography. I do not think that the realism itself can be understood unless it is read within two overlapping frames: the rhetoric of verisimilitude and the notion of fictional (possible) worlds. The picaresque journey (an ironized quest plot) demands to be studied as a frustrated rite of passage in the context of the dislocation of social structures. In Chapter 4 I offer a brief presentation of the logical model (or game) of "possible worlds" followed by an account of the "world" of each novel, as the actantial field of each protagonist, with its own criteria of plausibility and consistency. These novels have also been claimed to be the earliest examples of the representation of consciousness and of the representation of the self in fiction, and this is the subject of Chapter 5. Once again we find great variation among the texts, as well as very narrow conventional limits within which this representation was confined: Lázaro as a sequence of remembered roles and functions; Guzmán's retrospective monologues created from the discourses of scholastic psychology, prayer manuals, and the Augustinian ideology of memory; Quevedo's travesty of all forms of self-presentation. Chapters 6, on Cervantes, and 7, on the female rogues (*pícaras*), can be approached without prior explanation. Chapter 8 surveys a range of works that show the spreading fashion for low-life adventure and documentation, works in which picaresque turns picturesque, mere decor for fictions that flatter upper-class pretensions.

Chapter 9 returns to questions raised earlier, but from a different standpoint. In Part One I undertake to deconstruct the picaresque genre and to rehistoricize the individual texts; to restore to individual works levels of significance that have been repressed by their placement in linear sequence, as beads on the string of "the picaresque novel." I conclude with an attempt to historicize the literary picaresque enterprise as a whole, within an anthropology of the fiction and its culture. I do not know if we can ever answer satisfactorily all of the questions raised by this literature. Why these low-life actions and settings, for example? What did it (and

Preface

does it now) mean, this *nostalgie de la boue*, in a society that was so
addicted to propriety, so snobbish, so contemptuous of the low-
born, so obsessed with status, propriety, and decorum? Criticism
has emerged from its puritanical period of prohibition; referential
issues are back with new urgency.

I gratefully acknowledge the award of a fellowship from the
John Simon Guggenheim Foundation during the academic year
1990–91; it gave me the time and the encouragement to write in
difficult circumstances.

Some of these chapters contain pages that have appeared in
articles previously published. My grateful acknowledgments go to
the editors of *Dispositio, Bulletin of Hispanic Studies, Cervantes,* and
Revista de Estudios Hispánicos, and to the publisher Juan de la Cuesta for some pages in a festschrift volume.

I have received friendly encouragement and helpful comments
from colleagues and friends in the United States and in Great Brit-
ain. Chapter 1 began as a lecture, which they have heard in one
version or another over the years, and from their responses I concluded that the subject was in need of a book. I hope the book will
not disappoint them. I particularly thank those colleagues who
have given up their time to read and make helpful suggestions on
individual chapters: Mary M. Gaylord, Diana S. Goodrich, Yvonne
Jehenson.

All translations are my own.

PETER N. DUNN

Middletown, Connecticut

Abbreviations

Primary Texts

Cervantes   Miguel de Cervantes, *Novelas ejemplares*, ed. Harry Sieber, 2 vols. (Madrid: Cátedra, 1982).

DQ   Miguel de Cervantes, *Don Quixote*, ed. Luis Andrés Murillo, 2 vols. (Madrid: Castalia, 1982).

Estebanillo González   *La vida y hechos de Estebanillo González*, ed. Antonio Carreira and Jesús Antonio Cid, 2 vols. (Madrid: Cátedra, 1990).

Guía.   Antonio Liñán y Verdugo, *Guía y avisos de forasteros que vienen a la Corte de Madrid*. Madrid: Imprenta de la *Revista de Archivos, Bibliotecas y Museos*, 1923.

Guzmán   Mateo Alemán, *Guzmán de Alfarache*, in *La novela picaresca española*, ed. Francisco Rico (Barcelona: Planeta, 1967).

Lazarillo   *Lazarillo de Tormes*, in *La novela picaresca*, ed. Francisco Rico (Barcelona: Planeta, 1967).

Pinciano   Alonso López Pinciano, *Philosophia antigua poética*, ed. Alfredo Carballo Picazo, 3 vols. (Madrid: C.S.I.C., Instituto Miguel de Cervantes, 1973).

PL   *Patrologiae cursus completus: Series Latina*, ed. J. P. Migne, 221 vols. (Paris, 1884–1904.)

Abbreviations

Valbuena   *La novela picaresca española*, ed. Angel Valbuena Prat, 2d ed.
   (Madrid: 1946).
Viaje Agustín de Rojas Villandrando, *El viaje entretenido*, ed. Jean
   Pierre Ressot (Madrid: Castalia, 1972).

Secondary Sources

AC   *Anales Cervantinos*
BAE   Biblioteca de Autores Españoles
BHi   *Bulletin Hispanique*
BHS   *Bulletin of Hispanic Studies*
BRAE   *Boletín de la Real Academia Española*
CH   *Cuadernos Hispanoamericanos*
CI   *Critical Inquiry*
CL   *Comparative Literature*
HR   *Hispanic Review*
JAAC   *Journal of Aesthetics and Art Criticism*
JEEH   *Journal of European Economic History*
JHP   *Journal of Hispanic Philology*
KRQ   *Kentucky Romance Quarterly*
MLN   *MLN: Modern Language Notes*
MLR   *Modern Language Review*
NLH   *New Literary History*
NRFH   *Nueva Revista de Filología Hispánica*
P&P   *Past and Present*
Picaresca   *La picaresca: Orígenes, textos y estructuras*, ed. Manuel
            Criado de Val (Madrid: Fundación Universitaria Española,
            1979).
PMLA   *PMLA: Publications of the Modern Language Association of
            America*
RCEH   *Revista Canadiense de Estudios Hispánicos*
REH   *Revista de Estudios Hispánicos*
RFE   *Revista de Filología Española*
YFS   *Yale French Studies*

PART ONE

GENRE AND READING

1

Genre as Problem

Interest in picaresque literature has surged in tandem with the attention devoted to narrative by theorists and historians of literature.[1] For the historically minded reader, the attraction of Spanish picaresque narratives is not particularly surprising; these works have long been regarded as a highly sensitive mirror of the social conditions and mode of life of the time in which they were written, and this incorporation of material from the world of everyday has been seen as a formal rejection of the mode of romance and thus as an important step toward the institution of the modern novel.[2] Twentieth-century novelists have helped to intensify this interest by writing works to which the label "picaresque" can be attached. One might wish that genre identification were a simple matter of truth in labeling, and that questions could be referred to a bureau of standards. The fact is that the generic identity of "the Spanish picaresque novel" and the place accorded to it as a sort of

1. Joseph L. Laurenti's *Bibliography of Picaresque Literature* (1973) contains 2,439 items; the *Supplement* (1981) lists works published almost entirely between 1973 and 1978, and they number 1,009.
2. This is a recurrent motif in the literary history of picaresque fiction since Chandler's *Romances of Roguery* (1899). See more recently Reed 1981.

historic separator of novel from romance remain open to question. The opposition novel/romance that was broached in the eighteenth century no longer carries conviction.

Genres are instruments not simply of critical classification or prescription but of meaning and interpretation. Historically and institutionally they rest upon consensus. They mediate between writer and public by shaping a common "horizon of expectations"[3] that is rationalized as a set of consistency criteria. On the relation of reading to generic expectation, E. D. Hirsch has written that

> in most cases our expectations are not baffled and defeated. We found the types of meanings we expected to find because what we found was in fact powerfully influenced by what we expected. . . . Thus, while it is not acccurate to say that an interpretation is hopelessly dependent on the generic conception with which an interpreter happens to start, it is nonetheless true that his interpretation is dependent on the last, unrevised generic conception with which he starts. All understanding of verbal meaning is necessarily genre-bound. (1967:76)

Judgments of particular works are formed upon the basis of implicit assumptions about genre; conversely, or complementarily, a dominant theory of genre will favor this or that reading of the works in question. This circularity is not unfamiliar in criticism. Two conditions, however, are peculiar to discussions of Spanish picaresque fiction. First, a sense of ideological challenge has been evident in the responses of critics and commentators since the earliest comprehensive studies were made in the late nineteenth century. Second, the interplay, the mutual determining of the concept of genre and of the meaning and significance ascribed to texts, has been left largely unexamined. When we scrutinize the criteria by which the canonical works are identified and privileged, we note two kinds of violence that result from this demarcation. The first is the repression or devaluation of highly significant individual differences between these novels; the second is the failure to perceive the relation between them and the works not classified as picaresque. We find on the one hand the peculiar dynamics set up within

3. The phrase is borrowed from Jauss 1982.

the group, and on the other a rupture of continuity across the field of literary discourse. Discussion of picaresque literature has become trapped in the discursive categories that recent literary history has elaborated.

What is conveniently—I would say inconveniently—known as "the picaresque novel" consists of narrative fictions that vary in length, from novellas, such as *Lazarillo de Tormes* and a couple of short pieces by Cervantes, to the immensely long and complex *Guzmán de Alfarache* by Mateo Alemán. By the loosest and most inclusive criteria there are some twenty works in all.[4] They occupy a historical period that extends from the publication of *Lazarillo de Tormes* in 1554 to the mid-1640s. Since there is an almost complete hiatus between *Lazarillo* and Part I of *Guzmán de Alfarache* in 1599, the period of continuous creativity spans less than fifty years. The earliest works are written in the first person, and this autobiographical mode is assumed to be most characteristic. Many later ones, however, are composed in the third person. All the protagonists are nonheroic; some struggle in poverty, some become crimi-

4. Works commonly referred to as picaresque:
Anon., *Vida de Lazarillo de Tormes* (1554)
Anon., *Segunda parte de "Lazarillo de Tormes"* (1555)
Mateo Alemán, *Guzmán de Alfarache* (1599)
Mateo Luján de Sayavedra [pseud. of Juan Martí], *Segunda parte de "Guzmán de Alfarache"* (1602)
Mateo Alemán, *Segunda parte de "Guzmán de Alfarache"* (1604)
Gregorio González, "El guitón Honofre" (unpublished ms., 1605)
Francisco de Quevedo, *La vida del buscón* (ms. 1605?; published 1626)
Francisco López de Ubeda, *La pícara Justina* (1605)
Miguel de Cervantes, *Rinconete y Cortadillo* and *El coloquio de los perros* (1613)
Alonso Jerónimo de Salas Barbadillo, *La ingeniosa Elena, hija de Celestina* (1612, 1614)
Juan de Luna, *Segunda parte de "Lazarillo de Tormes"* (Paris, 1620)
Juan Cortés de Tolosa, *Lazarillo de Manzanares* (1620)
Vicente Espinel, *La vida de Marcos de Obregón* (1618)
Jerónimo de Alcalá Yáñez, *El donado hablador, Alonso, mozo de muchos amos* (Part I, 1624; Part II, 1626)
Alonso de Castillo Solórzano, *El proteo de Madrid* (1625); *Las harpías en Madrid* (1631); *La niña de los embustes, Teresa de Manzanares* (1632); *Las aventuras del bachiller Trapaza* (1637); *La garduña de Sevilla* (1642)
Antonio Enríquez Gómez, *La vida de don Gregorio Guadaña* (1644)
Vida y hechos de Estebanillo González, hombre de buen humor. Compuesto por el mismo (1646)

nals or confidence men, whereas others make good. Some are women who separate men from their money in the time-honored ways.

The problem became visible when the picaresque narrative, like the picaro himself, left home. From Charles Sorel's *Vraie histoire comique de Francion* (1623, 1626, 1633) and Alain-René Lesage's *Histoire de Gil Blas de Santillane* (1715, 1724, 1735) to Daniel Defoe and Tabias Smollett; from Hans von Grimmelshausen's *Simplicissimus* (1669) to Thomas Mann's *Confessions of Felix Krull* (1954) and Günther Grass's *Tin Drum* (1954) and a great swarm of twentieth-century fiction, the progeny is immense, if the paternity is acknowledged. In the last few decades reviewers have applied epithet "picaresque" so indiscriminately to any somewhat unscrupulous adventurer that it has little definition. This problem of international critical hijacking was summed up by W. M. Frohock in 1969, in an article with the apocalyptic title "The Failing Center," when he said that for every new novel there is a critic waiting to find something picaresque in it.[5]

Can the term "picaresque" be used with greater precision? In 1895 the Dutch scholar Fonger de Haan wrote a succinct description of picaresque narrative as he saw it, as "the prose autobiography of a person, real or imaginary, who strives, by fair means and by foul, to make a living, and in relating his experiences in various classes of society, points out the evils which come under his observation" (1903:8). This set—struggle, observation, social criticism—has a familiar ring and it vibrates in tune with the judicial character of much nineteenth-century criticism, and with that century's idea of what literature, following Honoré de Balzac, Charles Dickens, Benito Pérez Galdós, and Emile Zola, *should* present. The

---

5. Frohock 1969. The wide and loose application of the term "picaresque" to fiction of many periods and places has created a problem of a different order from the one I introduce here. Ulrich Wicks (1974) argues for a spectrum of narrative modes on which "picaresque" can occupy a place. His "picaresque mode" embodies an "essential picaresque situation" (242a) and, following Northrop Frye (1957), a vision of a world that is worse than the reader's. Wicks's concern is to restore credit to the word, to avoid "banishing the term 'picaresque' from all but the historically definable genre of *la novela picaresca*" (241b). I do not exempt the concept *novela picaresca* from examination but offer a critical review of what it covers, and question the assumption that it is no longer problematic.

progress of Lazarillo and some later protagonists from master to master was interpreted as indicating a novel of manners, and the portraits of the masters themselves constituted social satire.[6] (It was natural perhaps that readers who had imbibed nineteenth-century liberalism and who shared the Victorian faith in the civilizing and liberating power of humane letters should find themselves unable to contemplate representations of Catholic authoritarian Spain except as satire. The practice of reencoding was not new; the medievals could come to terms with the scandalous works of the pagan past only by reencoding them as allegory.)

The concept "picaresque novel" in fact was constituted during the second half of that century from a set of overlapping cultural matrices—the absolute singularity of individuals; the necessary struggles of individuals for freedom within their social bounds; the moral value of literature; and, on a lower level of generality, the decadence of Spanish society in the sixteenth and seventeenth centuries—and from a biological concept of the development of literature, which sometimes adopted the model of the growth, maturity, and decay of the individual organism, and at other times promoted an evolutionary progress. It is against the persistence of these historical fictions that critics and literary historians have had to struggle in our century.

The rise of various types of formalist criticism in this century drew attention away from the predominantly social and ideological concerns and toward narrative devices and patterns; phenomenological and existentialist readings have discovered the functioning of narrative time, the dual consciousness of the narrator who makes himself the subject of his own narration.[7] In the case of Lazarillo de Tormes's three principal masters—the blind man, the priest, and the squire—they do not cease to represent a society emblematically in its three estates. But by virtue of their presentation in Lázaro's first-person narrative, they are unified also on an

6. Notably Chandler (1899), but also earlier: e.g., George Ticknor's *History of Spanish Literature* (1849). David Rowland (1586/1924), *Lazarillo*'s first translator, recommends it, for "by reading hereof, such as have not travailed Spaine, may as well discerne much of the manners and customs of that country, as those that have there long time continued" (3).

7. Guillén 1957, Gilman 1966, Rico 1984. I mention these works as paradigmatic, not as a definitive list.

existential plane. They provide the hard experience of Lazarillo the boy, but they also shape the consciousness of Lázaro the man and the writer. So if in the early chapters his world is framed in satire, the figure of Lázaro feeds back into the satire through his activities as an adult and, most radically, through his activity as a writer constituting himself in words before his reader's eyes, in the expectation of the reader's indulgence and admiration. We now read *Lazarillo de Tormes* as a text that ensnares us in its own operations.

Critics have attempted to fix a typology or generic model for the picaresque novel. In what has become an influential paper, "Toward a Definition of the Picaresque,"[8] Claudio Guillén distinguishes four separate uses of "picaresque": (1) a picaresque genre; (2) a group of novels that (in his words) "deserve to be called picaresque in the strict sense—usually in agreement with the original Spanish pattern"; (3) another group that can be considered picaresque only "in a broader sense of the term"; and (4) a picaresque "myth": "an essential situation or structure derived from the novels themselves" (1971:71). These categories are not altogether clear; but rather than spend time on them individually, let us look at the second, the "Spanish pattern." Guillén ascribes to it the following formal and thematic properties:

The picaro protagonist is an orphan cast out into the world, who *becomes* a rascal (75–76).

The autobiographical mode enables us to view both the inner and the outer man (81–82).

The protagonist has to discover values anew, like "a godless Adam" (79).

He is "a half outsider, unable either to join or to reject his fellow men" (80).

The stress is on the material level of existence (83).

The plot is episodic (84–85).

Then, referring back to the picaro, Guillén characterizes him as a dissembler or a hypocrite, and in a lapidary phrase he says: "The picaresque novel is, quite simply, the autobiography of a liar" (92).

Some of the qualities attributed to the "Spanish pattern" are less essential—and less clearly defined—than others. I could add

8. Presented at the Third Congress of the International Comparative Literature Association, 1961. The paper is reprinted in Guillén's *Literature as System* (1971).

to the list: In *Lazarillo*, *Guzmán*, and *El buscón* the ending is an ironic echo or restatement of the situation at the beginning. But nothing that Guillén says can apply to more than a few of the novels that anthologists persist in calling picaresque, neither the autobiographical mode nor the outsider status (a concept whose precise field is difficult to determine when it is projected back into early modern Europe) nor the primal innocence.

Guillén's prescriptions were taken up and reformulated by Fernando Lázaro Carreter (1972)[9] and reinforced by Francisco Rico. Lázaro focused on the institution of the genre; a picaresque genre existed, he argued, when *Guzmán de Alfarache* incorporated structural elements derived from *Lazarillo*. Their common features then provided a paradigm for subsequent writers. As Rico observed, a genre is not initiated by the first work of its kind; it is constituted when characteristic structures are disclosed and found to operate with a generative energy in works that follow. In Lázaro Carreter's scheme, three of *Lazarillo*'s principal elements are developed in *Guzmán*:

1. The story purports to be the autobiography of "an unscrupulous wretch," narrated as a sequence of episodes.

2. The autobiography is articulated by means of a succession of masters, who also provide the pretext for social criticism.

3. The whole narrative is offered as an explanation for the final state of dishonor in which the protagonist finds himself (206–7).

Lázaro Carreter is aware of the possibilities for modification: a writer may develop this or that formal element and vary the relation between narrator and reader. Then, moving silently from theory to history, he maintains that whatever novelties and variations were introduced by later writers, the system continues to cohere; that however disruptive everything after Alemán may appear to be, opposing tendencies pull back to the center (228). Once more, that problematic "center" has escaped scrutiny.

This is a more economical and elegant formulation than Guillén's, though both display evident affinity with Russian formalist criticism.[10] Lázaro Carreter's in particular was an inevitable

9. First read as a paper at the III Congreso de la Asociación Internacional de Hispanistas, Mexico City, 1968.

10. This affinity is evident in their common perception of a dynamic, dialectical relation between coexistent literary forms. The Spanish critics barely

reaction against the heavy stress in earlier academic criticism on definition by reference to content (197). There was the stress on social satire. And the pervasive Christian doctrine of *Guzmán de Alfarache* caused some scholars to look for generic unity in a moral or religious program (e.g., Parker 1967). Also, critics had disagreed over whether *Lazarillo* or *Guzmán de Alfarache* should be regarded as the prototype of the genre. Those of the *Lazarillo* camp have seen in *Guzmán*, with its preoccupation with salvation, an art overwhelmed by the demands of the Counterreformation, or by the author's desire for acceptance (Del Monte 1971, Molho 1972), while Alemán's supporters have seen *Lazarillo* as merely a distant precursor, and confined it to the limbo of the unbaptized (Parker 1967). The solution offered by Lázaro and Rico was to place *Guzmán* over *Lazarillo* and to say that where the formal elements coincide, there is the nucleus of the picaresque genre. This has been the most influential model and is almost universally taken for granted. But the cost in discarded literature is high. The canon shrinks to but two or three "truly" picaresque works. Moreover, Guzmán writes to declare his final regeneration (not his dishonor), and has consistently rejected the notion of honor in its conventional sense, so Guillén ought logically to expel *Guzmán* from the canon!

Claudio Guillén was aware of possible difficulties with his generic model when he wrote that "on a certain level *Guzmán de Alfarache* (a didactic and dogmatic monolith) and *Lazarillo de Tormes* (compassionate and pluralistic) seem nearly antithetical" (1971:142). We should give the antithetical aspects of these and other works a fairer showing than they have so far received.

The dangers of reading our assumptions into the data we study are common to all branches of investigation. The selection and isolation of common factors among the novels introduces a bias into the readings because these common factors are held to constitute a system, a significant structure charged with value. Meanwhile, characteristics not shared by all of the novels lose significance. Generic characteristics are given priority over the specific, the model

---

sketch this connection between the new and the old, whereas the formalists are acutely aware of diachronic intertextuality. See Jauss, "Literary History as Challenge," in Jauss 1972:17.

is privileged over the works from which it is derived. If we take the three works that receive all the attention in studies of picaresque fiction and look at their intertextual relations, we can see clearly that Alemán was using the autobiography of a runaway in a very different way from that of the unknown author of *Lazarillo*, and that Quevedo's *Buscón* makes a social point totally alien to both of the earlier works by giving a travesty of their principal motifs. Identity (as we would expect) is the ground upon which differences are inscribed, while the differences rather than the identity are the vehicles of meaning.

A category overlooked by the creators of the formal model is that of extension, though the Russian formalists Boris Eichenbaum and Yury Tynyanov showed the importance of distinguishing between long and short literary forms.[11] *Guzmán* is about *twelve* times the length of *Lazarillo*. Such a difference must convey qualitative differences, distinct concepts of what the two works aim to achieve and their means of achieving it. One is a brief story in which a young boy, raised in poverty, is given to a blind man as a servant; the other is a very long story in which a boy raised in luxury leaves home of his own choice. Whereas Lázaro's composition is concise, laconic, astringent, Guzmán's is rhetorically expansive, self-revelatory, and overwhelming in its desire to persuade the reader to reject vanity and concern with honor, and to seek salvation and social reintegration. Lázaro is cynically disarming; Guzmán enfolds himself in self-accusation, in the vehemence of "this general confession."[12]

Were one to follow the course of Lazarillo's travels, from the time he leaves home until he establishes himself as a citizen of the "illustrious city of Toledo," one would find many gaps; even so, the scale is minute in comparison with the world of Guzmán, who goes from Seville to Madrid to Barcelona to Genoa to Rome and back to Spain (Alcalá, Madrid, Seville), then out to sea, where the writing ends. Lázaro assures us that he has made a comfortable place for himself; Guzmán writes as a convict on a galley and declares that he is now a new man as a result of his repentance.

11. Victor Erlich, *Russian Formalism: History-Doctrine*, 3rd ed. (New Haven: Yale University Press, 1981), 247.
12. *Guzmán*, II.1.i (484).

Guzmán's is a trajectory that conveys a freight of symbolic meaning, as it links the great political and commercial power centers of the Christian Mediterranean. Both of these novels force us to put problematic quotes around such terms as "success," "to rise," "a new man," but their biases could not be more radically opposed.

Fictional autobiography allows the narrator to develop a double perspective on his past self, but the possible relations between narrator, his past self, and his readers can be enormously variable. The narration may be centered upon the past experiences or upon the recollecting consciousness of the narrator, and may assume an unlimited range of modes and forms, from ribald farce to sentimental romance, from *Robinson Crusoe* to *Treasure Island* to *A la recherche du temps perdu* to *Krapp's Last Tape*. So autobiography, though it limits what can plausibly be presented, is not genre-specific. *Lazarillo* and *Guzmán* may be contrasted also in relation to the designated reader. Lázaro's reader, Vuestra Merced (Your Honor), never appears, and we know almost nothing about him or the authority he represents. Alemán, on the contrary, addresses you and me directly, in two prologues: we are *vulgo* (common) or *discreto* (perceptive) reader, according to how we read, according to whether we choose the story or the message, the *conseja* or the *consejo*. A small pun carries a great weight, but then salvation may turn upon our ability to tune our ear to the word that bears the message. These two books also handle the authority of the writer differently. Lázaro responds to an authority wielded by Vuestra Merced, but he reclaims authority for himself by appealing to experience, the great teacher, and to the "virtue" of having risen in the world. In so doing he relegates Vuestra Merced to the periphery of his narrative. This aspect of the novel, in which we see the act of writing as an attempt by Lázaro to wrest control from Vuestra Merced, is one of the many fascinating tensions in the book. And it is unique, for nowhere else that I am aware of do we find a narrator writing his life, making his claim to exist as he does, in an effort to efface his inquirer, the source of authority, making a book that denies its own first cause. Not, at least, until we come to Samuel Beckett. By comparison, Guzmán's Pauline compulsion to proclaim the truth in season and out of season, to call us to judgment, and to declare the possibility of salvation is relatively uncomplicated. The source to which Guzmán's conscience and his authoritative rhetoric insistently point is outside his life, outside his book. Stable and unmoving, it is God himself, the Author acknowledged by his Christian readers. If Alemán stands behind Guzmán, authorizes him, then behind Alemán is the ultimate Authority. In this relation of the narrator to his life and to his motives for writing, a vast conceptual distance separates *Lazarillo de Tormes* from *Guzmán de Alfarache*. Although they are both autobiographical in presentation, the first-person mode of telling differs structurally and functionally and conveys totally different ideological content in the two works.

The desire to establish a common formal model or typology, then, promotes a search for similar characteristics from which the paradigms for a system can be derived. As a result, it becomes difficult to read an individual text in a way that does not confirm its participation in the system. Insistence upon common structures and shared themes conditions us to offer an analogous response to each case. But such guiding metaphors as "life is a journey," such motifs as "ingenuous boy leaves home," and the first-person narrative are not charged with fixed meanings. On the contrary, they are semantically variable. The generic model is self-defeating insofar as it prevents us from evaluating the radically different meanings that are encoded in identical devices and in homologous patterns.

What I have said about the relation of *Guzmán* to *Lazarillo* can be repeated, with variations, for all the picaresque works that followed: Juan Martí's spurious Part II of *Guzmán* (1602), *La pícara Justina*, and so forth. Quevedo's *Buscón* can be seen as a travesty of Alemán's best-seller for Quevedo's own dyspeptic purposes, rather than as an awkward piece of the puzzle that we have called "the picaresque novel." We can note, too, how *La pícara Justina* (1605) is both a self-parody and also a parody of *Guzmán*: its action dissolves into endless prattle rather than sermons, and moralizings are put conveniently separate at the ends of chapters so the reader can skip them. The protagonist announces that she is about to marry Guzmán de Alfarache: so much for Guzmán's claim to be spiritually regenerated! There is nothing here to remind us of *Lazarillo*. Attention is here fixed not on the object of its messages but on its own codes.

The case of Cervantes would appear to have been settled by the combined authority of Américo Castro (first in 1925 and repeatedly during the rest of a long career) and Carlos Blanco Aguinaga in 1957, both of whom contrast Cervantes in ideological terms with Alemán.[13] I review their arguments in Chapter 6 and will not anticipate them. If critics have neglected the confrontational aspects of the intertextual relations between *Guzmán* and *Lazarillo* and between *Buscón* and *Guzmán* in order to emphasize generic continuity, the reverse has been the case in recent readings of Cervantes. Yet what Cervantes wrote in *Rinconete y Cortadillo* and the *Coloquio de Cipión y Berganza*, in episodes of *Don Quixote* and *Persiles y Sigismunda*, could not have been written without the presence of *Lazarillo* or *Guzmán de Alfarache*. Indeed, he goes much further than other writers in the creative recycling and transformation of the whole repertory of devices and motifs that are commonly referred to as picaresque—a repertory that had only recently been assembled, and that was just as rapidly being dismantled and recombined. The prevailing formalist model of the picaresque novel has had the effect of restricting the canon to a very small handful of works. To read Cervantes as antipicaresque is obviously to reinforce this state of things. By that means, Cervantes can be kept pure, and the ideal picaresque paradigm can be saved from the complication and disruption produced by the presence of Cervantes. The paradigm, however, is flawed and unstable, with or without Cervantes.

Let us now move away from this question of the repressive nature of the generic model and of the canon that it establishes, and turn very briefly to the historical constitution of "the picaresque." We need a clearer vision of the horizon of expectations of readers at specific moments of literary history. Much recent research on and around *Lazarillo*, especially in France, has revealed its relation to folk tales, to the *Golden Ass* of Apuleius, to Petronius, to dialogues of various kinds, as well as its setting in the political debates on poverty and rural migration.[14] It is evident that the first

13. Castro 1925, 1966, 1967; Blanco 1957 (abridged version translated as "Cervantes and the Picaresque Mode: Notes on Two Kinds of Realism," in *Cervantes: A Collection of Critical Essays*, ed. Lowry J. Nelson, 137–51, Twentieth-Century Views [Englewood Cliffs, N.J.: Prentice-Hall, 1967]).

14. Chevalier 1976, 1980; Cros in *Actes: Picaresque européenne* 1976:9–24; Lázaro 1972; Bataillon 1973b; Alexander Scobie, "Petronius, Apuleius, and the Spanish Picaresque Romance," *Words* 2 (1966): 92–100; Cavillac 1983.

14

readers saw it as a comic book. Thanks to Fernando Lázaro Carreter, Maxime Chevalier, and the late Marcel Bataillon, we begin to see what the institution of literature looked like around 1554, when *Lazarillo* appeared, and between that date and 1599, the date of the First Part of *Guzmán de Alfarache*. The institution of literature would look very different, obviously, in 1605 after the tremendous success of the complete *Guzmán*, after *Don Quixote*, *La pícara Justina*, and Lope de Vega's *Peregrino en su patria*. We should try to imagine how *Lazarillo* would be read by a new generation of readers, when it was republished during the 1600s, with much greater success than it had enjoyed previously. And so on, down through the 1620s, 1630s, and 1640s. Literature now would include, of course, the novels, and the semidocumentary fiction such as *Guía y avisos de forasteros que vienen a la Corte de Madrid* and *La desordenada codicia de los bienes ajenos*, because picaresque literature is not to be understood in isolation from such semidocumentary writings.

The vogue for low-life settings begun by *Celestina*, the marginal protagonists, the first-person narrative with its possibilities for irony, these come together in a few unusual works, but they are the means for the radical transformation of *existing* genres and not the installation of a new one. The long romance, which *Guzmán* essentially is, profoundly influences Cervantes' *Persiles y Sigismunda* and other long novels of the following decades that few people now read. In earlier fiction, the principal characters had been stable, and their relation to their world was given and narrowly defined. Their status was inseparable from their identity: a knight, a priest, a merchant, a prince, a man of law, a peasant. Picaresque fiction helps to change that. Picaresque characters and episodes can be found in short novels, poems, autobiographies, plays. Much of this writing is shallow or merely decorative, but then, so is most literature. At its best, this fiction probes the relation of self, role, and society in totally new ways by finding new ironic or parodic or tragicomic forms of the quest narrative.

First-person narration problematizes more than reality, for it offers the whole fictional world as the creation of a self-conscious subject. Discourse of a self-conscious subject, as the *only* discourse of a fictional text, is new in European literature and yet it does not so much create a new genre as revivify and transform existing ones. In addition, the fact that the self-conscious subject is not noble, is an antiheroic or low-life figure, indicates that the traditional authority of the narrator is being subverted. So, too, is the idea of decorum, of *bienséance*, which has always been underwritten by the seemingly objective valuation of social hierarchy. The canonical figures of respect and authority—knights, kings, beautiful ladies—are being abandoned at the same time that the authority of the narrative voice is becoming less absolute.

If that can be said, then it seems that we are talking about something essentially modern. But the features that we call picaresque develop not by forming a tightly self-contained organism of their own but rather by invading, in the manner of a virus, such diverse genres as travel literature, satiric poetry, romance, soldierly adventure, autobiography, ingenious swindles (male and female). A result of this invasion is to give to "verisimilitude" an abrupt shift in the direction of a discourse resembling reportage. Here we touch yet another problem, for topics such as the "picaresque" poverty and marginality and alienation that have been generated within the discourses of twentieth-century social sciences cannot be properly discussed so long as they continue to be presented in purely sociological terms. They must be analyzed in the context of a fundamental aesthetic question: whether what is often perceived as literary realism at that time is representational or expressive in mode. This analysis would carry us into sixteenth-century poetics, but also (and more interestingly and productively) into our contemporary philosophy of "possible worlds." The anthropological models of Victor Turner and his school can also enable us to reframe the aberrant individual in the context of cultural symbolism instead of as simple mimetic documentation.

My attempt at a literary history of picaresque narrative will trace relationships—formal and ideological—as they develop within the "horizon of expectations" of the writers and their readers. Hans Robert Jauss's (1982) formula has called forth some cautionary words from Jonathan Culler:

> . . . . perhaps because of the attraction of an original meaning, Jauss often seems to work from the text itself rather than from information about responses, emphasizing what is new in the themes and techniques of a work. If he began instead with information about responses, he might encounter greater diversity

and chaos; he might find that works are often the objects of fierce disputes rather than answers to questions posed by a homogeneous horizon of expectations. Of course, in many cases we may lack detailed responses from readers of earlier periods, but a *Rezeptionsästhetik* ought at least to exploit as thoroughly as possible any richness and diversity that is available, rather than positing a unified horizon in the hope of discovering the true meaning of a work in its own age. (1981:57)[15]

Despite the scarcity of detailed responses to more than a few works in Spain's "Golden Age," we must attempt to reread these narratives free from our acquired generic expectations.

The history of the concept of genre has wandered uncertainly between two extremes: on the one hand, Benedetto Croce's rejection of the idea of genre in defense of the unique individuality of each work of art and, on the other, the affirmation of the classical forms from Aristotle through Goethe to Northrop Frye. Three basic forms, the epic, the lyric, and the dramatic (Goethe's *Naturformen*), and their concomitant questions of mimesis have dominated Western discussion of the taxonomy of literary works. The attempt to classify literature according to formal criteria of voice and point of view (Frye's "radical of presentation") has serious drawbacks that we cannot overcome simply by multiplying "subgenres," since there is always a point at which subgenres prove to be incompatible one with another or violate the boundaries between the genres that contain them. Also, if there is to be a system, it should enclose the complete universe of genres, including that universe's antimatter and black holes. Appropriate space must be found for the nonrespectable, "parasitical" or "reverse" kinds of literature (parody, satire, riddle, nonsense, and the like) ignored by the restrictive classical systems of genre classification.

At those times when the arts have sought the closest conformity to antique classical canons of form and expression, critical theory has tended to ignore not only the newer forms but also the popular ones. The schema has become rigid, highly codified, hierarchical; many kinds of works are adjudged too lowly or too trivial

15. See also the cautions expressed in Suleiman/Crosman 1980:36–38.

to be admitted to it at all, despite the fact that they are evidently related to the canonical genres in some way. The intertextual relation may be parodic or it may be straight-faced, or it may threaten the social authority by which the established genre is sustained. The heroic epic clearly has enjoyed a superior status during a long period from classical Greek times until the eighteenth century, but a mock-heroic bawdy ballad, however formally accomplished it may be, is excluded from all consideration because of the "low" level of its discourse, its nonheroic action, and its destabilizing effect on the relation between canonical literature and the social order.

A reader of the treatises by Renaissance theorists on literature (Francesco Robortello, Lodovico Castelvetro, Joseph Justus Scaliger, Torquato Tasso, and others) can easily observe that their point of reference is Aristotle, so far as the division of the field of literature is concerned. They imposed ancient categories upon the modern practice and effectively dehistoricized it, much as the early grammarians of the modern vernacular languages had recourse to the paradigms of Latin. The result was the same for both systems: an ideal fixity and the assumption that, however flexible the rules governing the production of new works might be, the types were valid forever. Genres, however, do not remain forever the same, but are continually in a state of change and flux, however determinedly classically minded writers try to keep them bound in fixed rational categories. It is easy for literary historians to take at their own evaluation those categories and the declarations that support them, to privilege their values of order, clarity, and permanence. Literary history, too, has pursued the mirages of order, clarity, and recovery of permanent forms from a world of flux. It is tempting to view the less orderly periods of literary history as aberrations, to expose the ignorance of medieval writers' concepts of comedy and tragedy, for example, or to accept the Renaissance theory that all extensive narrative fiction could be classified as epic in prose.

Modern writing on genres can still become trammeled in the pursuit of eternal or essential characteristics, the search for objective and universal literary properties. Such pursuits, however, eventually lead to the embarrassing discovery that the same genre may be characterized by different qualities at different times in its history; as a result, no typology of, say, tragedy or epic or ode or elegy can claim to be definitive. For the same reason, any attempt to map the various genres and their relations will be valid only for the particular moment at which it is drawn, if at all. Alastair Fowler has referred to the many attempts to revise the Aristotelian system: "But still the genres seem to resist subdivision into any one set of 'universals.' Even what Austin Warren calls the 'ultimates'—poetry, fiction, and drama—cannot reach this taxonomic goal" (1982:239). Every genre has been theorized in terms of internal criteria, and at particular moments in history the practice has been trimmed to conform to these criteria. But when we look at all existing genres, or what are called genres in the universe of literature, we discover that they use *different kinds* of criteria: there are no criteria of consistency for the taxonomic criteria themselves.[16]

Genres not only change over time; they share the literary universe with other genres, they come into existence, expand, shrink, disappear within a continually shifting field. The classical moment of order and stasis is a myth. "A genre does not exist independently" Ralph Cohen points out; "it arises to compete or contrast with other genres, to complement, augment, interrelate with other genres . . . each is defined by reference to the system and its members" (1986:207). Genres are systems, and they, in their turn, are parts of a larger system, which is the world of literature, which in its turn forms part of the larger universe of discursive systems, and so on into other interlocking systems. It is useful to imagine them as an ecosystem, self-sustaining, in constant flux, rather than as a mechanistic or logical system. There is nothing inherently rigid in genre, although, as we have observed, genres have been

16. Paul Zumthor notes that this is part of an inescapable bind: no system will hold, but we cannot think without a system:

On le constate de toute manière: aucune définition n'a de validité universelle; aucune, au sein d'un même secteur spatiotemporel, ne s'applique dans la totalité des cas particuliers. On m'assurait récemment, en Haute-Volta, que pour la plupart des ethnies de ce pays, conte, proverbe et devinette constituent un ensemble fonctionnel dont les éléments se rangent en classes déterminées par l'âge, le sexe, la situation sociale de celui qui les prononce, et parfois le moment du jour ou de la nuit où il se fait entendre. Les exemples foisonnent, de cet incessant dérapage hors des catégories . . . quoique sans catégories aucune critique ne soit possible." ("Perspectives générales," in Demerson 1984:11–12).

rigidly defined by theorists at particular times, in response to social and ideological pressures, and under the influence of intellectual models that stress permanence and formal perfection. The greater part of European intellectual history has developed under the aegis of such models (Ptolemaic, Euclidean, distinction-making, and mechanistic paradigms) until the scientific and philosophical revolutions of the nineteenth century sponsored more open-ended and mutually regulating structures of thought. As Cohen declares, "Genres are open systems; they are groupings of texts by critics to fulfill certain ends. And each genre is related to and defined by others to which it is related" (210). Genres are not "natural forms," but that is not the whole story. Before they are taken over and developed as taxonomic systems by critics and historians of literature, they have a prior existence in the endless sequence of transactions that take place between the producers and the consumers of literature, most visibly between the oral performer and the audience, in more obscure and more complex ways between writers and readers. The expectations of both writers and readers have an active role not only in defining and establishing genres but also in continually modifying them, creating new possibilities, and, in periods of cultural assurance and reflexivity, turning genres against themselves.

The futility of the search for origins, exposed by Jacques Derrida and Michel Foucault, applies to the history of genres as well as to any other cultural practice. The question of the origin of genres makes sense only as a systematic problem, not as a problem of history; or, if it is a problem of history, it belongs to the history of naming, of taxonomy, not the history of forms. Looking at the question both historically and systematically, one can say only that genres come into existence by the transformation of existing genres (Fowler 1971, Todorov 1976). We can no more search for the "ultimate" origin of genres than we can penetrate to the historical beginnings of language. For Tzvetan Todorov, a genre is "nothing but [the] codification of discursive properties," and each one is related to or derived from a specific kind of speech act (1976:162, 164–66). I am not sure how helpful this hypothetical derivation of genres from speech acts is, but there is some advantage to be gained from supposing that genres are themselves speech acts within the discursive system of literature.[17] Speech act theory supposes that the speaker is always the originator of his utterances and is in complete control of them, because without such an assumption, the speaker cannot be held to have satisfied the "appropriateness conditions" that are mandated by the theory. But we know that in fact people make assertions or agree to propositions that they themselves are unable to verify, but accept by hearsay or assume on some vague, unsupported supposition that such is the case. What speech act theory overlooks, Thomas Pavel points out, is that speakers are often unreliable, that they may incompletely understand the implications of what they are saying, and that they are not, in short, in total command of their linguistic competence. "Speakers who are sincere by participation should not be expected to defend the truth of most of their utterances other than by reference to the community ('I don't know; my friends told me that,' 'It's in the newspapers,' etc.), nor to readily accept the consequences of what they say ('How should I know that saying "X is a good leader" entails endorsing concentration camps?')" (1981:170). Many of the conditions that supposedly are required for the felicity of a speech act are not possessed by the speaker. "In many cases the individual speakers behave as if their personal linguistic duties had somehow been *waived*. They need not scrupulously perform these duties, since at every failure to do so the community is there to cover for them" (170). If speech act theory must be modified by the recognition that the *langue*, the latent discourse of the community, speaks through individuals and enables their incomplete or imperfectly formed or thoughtless utterances to be encoded and transmitted, theories of literature that use the speech act model must also recognize the extent to which the community modifies its own cultural codes. Genres may be constituted, modulated, refined, or abandoned by a continual interplay of individual wit and creativity, but they exist only by virtue of a consensus that may be constituted by any group— readers *vulgos* or *discretos*—or by cross-currents between them.

17. For critiques of the application of speech act models to literature, see Stanley E. Fish, "How to Do Things with Austin and Searle: Speech Act Theory and Literary Criticism," *MLN* 91 (1976): 983–1025; Pavel 1981, 1986:18–25; also reviews of Pratt 1977 by Michael Hancher in *MLN* 92 (1977):1081–98 and Joseph Margolis in *JAAC* 87 (1979): 225–28.

As readers, we begin to find our way in the universe of literary artifacts with their feigned discourses by the recognition of genre; through this recognition we are able to train our expectations upon the experience that lies in wait for us. This need—to recognize things according to their kind or their categories in order to become receptive to them—is not an exclusively literary one. Indeed, our encounters with all the products of culture require that we recognize initially the kind to which they belong, within broad or narrow limits. Thus it is that we manage to perform the ongoing tasks of structuring our experience, of knowing what it is that we are doing, and of judging our performance. The fact that, in this country, there are banks that resemble churches and churches that look like banks (Colie 1973:5) may provoke a range of reactions: annoyance, cynical amusement, or witty speculation. The ordinary citizen expects to be able to tell which is which without having to read the sign outside, but this expectation is thwarted when two genres are found to share a common visual code, one that says "solid respectability and high standing in the community." Genres are more than a system of classification employed by historians and critics, and their function has always been something more than the ascription of themes and subjects to forms and styles.

From an anthropological standpoint, genres are a grid through which our nonreflexive experience of our culture can be mapped and its contents made accessible to conscious perception and eventually presented for critical reflection. From a different point of view, that of the phenomenology of the reader or the viewer of any cultural product, genre is that which enables us to make a provisional recognition of the thing and hence to adopt a decision as to what is the appropriate attitude of expectancy. Genre recognition is not only an essential part of the extremely complex process of reading, it is one of the first operations we perform when we open a book. From here it is no great distance to the pragmatic sense of genre as a kind of contract between the producer and the consumer, the artist and the public, as to what codes carry what significance. Pavel also offers an interesting and fruitful model for the transactional aspect of genres; namely, coordination behavior and coordination games. He cites the example (among others) of two persons rowing a boat together; each must adjust his actions to those of the other in order to realize a common expectation.

Thus "the horizon of expectations within which writers and their public operate can be seen as the background of various coordination games involving tacit cooperation between the members of the literary community" (1986:118–21). The advantage of the coordination behavior model is that it is dynamic, whereas the usual reference to a contract implies something fixed and stable, a preexistent paradigm whose products will be predictably identical.[18] Coordination games allow for both the expected and the unforeseen and therefore are more like what happens in the transaction between the artist and the public.

If, in the long run, new genres develop out of old ones, new and surprising effects can be achieved in the shorter run in the periods of greater sophistication that produce the self-reflexive forms such as parody by making combinations, inversions, substitutions. A traditional folk tale, a fabliau, or an adventure story can become newly significant when it is combined with or framed within another narrative, or when the traditional association between the social role of the protagonist (e.g., priest, knight, merchant) and the story type is broken. Recombinations, parodies, changes of social focus, and modulation of the level of discourse are basic methods of widening the range of narrative, of challenging the reader through disturbing or even disrupting the system of expectations (Fowler 1982:9, 10). The postmedieval, early modern period that witnessed so many innovations in social, religious, administrative, and technical fields saw correspondingly vigorous activity in the elaboration of its symbolic forms and in philosophic discussion of them.

Insofar as genres are classes of works, they are no less a part of the total signifying order of the culture than are the individual works that constitute them. Like other signifiers, they participate in a synchronic system that is the totality of the expressive modes that are operative in a culture at a given moment. The critic looks for order, process, structure, but writers and artists, besides being aware of the past of their art, are alert to the presence here and now of other expressive forms. Their principal criterion is practical: usability. They attempt not to map the literary or artistic ter-

18. See Paul Hernadi, *Beyond Genre* (Ithaca: Cornell University Press, 1972), 42–44.

rain but to live off the land. They may be hostile or indifferent to much of what they see, but inevitably it is all part of their own artistic horizon, shaping their world of possibilities.

In the chapters that follow I try to investigate and understand two principal questions. First, what were the possibilities that suddenly opened up to the Spanish writers when they incorporated the nonheroic picaro and his world into their established forms of fiction, some of them having their origins in the heroic tradition? Second, what challenges did these new and provocative works offer to the expectations of the readers? Further questions will naturally ensue as the picaro quickly becomes a familiar, even a conventional literary figure across the range of established genres, in prose fiction, in poetry, in political dialogue, in drama. Cervantes, as always, will merit a place apart, for it was he that possessed the genius to escape the narrowing horizons of convention. And he escaped them not by taking his picaros through ever more amazing escapades or ingenious swindles or grim hardships but by the very opposite procedure, by reducing them to an emblem of the world's banality, and yet making them the pretext for some of the most daring formal and technical experiments.

The presentation of picaresque novels as a separate and definable class of literature is relatively recent. It happened, not surprisingly, about the middle of the nineteenth century, after the invention of the history of literature as a cultural activity and a body of knowledge. History of literature followed the powerful models established by the new biohistorical sciences, biology, geology, paleontology, not only as systems of classification but as radically historical readings of the natural world. This historicizing of the sciences of nature, supported, however remotely, by the German post-Kantian philosophy with its belief in the evolution of mind, encouraged students of literature and the arts to seek analogous structures that would combine a consistent taxonomy with a historical process from lower to higher forms.[19] A typical and influential example is provided by the work of Jean-Charles-Léonard

19. The process could not be orderly, of course, or the model a perfect fit because of the powerful and widely held conviction that Greek art and literature represented an original perfection.

24

Simonde de Sismondi, who describes *Lazarillo de Tormes* as a "roman comique" and the initiator of a new kind of fiction: "A swarm of novels were written in imitation of *Lazarillo de Tormes*; this is what the Spaniards call the taste for the picaresque (or begging literature [le Genre de la Gueuserie]), and if they are to be believed, the beggars of no other country match theirs in ingenuity, swindles, camaraderie, obedience to an internal law in constant war against society's law."[20] The word "genre" is evidently employed here in a nontechnical sense, without any need for definition. Thomas Roscoe, in his English translation of Sismondi, offers "kind" or "class of novels" as equivalent to "genre"; also, he variously renders "roman" as "romance" and as "novel," terms that an experienced twentieth-century reader would be unlikely to use interchangeably.[21]

The earliest occurrence of the term *novela picaresca* in Spanish is, as far as I know, its use by Buenaventura Carlos Aribau in the "Discurso Preliminar" to his *Novelistas anteriores a Cervantes* (BAE 3). In the companion volume, *Novelistas posteriores a Cervantes*, Eustaquio Fernández de Navarrete also uses this phrase in his introductory "Bosquejo histórico sobre la novela española" (BAE 33). Surveys written in English use the phrase that we found in Sismondi, "gusto picaresco" (so Dunlop 1814) or "picaresque style" (Hallam 1837, Ticknor 1849). As late as 1887, an anonymous writer in *The Southern Review* published an article with the title "Picaresco Romances."[22] Frank W. Chandler's usage vacillated between "picaresque novels" and "romances of roguery." Not until the 1890s do we find "the picaresque novel" becoming standard, in its generalized singular number, preceded by the definite article, with all that this usage implies: an agreed-upon category, having fixed boundaries and an assured conceptual status, in a universe of solid referentiality.

20. "Une foule de romans ont été faits à l'imitation de *Lazarille de Tormes*; c'est ce que les Espagnols nomment *El Gusto Picaresco* (le Genre de la Gueuserie); et s'il faut les en croire, les mendiants d'aucun pays n'égalent les leurs en artifices, en fourberie, en esprit de corps, et en subordination à une police intérieure, toujours armée contre celle de la société": Simonde de Sismondi 1813: III, 293.
21. Thomas Roscoe, *The Spanish Novelists* (London: Warne, 1868).
22. *Southern Review* 2 (1887): 146–71.

For most of the nineteenth century, then, terminology was not fixed, and writers did not seem concerned to define closely what their labels referred to. When they came to describe what they found in the picaresque works, we have to wonder not only at the change of taste but at the shifts of perception and judgment. They quite obviously did not see what we see, nor did they refine their idea of the picaresque to the point of excluding works that do not conform to our definitions. Their response, in fact, seems to have been much closer to that of the seventeenth century than to ours. Dunlop found the "romance" of *Guzmán* composed of "comical adventures" (314b), for example. The more one reads of these nineteenth-century judgments on picaresque fiction, the more one is struck by the fact that the writers stress three constant characteristics: comicality and a merry style; the protagonist as an amusing cheat; the books as faithful portraits of the customs of the beggars and vagrants who are said to have swarmed over Spain.

Since that time we have entered a period of insistent questioning. The constitution and the stability of the genre have been called into question. Literary history has lost its innocence: it can no longer be assembled as a chronicle of great authors and their works, or as a narrative of the progress of literature, or as a sequence of appraisals, varying in extent according to the writer's judgment of the works' importance. We are not objective observers of the processes that we call historical; rather, they are the mental constructs with which we attempt to frame an intelligible and usable past. Our judgments as well as our understanding of the past, whether as process or as narrative, are themselves historically grounded and consequently historicizable. E. H. Carr has described the study of history as a process of interaction, a dialogue of the historian with the facts of the past, the facts being inseparable from their interpretation. The historian's point of view enters irrevocably into every observation he makes; "the process of observation affects and modifies what is being observed."[23]

Moreover, the paradigms we employ in our construction of lit-

---

23. E. H. Carr, *What Is History?* (New York: Knopf, 1962), 90. Observations of this kind were already commonplace before Hayden White's exposé of the rhetoric of history in his *Metahistory* (Baltimore: Johns Hopkins University Press, 1972).

erary history, like those in the sciences, become unusable when they cannot absorb the empirical strain placed upon them by anomalous data or contradictory perceptions.[24] Any formulation, however stable it may appear, is condemned eventually to become historical, detached from the present cultural systems when their discourses can no longer lend it explanatory force. An egregious example is the late nineteenth-century idea of the picaresque as the product of a vainglorious empire whose subjects were too proud or too idle to work. Such an account was acceptable within the energetic capitalism (and rival imperialism) of the Anglo-American linguistic ambit; not surprisingly, the Hispanic world did not favor this "obvious" explanation. Paradigms shift less promptly and less efficiently in the historical disciplines and the historically describable humanities than in the sciences. As soon as the nonviability of the scientific model can be demonstrated, it is recognized as useless in the scientific community by procedures that ensure a relatively rapid consensus; a literary historical model may continue to be tenaciously affirmed, or simply allowed to stand unexamined, even though the field around it may have changed. This is the case, I believe, with our hypostatized trans-textual concepts of "the picaro" and "the picaresque."

To an unprecedented degree we are able to retrieve information about the past and to reconstruct former ways of thinking about familiar material. As Jauss has put it, citations "can . . . remind us of a former way of posing a question, to prove that an answer that has become classic is no longer satisfactory, that it has become historical again and demands of us a renewal of the process of question and answer" (1982:5). The nineteenth century's "gusto picaresco" is not the answer to our problem, but it does have the fortuitous virtue of being just the kind of catalyst that Jauss describes. It can make us aware that our pursuit of ever more exact definitions of this "genre" has left us almost no example of a typical picaresque plot structure, or of a typical picaro other than the fact that he leaves home and that he does not have a title of nobility. Nineteenth-century criticism was also deeply committed to a belief in literature as representation, exemplified in the strong cur-

24. Thomas S. Kuhn, *The Structure of Scientific Revolutions*, 2d ed. (Chicago: University of Chicago Press, 1970).

rent of *costumbrismo* (literature of manners) the abundant documentation, and the frequent validation of the truth of a fiction by the accuracy and richness of its observation. In order to avoid that kind of identification, we must remember that writers do not simply represent the world of objects that they share with the reader but rather mediate between consciousness and its objects, and may stand in any of the possible relations that consciousness has with the universe of objects. Our problem, or one formulation of it, should be: How do we remain responsible to both historical consciousness and the singularity of the work of art (White 1970: 173–74)? I shall attempt to deal with this problem in Part Two, "Fictive Worlds."

Novels written in the first person raise some peculiar questions of their own. One of them is the problem of how to identify the formal mimetics. As far as the first-person picaresque works are concerned (and by no means all picaresque fiction is written in the first person), it is not possible to propose a single narrative model for them all. They cannot all be said to imitate formally a confession, or a *carta de relación*, or a memoir, or a report. Moreover, there is disagreement as to what individual narratives do imitate, if anything at all. And if a model is clearly visible through the text, we must bear in mind that the fictional work does not merely imitate the model: it *novelizes* it (Glowinski 1977). And in the process of novelizing, it has to draw upon conventions and practices found in the third-person fictions that form the literary horizon at the moment of its production. Hayden White has said that the task of the literary historian is to restore to the classics their original strangeness (1970:181–83). How to achieve that aim is a problem unique to each case. Beyond that challenge, however, lies another, made explicit by Robert Weimann (1976:56): We must attend to both the past meaning and the present significance of the work of literature, and also to the tensions and the contradictions between them. Fredric Jameson's rallying call "Always historicize!" (1981) has far-reaching consequences for our critical practice.[25]

25. For the difficulties and pitfalls in relating the text to its historical and ideological situation and to the system of power relations—and to the reader's —see Edward Pechter, "The New Historicism and Its Discontents: Politicizing Renaissance Drama," *PMLA* 102 (1987):292–303.

2

The Canonical Texts

This chapter deals with several questions that bear upon the problematics of reading *Lazarillo de Tormes*, *Guzmán de Alfarache*, and *El buscón*. One of them is the history of their readings. In each case I attempt to recover the contextual moment of the work's first appearance, to observe the cultural and discursive norms that foster its reception, and also those which it is designed to transgress. I give attention to ways in which we, in our here and now, may be constrained both by previous readings and by the critical fields in which we operate. Reading codes have shifted over historical time, and changes in critical practice have brought to the surface new indeterminacies that have implications for our choice of reading strategies. That being the case, I attempt to provide what might be called a minimal reading or interpretive base.

Reading *Lazarillo de Tormes*

We read *Lazarillo de Tormes* as a "novel", a term that already implies some broad expectations on the part of a twentieth-century public in relation to the unity of the story, the focusing of the narrative upon the central character, the continuity of the protagonist's identity, and the mutual definition of identity and experience in the protagonist. And yet such terms are remote from the world of sixteenth-century readers. The narrative of *Lazarillo* can be separated into numerous episodes, events, anecdotes, jokes taken from the existing store of oral tradition as well as from the written collections of stories that accumulated in the late Middle Ages and early modern era (Bataillon 1973b; Chevalier 1976, 1980; Lázaro 1972). Furthermore, as Fernando Lázaro Carreter has well demonstrated (1972), the methods of articulating these diverse elements are also drawn from the techniques of traditional storytelling. Finally, the protagonist himself is constructed in accordance with familiar folk-tale antecedents. All of these various ready-made elements could have been easily recognized for what they were by the original readers; indeed, a large part of whatever appeal the book had would have been found precisely in the recognition of the familiar in a new form, assimilated to a new process.

The unknown author incorporated into his fiction the following anecdotes: the baby brother's "Madre, coco" ("Mommy, the bogeyman!"); the practical joke of the stone bull, and Lazarillo's revenge at the post; the trick with the wine jar; the boy's confusion of the empty house with a tomb; the counting of the grapes; the priest's onions; the play with the chest of bread; the escape of the *escudero* (squire) from his creditors and the master's abandonment of his servant boy; the theatrical deception of the public by the *buldero* (pardoner) in his sale of indulgences. The book also sets in dramatic motion such proverbial situations as the curing of the boy with the wine. Such proverbial phrases as "arrimarse a los buenos" (stick to the good sort of people) also provide motivation and an implied scale of judgment by which the conduct of mother and son can be compared and assessed, both by the protagonist and by the reader. The *escudero*'s claim to own landed property far away in the north country would evoke a popular witticism: "A man from out of town prided himself on being an hidalgo [pure-blooded], and when a tailor became irritated by this, the man said: 'Do you know what it is to be an hidalgo?' To which the tailor replied, 'To be from fifty leagues away'" (Bataillon 1973b:42).

Lazarillo de Tormes incorporates many prefabricated units that had existed as self-contained anecdotes within a long tradition of storytelling (Soons 1976). This tradition included the jests of clowns as well as the literary progeny of the *Disciplina clericalis*, the *Conde Lucanor* of Don Juan Manuel, the short farces of Lope de Rueda, and the *Cancionero de obras de burlas provocantes a risa* (Valencia, 1519). The *Decameron* of Giovanni Boccaccio (translated into Castilian in 1496) was pillaged for individual stories, and so were the collections of other Italian writers, notably Matteo Bandello, Giovanni Francesco Straparola, Franco Sacchetti, Masuccio Salernitano, and Francesco Sansovino (Bourland 1905, 1927; Dunn 1952). Anecdotes and funny stories became part of many longer works, such as *Retrato de la Lozana andaluza* and *El crotalón*, but they were also made into collections without the artistic organization that Boccaccio gave to his *Decameron*. Pero Mexía's *Silva de varia lección* (Seville, 1540) was a miscellany of stories and information, the fabulous mixed with the true. Collections of stories continued to be published into the next century: Juan de Mal Lara, *Philosophia vulgar* (1568); Melchor de Santa Cruz, *Floresta española* (1574); Gonzalo Fernandes Trancoso, *Contos e historias de proveito* (Lisbon 1575); Juan Timoneda, *Sobremesa y alivio de caminantes* (1563); *El buen aviso y portacuentos* (1564); Luis Pinedo, *Libro de chistes* and *El patrañuelo* (1565); Gaspar Lucas Hidalgo, *Diálogos de apacible entretenimiento* (1606); Sebastián Mey, *Fabulario* (1613). All of these works attest to the continuing vitality of the storytelling tradition and of its ancient and medieval sources, from Aulus Gellius and Valerius Maximus through the medieval exempla.

Maxime Chevalier's research leaves no room for doubt on this point. The incorporation of jokes, anecdotes, and folk tales into works of the literary imagination began in Italy and France in the fourteenth and fifteenth centuries, and had passed to Spain and become a flood by the sixteenth.[1] This abundance of material was exploited by erudite as well as inventive minds: university professors such as Hernán Núñez, Lorenzo Palmireno, Juan de Mal Lara, and Gonzalo Correas; physicians such as Andrés Laguna,

---

1. ". . . la oleada de cuentos que por todas partes surgen en los textos de los siglos XVI y XVII: refraneros, diccionarios, recopilaciones, misceláneas, diálogos, tratados didácticos, entremeses, comedias, novelas. Un terremoto sacude la literatura española" (Chevalier 1980:6).

Alonso López Pinciano, and Jerónimo de Alcalá Yáñez; friars and clerics such as Juan de Pineda, Sebastián de Covarrubias, Juan Farfán, and Juan de Robles, as well as some men of noble birth (Chevalier 1980:6).

Brief stories were not confined to oral tradition or to a vulgar audience. Giovanni Pontano's *De sermone* (Naples 1509) devotes space to the quality that he calls *facetudo*, or the art of telling amusing stories (Soons 1976:24). *Facetudo*, a neologism unknown in traditional rhetoric, responded to the timely need to define a quality that was both artistic and social. The skill consisted not only in telling jokes and stories but in judging the appropriate moment for the story and the appropriate story for the moment, suiting the style to the company. This social art enabled the most ribald story to be told without offense and sardonic comments to be made without wounding. The urbane skill prescribed in *De sermone* is represented by Castiglione in *The Courtier* (translated by Juan Boscán in 1534) and later, in Spain, in *El cortesano* by Luis Milán and *El galateo español* (1582?) by Lucas Gracián Dantisco. A reprint of *Lazarillo* in the following century, interestingly, was bound in the same volume with the *Galateo* (1603, etc.).

Lazarillo resembles other contemporaneous forms of literature in its incorporation of *facetiae* and other brief stories, but is unlike them in its manner of incorporating and articulating these materials. They are not part of a conversation, as in *The Courtier* or the *Viaje de Turquía*, or occasional diversions from the principal course of events, as in *El libro del caballero Zifar*, in *Don Quixote*, and in later picaresque novels: they *are* the events, most obviously in the first two chapters. These preexisting, ready-made pieces, however, are ordered on more than one level of organization. At the first level, they are attached to figures (miller, blind man, priest, etc.) who are recognizable as stock types. These stock figures, with the acts and events that accompany them, are organized into a sequence by a comic autobiography. The narrating "I" that articulates its own past acts and those that it reports has its identity established in turn by reference to an "other": Vuestra Merced, that anonymous *destinataire* or recipient of Lázaro's text, who is also its originating authority. In structural terms, those figures are units of intermediate organization between the single incident and the whole life story. Apparently outside of this whole construction stands the Prólogo. In fact, it is as much a product of the narrative "I" as anything else in the book: it is a reframing device that ensures that our reading of the *Vida* will not be identical with Vuestra Merced's.

The frequency and density of these preexisting motifs is greatest in *Lazarillo*'s first *tratado*, or chapter, the one in which he is a child at home, and then is put into the service of the blind man. With the exception of the extended narration of the false miracle by the indulgence seller (in *tratado* 5), the rest of the story presents his rising fortunes and the relationships that define his ultimate state of "good fortune." Stories, jokes, and anecdotes simply succeed one another in the narrative, though they may also contribute to the establishment of formal contrasts and symmetries in the mind of the reader. Other traditional materials serve to give consistency or continuity to a whole section of the book. These are principally the stereotypical characters, beginning with Lazarillo himself. The name Lázaro proverbially signified poverty ("Por Lázaro laceramos" [old Castilian *lazrar*, *lacerar* = to suffer poverty]; "más pobre que Lázaro" [poorer than Lázaro]; "más pobre que Lázaro y que Job" [poorer than Lázaro and Job]) and would recall to mind the beggar Lazarus in Luke 16:20–31 (Bataillon 1973b:27). Whether his name already signified "blind man's boy" or whether this meaning was derived from the book is uncertain (Bataillon 1973b:29–30). But there is visible evidence that the blind man with his guide boy was a familiar image (as the pair no doubt was in the cities of Europe) and that the boy was depicted as tricking his blind master (Cros, in *Actes: Picaresque européenne*, 1976:9–15). At the point in the first *tratado* where the mother gives her son to the blind man, tales of trickery can be expected to follow.

Each episode within the chapter states a need, a problem for which Lazarillo must find a solution in a course of action. So a familiar sequence is established: problem-trick/solution-outcome. The first such encounter with the blind man, the stone bull incident, makes him realize that his relation with his new master will be continually problematic: in the words of the blind man himself, "You've got to know one trick more than the devil." Lazarillo is more complex than the popular stereotype of a guide boy taking advantage the man's blindness. He is doubly determined—first by the basic need not to die of starvation, but then by a formal motive. In the trick with the stone bull the blind man defines the mode of their existence together; Lazarillo's sore head turns the blind man's words about going one better into an existential need for revenge that is satisfied when Lazarillo has his master crash his head against the post. Everything that happens between these two events enables Lazarillo to eat, drink, and survive, but it also is preparation for the triumphal moment. Each trick enables an immediate problem to find an outcome, and it also attests to the power of the blind man, and so defers further solution.

The blind man lacks sight, but he has power and experience in addition to the insight attributed to the blind in lore and literature. The reader's scruples with respect to deceiving the blind are canceled by the man's rough exploitation of the boy, his demonic intelligence, and his malice. Lazarillo's role as underdog is to turn the tables in a final reversal. In the interim, however, the forces remain balanced, the struggle inconclusive. The man's blindness is matched by the boy's inexperience, the man's stinginess by the boy's acquisitiveness and addiction to wine. Balances and imbalances serve to keep the relation a dynamic one within which the traditional tricks and jokes appear not only plausible but artistically necessary. The second master, the priest, is even stingier and is hypocritical besides. Again master and boy are engaged in silent warfare; once again Lazarillo's defiance of a figure of paternal authority (and of ostensible spiritual authority) is justified by the need to survive. Next comes the squire and a reversal of roles, since the boy now provides for his master. Each of these first three masters is a traditional type, satirically conceived, the embodiment of a characteristic vice, and nameless. The miserly priest and the famished hidalgo who lives only for his "honor" can both be found represented in prose and poetry. The pardoner is a familiar type of charlatan, and lecherous archpriests are not new in literature (Thompson 1957: no.211). This string of characters are all recognizable types, as familiar in the world of the raconteur as "an Englishman, a Scotsman, and an Irishman" or persons who change light bulbs. After the encounter with the squire, Lazarillo effectively ceases to be involved in jokes, either as perpetrator or as victim. He recounts the story of the pardoner as a witness, and from then on he tells us merely of the petty trades by which he earned a living.

Persons in jokes who carry off a deception, or who turn tables on a persecutor or a bully, hold no interest in and of themselves, but exist merely as a function in the story.[2] They have no qualities beyond the need to deceive, the ability to escape, and so forth. They are pure role, and Alan Soons's (1976) term *figura* for such a type is apt. Lazarillo is just such a *figura* during most of the first three chapters. In his relation with the first three masters, he has no definition, no qualities. It is the masters who are defined, generically and socially: the blind man, the priest, the squire. After this point the function of Lazarillo changes as he seeks a social definition of his own, and the nature of his relationships also changes. He begins to enter and leave the service of masters by his own choice: the friar, the pardoner, the painter, the chaplain, the constable. His situations become more obviously contractual, his relations less coercive and adversarial, a matter of cooperation and finally of complicity. The transition began in the service of the squire, when the recognition of mutual need led to the the first exercise in complicity and bad faith.[3] In his relation with the archpriest the complicity has become gratuitous. He has already become settled in his various occupations of wine merchant, broker, and town crier before marrying the archpriest's mistress. Upon gaining his freedom to contract relations of his own choosing, Lázaro surrenders it, creating a new nexus of indebtedness as he dances to the tune of his wife, his patron the archpriest, and, most powerful of all, *el qué dirán*, "what they will say." Hovering in the shadows is the nameless Vuestra Merced, a new coercive authority in whose presence Lázaro once again becomes a *figura*. The circle is closed when the one who did learn a trick more than the devil finds himself snared in his own desires.

The view of *Lazarillo* as a sequence of brief comic stories strung together by an amusing narrator (Chevalier 1976:192) seems to have been shared by foreign readers.[4] The dates of the few reprints that appeared in the sixteenth century[5] fit well with those of the

2. For "function" as a basic component of a tale, see Propp 1968: "Function is understood as an act of a character, defined from the point of view of its significance for the action" (21).

3. "Señor, mozo soy, que no me fatigo mucho por comer, bendito Dios. Deso me podré loar entre todos mis iguales . . . "; "Yo, por hacer del continente, dije:—Señor, no bebo vino" (45, 46).

4. This judgment is also to be found in the prefaces to the earliest English and French translations of *Lazarillo*.

5. Madrid 1573, Milan 1587, Antwerp 1595.

books of jests and anecdotes that became popular during the same period. They reinforce the impression that *Lazarillo* was read as a collection of facetiae.[6] Its favorite episodes were received back into the repertory of oral tales (Chevalier 1976:194–97). It is no coincidence that it was composed at a moment in the history of Spain when the most characteristic and widely diffused contents of the culture were shifting from oral to written transmission and from script to print: *cancioneros, romanceros, refraneros* (collections, respectively, of lyrics, ballads, and proverbs), as well as books of jests and stories.

We must suppose that early readers were capable of seeing the whole as well as the parts, of reading the comic *Bildungsroman* that gives them their distinctively sardonic edge. Devices of repetition, of foreshadowing, hindsight, and circularity occur in each episode and also embrace the whole, tying the end to the beginning. Lazarillo takes his mother's maxim, *arrimarse a los buenos*, and makes it his own, and the lapidary phrase in which he weighs his success, *llegar a buen puerto*, (make it to port), invites his readers to envision his life in the exemplary metaphor of a journey. And the interpolation of additional foreshadowings in the Alcalá edition (1554) shows that at least one reader grasped the story as a progress. Lázaro's progress from submission to the violence of authority to accommodation and complicity coincides with the moment when the text ceases to depend on the materials of jest and anecdote. At this moment the text is released from its dependence on tradition and acquires its own authority, marked by a profound change in its actantial features.

Of fundamental importance in our assessment of the book's novelty and its enduring fecundity of interpretation is the first-person narration. The first-person narration tends to make everything that it relates into part of the experience of the "narrating I," and for this reason Marcel Bataillon observed that "the autobiographical form is itself a factor of 'realismo'" (1973b:50). The "I" of the narrator unifies what it narrates, imposes a standard of internal consistency, and creates the illusion of immediacy from which a realist aesthetic can begin to develop.

6. Chevalier 1976:193 has a table showing nine editions of Melchor de Santa Cruz's *Floresta*, from 1574 to 1598.

It is interesting to compare the autobiographical narrative of Cingar in the Castilian version of Teofilo Folengo's *Baldus* (1542) with *Lazarillo*, as Alberto Blecua (1971) has done. Cingar's story is told orally, beginning with his ignoble ancestry and detailing the family career of thieving that he has pursued on the roads and in the inns and cities of Italy. It, too, can be broken down into traditional stories, and its author evidently knew *The Golden Ass*. But it is, in Blecua's term, an "anti-*Lazarillo*" (203) because the speaker offers his story as a negative model, an example to be avoided. Cingar is a "repentant pícaro" (206) who later becomes a knight, and an exemplary one, in spite of his low origins.

In his influential *Rise of the Novel*, Ian Watt makes "formal realism" the defining quality that distinguishes the novel from earlier kinds of prose fiction. Watt grounds the representational mode of the novel in the epistemological and linguistic ideas of the period. The fictional place, the time, the whole physical and moral environment of the action, the authenticity of the manifold aspects of life depicted were underwritten by a referential theory of language and a philosophical belief in the particularity of experience as the basis of reality. Plots were accordingly derived, not from myth or legend or history but from contemporary life (12–35). On the philosophical ground provided by Locke and Hume, Watt writes:

> Locke had defined personal identity as an identity of consciousness through duration in time; the individual was in touch with his own continuing identity through memory of his past thoughts and actions. This location of the source of personal identity in the repertoire of its memories was continued by Hume: "Had we no memory, we never should have any notion of causation, nor consequently of that chain of causes and effects, which constitutes our self or person." (1962:21)

This constitution of a self through recollection, the awareness of identity in a sequence of acts seen as events in a causal chain, has already found imaginative representation in outline in *Lazarillo de Tormes* and, more elaborately, in *Guzmán de Alfarache*, which draws explicitly on a philosophical tradition.

By the middle of the sixteenth century, first-person narration had become more common in a variety of fictional genres, but no other work presses into so concise a form such a variety of effects derived from that one technical choice. As we read, we divide our attention between the subject and the object of the discourse, the man who weaves the story and the boy whose image is given shape by it. But these are discriminations that have only recently been defined and named. We read the same words that sixteenth-century readers read, but the "text" is not the same for us as for them.[7] Our critical language, the tools of narratology, explores spaces in the text that we assume to have been present to the first readers, but those spaces would not have been discovered without these tools. What we discover is conditioned by the questions we ask, the assumptions we make about "reality," what we believe to be possible in any given situation. Our reading is governed in part by our broad expectations of the kind of work we are reading, and in part also by our response to the text itself in a continuing dialectic or transaction. The discontinuities in a narrative, the uncertainties of social and ethical approbation, for example, may be left inconclusive, "gaps" for the reader to negotiate, in the terminology of Wolfgang Iser.

> These gaps have a different effect on the process of anticipation and retrospection, and thus on the "gestalt" of the virtual dimension, for they may be filled in different ways. For this reason, one text is potentially capable of several different realizations, and no reading can ever exhaust the full potential, for each individual reader will fill in the gaps in his own way, thereby excluding the various other possibilities; as he reads he will make his own decision as to how the gap is to be filled. . . . By making his decision he implicitly acknowledges the inexhaustibility of the text; at the same time it is this very inexhaustibility that forces him to make the decision. (1974:280)

What is true for the individual reader is true for the reading community. What a reader "sees" in the text as a member of one cultural community may pass unrecognized by a reader in a different community, and such cultural biases operate as constraints

7. Louise Rosenblatt (1978) discriminates between these readings, referring to them as "text" and "poem," respectively.

upon interpretation. The early reader would not have decoded the text existentially and taken the protagonist seriously as a human being. Conversely, that reader's view of *Lazarillo* as a collection of anecdotes is not normally present to the modern reader unless the latter belongs to that tiny community that has made a special study of the book's intertextuality. The early reader could have seen the first-person address as a new way of giving immediacy to old material; the modern reader is more likely to see it as the discourse of personal hardship and victimization (Herrero 1979) or of cynical obfuscation (Shipley 1982, 1983) or of the social construction of the self. Narrative, especially when it is given in the first person, is nothing if not problematic for us, and much criticism of both *Lazarillo* and *Guzmán de Alfarache* rests explicitly or implicitly on the constitution of the narrator's identity as it is projected in the act of writing. We may find that the persona of Lázaro is constructed of gaps that stand between us and his text and that we attempt to fill, being no longer satisfied with anything less subtle than what the tools of our narratology can provide us.

The varied readings of *Lazarillo* in our time have reflected the literary culture, the philosophical, sociological, or other theoretical interests and preoccupations of the interpreters, and in so doing they have not merely made the Spanish book accessible to a modern reader but inscribed it in the plural worlds in which we move, think, and feel. The fact that many of these readings contradict one another merely underscores what we already knew, that our culture is a cacophony of many voices. At this point it is of greater interest to note that this work which is so brief, organized so tightly around symmetries and polarities, can nonetheless remain so open. We are not surprised at the inexhaustible meanings that can be generated from within so large and varied a novel as *Don Quixote*, but the modest level of discourse of *Lazarillo*, the relatively narrow range of its experiences, the fewness of the voices and their restricted register would seem to preclude its openness to varied readings. Nonetheless, modern readers have found indeterminacies and gaps in its structural syntax that allow for different elements to be foregrounded, or the same ones to be given very different significance. This alone marks a radical distinction between *Lazarillo* and the other picaresque works. *Guzmán de Alfarache*, for example, for all its length, discursiveness, variety of incident, and subordinate narratives, is far less permeable by the reader's inferences, and the reader is much more constrained by authorial directives. One may find in *Lazarillo* the coordinates for an existential reading (self-awareness, sense of time, of death, of the urgency of making choices). The versatility of the book in fitting extraliterary paradigms, whether psychological (Erik Erikson's "stages of development" or Abraham Maslow's "hierarchy of needs") or sociohistorical (the "rising middle class," the "frustrated Castilian capitalism," or the "marginalization of the poor")—not *one* model but a variety of models—raises the question from a different angle. The generic uncertainty or instability implied in the variety of modern interpretations of *Lazarillo* is also related to our current difficulties with the history and theory of genre and with the uncontrolled expansion in our time of the concept of irony.

If we were to peel away the conceptual layers that sustain our current interpretive schemes (layers derived from Nietzsche, Dilthey, Bergson, Saussure, Barthes) and to suffer total critical amnesia, we could not read the same *Lazarillo* as we do now. In the absence of our current analytical tools sharpened by narratology and semiotics, the text would lose much of its layered complexity, since in literary criticism works take the shape of the tools that are brought to bear upon them. For example: before the 1960s readers appear not to have concerned themselves with identifying precisely the *caso* that Lázaro is supposedly writing to explain (Rico 1966:277). Nor was Vuestra Merced, the addressee or designated reader of Lázaro's narrative, seen as having a function beyond this stated role. That his request to Lázaro might have caused the latter to slant his story and adjust his style apparently had not yet occurred to anyone.

The rhetorical theory and practice that readers shared with writers in the sixteenth century had almost nothing to say about prose fiction. We may suppose that, like readers at all times, they perceived and responded to cues in the text derived from accumulated reading experience —the "repertoire of the familiar" (Iser 1974:32–34)—but we cannot recover their evaluation of them. Did the evocation of a familiar urban setting reinforce the laughter provoked by the incidents, or did it give a startling new verisimilitude to the narrative of an individual's existence? Could the assembling of such materials into the life story of an ignoble individual have struck those discordant notes upon which complex modern interpretations have been built? Let us note some codes that might perhaps have guided the reader at the very beginning. The book is titled *La vida de Lazarillo de Tormes, y de sus fortunas y adversidades*, and it has been shown that the only literary genre that regularly appeared with such a title (*The Life of* . . .) since the thirteenth century was the saint's life (Jones 1979). Fictional narratives were usually called *Historia, Libro, Hechos, Crónica*. The ironic allusion in the title to a saintly model is an indicator that the comic mode extends to the whole work, not just to its parts. The surname de Tormes, as has often been noted, is a trivializing parody of the chivalric nomenclature (Amadís de Gaula, Palmerín de Inglaterra, etc.). Lázaro's life is therefore set up in a parodic relation to two exemplary traditional models: the real-life saint and the fictional knightly hero.

Given these generic coordinates and these discursive fields, the reader would have the delicate task of deciding whether the career of Lázaro was being ridiculed by contrast with the exemplary models or whether the models were being satirized by contamination with Lázaro's squalid life. It is attractive to imagine a skeptical author, Erasmian perhaps, confronting the chivalric and the saintly heroes on their own ground. Here is young Lázaro encountering evil in its mean and pervasive forms and in the social guises that all readers can recognize, rather than in cardboard villains, fabulous monsters, and unreal locations. He suffers cold, hunger, cruelty, and neglect in the muddy streets of Castilian towns instead of parrying mighty blows beneath the inspiring gaze of a beautiful lady. Shift the angle again, and here is a boy about to become a man, struggling to find his own truth amid all the hypocrisy, deception, and lies in which the world entangles him. He is kept so ignorant of God (by a man of religion) that he can be tempted without being conscious of what temptation is, and be corrupted in the mere attempt to survive. No villains or demons here, no marvelous interventions, no celestial applause, just the world as it is. With such a reading, *Lazarillo* could have served to show up the rhetorical conventions of both kinds of representation, that of fictional heroism and that of heroic virtue. If this novel makes us conscious of some of the cant that adheres to noble heroes and to models of virtue, it continually ironizes itself in the process. No sharp lines are drawn, there are no dramatic confrontations between good and evil, nothing redemptive can be read into the circularity of its plot. One does not emerge from the tunnel into daylight; rather the tunnel becomes broader, easier, more comfortable, better illuminated. In real life, artful dodgers are more often encountered than doughty heroes or saints, and may be more amusing company. Lázaro is certainly a good storyteller, and his story is resolutely undercut with irony, from the "remarkable things, never before heard or seen" promised in his prologue right to the end of the narration.

Lázaro's assertion that the writer has an obligation to preserve noble deeds from oblivion is common to writers of true historical chronicles and biographies and to books of chivalry with their pretense of historical veracity.[8] Plots of romance typically end by revealing a structure of familial relations that either reflects and reaffirms an implicit ideal or repeats that which presided at the hero's origin before he set out on his quest. In the case of *Lazarillo*, that common structure uniting beginning and end is antiheroic; it is the comically ignoble one of the ménage à trois. Other models of narrative are present, and there is no need to choose between them, because it is a question not of finding "the source" but of charting the range of intertextual play. We can find all the current exemplary modes of writing, from confessional memoir to heroic fiction, being raided for ideologically encoded key words, phrases, or narrative strategies, with the purpose of composing a story and a self that negate them all.

Modern readings of *Lazarillo* have shifted the center of interest from the boy to the man, from the actor to the writer, from the liver of the story to the artful planner and justifier of his life as representation. This series of shifts has resulted from the discovery of gaps within the text: the time that has elapsed between the events of the narrative and the construction of the narrative itself; the undisclosed identity of the designated reader, Vuestra Merced,

8. Juan Pérez de Guzmán, *Generaciones y semblanzas*, ed. R[obert] B[rian] Tate (London: Tamesis, 1965); Hernando del Pulgar, *Claros varones de Castilla*, ed. Robert Brian Tate (London: Oxford University Press, 1971); *Amadís de Gaula*, I.i.

and Lázaro's relation to him. In his Prólogo Lázaro acknowledges that Vuestra Merced wants him to write about *el caso*; what is this "matter," and why does it have to be explained? Indeterminacies multiply and so do the possible lines of causality: Has Vuestra Merced issued a request, or is it a command? Whose conduct does he seek to investigate, Lázaro's or the archpriest's? Is this a serious investigation? What are Vuestra Merced's expectations: a serious deposition? a cover-up? an amusing story? What consequences are entailed? Could he deprive Lázaro of his post as town crier? How has Lázaro adjusted his response to the demand? What has he *not* said? Did his self-consciousness as a writer come to him only as he penned the Prologue, looking back, or did Vuestra Merced's order stimulate it from the first? Or (since everything seems to be possible) did Lázaro himself invent the occasion, including Vuestra Merced, in order to have a pretext for writing? Questions can proliferate out of control. We must not extend the list of questions or attempt to answer them, because to do either of these things is to fall into the trap Lázaro has laid for us in his text. Later writers of picaresque were careful to make their texts less open to uninvited creative readings.

Francisco Rico (1966, 1970, 1984) first argued that the "matter" that prompted Vuestra Merced's request for information was the ménage à trois, in which Lázaro's wife is the archpriest's mistress. Dissenters find it unlikely that a highly placed Vuestra Merced would display an interest in this dubious character and his story (Hitchcock 1971, Sobejano 1975, Archer 1985). The search for an answer, however, can only entangle us even more inextricably in Lázaro's rhetoric. Most important for him, and implicitly for us, is that during or after complying with the authority, he discovers that he is an author. The *relación* or personal memoir becomes a book addressed to the public. The Prologue records his fascination with the double image of himself as author and as protagonist of his story. In it he adopts authorial clichés and platitudes much as he had earlier acquired secondhand clothes and a sword and thereupon assumed the posture and platitudes of a man of honor, and one who is master of himself. If that independence and that honor were derived and derisory, so is his new authority as self-publicist. The space of art is the space of its freedom, but the authority, which he would like us to believe is earned by merit, is really derived from the authority of Vuestra Merced. These questions—Lázaro's construction of himself as author, the appropriation of his text, and the effacement of the authorizing presence of Vuestra Merced—are taken further in Chapter 5.

When questions multiply without the possibility of answers, we must suspect that they are created by our assumptions about reading. Questions concerning Vuestra Merced, *el caso*, and so forth imply that this is a work of mimetic realism that can be pressed to yield the "facts of the matter." Vuestra Merced is forever outside the text of the story, being its authority and its only authorized reader; *el caso* is an extratextual event that the text supposedly interprets by contextualizing it. The reader is trapped, because any attempt to escape by explaining these primal events merely extends the fiction and creates more questions. For any reader of *Lazarillo de Tormes*, two terms are missing. The first is the real author, whose impenetrable anonymity has led some readers to identify him and his intentionality with the fictional author, Lázaro. But of course his *Vida* was written not for us but for the invisible Vuestra Merced, who is fictionally anonymous. On whichever level we approach the text we encounter an aporia. Whether we seek to examine the *Lazarillo* in the context of the real world within the system author-text-reader or in the context of the fictive world within the system narrator–text–Vuestra Merced, one necessary term is absent in each case: the real author in the first, the narratee or fictive reader in the second. Any analysis has to operate without consideration of the author's production of the text, and without the text as received and reconstituted by the inscribed reader for whom it was encoded.

If we were to fill all the gaps, we would simply enclose *Lazarillo* in an envelope of larger and larger fictions. We would eventually demand answers to such questions as: Who taught Lázaro to write? What did he do with all the small change that he hid from the blind man and stored in his mouth? How did they make their way through the mountains of Toledo? If we press against these empty places, the work threatens to fall apart, and if we fill them we shall have made for ourselves a text that is realist, nonironic, and too easy. Given the discontinuities of the "experiencing I" and the "narrating I," we must assume that their indeterminate relation to the silent phantom author who resides outside his work is both intended and functional. We know from our reading experience that the relation between Lázaro-the-told and Vuestra Merced is inaccessible. Once we accept the inaccessibility as a datum of the text rather than as a lack, we are able to see it as a part of Lázaro-the-teller's strategy of self-representation. The primary object of this strategy is the effacement of Vuestra Merced as authorizer of his text so that Lázaro may assume complete authority for himself; this much can be inferred from the Prólogo. But the more Lázaro attempts to suppress the other's authority, the more he testifies to his power, which is made evident each time he addresses Vuestra Merced. These instances of direct address are rendered more obtrusive, not less, by Lázaro's bid for authorship. Functionally, these apostrophes serve as markers of the first-person mode of presentation; by establishing the "presence" of the addressee they reinforce the continuity of Lázaro as the center of narrative consciousness. They also dramatize the act of the book of narration, creating the temporal space, the narrative present, in which it is located (Gómez-Moriana 1983:140). Finally, Lázaro remains ensnared in a paradox that even his act of appropriation (in seizing the text he has composed for Vuestra Merced and redirecting it to us, as his *Vida*) cannot remove: his words are inevitably the traces of the originating text (Vuestra Merced's request or command) that he has suppressed. As for Lázaro himself, his ambiguous relation to his text—he is both outside and inside, teller and told, impresario and puppet, tied to his text and liberated by it—places the reader in dilemma upon dilemma. We have to decide not only how far to trust him as the narrator of his life but how far we can accept him as the interpretant within his own text.[9]

I have dealt with the Prologue last because it is really a device *at the end*, which compels us to reread the whole. The reader has had to negotiate not one but two "versions" of Lázaro's story and attempt to adjust them. They are the *relación* or report that is read by Vuestra Merced and the *Vida* read by the public. Though verbally identical, they are generically distinct, and as different as the *Don Quixote* written by Jorge Luis Borges' Pierre Menard is from the *Don Quixote* written by Cervantes. Like Borges' story, *Lazarillo* thematizes its own reception. In the case of *Pierre Menard, autor del*

9. "Interpretant" is the term suggested by Naomi Schor for the interpreting character within the text: "Fiction as Interpretation/Interpretation as Fiction," in Suleiman/Crosman 1980:168–69.

Quijote, John Frow points out, "what is at stake is the historicity of a single, verbally self-identical text," and that "'textual identity' under changing conditions becomes 'difference.'"[10] In the case of *Lazarillo,* it is the self-identity of the text *at the same* historical moment that is put into question, depending on whether it is viewed in the conditions of its production or whether it is construed in the place of its reception. This demonstration of how a text may be transformed and transvalued by publication left no mark on the literature of its generation, but Alemán and Cervantes both saw its import, and the radical dislocation of "truth" that it implies. For if *Lazarillo* should be understood not as the product of its absent author but in terms of the play between "real" and "fictional" readers within the text, the status of its self-representation (history or fiction? true or false?) is rendered irrevocably ambivalent. It is not difficult to perceive the significance of this precedent for Cervantes as he conceived his *Casamiento engañoso y coloquio de los perros.*

In summary, readers before our time appear to have assumed that the author invented the narrative devices of Vuestra Merced and *el caso* with no other intention than to get the autobiographical fiction moving. Vuestra Merced's request is left imprecise as to its motive, its force, its possible consequences, perhaps to leave the narrator free to compose his story, and not to direct the reader's expectations toward any particular outcome. Such "laying bare of the devices" (in the term dear to the Russian formalists [Erlich 1981:190–194]) is one means, though not the only one, to attain textual reflexivity. Combined with the gaps and indeterminacies, it has confused generations of positivist critics who have gone questing for a mimetic realism. Among later writers only Cervantes, whose interest in picaresque material has so often been questioned, will take up and further complicate narrative gaps and uncertainties in marvelously ingenious ways.

Reading *Guzmán de Alfarache*

Mateo Alemán's *Guzmán de Alfarache* became a much more immediate success than *Lazarillo de Tormes* had been. The First Part

10. John Frow, *Marxism and Literary History* (Cambridge: Harvard University Press, 1986), 171.

(1599) went through more than twenty editions before the appearance of the Second Part (1604), and the latter had a half-dozen editions during the years 1604–1607. Even the spurious Part Two, published in 1602 by the pseudonymous Mateo Luján de Sayavedra (Juan Martí), went through eight editions by 1604. This work appealed to a wider public than *Lazarillo* did in its time. Within a very few years it was printed in Madrid, Barcelona, Zaragoza, Burgos, Valencia, Seville, Tarragona, Lisbon, Coimbra, Brussels, Paris, and Antwerp.[11] Printers in a broad spread of cities cashed in on the success of *Guzmán*, and they ensured that this success would be wide and general.

Guzmán de Alfarache appeared at a moment of great creative energy and of enormous consequence in the literary history of Spain. Aside from Alemán's *Guzmán* Part I (1599) and Part II (1604) and the spurious Part II (1602), López de Ubeda's *Pícara Justina* and Lope de Vega's *Peregrino en su patria* both appeared in 1604, and Cervantes was writing *Don Quixote* (Part I, 1605; Part II, 1615) and some of the *Novelas ejemplares* (1613). Lope de Vega was reshaping the Spanish theater to his own manner, mixing styles and creating such dramatic genres as the *comedia de capa y espada* (cape-and-sword comedy). The chivalric and the pastoral literature that had represented the values of a noble readership, through heroic prowess in archaic modes of adventure and constancy in love, were losing their appeal.[12] The absence of novelistic norms provokes both theoretical anxiety and creative innovation, since each new work of fiction is sui generis.[13] If such values as patience and endurance and courage and fidelity were to be reaffirmed, they had to be liberated from aristocratic fantasies and tested in

11. Madrid (Várez de Castro, 1599), Barcelona (Sebastián de Cormellas, 1599; Graells & Dotil, two printings, 1599), Zaragoza (Pérez de Valdivielso, 1599), Lisbon (Carvalho, 1600), Coimbra (Mariz, 1600), Brussels (Mommarte, 1600), Paris (Bonfons, 1600), Antwerp (Bellero [?], 1600), Madrid (Martínez, 1601), Seville (León, 1602), Tarragona (Roberto, 1603), Milan (Bordón, 1603). Part II, originally published in Lisbon (Crasbeeck, 1604), also appeared in Valencia (Mey, 1605). In Burgos both parts appeared together for the first time (Gómez de Valdivielso, 1619).

12. ". . .las acciones de personajes que llevan al límite la experiencia de la guerra y del amor hasta constituirse en arquetipos de sus respectivos ámbitos": Rodríguez Pérez 1983:9.

13. For discussion of the arguments concerning the rules and the possibilities of fiction, see Riley 1962, Gilbert 1940, Parker/Quint 1986. The term "theoretical anxiety" is mine, not theirs.

more problematic everyday situations that resembled the worlds of the new readers. This was one of the challenges facing writers of the generation of Cervantes and Alemán.

The success of *Guzmán* inspired printers and booksellers to bring out new editions of *Lazarillo*, and this revival of the earlier work followed the same initial itinerary: Madrid, Barcelona, Zaragoza (Guillén 1971:145–46). The revival of *Lazarillo* gave it a wider public than it had previously enjoyed. New editions of *Lazarillo* made their appearance also in cities where *Guzmán de Alfarache* had not been printed (Rome, 1600; Valladolid, 1603; Medina, 1603; Alcalá, 1607). The printers and booksellers must have speculated that a public that received *Guzmán* with such enthusiasm would buy a reissue of an earlier tale with which it had some formal qualities in common. Lázaro Carreter has argued that Alemán saw in *Lazarillo* great, but frustrated, potential (1972:206). But while Alemán adopted the basic schema of *Lazarillo*, his project was worlds away from that of the anonymous author with its subversive ironies, its discourse of insolence, its proposition that duplicity is a condition of art. Their readers could not have perceived the two works as being generically identical. It happens that the first expurgated *Lazarillo* (*Lazarillo de Tormes castigado*, 1573) was printed and bound in one volume with the *Propalladia* of Bartolomé de Torres Naharro (Laurenti 1973: item 511). Presumably this printer also hoped to exploit their common anticlerical and anti-aristocratic satire and their attention to the physical sense of the life of low-class people—a characteristic they both share with *La Celestina*, which was a true best-seller.[14]

The ambience in which *Guzmán* and *Don Quixote* become best-sellers implies a larger and more diverse community of readers than could have existed in the middle decades of the sixteenth century. As this new community of readers reappropriated *Lazarillo*, they would read it differently from the way their predecessors did. The intertextual relations and discursive norms presupposed in *Guzmán de Alfarache* and *Don Quixote* would sensitize new readers to aspects of *Lazarillo* that were not apparent before,

14. Clara Louise Penney, *The Book Called "Celestina" in the Library of the Hispanic Society of America* (New York: Hispanic Society of America, 1954). Penney lists and describes more than a 100 editions from the sixteenth century.

in a different literary and intellectual setting. It was as if Ernest Hemingway's *Old Man and the Sea* had first appeared forty-five years before Melville's *Moby Dick*, then been forgotten, then dusted off to exploit the latter's success.[15]

It is easy to find "family resemblances" between *Guzmán* and *Lazarillo* (to use Ludwig Wittgenstein's colloquial mode of characterizing what holds a genre together).[16] In each one the protagonist narrates his life, beginning with his childhood with parents of dubious virtue. Their stories are organized in a similar way: movement from master to master, place to place, episodically, with stories or anecdotes developing from the relationships or the locations. Detachment and reattachment are one dynamic that governs the development of these narratives, Both narratives achieve their end in the act of writing itself, and both narrators reach a final stasis that resolves the earlier striving. Here the resemblance ends, for they move through very different worlds, and Lázaro's final ménage à trois offers comfortable satisfactions and an easygoing hypocrisy; Guzmán is a convict condemned to serve in the royal galleys, experiences the desire to reform, and is tortured and flogged nearly to death before he is pardoned, at which point he writes his story, for the edification of readers. It is unmistakably a *roman à thèse*. Genres, like individual texts, are subject to the constraints of the cultural formation. Rosalie Colie mentions many hybrids and sports from this period, works without precedent or succession. Generic categories were often vague, and in some cases were no more than formal descriptions of poetic subtypes. If *Lazarillo* had not been trapped retroactively in our picaresque net, we would not know where to place it. It is difficult even now to bring *Lazarillo* into generic focus, to see that the agency of transformation by which the boy becomes a man is a late-medieval

15. "[A] literary past can return only when a new reception draws it back into the present, whether an altered aesthetic attitude wilfully reaches back to reappropriate the past, or an unexpected light falls back on forgotten literature from the new moment of literary evolution, allowing something to be found that one previously could not have sought in it": Jauss 1982:35.

16. Ludwig Wittgenstein, *Philosophical Investigations*, trans. G. E. M. Anscombe (London: Oxford University Press, 1953), §§65–77; adopted in Fowler 1982:40–42. For a critique, see Earl Miner, "Some Issues of Literary 'Species or Distinct Kinds,'" in Lewalski 1986.

49

aggregation of facetiae.[17] But this knowledge does not help us to read *Guzmán de Alfarache*. Accustomed to reading it as the necessary sequel in the formation of a genre called the picaresque novel, we fail to see in it the witty transformation of prose romance that Baltasar Gracián saw. Ernst Gombrich's observation that "an existing representation will always exert its spell over the artist even while he strives to record the truth" is as true of the critic and the historian as it is of the artist.[18] Even further from our modern expectations and from our idea of pleasure in reading are the collections of sermons and meditations that were the outright best-sellers in the sixteenth and seventeenth centuries throughout Europe (Whinnom 1980). These didactic, consciously literate pieces are to *Guzmán* what the preliterate, oral tales and jokes were to *Lazarillo*: the writing self could not have been constituted without them. At the level of both the generic framing and the discourse, the distance between the two works is vast.[19]

Guzmán de Alfarache, as I noted earlier, is about twelve times as long as *Lazarillo de Tormes*. Such disparity of scale implies difference of kind.

> As every kind has a formal structure, so it must have a *size*. This corollary of the doctrine of quantitative parts is by no means trivial. . . . Here literary and linguistic organizations diverge. There are no linguistic constraints on the length of an utterance, whereas genre often determines length precisely (sonnet; computistic verse) and always exerts constraints on it. . . . A specific magnitude, then, is a *sine qua non* of every kind. (Fowler 1982: 62–63)

Scale is also a sensitive generic indicator, as Russian formalist critics recognized.[20] Such episodes in *Guzmán* as the picaro's residence with the cardinal in Rome cover many pages and contain anecdotes, conversations, scenes of drama and tension; their tell-

17. Chevalier 1976, Lázaro Carreter 1972.
18. Ernst H. Gombrich, *Art and Illusion: A Study in the Psychology of Pictorial Representation*, rev. ed. (Princeton: Princeton University Press, 1961), 82.
19. See Fowler's observation: "The sermon, the 'character', the scientific treatise, and the history . . . have changed not only their own parameters but their relations to neighboring genres" (1982:11).
20. In particular, Boris Eichenbaum. See Erlich, 1981:247.

ing is interrupted by the comments of the narrator; there is an extensive cast of characters: stewards, servants, cooks, visitors who participate in the day-to-day flow of events. Guzmán's residence with the French ambassador, with its intercalated stories, is longer than the entire *Lazarillo*. The balances and symmetries are massive, too: seven years spent in Italy questing for his family identity (Part I); seven years spent as a student in a vain quest for a vocation (Part II).

These episodes are long because Alemán contextualizes his novel in a grander narrative tradition than that of *Lazarillo*: the wandering hero who is made welcome in a great palace and beguiled by luxurious entertainment, from Odysseus and Aeneas to Apollonius and Amadís and Cifar. The picaro is an antihero not because he disregards the ostensible public values of his society or because he chooses to occupy the margin rather than the center. In fact, he is closer than anyone else in his fictional world to the truth of that society insofar as his past life embodies its bad faith and reveals the hollowness of the ideology that underlies its pretensions to honor and virtue. He is an antihero because in the interdiscursive universe, his story plays its parody against the heroic tradition, forcing the reader to ask where is the center and where the margin. And since that tradition has, by the end of the sixteenth century, become remote from the realities of the culture, the parody acquires the ring of a subversive truth.

With *Guzmán*, as with *Don Quixote*, the heroic scale of the work is essential to its being antiheroic. Within the massive frame of epic, this scale is manifested in particular episodes, and not only in their extension but in their dynamic, in the development of their tensions and their readerly expectations and resolution. The hero of epic or romance cannot settle and become absorbed in the static world in which he is a guest; neither can Guzmán or Don Quixote. The true hero's destiny and his high endeavor forbid him, no matter how gentle his birth and courtly his training, to remain among the allurements of the domestic order represented by the hospitable table, the great hall, the fair linen, and the beautiful lady. He must practice a fine duplicity, exercising the courtesy that befits his noble blood and station and observing the elaborate decorum of the place while remaining ever alert to the duty, the pledged word, the challenge, or the fateful meeting that draws him forward. Until he has accomplished his mission, whatever it may be, his identity is defined by a mode of being that sets him apart from his hosts; welcome everywhere, he is everywhere a stranger. The picaro Guzmán, too, is impelled by his destiny. Like more reputable heroes, he has vowed to follow a way of life. Serving, becoming domesticated in the household of the cardinal or the French ambassador (*Guzmán*, 1. iii. 6–11, i, 7), offers him the opportunity to display the wit and the vivacity that have enabled him to survive as a picaro, much as the noble knight displays as a guest the courtesy and discretion that make him worthy to be a champion. But the picaro can no more afford to risk his freedom by remaining under the welcoming roof than the knight could. He must not yield to order and routine, but move on in pursuit of his "adventure," to realize a self that always eludes him. The knight knows that once his mission is accomplished he may return to his place of origin, as did Odysseus, or he may found a new one, as did Aeneas. Only then can he be reintegrated with the domestic order as it is constituted by location, name, and continuity. Each stay in a hospitable castle or palace is both a reminder of what he must renounce and a promise of the inheritance to which he will ultimately be rejoined.

The picaro's consciousness is split along a different line, since he pursues a desire that contradicts and attempts to erase his origin. He cannot deny its pull, even as he attempts to repress it. Guzmán recognizes the illusory nature of his pursuit of freedom from the beginning, confessing his regret that he was unable to face reality and turn back (1.ii.1). After his rejection by rich relatives in Genoa, who refuse to accept such a ragged fellow, his mission is to wait and plot revenge. In contrast to a knight's vindication of the good and the innocent against the bully and the evil monster, the picaro Guzmán proposes to rob and humiliate those pillars of respectable society who humiliated him. Here the contrast is to be found not in revenge as such but in the absence of a good to be vindicated. There is no honor to be retrieved. His mission will simply cancel the difference between himself and the enemy. Rather than make knightly values prevail for a shining moment in a gloomy world, he will confirm the world's *picardía*, its rascality and treachery, by participating in it.

The contrast in this respect between *Guzmán* and *Lazarillo* is sharp. If Lazarillo enters a house, there is no one else in it except the master. His condition of servitude is starkly evident, and he must engage in a battle of wits and create ingenious subterfuges in order to survive. He succeeds by inventing fictions, possible worlds that can explain the disappearance of food or (in the case of his relation with the squire) the unexpected production of it. These fictions refer exclusively to Lazarillo's transactions with food and drink, and they mediate between the boy and his current master's acceptance of things as they are. Guzmán in the cardinal's palace and in the French ambassador's becomes an entertainer and a protégé. He is also a participant in a very complex social structure. In *Lazarillo*, however subtle the variations from episode to episode, power remains a straighforwardly reciprocal play.[21] Guzmán, from the time of his first employment, enters a more complex set of relations, and in the great houses of Rome we find an intricate play of authority among servants, stewards, kitchen staff, secretaries, and the master himself, a play in which Guzmán becomes an adept performer and manipulator of forces.

The size and scale of *Guzmán de Alfarache* allow separate episodes to be developed in great detail, in the activities of a large cast of characters. The palaces of the cardinal and the French ambassador are societies in miniature. The loftiness of the persons and the complexity of the economic and political relations contribute to the creation of a world that is inconceivable in *Lazarillo* and a literary form that is correspondingly remote from it. Within this form the focus shifts back and forth between the complex swindles, the travels, the conversations, the buffoonery, and the narrator's reflections on all of them. Some of the reflections are part of the act of writing, others are retrieved from memory and convey decisions not taken, misgivings and regrets for his failure to follow his better judgment. So ample is the structure that there is room in it for characters to tell extensive *novelas* whose relation to the principal narrative is thematic or analogical rather than organic (Cros 1971:106–9; Cavillac 1983, 1990). Both *Lazarillo* and *Guzmán* are an-

21. I do not wish to underestimate the subtlety: the blind man's and the priest's appeal to the consensus of neighbors on Lazarillo's conduct and the boy's discovery of the power of food and of words in the house of the squire are notable examples.

53

tiheroic, but the former's satirical mode is not repeated in *Guzmán*. The blind man, priest, squire are social emblems who also embody vices and lack individuality. The satire is enhanced by the verbal concision and by the sharply defined sequence in which the characters are presented. This satire depends on the smallness of scale and flatness of perspective that make *Lazarillo* so unlike *Guzmán*. *Lazarillo*'s textual duplicity, its threat to the status of the author and to the decidability of meaning, is countered vigorously by Alemán. In preface after preface and in testimonial verses and prologues from his friends he insists on the writer's authority to declare *the* meaning of his work. Alemán proclaims that his picaro has become a new man, calls the book a *general confesión*, and gives great weight to sermons and spiritual reflections, for these above all represent the validating form of utterance, the universally recognized vehicle for truthtelling. He takes deliberate pains to establish his narrator's credentials, to have the new self discourse upon the old, to speak in his own name, and not to let his narrator make any comments *hors texte*.

In one preface ("Al vulgo") Alemán dissociates himself from the "ignorant rabble" who misjudge and slander the good intentions of others and are content with external appearances.

> You are the country mouse, you devour the hard rind of the melon, which is bitter and tasteless, and when you reach the sweet part, you have no stomach for it. . . . You give no attention to the lofty moral truths of the highest minds, and are satisfied with what the dog said and the fox replied.

The analogy shifts to a more destructive and repugnant animal, the wild boar:

> You are free, and you are unbridled, and I'm giving you occasion: charge, mangle, smash and rip to your heart's content; the flowers you trample on encircle the brow and perfume the nostrils of the virtuous. The deadly thrust of your tusks and the wounds inflicted by your hands will be healed by the hands of the man of discretion. (92)

The following preface ("Del mismo al discreto lector") makes the punning distinction between the *conseja* (the tale) and the *consejo*

54

(the wise counsel). We are to consider the paradox that, though the subject be ignoble, "these sweepings may be precious. Gather up this dust, put it into the crucible of your thought, apply the heat of your mind, and I promise you will find some gold that will make you rich" (94). The matter of the sermons is not all original; he has taken much of it from learned divines and saints, which is to say, the authoritative sources of wisdom. "I recommend it. . . . You can moralize as much as you need; there is lots of room for that" (94). Eulogies from Alemán's important friends, in Spanish, Latin, and Italian, stress the book's exemplary quality. He could go no further in laying down how his book was to be read or enlisting testimony to his intentions. His adoption of the discourse of the "doctos varones y santos" (learned men and saints) was more than a declaration of seriousness; as the discourse of spiritual truth, it would not be taken in vain or travestied. Alemán has hedged his writing and the reader within the most deliberate of textual and contextual constraints.

Here is the first diametrical departure from the unstable ironies of Lázaro's presentation of his *Vida*. Within the world of the text are other divergences, notably at the scene of writing. In the Prologue, Lázaro claims that his explanatory letter is now a work of art; he has reappropriated what he wrote privately for Vuestra Merced and readdressed it to us, the public. Guzmán presents himself in the act of writing, declaring that what he has written so far is defective:

> The desire *I had*, inquisitive reader, to tell you my life, *made me* so impatient to plunge you into it . . . that I *forgot* to close a little gap, through which some logic-chopper [*terminista*] might accuse me of faulty Latin [= rhetoric] . . . because I *didn't go* from the definition to the thing defined, and before relating my life I *didn't declare* who and what kind of people my parents were, and my dubious origin. . . . (105–6).

I emphasize the past tense; it tells us that Guzmán is dissatisfied with what he *previously* wrote, that there was an earlier text that no longer exists, except as a trace, an absence, in his reference to its inadequacy. The hesitation and rewriting respond to two absences: first, the parents, a lack that he is now about to remedy;

second, the hypothetical *terminista* who might pedantically call him to account for his lack of method. The omission of his parents is, for the modern reader, the more significant absence: the repression is obvious in the extensive and detailed recollection of them and the Edenic world they created at Alfarache. As for the logic-chopper over his shoulder, he stands metonymically for a more numerous "they," those others who would like to control the discursive practice. Curiously, those recent critics who are unsympathetic to Alemán, finding *Guzmán* to be rigid and dogmatic, cite the phrase "de la difinición al difinido" (from the definition to the defined) as being typical of Alemán's mode of argument (Blanco Aguinaga 1957:317–18; Bataillon 1973c:229). In fact, Guzmán does not present his matter in this fashion, but quite the reverse: throughout his narrative he proceeds not deductively but inferentially, not from precept to example but from example to principle, from his experience to his meditation on it. This initial textual archaeology, his erasure and rewriting, opposes Lázaro's confident transmutation of his text, for it exemplifies the difficulty of writing, of assuming a posture both before that unknown audience and before oneself. It is also testimony to the importance of memory in the act of writing (and confessing) and the composition of memory's contents. I consider the matter of memory in a later chapter.

There are differences within apparent similarities. Though Lazarillo and Guzmán both leave home, the circumstances are quite different. Lazarillo was the child of poor parents, whereas Guzmán was brought up in luxury. Lázaro's father, a country miller (a stereotypical cheat in traditional folklore), was sentenced for petty larceny;[22] Guzmán's father was a shady financial manipulator from Genoa, of uncertain eastern Mediterranean origin. Guzmán was brought up in Seville, the city of riches. Everything is magnified. The economic difference between the marginal poverty of *Lazarillo* and the dishonest wealth of Guzmán's parents is blatant. By such means Alemán keys his moralistic and mercantilist attitude toward work and wealth into the meaning of his book (Cavillac 1983, 1990). The departure from home also is motivated differently in

22. Hale 1971:192–93. For jokes about cheating millers, see Thompson, 1957: vol. 5, items X210–12.

the two works, and obeys very different structural and ideological conceptions.

Unlike *Lazarillo*, *Guzmán* was enjoyed for its eloquent commentaries.[23] All literature of this epoch is sententious, relating actions or events to moral truisms and proverbial wisdom as a form of validation. If modern readers find such passages redundant, referentiality and its discontents are always with us. For the seventeenth-century reader or theater audience, the consensus invoked by sententious phrases established an important level of verisimilitude.[24] The common discourse of fiction and of the socially constituted self-image was underwritten by a system of expectations and sanctions. But *Guzmán de Alfarache* does more than invoke public assent by means of well-placed *sentencias*. Here are extended meditations in which a vast homiletic literature is brought to bear upon the protagonist's thoughts, motives, and actions. As a result, *Guzmán* may be read (following Alemán's direction) as a collection of sermons that takes the life of the protagonist as its text and uses the individual episodes of that life as *exempla*.[25]

This book's publication history shows that early European readers of the time were able to reconcile the sordid story with the chastened self that tells it, and to experience pleasure in both. Arthur Pollard noted that in England, from the Elizabethans to the

23. Besides the praise that is contained in the prefatory verses, we may note the eulogies of the English contributors in James Mabbe's version (London, 1623). As if to underscore the point, Mabbe also translated Fray Cristóbal de Fonseca's *Devout Contemplations Expressed in Two and Fortie Sermons*. See also Russell 1953.

24. Pring-Mill (1962) found 63 sentential statements in Lope de Vega's *Fuenteovejuna*, and examined them as one of three ways in which the dramatist related the action "outwards to the general framework of belief" (6).

25. Miguel Herrero García's description of picaresque literature as a "sermón con alteración de las proporciones de los elementos que entran en su combinación" is not inappropriate to the *Guzmán*, though it makes no sense when applied to the rest of that literature: "Nueva interpretación de la novela picaresca," *RFE* 24 (1937 [1940]): 343–62. Herrero was one of a sequence of writers extending over a century and a half who, stung by the European indifference to or disdain for Spanish life and thought (Masson Morvilliers's "Que doit-on à Espagne?" [1782]), seized the moral high ground by asserting that Spanish (i.e., Castilian) cultural production was essentially moral and ascetic, and was directly responsive to the doctrinal pronouncements of the Council of Trent (in which Spanish theologians had, of course, taken a leading part).

Victorians, printed sermons were "a perennial best seller,"[26] as they were in sixteenth- and seventeenth-century Spain. *Guzmán* derived a great part of its success from Alemán's unprecedented appropriation of the literature of confession, of spiritual meditation, and of moral exhortation, at a time when men and women found public sermons as exciting as political rallies are now. "Catholics and Protestants seem to have been possessed of an equally voracious appetite for sermons," Hilary Smith writes, "to judge by the numbers of them to appear in print as the century progresses, and by the persistent homiletic strain which runs through contemporary prose fiction, particularly in Spain" (1978:5).[27] Sermons not only were preached in churches, convents, and monasteries as part of the religious office, but also were delivered in streets, squares, and other public places. Priests officiated and spoke at many public functions, and particularly at the frequent acts of public justice. Sermons were preached in the galleys, in the *mancebía* or whorehouse district of Seville, in hospitals, in hospices for the poor. All over Europe scribes took down sermons as they were being delivered, so that they could be printed as broadsides (*sueltas*), and preachers kept their own sermons for publication. Guzmán testifies to this practice: "In Seville I met a man who . . . though not of good reputation, his sole occupation was to take down sermons, and they paid him half a real per sheet" (829). Even as *the* best-selling novel, *Guzmán* could not rival the popularity of devotional and homiletic literature. The wit and eloquence of the sermons and meditations contributed to the book's universal appeal, as the preliminaries to James Mabbe's English version declare. The provocative combination of commonplace events, subtle commentary, and teleological structure made it highly original as fiction yet profoundly familiar as a set of propositions.

In 1948 Enrique Moreno Báez published *Lección y sentido del "Guzmán de Alfarache."* He codified the topics of the meditations and correlated them with the conduct of the protagonist, and pronounced the work "baroque"; following Werner Weisbach, Giu-

26. Arthur Pollard, *English Sermons* (London: Longmans, 1963), 7.
27. In England, France, and Germany, where sectarian conflicts could erupt into riots, martyrdom, and war, sermons often *were* political rallies.

seppe Toffanin, and others, he took "baroque" to mean the art of the Counterreformation, designed to exemplify and propagate Catholic doctrine after the decrees of the Council of Trent. Guzmán's moralizing reflections are a means of representing his awareness of himself as sharing the human condition, with its propensity to sin, to nourish illusions, and to be governed by passions. Relating the novel to the debates on original sin, predestination, and freedom of the will, Moreno claimed that Alemán conveyed a specifically Catholic view of the human condition in the ideological war against Protestantism. In brief, the novel simulates a credible experience that illustrates the doctrine that, though humankind is inevitably depraved, even the greatest offender may be redeemed through a desire to change, with the aid of God's grace.

Moreno's analysis of the doctrinal content is thorough, but his interpretation of it is disputable. His insistence that the novel is an anti-Protestant text (1948:11–13, 44, 168–69) was controverted by Peter Russell (1953), who showed that it was admired in Protestant England precisely for its sermons and meditations. There is nothing specifically Christian in a narrative that assumes, on the one hand, that we can seldom control our nature as we wish, and on the other, that we may experience a moment when we suddenly "find ourselves" and are able, we know not how, to break free, to turn our lives around. Magazines and television shows supply a steady stream of such upbeat stories of addicts, jailed criminals, and the like who have touched bottom and then emerged to become new people in their community. Notwithstanding the commentators who present *Guzmán* as an example of "*converso* pessimism," it really belongs to this mode of upbeat storytelling.[28] After

28. The presumption that pessimism and worldly disillusion are intrinsic to writings by converted Jews and their descendants is widespread among Hispanic critics, especially those influenced by the writings of Américo Castro and Stephen Gilman. They usually fail to take account of the tradition of *contemptus mundi* or *de miseria humanae conditionis*, which continued to dominate popular devotional reading throughout Europe at this time (see below, chap. 4).

Whether Mateo Alemán had Jewish ancestry or not is an open question, although most critics assume, without evidence, that he had. The only source that is cited for Alemán's ancestry is not reliable: F. Rodríguez Marín, "Documentos referentes a Mateo Alemán y a sus deudos más cercanos," *BRAE* 20 (1933): 167–217, also published separately (Madrid: Tipografía Archivos, 1933);

his moment of "conversion," of lucidity and decision, Guzmán is tested to the utmost: his fellow convicts intend to murder him if their plan to mutiny succeeds. The officers believe him to be guilty of a theft he did not commit, so he is totally isolated, abandoned, and subjected to the most extreme torture. Nothing in his earlier life leads us to suppose that he will remain firm in the face of excruciating adversity; his story until now has been one of endless failure, in much easier circumstances, to stay whatever course he has chosen. But he does remain firm, and this is an emphatic sign that Alemán underwrites his protagonist's reform. The book addresses you, reader; it says that if a Guzmán can turn his life

---

my page references are to the *BRAE*. In a note to the final document (no. 80) he refers to the maternal surname, Enero, and adds the offensive comment that in Seville this name "olía a judío a cien leguas." Claudio Guillén (1960) has established the mother's Italian origin, which throws more light on Alemán's connection with the commercial world of Florence. Rodríguez Marín made other assertions (216–17) concerning Alemán's supposed deviousness in hiding his origins, which have been corrected by the letters published by Edmond Cros (1970). One might suppose that Rodríguez Marín's credibility in this matter would have suffered, but apparently not. His assertion that "éste y todos los sevillanos de este apellido eran de un linaje y descendientes de aquel Alemán, mayordomo de la ciudad de Sevilla, en el tiempo de los Reyes Católicos . . . que murió quemado en el brasero de la Inquisición a los pocos años de instalado este tribunal" (216) is widely accepted, although (once again) he never provided the documentary proof he promised: "Para las genealogías materna y paterna de Mateo Alemán tengo allegados muchos datos documentales, que publicaré, Dios mediante" (216). It is strange that a scholar who had carefully collected and edited eighty letters, bills, memos, affidavits, etc. could not find time to produce documents that he claimed to have in his possession, and that would be of crucial interest for the biography of Alemán. More strange is the willingness of critics to accept Rodríguez Marín's uncorroborated statements, in view of the unreliability of his other assertions, and without expressing any reservations about the offensive tone in which he presented them.

Alemán was indeed one of the surnames adopted by converted Jews in Seville (Guillén 1963), but it does not follow that everyone called Alemán was therefore a *converso*. There was a community of German (*alemanes*) tradesmen, artisans, printers, etc. who had been attracted by that city's opportunities. And a *converso* would have been unlikely to adopt the name unless there were a significant population of non-*conversos* of the same name into which he could merge. Obviously, the question of Mateo Alemán's ancestry cannot be settled one way or the other at present. His clear and public links with Italian commercial families, together with his activism and the reformist circles in which he moved, can be much more certainly construed for the kind of world he envisaged. The possibility that there may be a *converso* connection too is cautiously and plausibly argued by Cavillac (1983:22–38 and 1990:183).

around, you can too. The message is put in Christian terms, "salvarte puedes en tu estado" (you can win salvation whatever your circumstances) (275), but it dramatizes a tragic split in our nature that is universally experienced: *video meliora, proboque; deteriora sequor* (I see and approve better things, but follow the worse), in Ovid's lapidary verse (*Metamorphoses*, vii, 70). The biblical quotations and the urgent homiletic rhetoric gloss the life, but the life is not pressed into the mold of sectarian dogma. Moreno overstated his case by putting Alemán's novelistic discourse at the service of religious polemics.

If *Guzmán* is contentious, it is not in the *roman à thèse*, whose first level of allegoresis is the availability of grace and salvation, a Christian commonplace. Guzmán's repentance and turnaround are not only spiritual. There are other levels: the *whole* man is turned around—Guzmán as economic man, political man, social man. Gonzalo Sobejano (1967) distinguished between the novel seen from the perspective of its resolution and the same novel seen from the perspective of its genesis. Its intention was pedagogical, one aspect being to show a life that was to be avoided, the other to suggest through its criticism how society might better serve the common good. "The work's thesis is neither philosophical nor religious, but educational: to banish injustice and idleness" (53). The difference between the initial intention and the outcome is, according to Sobejano, the result of the intervention of Martí's spurious Part ii. He finds Martí's writing more dour and moralistic than Aleman's, so that the latter was induced to go the same way in his own Part ii. The real *Guzmán*, then, is not the "ascetic treatise" to which a religious reading reduces it but "a poetic fiction of splendid narrative qualities, and a satire upon the conditions of its time, with an educational purpose" (55). I see no need to deny the religious sense in order to stress other senses. As for Martí's moralizing, it can have had no influence at all on Alemán: it is sporadic, unorganized, and routinely conventional. It is also overshadowed by the legal pedantry and garrulous anecdotage that, thankfully, Alemán did not attempt to emulate (see below, Chapter 8). Moreover, Alemán's plan had already been sketched in the 1599 preliminaries.

Moreno (1948:126–37) also noted the abundant criticism directed at all levels of society, and concluded that it was directed at people in general, and that Alemán's eye was philosophical rather than political.[29] In that reading, Guzmán is a reformed picaro looking back not only on his past *picardías* but on the whole wicked world that they stand for. But if the object of his criticism is humankind as a whole, seen "with the eyes of a philosopher" (and with a philosophical shrug?), we need not expect things to get any better or any worse, whatever anyone does. So what would be the point of Guzmán's reform, and why should it matter to the reader? If the salvation of one's own soul is the book's single objective, then criticism of the rich, the magistrates, the royal officials, and so forth is superfluous. And it should be stressed that Alemán *criticizes*, in contrast to Quevedo, who lampoons and caricatures a predictable range of safe targets. Quevedo views his victims with ridicule and contempt: he neither expects nor desires change; indeed, the world has changed too much already for his comfort. Alemán, as Moreno noted, attacks men who wield authority, and particularly the rich and the powerful.[30] This is surely significant, since abuses of power and wealth are not cured by appeals to the abusers to become better persons.

Edmond Cros (1967) examined the book's rhetoric at great length and showed how it serves what he defines as the "dialectic of justice and mercy." Earlier (1965) he had drawn attention to the close friendship between Alemán and the reformer Cristóbal Pérez de Herrera, and published a letter from Alemán which stated his pedagogical intention in writing his novel. Behind Guzmán's attacks on the rich and powerful lies an implicit concept of the public good, the *bien público*, which Alemán shared with eminent proponents of adminstrative and fiscal reform. Guzmán's comments are consistent with the mercantilist ideas that were being propounded in the circles in which Alemán moved. In his profoundly revisionary reading of the novel, Michel Cavillac (1983) has clarified these relations, and shown that becoming "new" is not con-

29. ". . . simplemente . . . veía en las personas que le rodeaban más a los hombres que a los españoles y que miraba la sociedad con ojos de filósofo y no de político o reformador" (137).

30. "Conforme vamos descendiendo por la llamada escala social vemos que sus ataques son menos frecuentes y pierden mucho de su acritud, como si sólo le interesaran para estos fines aquellas clases que están revestidas de prestigio o autoridad" (132); ". . . como vemos, Mateo Alemán apunta en sus discursos siempre hacia arriba" (133). See also 134, "Ricos y pobres."

fined to the spiritual life of the picaro. The picaro's life will be redirected to productive work. He is converted from his adherence to *honor* as the badge of a caste, of *otium*, to *dignity* as the reward for productive activity, social and economic virtue, *negotium*. The religious discourse of salvation is a metadiscourse that subsumes the economic discourse of the salvation of a nation. The language of reform and renewal is rich with commercial vocabulary: "Try to profit from your life [ser usufrutuario de tu vida]; if you make something of it, you can win salvation whatever your circumstances [salvarte puedes en tu estado]" (*Guzmán*, 275). Guzmán's travels are not directionless wandering; they advance Alemán's pedagogical project: the commercial city-states of Italy have economic lessons for Spain, and the French ambassador has administrative ones. Cavillac shows that the influence of Tacitus was present in Spain long before any of his works were printed or translated there (1983:289–304).

Guzmán de Alfarache also presented a more general miscellany of observations and information. Edmond Cros called attention to this variety, and to the fact that when Barezzo Barezzi and James Mabbe translated the book, they tabulated topics (such as love, hunger, friendship, mythological references), stories, rhetorical devices, places, names, and so forth as if it were a *silva* or miscellany, "crushing the substance of the work into small bits" (1967:111). Learned miscellanies had enjoyed a long and varied history, from Aulus Gellius and Valerius Maximus down through the Middle Ages (Colie 1973: chap. 3). The wide erudition, philosophical curiosity, and rhetorical skill that these works attempt to display were recommended to authors of serious works of fiction. In his *Philosophia antigua poética*, Alonso López Pinciano claims that poetry embraces all the speculative and practical sciences, and that epic poetry in particular calls upon the poet's knowledge of politics, astrology, economics, medicine, navigation (I.216–19). Homer was not only the primordial poet but a universal sage. The poetics of the late sixteenth century allowed extended episodic fiction to be classified as epic, whether composed in verse or in prose, so erudition was demanded of prose fiction.[31] Such novelistic titles as

31. Francesco Robortelli, *In librum Aristotelis de Arte Poetica explicationes* (1548); G. B. Giraldi Cinthio, *De' romanzi* (1554); Giangiorgio Trissino, *Poetica* (1529); Torquato Tasso, *Del poema eroico* (1594). The texts are translated in Gil-

Gonzalo de Céspedes y Meneses' *Poema trágico del español Gerardo* (1615) are evidence of this weakening of generic boundaries within a totalizing field of "poetry"; so are those that apply the categories of fact to the world of fiction and call themselves *vidas, historias, aventuras, desengaños*. Generic taxonomy had become a nonserious do-it-yourself activity for writers long before Henry Fielding playfully went through the permutations in the Preface to *Joseph Andrews* (1742), which he commended to his readers as a "comic epic poem in prose." Alemán offers his book with the un-Aristotelean phrase "this poetic history" (95).

In *Guzmán de Alfarache* Alemán has pursued some of the same formal and rhetorical ideals that were prescribed for heroic romance by the Canon of Toledo (*DQ*, 1.47). There are journeys by land and sea, storms and calms, mistakes and misfortunes, triumphs and failures. The acts of the protagonist are minutely examined and their significance for his moral understanding and the readers' is urged upon us tirelessly. The divergences from heroic epic and romance are obvious; they are also part of the novel's system of signification. Guzmán is no Hector or Alexander, but he is peerless in his "field" of deception, without being brutal, as Soto is. He displays ingenuity and cunning, though not the magnificent cunning of the culture hero Ulysses. The author's expertise is revealed not in the maneuvering of ships or armies but in the conditions of life and the routines of the convicts. His field of operations is not the camp but the public squares and streets of the cities of Spain and Italy, and his arms are not the sword and the shield but the promissory note, the forged letter of credit, with all of which the author shows a familiarity equal to that displayed by Homer in the skills of war. There is no respected adversary, but other types familiar in romance are present: the perfidious friend (Sayavedra) and the ruthless rival (Soto), as well as the temptations of a life of ease in a corrupt world. *Guzmán* lacks the thing that makes many ancient and medieval romances romantic: a pair of lovers whose union is agonizingly deferred by trials and mischance until the last chapter of the book. It also lacks epic's indispensable comrade, or double. The protagonist is solitary, and this is the one picaresque

---

bert 1940 and discussed in Spingarn 1899:46–52; Weinberg 1961; Riley 1964: chap. 2; Forcione 1970; and Lewalski 1986.

work in which solitariness is thematized rather than being simply a necessary accident of the plot.[32] No lady waits for him, there is no home to which he can return. He rejoins his mother, but only to form a nefarious partnership that soon ends in betrayal. Guzmán's reintegration at the end of the book is not merely inward and spiritual but social and dynamic. In crucial ways, then, this work travesties or inverts the forms, devices, and motifs of the epic-romance tradition, and in doing so it declares its dependence on that tradition. It conforms to the inclusive, encyclopedic idea of romance or "prose epic," though the range of material is limited by the satiric, antiheroic mode in which it is conceived and by the limited and contingent knowledge of the protagonist, which has replaced the panoramic omniscience of the Olympian narrator.[33]

Lazarillo had satirized and trivialized chivalric romance. Alemán, however, retrieves the length, the spaciousness, the variety of materials, the internal islands of story, the wandering "hero" characteristic of the genre from the *Odyssey* to the recently translated works of Heliodorus and Achilles Tatius. Like Odysseus, Guzmán crosses the Mediterranean, though in the reverse direction. He goes to Genoa in search of his family origins but, being poor and ragged, is rejected as an imposter. After a long stay in Rome he returns looking prosperous and is welcomed by those who earlier rejected him. He takes revenge by swindling them, with the assistance of Sayavedra. We recall Lazarillo's revenge against the blind man as we watch Alemán playing his false homecoming against the generic expectations of a real return and recovery of the past. The travesty of these expectations is sharpened because of the contemporary setting. Guzmán, like his fatherland

32. For Alemán, as for Cervantes, solipsism is perhaps the worst of sins, though the perspectives of these two writers are quite different: Alemán's is religious, social, and economic, Cervantes' is existential. The dynamic of separation/integration is fundamental to the artistic vision of Shakespeare also.

33. In his study of the Greek romances, Ben Edwin Perry (1967) also noted that romance, as proto-novel, tends to be an encyclopedic genre. It has the novel's voraciousness and, as it absorbs other literary forms, it effaces its generic boundaries. "That which reaches out for everything loses its own shape; hence the novel, like the epic, is the least defined, the least concentrated, the least organic. . . . Like the epic in its day, it has everything for everybody and the range of its thought-content is, or tends to be, coextensive with that of the world for which it was produced" (47).

Spain, is humiliated by Genoese bankers; later the hated exploiters are humiliated in their turn by an act of expropriation which is no more immoral and scarcely more violent than their normal business operations. Readers are put into the ambiguous position of sympathizing with Guzmán in a political sense while distancing themselves ethically and socially from both victors and victims. Having rejected the past on his father's side, he will finally be rejected by his mother in his home city of Seville. They collaborate in a swindle, he is arrested, and she departs with the money. Earlier, each of his marriages ended when he prostituted his wife. So the epic-romance motif of a woman who remains faithfully waiting, nurturing the precarious domestic order while the hero pursues his destiny or finds his labyrinthine way home, is savagely mishandled.

The geographical turning point of Guzmán's travels is Rome; it is also the midpoint of the novel, where the events of the end of Part I and the beginning of Part II take place. Soon after his arrival there, he is taken off the street in his rags to the cardinal's palace, where he is treated as a favored guest. In the middle section of the *Odyssey*, the hero is washed ashore naked, the sole survivor of his wrecked ship, and is feted and treated royally by Alcinous, king of the Phaeacians. The middle section of our novel is likewise where Guzmán achieves great social success, as servant and entertainer, first to a cardinal and second to the French ambassador. A prince of the church and a great secular authority fill the middle of the picaro's career and are twin peaks of his fortune. His fortune is delusory: he passes from being a favored object of the cardinal's charity to practical joker, then hired buffoon and pimp for the ambassador. Guzmán next retraces his route to Spain and, within Spain, to Seville. The course of his career, Seville-Madrid-Genoa-Rome-Genoa-Madrid-Seville, repeats the circular movement of epic, its west-east loop being a reverse image of the east-west loop described by the career of Odysseus. We also find mirror structures in the *Guzmán* itself, the back-to-back pairing of the ecclesiastical and the secular authorities, for example. On the return part of his loop Guzmán meets characters who recall ones he met earlier: an army captain in each of his two sea crossings. Ironic repetitions also occur, such as his marriage, near the end, to the daughter of an innkeeper, although he has suffered unforgettable humiliations at the hands of innkeepers.

66

In heroic narratives the wanderings and encounters serve to test and to temper the hero. Aeneas had to become worthy of the final restoration of harmony, the rejoining of ties and linking of the heroic past with a heroic dynasty in the future. Guzmán goes from shame to shame, renewing his ignominy in new swindles, new betrayals of his good intentions. When his marriage to Gracia destroys seven years of study, he comments: "Just when I was at the summit of my labors, and had earned my rest from them, I found myself like Sysiphus, pushing my stone once again" (822). This protagonist's journey and return have measured not a hero's growth in experience and control but a closed system, a vicious cycle. (This structure is appropriated by Quevedo in *La vida del buscón*.) But Guzmán finally breaks the cycle in a moment of inner crisis that occurs in the last chapter of the book, while he is a convict serving time in a galley of King Philip's navy.

Readers of Northrop Frye will be familiar with his use of the concept of "displacement," a term he adopted from Freud's theory of dream symbolism.[34] The basic units from which the imagination creates a *mythos*, a formed narrative, do not change, but are combined and recombined in new encounters with reality. Myths are displaced when units and significant patterns are dispersed and reembodied in drama or romance. Frye's notion of displacement as "the adjusting of formulaic structures to a roughly credible context"(1976:36) points to an important aspect of literature as a historical phenomenon, namely, that originality is mostly a matter of recombining and recontextualizing usable parts. Rather than maintain a firm distinction between romance and novel, we should note fundamental identities and continuities between them. The patterns of romance—the questing hero; the female as sacrifice or as prize; the search for fame and fortune; the return to the home or the place of origin and recovery of identity—are as frequently embodied in nineteenth- and twentieth-century novels as in Alexandrian or medieval or baroque romances. The displacement of romance themes and patterns onto a more realistic fiction often

34. In *The Secular Scripture* (1976) Frye no longer tries to present literature as the forms and expression of seasonal myths, as he did in the *Anatomy of Criticism* (1957) and in *Fables of Identity* (New York: Harcourt Brace, 1963). In fact, one is left with the implication that myths are no longer thought of as primary except in the sense that they represent collectively significant narratives formed during the preliterate period of a culture (cf. Lotman 1979a, Todorov 1976).

leads to parody, especially when romance with its foregrounded symbolism and heightened language is still vigorously alive. *Don Quixote* thematizes the displacement of chivalric romance into a more realistic narrative, and the fictive "author's" performance of the act of displacement is also made part of the fiction.

Though it lacks some conventions, stock figures, and erotic interest, *Guzmán* reveals its dependence on the romance tradition. The containing structures (life's journey, the cyclical plot, the repetitions) are firmly present. Baltasar Gracián, an admirer of Alemán and a penetrating observer of how literary signs operate, said that *Guzmán de Alfarache* was "so superior in its craft and writing that it encompassed Greek invention, Italian eloquence, French learning, and Spanish wit."[35] In its context, the Greek "invention" or "inventiveness" can refer only to the overall plan of the work. If an important part of Alemán's ingenious wit was what he did with the "Greek" romance conventions, the deviations may be as significant as the points of conformity. Given the primary frame structures, the absence of a constituent conventional element is not irrelevant but may be a deliberately created negative space.

The picaro is not reintegrated with woman and home, he has no posterity. Whereas traditional romance satisfies in fantasy the craving for identity and an assured place in the world, picaresque "antiromance" intensifies these anxieties. The quest structure of romance is a spiral rather than a circle: the hero returns to the starting point in order to show that he is both the same and a different man from the one who first set out. As Frye puts it: "The past is not returned to; it is recreated, and when time in Proust is found again (*retrouvé*), the return to the beginning is a metaphor for creative repetition" (1976:175). Lázaro returns the same; he ends by repeating the pattern, the ménage à trois, in which he first became conscious of himself. Guzmán's return to his mother in Seville mocks the expected ending. The story will end, when it does, not at home but on a ship in the middle of nowhere, on the ocean, whence comes new life. But in this work, it is the mark of the picaro that everywhere and nowhere are for him interchangeable. Here *Lazarillo* and *Guzmán* diverge sharply. Lázaro pursued definable goals: mere survival at first, then security and a position

35. Baltasar Gracián, *Agudeza y arte de ingenio* (Huesca, 1648), discurso 56.

in the world, and the honor that accrues from these achievements. He is proud that he has succeeded in "making it to port" and now claims the fame that is his reward (Prólogo). Guzmán's moments of success have been both ignominious and temporary, but he does not want to be a criminal. This loss of control over his identity is concentrated in the final episode in the galley, where Soto plants stolen goods among his belongings and Guzmán is flogged nearly to death. For once, he is not the thief that everyone takes him for.

The dramatic reversal that marks the end, the turning point on which the two levels of narrative—story and discourse—converge, broadly confirms Alemán's initial promise. But the ending does not fit some forward glimpses of it that have been given from time to time. Guzmán writes from the galley where he is under sentence for the crimes he has committed ("Declaración," 96), "in irons" (490). In fact, Guzmán is freed from his bench and his chains before the close of Part II, as a reward for uncovering the conspiracy. Then, at intervals during Part II, we are promised a Part III. How it would be related temporally to Part II we are not told. It is impossible to say what Alemán's Part III would have been like had he written it. "Throughout the Middle Ages," writes Alexander Parker, "the natural thing for a notorious sinner to do after repentance was to atone for his sins by pilgrimage," and he declares that Alemán "would without any shadow of doubt have made Guzmán a pilgrim and, after that, a hermit." This indeed is how Felix Machado ends his continuation, and how Grimmelshausen ends his *Simplicissimus*. Parker adds that a pilgimage "fitted into the peripatetic framework of the picaresque narrative" (1967: 80). I doubt, in view of Machado's tedious tale, that Alemán would have wanted to write that kind of novel. The tension between the narrator and the narrated selves, so typical of Alemán's fiction, would cease to exist. Unless Guzmán were to be repeatedly made the victim of a wicked world, the tension between "is" and "ought" would disappear too. What we know of Alemán, his activism on behalf of the convicts in the mercury mines (Bleiberg 1966), his association with the social planner and publicist Pérez de Herrera, his political friendships, all suggest that he would have wanted his ex-picaro to rehabilitate himself *in* the world, not withdraw from it.

About a half century after Alemán published Part 1 of *Guzmán de Alfarache*, a Portuguese nobleman who had lived in Madrid wrote a continuation. Felix Machado de Silva's *Tercera parte de "Guzmán de Alfarache"* remained virtually unknown until Gerhard Moldenhauer published it (in *Revue Hispanique*, 69[1927]:1–340). Its importance in literary history is slim, but it shows that a cultured reader, a writer living in the mainstream of Portuguese and Spanish literary life, took Alemán's work seriously. It indicates that Guzmán's change of heart was taken seriously, as we would expect, and it reveals how limited were the choices and how difficult the formal and other technical problems that beset the attempt. The *Tercera parte* is no worse than much Spanish fiction of the mid–seventeenth century, but it may be read as a cautionary illustration of why Alemán chose not to write a sequel.

Unlike the continuator of *Lazarillo*, Machado is careful to start exactly where Alemán left off, and to write from within the same situation. As Guzmán waits in suspense for the royal pardon that the captain of the galley has requested, he prays, plays harmless games, and meditates on the follies of human life. The intolerable strain of waiting leads him to consider how many men surrender peace of mind to uncertain hopes of advancement, ambitions, illusory pretensions.[36] He expresses his surprise at the change in himself with such exclamations as "How different I feel now!" ("¡Qué diferente oy lo siento!") The change, of course, is in the narrated self, not in the narrating self; the latter is continuous with Alemán's narrating consciousness, as far as Machado is able to make it. The same sententious, self-critical, disillusioned gaze is turned upon his own and others' lives, though it is more urbane, less scalding than in Alemán's work, and he continues to scatter the pearls of wisdom that readers expect.

It is easier to achieve the initial splicing than to modulate the previous experiences into a new narrative. The first few chapters are devoted to establishing a new relationship with the past. Guzmán returns to Seville to look for his mother, but she has died.

36. "El officio de mayor utilidad es governarse el hombre con prudencia; el abito de mayor estimación, es el de la virtud. . . . Gran dicha es heredarla con riquezas, pero no es menor el poseerla, aunque no las aya, pues excede la virtud a todas ellas, y no ay ningunas que con ella se comparen" (30–31).

The chaplain who has been the Guzmáns' unwitting accomplice has a letter from his mother, who died repentant, informing him that he really is Don Juan Guzmán, her son by an aristocratic lover! In order to write his own novel, a continuator not only must splice his story effectively onto the existing one but must integrate the earlier one as the new one progresses. This task is easier when a well-defined genre exists, as in the case of the romances of chivalry, where plots, motifs, and codes are so clearly established that a new writer will feel the assurance of one who is joining a collective enterprise. But *Guzmán* does not share a generic repertory, and a writer can continue it only by turning one of its own premises upside down. Therefore any sequel must both splice into and block off the original work. It is easy to see what Guzmán is converted *from*, but not what he ought to be converted *to*. That "ought" is an aesthetic imperative rather than a moral or social one. The premise of Machado's *Tercera parte* is that the picaro has changed but the world has not. But Guzmán is generically incapable of romantic adventure, courtly intrigue, or amorous pursuit. Therefore he will be confined to the sidelines as spectator of the follies and rascality of other people, more stories will be told as set pieces, and pages will be devoted to descriptions of notable places. The story is that of a pilgrimage of an ambling sort that proceeds up from Seville through Portugal to Santiago de Compostela. We meet more nice people here than in Alemán's fiction, but the public's taste for *picardías*, scornfully noted in the 1626 prologue to *El Buscón*, has still to be satisfied. Machado sustains the interest in the picaresque with what by 1640 had become standard motifs of fiction: the picaresque cleric who tells racy stories, and sharp-witted, quick-fingered students who rob Guzmán on the way. But Machado reaches into the bag of romance tricks again, inventing for Guzmán a twin brother who appears along the road, coming from the opposite direction. Since this hitherto unknown twin is a criminal called Guzmán de Alfarache(!), our protagonist finds himself thrown into jail. Eventually he enters the Third Order of St. Francis, retires from the world as a hermit, tends lepers, and gains a reputation for saintliness. When we read Machado de Silva's *Tercera parte*, we see clearly what problems would face any writer who attempted to continue where Alemán left off and also, perhaps, why Alemán chose not to do so. Machado de Silva's text is an example of what had become, by mid-century, the standard stuff of fiction: part pious narrative, part travelogue, part episodic adventure of the picaresque or cloak-and-sword kind. All fiction becomes hybrid in the seventeenth century, as picaros get rich and move up socially, as wandering soldiers become temporary picaros, as runaway lovers fall in with rogues, as rogues repent and become hermits.

Reading *El buscón*

It is characteristic of Francisco Gómez de Quevedo that everything about *La vida del buscón* is cause for scandal. The circumstances of its publication in 1626 are obscure, and Quevedo seems not to have intended originally to publish it but to circulate it in manuscript. It is not known with any certainty when he wrote the first version. In the absence of factual evidence, disinterested scholarship is easily compromised; arguments for or against dates of composition may be based upon the scholar's sense of the "maturity" or "immaturity" or "youthful spirit" or "weariness" of the author in his work, criteria that are impossible to objectify.[37] The clash between discrepant interpretations over the past few decades is remarkable for the irreconcilability of the views represented. The claims to a correct interpretation that have been put forward not merely are incompatible with one another but share no common basis. Readers have been unable to agree on the text's basic elements, from which its interpretation, and ultimately its significance, must be derived. The different interpretations of classic works within various paradigms (religious, political, Freudian, existential) may be reconcilable at some level of analysis, but read-

37. Some critics supposed Cervantes' *Trabajos de Persiles y Sigismunda* to be the product of his youth, for example, because they found its whole conception to be childish in comparison with that of *Don Quixote*. For Quevedo, see the polemic between Parker and Lázaro Carreter in the following publications: Parker 1967 and the Spanish version, *Los pícaros en la literatura* (Madrid: Gredos, 1971); Lázaro Carreter, "Glosas críticas a *Los pícaros en la literatura* de Alexander Parker," *HR*, 41 (1973): 469–97; Parker, "Sobre las *Glosas críticas* de Fernando Lázaro Carreter," *HR* 42 (1974): 235–39, and Lázaro's "Contrarréplica," 239–42 in the same issue.

ings of *El buscón* do not even speak to one another. How is it that our critical equipment appears to be so fallible? How can readers' perceptions be so capricious, so scattered, yet so firm in their singularity that few can agree about what happens at crucial points in the text, much less about what it conveys?

To begin with the protagonist, Frank Chandler (1899:279) saw Pablos as "simply an adventurer," whereas for Terence May (1950:331–33) and Parker (1967:62–74) he is of profound spiritual significance, and his turning to the picaresque life is a symbolic refusal of Christian suffering and consequently of salvation. For Lázaro Carreter (1961), the book has no edifying intent. For some readers, such as Stuart Miller (1967), his life is chaotic, with meaningless repetitions, while for others, such as C. B. Morris (1965), the repetitions are signs of a deeper structure of meaning. We do not find agreement on the mode of fiction presented (other than that it is a narrative) or on the theme encoded in it. What is for Parker the greatest of the picaresque novels and a profound study in the psychology of delinquency is for others a carelessly constructed story that exists only to be destroyed, dissolved in its own corrosive wit (Lida 1972). "A work of genius," says Francisco Rico, "and a very bad picaresc novel" (1984:74, 96). A game of masks, says Edmond Cros (1975). The concluding phrase of the book, the sententious adage on the folly of expecting fortune to change if you change location but not your way of life, is taken by some readers as a self-judgment, to be understood in Christian or in Stoic terms, while others read it as burlesque, as one more example of Quevedo's rejection of the pious solemnity of *Guzmán de Alfarache*, or as an affront to the reader because it is out of tune with everything that has preceded it.)[38]

Modern writers such as Alain Robbe-Grillet, Julio Cortázar, Witold Gombrowicz, and Fernando Arrabal have disoriented readers by flouting the reigning generic paradigms. Flouting, however, requires that both writer and reader recognize and share an understanding of what is being flouted. What has become known as

---

38. For more samples of critical opinion, see Frohock 1971. I plead guilty to having contributed to this confusion with an expanded undergraduate essay (1950) that still returns to haunt me in other writers' footnotes. It had some originality in giving significance to the structural repetitions (382–87), but most of the article now seems to me to be inappropriate.

"the Spanish picaresque novel" could have had no meaning for Quevedo around 1604.[39] What were present to him were some provocative writings (particularly *Guzmán de Alfarache*) and a great range of parodic modes of representation, from carnival to *celestinesque* to *entremés* to *poesía germanesca* to *pliegos de cordel*.[40] Alemán's two parts of *Guzmán de Alfarache* and Martí's continuation constitute a sizable mass of antiromance, structured on the metaphor of life as a journey. Antiromance and journey structure are shared also by *La pícara Justina* and *Don Quixote*, both of 1605, though both were licensed in 1604.

Let us briefly recall the most widely held thesis for the constitution of the picaresque genre: that when Alemán's *Guzmán de Alfarache* incorporates and transforms structural elements derived from *Lazarillo de Tormes*, a paradigm exists for later writers to accept or variously adapt. The principal elements held in common by *Lazarillo* and *Guzmán* are (1) the lowborn and even shameful origins of the central character; (2) organization of the episodes as part of a life rather than as history, anecdotes, or cluster of events; and (3) the autobiographical mode of narration. It is by this model of generic structure and continuity that Quevedo's novel is usually read and judged. Such characteristics as are not held in common lose significance by reason of being outside the system. But where parody and satire are concerned, the identity of signs between the model and the "copy" is not evidence of conformity to a model but rather the vehicle of a radical *difference* in meaning.

I shall argue, as Maurice Molho (1972) and as Michel and Cécile Cavillac (1973) have done, that Quevedo adopted the brevity of *Lazarillo* (concision of form, ironic structure, agility of plot and style) to set it against *Guzmán*, both to distance himself from and to subvert Alemán's great and ponderous creation that loomed over the literary universe in 1600. Alemán's picaro moralizes; Quevedo's Pablos will not, except in one resounding platitude at the end. Guzmán makes a fresh start; Pablos is condemned to repeat himself endlessly. Guzmán's change of life is simply the most obvious, structural sign of Alemán's thesis (part of his Italian heri-

39. F. Lázaro Carreter places the earliest redaction of *El buscón* in the year 1604; see his edition (Salamanca: C.S.I.C. 1965), pp. lii–lv.

40. For the extraordinary intertextual range of the *Buscón*, see Lázaro Carreter 1961, and Aurora Egido's excellent review article (1978) on Edmond Cros, *L'Aristocrate*, which goes far beyond its ostensible subject.

tage, perhaps) that men can change their lives and their institutions (Cros 1967; Cavillac 1973, 1983). Quevedo, xenophobe and snob, condemns his base creature to be forever base. To Alemán the first person is an exemplary pulpit to preach from; Quevedo employs the first-person narrative as a means of striking the reader more forcefully with the carnivalesque, the scatological, the guignolesque, as part of his satirical project. Rather than judge *El buscón* as the keystone that fixes the picaresque model and confirms the genre, we should regard it as the exploiter of oppositions and tensions and the instigator of new ones. "When we restrict ourselves to recognizing what we expect to find, it almost always happens that the most important thing has escaped us: the specific and the distinctive" (Lázaro 1961:319). That is the argument of this chapter.

Pablos is born in Segovia; after his residence at the University of Alcalá he moves briefly back to Segovia, then to Madrid, to Seville, and finally to the American colonies. Quevedo incorporates the by now familiar urban jungles of Madrid and Seville into his protagonist's itinerary. In literature, Seville is stereotyped as a mecca for runaways, thieves, and swindlers. From there Pablos crosses to the Indies, confirming Cervantes' comment in *El celoso extremeño*: "the Indies, a refuge and a cloak for desperados from Spain, a sanctuary for men on the run, safe-conduct for murderers, a shelter for gamblers, . . . a lure for loose women, a general snare for many and specific remedy for few" (Cervantes 2:99). His career is more violent than Lazarillo's, less varied than Guzmán's, more repugnant than either of them. Like Guzmán, he is not given to a master, but he insists on going to school; from the local school he goes to boarding school, then to the university as servant to his young master, Diego Coronel. Until the Coronel family dismisses Pablos as an undesirable companion, he is marked off from other picaresque figures by his desire for an education as a means to advance socially. The pranks performed on landladies and shopkeepers derive from the literary stereotype of students as tricksters, familiar in farces and jocose verse. In the second half of the story, he joins with mountebanks, showmen, gamblers, false cripples, sharpers of all kinds, ridiculous poets, crazy planners (*arbitristas*), and other familiar objects of Quevedo's satire. Apart from the social milieu of petty rascals and bullies into which they merge at times, *El buscón* and *Guzmán* have little in common.

Schooling gives Pablos the means to make his way in the world. But Quevedo gives him this degree of freedom, greater than is granted apparently to either Lazarillo or Guzmán, only to demonstrate that it is useless. Pablos's failure is overdetermined. Obeying his own nature, he squanders his opportunity in futility. Throughout his narrative, Pablos engages in self-destructive acts that defeat his proclaimed intention to be different from his unimaginably sordid parents, and he narrates them with irrepressible facetiousness. But Pablos' fate is determined not by his own nature alone, for Quevedo ensures that his world will have no place for educated upstarts.

Pablos' story cannot be read as a success, even in the ironic mode of *Lazarillo*, whose protagonist undeniably ends by being more than the starveling that he was at the beginning. Pablos might have achieved success in an advantageous marriage, posing as a rich nobleman, had he not been recognized by his former patron Don Diego, who then had him attacked and beaten and his face slashed: "That's how you pay for being a lowborn picaro!" (241). Pablos does not recover from this humiliation; the rest is anticlimax and a treadmill of futile repetitions. In the final sentence, referring to his poor luck in the colonies, he comments that "things only got worse, as Your Honor will see in the second part, because anyone who changes only his location and not his life and his ways never improves his lot" (280). This sententious closure, a commonplace observation attributable to Horace, Cicero, Seneca, Augustine, and doubtless other worthies, is the nearest that the narrator gets to moralizing upon his life.[41] Coming at the end of a book that is full of self-exposure, frenetic movement, flippantly detailed physical humiliations, excesses of the mouth and the bowels, it must shock the reader with its banality. This closing phrase, singular and unexpected, makes clear that the youthful parodist's only use for moralistic fiction is to expose it to ridicule.[42] Its significance lies not in its truth content but in the part it plays in the author's intertextual parody.

41. Edward M. Wilson and José Manuel Blecua, *Lágrimas de Hieremías castellanas*, RFE, anejo 55 (1953), cxxx, cxxxvi; Henry Ettinghausen, *Francisco de Quevedo and the Neostoic Movement* (Oxford: Oxford University Press, 1972), 172.

42. This vogue had hardened into a sterile convention by the time of the book's publication in 1626.

76

El buscón has a plot that is minimal but sufficient: Pablos tries to rise socially and efface his family origin, and is defeated by his own self-destructive strategies and by the defensive violence of the society. What strikes the reader most forcibly and immediately, however, is the surface; it is from the very first a display of parodic virtuosity, a violent joke that seems designed to absorb and dissipate the political and social violence of the story by dissolving it in "mere" words. This feint on Quevedo's part to mask the political and social violence, either by displacing them from the center of the narrative or by dissolving them in the aggressively facetious discourse, demystifies itself, however. The lexical and rhetorical violence with which Quevedo constitutes his fictive world does not succeed in displacing the political and social violence of the story; it confronts them, but yields under their pressure and turns against itself to become, in the discourse of the narrator, a linguistic self-laceration (to be read as comedy), and on the authorial plane a vindication of the action (to be read as poetic justice).

The episode of Pablos' initiation among the students at Alcalá is important for any reading, since it marks a decisive moment in his career. "Look out for yourself," says Don Diego (67); "Careful, Pablos, watch it," says Pablos to himself (73). A threshold of awareness is crossed, but the move is from one extreme posture to another, from impossible aristocratic ambition and shame for his origins to undisguised mischief and identification with his tormentors. This is the most emphatic and structurally significant example of the work's characteristic rhythm. The alternate denial and embracing of the world he detests (a dialectic similar to that in Quevedo's poetry) implies an alternate affirmation and rejection of innocence. Here is the work's pulse, and it is manifested in the way the episodes are put together and shadow one another. After having ridiculed the bad poets, false cripples, card-sharping hermits, and other parasites, he goes on to imitate them. He is aloof and satirical in the early part of his *Vida*, evaluating stupidity and hypocrisy for what they are, but in the latter half he embodies all that he has rejected. The innocence, however, is an unconvincing simulacrum, mocking itself through the insistent flippancy of its discourse. It is called into question by the very linguistic mystification, the multilevel puns and conceits that have constructed it.

These devices of repetition and self-parody have been read as signs of a character that is in the process of demoralization and disintegration (Dunn 1950, Morris 1965). But Quevedo did not employ "character" as the basis for narrative composition. In Alemán's *Guzmán de Alfarache* one can observe similar swings from acceptance to rejection of his self and his world and back again, self being a metonym for world, and world being a projection of self. In *Guzmán*, however, self and world are mutually constitutive, not mutually solvent, as in the *Buscón*. Some of Quevedo's satirical works express strong indignation, but most often this indignation is political and social, and it is visceral, arising from frustration and insecurity as he sees men of less pure blood and less talent than himself win preferment. Often his indignation is aesthetic, but it is notorious that what Quevedo finds ugly or repulsive, and so deserving of ridicule, is invariably socially inferior, conventionally farcical, or politically powerless. His targets (poets, prostitutes, pimps, braggarts, beggars, barbers, misers, foreign bankers, bullies, constables, notaries, most women, any physically impaired or ugly person, etc., etc.) are all predictable, conventional, and safe. They are the victims of what Fernando Lázaro has called his "almost demonic desire to show off his wit" (1961:322).[43] Nothing in his work leads us to suppose he would dignify grotesque narrative invention by making it the vehicle for serious moral or religious reflection. Stories are too semantically ambivalent to be trusted; that lesson of *Lazarillo* was not lost on Quevedo. For the author of *Política de Dios*, a serious moral or religious treatise would have to stand upon its own evident truth, supported perhaps by rigorously contextualized exempla or fables. Entrusting a serious freight to a scurrilous, entertaining, and unstable fiction is not a practice that Quevedo risks anywhere in his oeuvre. Whenever we may think some psychological depth or a moral superstructure is being disclosed in *El buscón*, his relentless punning and outrageous conceits and his indifference to consistency of levels of narration must make us pause.

43. I agree with Lázaro that Quevedo is a parodist rather than a satirist (1961:335–36). His is an art of caricature, of distorted mimicry, and is mediated predominantly through literature. Its referents are rarely to be found in the real world, and almost always in that *literatura marginada*, the *poesía germanesca*, lampoons, *pliegos de cordel*, *jácaras*, *entremeses*, continuations of *Celestina*, etc. His slang-laden vocabulary refers not to the life of the city and its streets but to the ephemeral *literature* of the city and its heroes.

Here we must try again to see both story and discourse, a task that Quevedo deliberately made difficult for the reader. *El buscón* is a reckless aggregation of fiendishly clever witticisms, but it is more than that. The wit, appropriately emphasized by Lida and Lázaro, is exemplified not only in the verbal play but also in the story and its intertextual dimension. The plot is intelligible; Pablos' career has a clear trajectory. His project is to fulfill his "idea of becoming a gentleman" and "deny his blood," and to do so in a world where such advancement is taboo and such forgetting impossible. Put as baldly as that, Pablos' story sounds uncomfortably like tragedy. But for Quevedo, the atrabilious blueblooded conservative, the tragedy (if he were to use the term thus loosely) is in the fact that such things are *not* impossible, the ignoble *do* rise, and the world is full of duplicity and concessions to money and influence. If Pablos had been only a little bit smarter and a little less unlucky, he could have made it, too. Therefore, we must recognize the overwhelming power of Quevedo's wit, his *ingenio*, without ignoring the story. Rather, the full force and direction of the wit, its destructive power are not felt until we see that they are necessary to the story, as Quevedo wants it told. In *his* story of a poor boy attempting to rise, there must be absolutely no place where any reader could feel the slightest temptation to ask, "And why not?" Hence, I suggest, the necessity of the lexical violence at the level of the discourse, which is an instrument of mystification insofar as it prevents the reader from deconstructing the mechanism of "poetic justice" as social-political violence, or reconstructing Pablos' story in a melioristic or possibilistic reading, as readers of *Guzmán* were invited to do.

The intelligible trajectory consists of more than the protagonist's thwarted ambition, for it includes his relation to Don Diego Coronel, Pablos' social superior and, up to a point, his friend and patron. What this point is, and what forces bear upon it; the ambivalence of the patrician (and/but) *converso* Coronel family; how these crucial moments and signifiers may be interrogated so as to reveal the duplicity in Quevedo's relation to the social world that structures his fiction; these are topics that will be taken up later, in Chapter 4.

I turn now to the episode that is most decisive for the direction Pablos' life takes: the repellent sequence of events that follows upon Pablos' arrival at the university, when he is spat upon by a crowd of students, suffers a beating, and cowers under his bed as students defecate in it. Here Quevedo's wit is at its most brutal. The description is both repulsive and flippantly hyperbolic, and it is rendered, like the rest of the narrative, in Pablos' voice. As a consequence of this event, he heeds Don Diego's warning, "Keep your eyes open, Pablos, they're roasting flesh. Watch out for yourself, there's no father and mother here" (67), and decides to make a new start: "'When in Rome,' as they say, and it's true. After thinking it over, I decided to be a rogue among rogues, and to outdo them all, if I could" (74). But this resolve to outdo everyone else in knavery is quite gratuitous, for once the ritual humiliations of the freshman are over, there is peace between him and the other students: "We made friends and lived together in the house like brothers from then on, and noone bothered me again in the colleges and quadrangles" (73). By virtue of this ceremony, this *rite de passage*, he is now one of them, a status he could quietly enjoy without any obligation to be the greatest knave of them all.

This is the point from which attempts to give the work an explicit Christian meaning take off, by investing this repugnant sequence of events with symbolism. Terence May 1950 stressed the following details: the phrase "I'm no *Eccehomo*" (65), addressed by Pablos to the owner of his lodging (a Morisco) when he returns covered with the spittle that the students have showered on him; the students' derisive "This Lazarus is ready for resurrection, to judge by the stink" (63); Pablos' inexplicable falling asleep in the middle of the day; his being awakened by the voice of Don Diego saying "Ya es otra vida" (This is a new life [or the next life]) (66) and imagining that he is dead. May viewed these details as part of a whole sequence of unmotivated sufferings and humiliations. Putting it all together, he sees a deliberate travesty of the humiliation and crucifixion of Christ, not as a mockery of the Christian story but as a measure of the inadequacy of Pablos. Quevedo is representing a moment at which the subject is offered an opportunity to enact existentially an *imitatio Christi*. So, whereas Christ is the model for accepting unmerited suffering as an inescapable condition of life, Pablos' rage and shame and his decision to avenge himself upon society are a symbolic rejection of salvation and of God's presence in individual lives. According to this reading, the episodes of humiliation through which Pablos passes, reproducing the familiar pattern of the scapegoat suffering at the hands of the malicious crowd, recall the *improperia* and persecution of Christ. This is the challenge—the most profound challenge, in the judgment of a devout Christian—that Pablos fails to meet. Alexander Parker (1967) accepted and incorporated this argument. A picaresque frame does not of itself prevent the formation of religious imagery; if Alemán could show a chastened Guzmán finally accepting the challenge that he had spent his life rejecting, why should Quevedo not show Pablos' rejection of the challenge and the consequent destruction of his integrity as a sort of tragedy? *El buscón* could then join *Guzmán de Alfarache* as a model Christian fiction, the two together illustrating two sides of the same choice in a depraved world.

Even if we grant that the figural mode of signification remained operative for Quevedo's public, *El buscón* has too many discordant features for such an explanation to hold; the codes are horribly confused. An exemplary story of the rejection of salvation through failure to recognize one's share in a world of guilt and suffering does not fit with the scurrility and authorial arrogance that characterize the whole work. On the contrary, since the allusions to the Passion are confined to this one place, we may rather conclude that Quevedo is setting up an empty display of Christian signs and tokens for the purpose of making a travesty of fictional conversions; that Pablos, far from being an autonomous character with a soul to be saved, exists in part to ridicule the aesthetic of Alemán's pious epic.

The titles of Chapters 2 and 3 in Parker's book are "The Delinquent Emerges" and "Zenith and Nadir in Spain." What is implied here is the familiar trajectory of emergence, rise, climax, and fall that we are accustomed to find as the pattern of empires, dynasties, and other human institutions. This metaphor could not have been deployed if picaresque fiction had not already been cast in the image of a definable institution with a history, a founding text, an internal dynamic, and an institutional self-consciousness. Rise and fall are easily hypostatized as hierarchy: which work, then, shall occupy the peak, the place of honor? Parker (1967) says of *El buscón*: "For these reasons [i.e., its figural religious imagery combined with rounded character, satirical wit, and insight into the psychology of a delinquent], *El buscón* must be considered the masterpiece of the picaresque tradition. It is the zenith to which *Guzmán* marked the rise" (72). May's article served Parker to double purpose; once an explicit and exemplary ideological bond can be established between *El buscón* and *Guzmán*, all the ugly and unruly elements of Quevedo's work can be subordinated to it. It is then given pride of place in the picaresque sequence, and the genre is thereby reconstituted, typified by an overriding moral seriousness; by this criterion *Lazarillo* has to be excluded as a "precursor." As so often in Parker's work, theme, and particularly the ideological content of the theme, is doubly privileged, at the level both of taxonomy and of evaluation, in a tight circle of tautology.

El buscón gives no reason to suppose that Quevedo had formed in his mind a generic model derived from *Lazarillo* and *Guzmán*, to which he shaped his text. He made use of episodes and adopted set pieces (the tax on stupidities, for example) from both Alemán and Martí (Lázaro 1961:326–32). In language, expressive range, and satirical objects, *El buscón* is also close to Quevedo's own first prose pieces, such as *Vida de la Corte* and the early *Sueños*. For Quevedo, to write this work was not to move into a literary mode that was radically different from what he had done already (Lázaro 1961:336–37). He moved into the narrative *Vida*, which enabled him to organize his stock of facetiae, his unrivaled genius for caricature, his unique facility for verbal wit, making his readers leap conceptually by contrapuntal wordplay rather than move them by causality or teleology. As an *active* text, *El buscón* does not perform very differently from the way *Lazarillo* did in its own time and literary setting. As *Lazarillo* stands to romances of chivalry, so stands *El buscón* to *Guzmán*. Each of them offers an insolent riposte to a vast work whose popularity endorsed its ideology and conferred moral authority upon it. *Lazarillo*, moreover, was reprinted in the wake of *Guzmán's* success (Guillén 1971:144–45), and so could be read not only as a forerunner but as a pattern by which to cut *Guzmán* down to size. The life story that Pablos narrates plumbs surreal depths of degradation and repellent humor beyond anything Alemán conceived.

The protagonist exposes his humiliations to us in a style of continuous self-destructive flippancy that contradicts any claims we may make for verisimilitude on the level of character.[44] Consider, for example, the moment when Pablos receives a letter from his uncle with the news that his father has died (*Buscón*, 1.,7). This

---

44. Parker (1947) thought otherwise.

uncle, Alonso Ramplón, is the executioner for the city of Segovia and he has just executed Pablos' father, whose death he recounts (hanging, quartering, scattering of the remains) as if it were heroic, but (he goes on) "I'm sure the pastry cooks of this place will console us by burying him in their fourpenny pies" (92). His mother, he learns from the same letter, is held as a witch by the Inquisition in Toledo, and will be burned. Pablos' comment on this news is: "I don't deny that this new shame touched me deeply" (93), and later, in Segovia, he tells repeatedly how he felt ashamed and humiliated by his uncle, by being seen in his uncle's company, by the circumstances, by his uncle's coarse companions . . . (II.4). When shame is expressed by a shameless narrator over his grotesquely caricatured family, the narrator's shame can be read only as comic. Laughingly he tells Don Diego of his newfound independence, and of the death of the father that has made it possible, in a torrent of brilliantly flippant puns—terms in which no son ever did or ever will report the death of a father.[45] At the party in his uncle's house in Segovia, meat pies are brought in from the bakery:

Five meat pies appeared on the table. After removing the crusts he took an aspergillum and everyone intoned a *requiem aeternam* for the souls of those whose flesh was buried there. My uncle said, "You remember, nephew, what I wrote you about your father." It came back to me; they ate, but I only took the pastry, and that has been my habit ever since. Whenever I eat meat pie, I say an Ave Maria for the soul of the departed. (139–40)

Such passages are what make *El buscón* a "book of jests": its seizure of topics that are not only beyond the bounds of propriety (Pablos' mother, a witch, is said to have committed sodomy every night with a goat)[46] but beyond all verisimilitude; its macabre fantasy, its brilliant play with words. Some of the puns have a long reach: in the first passage quoted, the verb used for the cutting up

45. "'Señor, ya soy otro, y otros son mis pensamientos: más alto pico, y más autoridad me importa tener. Porque, si hasta ahora tenía como cada cual mi piedra en el rollo, ahora tengo mi padre.' Declaréle cómo había muerto tan honradamente como el más estirado, cómo le trincharon y le hicieron moneda, cómo me había escrito mi señor tío, el verdugo, desto" (94).
46. ". . . daba paz cada noche a un cabrón con el ojo que no tiene niña" (93).

and quartering of the father after his execution ("le trincharon") is the one used for carving up meat at table; thus it anticipates the unappetizing joke about meat pies as the coffins of dead men many pages later. This scathing discourse (the nearest modern equivalent is perhaps to be found in the theater of Joe Orton) is comprehensible as an attack on the sensibilities of Quevedo's public while he caricatures some familiar trades and activities, but not as the unmotivated memoirs of an autonomous narrator or of a "rounded character . . . who can arouse our compassion and understanding" (Parker 1947:72). Pablos' insistence on his feelings of shame and humiliation set up expectations of consistency which are violently transgressed in his report to Don Diego of his father's death. The shame/compensation dynamic can be understood only as a mechanism engineered to produce the absurd social ambition that will predictably bring his downfall. Linguistic virtuosity has detached itself from both subject and object, and also from generic convention. Claudio Guillén (1982) accurately describes Quevedo's "privileging of writing (over literature) and of style (over genre)." *El Buscón* shares with other burlesque works their "triumph of language—euphoric, unbridled, arrogant, defiant, unrestrained" (6–7).

Gonzalo Díaz-Migoyo (1978) attempted to reconcile these levels of discourse, arguing that the whole novel is full of duplicity. Who among us would offer our own grotesquely bad luck and an unspeakably repugnant family—parents, uncle, and others—as material for light entertainment, as a good story for idle moments?[47] Such a story is not tellable without a radical editing and revision not of the story but of the self that tells it. The "I" must first be fictionalized and depersonalized and put into a highly self-conscious relation with the interlocutor. In this reading, Pablos' relation to Vuestra Merced can be seen as both ingratiating and full of duplicity. If he would present his misfortunes as matter for laughter, he has to display whatever is on the tongues of the gossips. To resolve this dilemma, he adopts a mode of discourse that will

47. In Pablos' "Carta dedicatoria" addressed to "V. M." he offers the various "discursos de mi vida" so that he may see "cuan corto he sido de ventura" and enjoy it as "alivio para los ratos tristes." Also he expresses his desire to deflect lying gossips ("por no dejar lugar a que otro mienta").

make the painful funny; the shameless way he chooses to write about his shame is the last line of defense. By appearing not to care about what has tormented him, he avoids repeated humiliation. The real reader, however, is not deceived. The verbal mask confirms that Pablos is still the picaro: he has created "a shameful present that feigns dignity by an ostentatious display of indifference toward his shame" (100). The act of narration then becomes the last in the sequence of picaresque deceits, and the writing becomes continuous with the living (101). Ingenious as this explanation is, it is flawed. It requires that we read the "Carta dedicatoria," like Lázaro's Prólogo, as an integral part of the text, though it was not part of the original text and probably was not written by Quevedo. But the argument is, in the final analysis, one more hopeless, if ingenious, attempt to read Pablos as a self-conscious autonomous character in the realist tradition, one who manipulates his discourse in order to reconcile himself to his life and make it tellable. Pablos is a trajectory, and he is perfectly describable as a Proppian function. He is also readable as the confluence of intertextual traces, within a complex intergeneric web.

Besides having a story to tell, Pablos is the mediating eyes and ears that scan the scenes of urban low life and itinerant vagrants that fascinated respectable readers throughout Europe. Through Pablos' fictive pen Quevedo practices his virtuoso art of caricature. But we must not think of Pablos as an observer of scenes in the real world, which are transformed by Quevedo's verbal art. Independent of the picaresque autobiographies of Alemán and Martí there existed a vast literature of low life and trickery in their many forms and variations. An increasingly popular and voluminous poetry, the *poesía germanesca* (poetry in street slang) celebrated, sometimes satirically, sometimes not, the exploits and the lifestyles of braggarts, pimps, cutthroats, and similar figures of the rowdy, brawling world of the metropolis. *Romances de ciego* (songs of blind beggars) reported crimes, notorious swindles, hoaxes, and executions, and these were the stuff of the increasing traffic in chapbooks. The pranks and the predatory lives of students were celebrated in verses and anecdotes. These social types and their tricks, their locations, their gestures, their songs, their dances, their pairings and microcommunities with their dialects, had already constituted the characteristic world and language of the *entremeses* (farces).[48] The existence of all these genres and subgenres representing the worlds of these sharpers, swaggering bullies, and the rest, beyond the confines of narrative but increasingly present in all narrative kinds, is of fundamental importance to the reading of *El buscón*. The "picaresque world" of Quevedo's text is not substantially different from that of his other prose pieces, or of his *jácaras* (verses in thieves' jargon) (Lázaro 1961, Lida 1972). Moreover, it is a second-order representation: Quevedo's verbal elaboration is not of the real world but of multiple existing literary conventions, a literary transformation not of life but of earlier literature. This fact is more useful for reconstructing the context of *La vida del buscón* than seeking a hypothetical moment of origin for the "picaresque novel" and relating Quevedo's text to it.

As a part of his enterprise, Mateo Alemán had mediated some of that subworld and its oral culture to his readers, but not as an entertaining spectacle; that shady world was necessary to his dark romance. For Alemán, the vertical axis is clearly the important one; the enticement of his protagonist into that world is a plunge into the lower depths, an addiction to evils; either he must lose himself in it and be absorbed without trace or he will begin to emerge from it as from a journey of purgation. His immersion and corruption were necessary if Guzmán was eventually to acquire significance in this familiar symbolic mode of descent and rise. The young Quevedo was not seduced by that model. It is easier to imagine him being incensed by that quasi allegorization of a world that offered to his insatiable satiric muse the rich dredgings of its scurrilous dialect, its grotesque or repugnant models with which he could not only lampoon hypocrisy and affectation but pitilessly dismember those who were unfortunate enough to be old or to deviate from physical and aesthetic norms. The signs of redemption have been ostentatiously trailed before us at an early stage of the narrative, and just as ostentatiously rejected ("I'm no *Ecce homo*," etc.). Equally if not more obnoxious to Quevedo would have been Alemán's political agenda. The political context has

48. Asensio, *Itinerario del entremés* (Madrid: Gredos, 1965); noted also by Mariano Baquero Goyanes, "El entremés y la novela picaresca," in *Estudios dedicados a Menéndez Pidal*, vol. 6 (Madrid: C.S.I.C., 1956), 215–46; Lida 1972; Egido 1978.

been lost in the critical tradition until very recently, obscured by religious issues and reliance on such literary-historical shibboleths as the Counterreformation. The "Why not?" question that Quevedo's reader must be prevented by every rhetorical means from asking is the very one that is implicit in the possibilistic world of *Guzmán de Alfarache*—that work being, among other things, the epic of self-vindication by Alemán the administrative reformer, friend of such well-placed critics and government functionaries as Pérez de Herrera (schemers all, to the sarcastic eye of a Quevedo). Alemán's less discriminatory concept of honor, his distinction between the creative activity of industry and commerce and the destructive effect of privileging financial dealings, would have alienated the landed gentry, who would disdain both kinds of activity. In Pablos' career there is no upward turn, no return to a point of departure, no reintegration on any level. Rather than the narrator's journey of self-recollection, it is the sign of the writer's violent rejection of any such exemplary claims for the practice of narrative fiction.

3

Beyond the Texts

Models

Autobiography has received increasing theoretical attention in recent years, and as a consequence of this interest, attempts are made to read picaresque fictions as if they were true autobiographies.[1] This move is a mistake, for two reasons. In the first place, theory of autobiography is drawn from modern writings. This was

1. Studies of autobiography: Roy Pascal, *Design and Truth in Autobiography* (Cambridge: Harvard University Press, 1960); William L. Howarth, "Some Principles of Autobiography," *NLH* 5 (1974): 363–81; Philippe Lejeune, *Le Pacte autobiographique* (Paris: Seuil, 1975); Elizabeth Bruss, *Autobiographical Acts: The Changing Situation of a Literary Genre* (Baltimore: Johns Hopkins University Press, 1976); Paul de Man, "Autobiography as De-facement," *MLN* 94 (1979): 919–30; Georges Gusdorf, *Autobiography: Essays Theoretical and Critical*, trans. James Olney (Princeton University Press, 1980); William C. Spengemann, *The Forms of Autobiography* (New Haven: Yale University Press, 1980). There is also the massive history of autobiography by Georg Misch, *Geschichte der Autobiographie*, the volumes published variously in Berlin, Bern, and Frankfurt, 1907–1969. For Spain, Pope 1974; *L'Autobiographie; L'Autobiographie en Espagne*; Nicholas Spadaccini and Jenaro Talens, eds., *Autobiography in Early Modern Spain* (Minneapolis: Prisma Institute, 1988).

to be expected, since autobiography as fully self-conscious self-portrait cannot be said to exist before Rousseau. As a minimal definition one can adopt that of Jean Molino: "a retrospective account by a real person of part of his or her existence," of which both the origin and the direction are "self-examination."[2] Autobiography obeys a double impulse: first, to reveal a self and to show it being constituted over time through interaction with its world; second, to be understood and justified before the reader, who may stand metonymically for that world with which the self has been engaged. Attitudes and motives are infinitely variable, ranging from gratitude for opportunities for a life well lived to grim stories of hardships suffered, from self-congratulation to assaults on enemies, real or imagined, and from honest accounting of public service to bitter settling of old scores. The boundaries of autobiography are even less clear than are those of the novel. Our century has witnessed an explosion of the self into print, though the revelations have often to be written "with" another. This also appears to be the case with *Estebanillo González* (lxxxii–cxxxvi). Readers commonly seek the "real" person behind the public image, the intimate self of the public figure, the real presence of the writer in the text. Nowhere is the illusion of presence cultivated so assiduously by writers and sought with such fervor by readers as in autobiography. It was inevitable, therefore, that autobiography would become the object of deconstructive practice, and Paul de Man declared that "it appears that the distinction between fiction and autobiography is not an either/or polarity but that it is undecidable" (1979:321). Critics, ever watchful for evidences of blindness, bad faith, self-exoneration, and the like in the few classical texts before Rousseau, easily discover in their "I" the encoding of desire beyond the self, and so assimilate autobiography to the universe of fiction.

In autobiography there can be no objectivity with reference to the object of the narration, nor can there be a total unveiling of the self. There is no self beyond the text, however powerfully the reader is lured into the illusory gap between the "I" of the *énoncé* and the "I" of the *énonciation*, between the discursive self and its rhetorical shadow games. In the feigned life of a first-person

2. *L'Autobiographie en Espagne*, 115–16.

novel, on the contrary, there can be no illusion of a self to be discovered behind the narration. The problematic conflation of author and narrator that is part of the game in autobiography, teasing the reader to judge the distance between them, is not simply problematic in fiction: it is inconceivable. To fail to see the horizon beyond which the author of a first-person novel has withdrawn would be to fail as a reader.

The first-person novel demands to be read as if it were autobiography, just as romances and novels once demanded to be read as if they were chronicles or letters or diaries. Its mode of presentation, its temporal structure, its expectations of the reader, and the rhetorical resources by which they are signaled are identical to those of true first-person narration. But whereas in true autobiography the author's expectation is identical with the narrator's, in fictional autobiography the narrator's expectations of the reader are not the same as the author's. It is left to the reader to judge the distance between implied author and narrator, as well as between narrator and narratee (the self writing and the self written about) and to observe how these distances are handled rhetorically. The space may be closed almost to nothing by the author's evident approval, or opened wide by authorial dissociation, or modulated by indulgence or by irony, to mention a few possibilities. First-person narration is to autobiography as third-person narration is to history or chronicle. For while the dominant third-person mode bears the traces of its ancestry (epic, romance, fabliau, myth, folk tale, etc.) but feigns the truth claims and the logic of history, the first-person narrative tells a story with the same genetic ancestry but with the narrow focus and the limited range, explanatory power, and credibility of the single "I."

In the twentieth century, a growing awareness of the subjectivity of all forms of knowledge and the intersubjectivity of cultures has been accompanied by a subtle assimilation of all narrative modes to the first person. Gustave Flaubert, Benito Pérez Galdós, and Thomas Hardy extended the use of the *style indirecte libre* so as to place the narrator's recording machine within the character itself, and Marcel Proust and Henry James split the narrator off from the author to such a degree, and allowed him such freedom to comment and speculate on the gaps and uncertainties, that the narrative as "retold" by the narrator becomes essentially the narrator's own story.

As an example of the difference in the reader's response to third- and first-person narration, Michal Glowinski cites the sentence "For Mr Ignacy Rzecki, the time of concern and amazement came again." Statements of personal feelings are implicitly validated by a third-person narrator, and Glowinski shows that problems of truthfulness arise only when we reformulate such statements in the first person. According to Glowinski, the narrator's information in its third-person enunciation, being "an objectified statement of fact . . . could be subject to verification by the narrator. The recipient could find out whether he ought to accept in good faith Mr Rzecki's words." A reader "does not enjoy the advantage of such a privileged situation" in a first-person novel. "He is doomed to a peculiar uncertainty as to the informational content of the sentence. He cannot refer to an authoritative narrator" (1977:103–4). A narrator who is established as the source of true and appropriately phrased information will be trusted to relay the truth about a character's emotions, whereas the character itself might not be able to do so.

In recent narratology what has often been in question is the reliability of the narrator, as if critics were unable to shake off the nineteenth-century concern with sincerity, truthtelling, and other values by which literature may be redeemed from frivolity, or worse. But if we shift our perspective back to the sixteenth century and look at the question raised by Glowinski in that historical frame, what matters is no longer the integrity of the messenger but rather the significance of the message. The long self-declarations of the sentimental novels and the monologues of shepherds in pastoral romances were perused not for their reliability but for their encoding of a social theory of the emotions. The matter was cogently expressed many years ago by Rosemond Tuve in regard to the truth of the feelings in Renaissance poetry:

Discussions are little preoccupied with [the poet's] feelings, greatly preoccupied with those that he will evoke. The critical question of "sincerity" is neglected in favor of the poetic problem of efficacy through credibility. The truth of the affections was a serious matter, but it stood to be answered less in terms of the question "did the poet feel it?" than "will the reader feel it, and why should he?"[3]

In this matter of the credibility of narrative, what would happen if we tried to imagine a heroic narrative subjected to the transformation from third person to first person? What would it be like to have Amadís tell his own story? First-person narration fatally ironizes the discourse of heroic romance, so that a hero telling his own story from start to finish would have to be either a god (beyond irony's reach) or a braggart. When Odysseus and Aeneas tell parts of their life stories, they do so within a discourse that is well established by the narrator, and with a well-defined relation to a listening audience within the poem. Indeed, it is not only heroic romance that is subject to ironic transformation, but any narrative in which the speaker claims to have excelled in a world where the claim cannot be validated. The author of *Lazarillo* saw this openness to irony, and made it work for him. Alemán saw it too; his antihero has no heroic dimension, for even as a criminal he is not the most monstrous or the most spectacular that could be imagined, nor should he be if he is to play the role of Everyman. The ironizing first person would reduce his offenses to tricksterism and banality were it not for the second level of discourse. The narrator's discourse of self-exposure is insulated from irony by the metadiscourse of commentary. This scholastic, Augustinian metadiscourse is *the* authorizing discourse that valorizes not only this novel but all experience, all activity, all history.

So the problematics of first-person narration, well known to us from the narratological analysis of much twentieth-century fiction, become problematic themselves when they are read back into works of the sixteenth or seventeenth century. There the protocols of reading are different; the story is a given, its "truth" is not at issue, and this stability in the discourse enables the reader to detect any deviations by the characters. We are required to ponder the meaning of what we are being told rather than whether the teller deserves our trust, unless untrustworthiness is textualized in

3. Rosemond Tuve, *Elizabethan and Metaphysical Imagery* (Chicago: University of Chicago Press, 1947), 183.

his comic role and his ironic winks and grimaces, as it is in *Lazarillo*. Lázaro's duplicities are not really mystifications, because they so clearly call attention to themselves at the surface of the discourse, through the characteristic use of euphemism, puns, and similar verbal tricks. After the father dies "like a faithful servant," the mother decides to "keep good company"; this phrase and "reach a safe haven" are made emblematic, referring both forward and backward. That is to say, they are programmatic phrases announcing Lazarillo's desire to make his way in life, and they are also lapidary ones that announce his satisfaction as he writes himself and his life into a book (*tratado* 7:79; Prólogo, 7). These facetious phrases are easily seen for what they are: markers that enable the reader to judge the ironic gap between intention and achievement, and, more particularly, essential tropes in the discourse of insolence.

This authorial strategy for revealing distance between the protagonist's intention and his achievement is one of the simple but far-reaching discoveries made by the unknown author. Its importance was evidently noted by Alemán, who adopted it and developed it on each level of his discourse. In *Guzmán de Alfarache*, the narrator's telling of the past events is structured on a dialectical tension between desire or expectation and the frustrated outcome, between resolve and remorse. This is the pattern, sustained episode by episode, whether Guzmán's intention is to achieve success by trickery or to rise by ingratiating himself with a powerful master or to follow an honorable course. The narrator tells us repeatedly that this pattern of rising expectation followed by defeat and shame caused him to reflect upon it at that past time; it is the motive for the commentary that he writes upon his life as he tells it in the present. Of all the picaresque works, this one offers the most successful and sustained attempt to represent a coherent subject, and it does so through the fusion of separate levels, as we have observed. Its rhetorical virtuosity brings it closest to the simulation of a subject that both manipulates and is manipulated in the telling.

Later novels use the first-person mode of presentation in an increasingly mechanical way, and some drop it altogether. But the most intriguing is the last, the *Vida y hechos de Estebanillo González* (1646), whose fictional status is obstinately indeterminate. It is im-

possible to know with certainty whether we are reading an anonymous fiction that has incorporated public events and simulated a
self that makes his life into a joke or genuine autobiographical
memoirs of a man who possesses the self-immolating wit of a buffoon and whose name really was that of the title.

The second objection to the use of autobiography as a theoretical model for picaresque narrative is that it assumes, again, that
picaresque exists as a stable self-consistent genre, and that one
paradigm fits all. This implicit assumption mars the otherwise useful essays of Jean Starobinski (1980) and Edward Friedman (1988).
Autobiography never has been a self-consistent genre. The autobiographical impulse of Renaissance writers was modeled in some
cases on the medieval confessional tradition (e.g., Petrarch's *Secretum*) and in others on the personal chronicle. Some scholars
have reacted against the established opinion that Spain has lacked
autobiography by pointing to the *Autobiografías* volume of the Biblioteca de Autores Españoles (vol. 90). Jean Molino refers to "that
véritable explosion" and claims that "Spain is the crucible in which
modern autobiography takes form."[4] Yet, as Margaret Levisi ad-
mits in an essay on the soldiers' *Lives* (which is what most of these
documents are), they are not what we would now call autobiography, but memoir, report, or deposition. "What is lacking is the
stress on the history of their personality" (Spaddacini/Talens, 98).
Jerónimo Contreras, for example, "narrates adventures without
the slightest allusion to his inner self or its development" (104).
These narratives are highly selective, concentrating attention upon
the *public* acts of the subject, acts of courage and endurance that,
in his opinion, should earn him public respect and reward. We
cannot expect to find a fully developed interiority either in autobiography or in first-person fiction modeled upon it. Montaigne
wrote of the dangers of "private fantasy," which must be checked
by the order of the public realm. In the words of Timothy Reiss:
"There are two subjects: one is nothing more than an inconstant
passage; the other is reasonable and is defined only by its insertion
into the sociopolitical realm. . . . The lack of fixity of the private
subject guarantees the stability of the state and the place of the
public subject; for that becomes the *only* possible place in which

4. *L'Autobiographie en Espagne*, 125.

something like an 'individual' with a more or less secure status can situate itself."[5]

Part of the fascination of *Lazarillo de Tormes* resides in its indeterminate relation to all of the narrative models that have been proposed for it: confession, deposition before a magistrate or an officer of the Inquisition, ironized heroic narrative, or personal chronicle. For *Guzmán de Alfarache*, the models of romance and of confession are examined elsewhere. Quevedo's *Buscón* will be seen to have a parodic relation to both *Lazarillo* and *Guzmán* and at the same time to be continuous with the author's practice of satire and burlesque; it has no need to draw upon other models to accomplish Quevedo's disruptive goals. *La pícara Justina* is a travesty of many kinds of activity, not all of them literary: court buffoonery, in-jokes, journeys, tall stories, loosely held together by the garrulous personal narrative that seems to have no more justification than the human urge to talk. It is sequential narrative mocking itself as gossip. In short, one cannot claim that sixteenth-century autobiography (a dubious concept in any case) is *the* generic model for picaresque fictions. One can say with some certainty, however, that beyond the common structural frame of the life-as-journey that derives from romance, each of the principal innovating picaresque works creates its own form, and does so by raiding genres and discourses that were not canonical or (in some cases) literary.

When we scan the field of fiction, long and short, at the turn of the century, we find that it almost always presents an image of a world that is *urban* and *contemporary*, the events generated by luck, coincidence, and cunning, but reliably within the saving postulate of a providential order. The providential order was ironized in *Lazarillo*, and will be again by Cervantes in *Don Quixote*, but for most other writers, whether of picaresque or of the kind called *novela cortesana*, it will become a conventional formula for bringing matters to a conclusion that will satisfy the prejudices of a mass readership. The contemporaneity that has come to characterize fiction of this period suggests that the public's hunger for news of the here and now, fed by cheap printings of *pliegos de cordel*, *relaciones*,

---

5. Timothy Reiss, "Montaigne and the Subject of Polity," in Parker/Quint 1986:137, 140–41.

sucesos in prose and in verse, news sheets of many kinds, had indelibly marked fiction as well as theater.[6]

Exemplary Shapes

The assumptions concerning the exemplary functions of literature that prevailed when the picaresque novels were composed not only favored some kinds of content over others but also privileged some narrative forms, particularly those that are designed to display the working of a providential order: romance is the preeminent example. Much of this literature is factitious: stereotyped stories of violence for the sake of honor, of love and pursuit, of wish fulfillment, for a public eager to share in or to pry into the new affluent urban aristocracy. It also prolongs and appropriates the prurient taste for low-life scenes (set at a safe distance) that sustained the picaresque. These texts enable us to understand how the imaginative originality and the powerful reformist impulse in *Guzmán de Alfarache* could be swiftly dissipated in a vulgarized concept of the exemplary that prioritizes kitsch. We do not find picaresque as one among several well-differentiated novelistic forms; rather, writings in a broad field of narrative share discursive properties, among them the traditional structure of romance. Within that field the kind of short fiction that is usually known as *novela cortesana* comes increasingly to dominate the public demand of the seventeenth century; it is eminently marketable, and its public is reflected within the literature itself, both literally and in wish fulfillment.

Spain participated in the European debate over the language of literature, and about rules of composition.[7] At issue were the aesthetic values of difficult or special vocabulary and syntactic complexity in poetry as against simpler speech and rhythms, as well as

6. For a similar phenomenon in England, see Hunter 1988 and Michael McKeon, *The Origins of the English Novel, 1600–1740* (Baltimore: Johns Hopkins University Press, 1987), 55–64.

7. Bibliographical information for Spain may be found in Riley 1964; Jones 1971; Bruce W. Wardropper, *Siglos de Oro: Barroco*, vol. 1 of *Historia y crítica de la literatura española*, ed. Francisco Rico (Barcelona: Editorial Crítica, 1983).

the question of the superiority of classical Greek plots and the
Aristotelian rules in drama. These debates were ostensibly literary,
but they were clearly engaged with questions of hierarchy and cultural preeminence, with the social status of the literary canon. Beyond these questions lay the perennial ones of the defense of literature itself and the terms in which it might be justified.[8] At what
we might call the conservative extreme were those who, like Juan
Luis Vives, would discourage all young and impressionable persons, especially females, from reading anything but pious and edifying works.[9] The power that literature could exercise through fantasy upon the desires and emotions was taken for granted.
Indeed, this power had to be assumed, for the art of literary composition was but a branch of rhetoric, and rhetoric was the art of
persuading, of subduing the mind of the receiver in as pleasurable
a way as possible. The evident sympathy of Juan Palomeque's
daughter (DQ, I.32) for the enamored female characters in the
books of chivalry would have confirmed Vives in his declaration
that the woman who lets her mind dwell on weapons and on the
strength of a man's arm is not a good Christian.

Other writers and critics differed from Vives less in substance
than in the degree of their tolerance. If nobody disputed the assumption that literature could stimulate desires, neither did anyone deny that it could stir noble and generous feelings. The novel
Don Quixote displays the power of fiction—romances, myths, folk
tales, received opinions—not only upon the central character but
upon everybody who appears in it. The effect of the magic presence of Don Quixote—himself a fiction of his own making—is to
bring everyone else's fiction-making to a curative level of self-
awareness. The Stoic ideal of self-awareness, "know thyself,"
makes the reader share responsibility with the writer, rather than
demand the intervention of an institutional censor.

If it was a commonplace to declare that no one should waste
time on frivolous stories and fancies, it was also a highly respectable commonplace to affirm (after Pliny, Epistle III.v.10) that there

8. In these paragraphs I cannot represent the variety of argument and the
range of authorities that were arrayed by the opponents of imaginative literature in Spain. Good accounts can be found in Riley 1964, Forcione 1970, Ife
1985.
9. Juan Luis Vives, De institutione foeminae christianae (Antwerp, 1524).

is no book so bad that some good cannot be found in it.[10] This affirmation assumes that readers read for the good they will derive from the experience as well as for the pleasure of it, and it underscores Horace's exhortation to writers to seek to instruct readers as well as to delight them. Axiomatic expressions such as *enseñar deleitando, deleitar aprovechando* (delightful teaching, mixing profit with pleasure) occur with mechanical regularity in support of the didactic function of literature.[11]

While moralists excoriated the romances of chivalry for their excesses and implausibilities and for their effect on young readers, the authors claimed to represent models of chivalrous conduct and prowess. If the writers of romances took liberties with historical fact, it could be claimed that "the poet . . . does not write of things as they were or are, but as they should be, in order to give at once profit and delight by satisfying the men of that age in which they write, a thing that is not permitted to those who write histories."[12] And Don Quixote would have applauded the words of another soldier and poet, had he known them: "Truly, I have known men, that even with reading *Amadis de Gaule* (which God knoweth wanteth much of a perfect poesy) have found their hearts moved to the exercise of courtesy, liberality, and especially courage. Who readeth Aeneas carrying old Anchises on his back, that wisheth not it were his fortune to perform so excellent an act?"[13]

These words of Sir Philip Sidney display the mode of exemplification by which literature was held to instruct its readers; namely, by exciting them to emulation of the good, wonder at the extraordinary, aversion to the ugly and the wicked. We may doubt by how much minds, morals, or sensibilities were improved by the

10. For references, see *Guzmán*, p. 5n.
11. Representative texts are given in Gilbert 1940. The conflation of Aristotelian formalism and Horatian moralism that underwrites these familiar formulas is traced in Marvin T. Herrick, *The Fusion of Horatian and Aristotelian Literary Criticism, 1531–1555*, University of Illinois Studies in Language and Literature, 32 (Urbana: University of Illinois Press, 1946). See also Ife 1985: chaps. 2 and 3.
12. Giovambattista Giraldi Cinthio, *Discorsi intorno al comporre dei romanzi, delle commedie, e delle tragedie, etc.* (Venice, 1554), 57; English version in Gilbert 1940: 271.
13. Sir Philip Sidney, *The Defense of Poesie* (also known as the *Apologie for Poetrie*), in Gilbert 1962:428.

romances of chivalry that inspired Don Quixote to emulation, with their huge slaughter against absurd odds. The same may be said of the sentimental novels of the fifteenth century (notably those of Juan de Flores, Juan Rodríguez del Padrón, Diego de San Pedro) with their feverish abandonment to the extremes of adoration and despair, in a bleak novelistic world confined almost entirely to the subjectivity of the lovers. In comparison with some of these indulgent and fatalistic presentations of the violence of the human emotions of love, jealousy, and family honor, *La Celestina* must strike the reader as being no less exemplary than its author, Fernando de Rojas, claimed that it was. Jorge de Montemayor's pastoral novel *La Diana* follows in the same tradition as the *novelas sentimentales* in its concentration upon the hopeless condition of lovesickness. However, by eliminating the courtly social setting and setting up a pastoral world as one that permits free discourse between equals, the pastoral novel allowed full play to an erotic fatalism, unmitigated by other motives for conflict. As Maxime Chevalier (1976) has shown, *La Diana* displays Montemayor's skill in pleasing every kind of audience by his choice of characters and episodes. Between this flattery of his several publics and his portrayal of a romantic passion that leaves lovers in such hopeless despair that only the sorceress Felicia can cure it with the water of oblivion, Montemayor achieved a success that angered moralistic readers. This not-for-profit episode in the history of fiction ended when Cervantes and Gil Polo redirected the alternating dialogue and monologue that structure the characteristic discourse of pastoral and made its central issue the avoidance of erotic destruction through reflective self-awareness.

In discussing the generic characteristics of heroic romance, we noted that it was valued for its didactic potential. The cultivation of so encyclopedic a form of literature offered the writer the greatest prestige except for that which was conferred by the epic in verse. This broad and very loose concept of instruction called upon the author's knowledge of times, places, activities, and artifacts, and so it could equally well be classed as the creation of verisimilitude or as a manifest of the author's model relation to the reader. More essential to romance is the heroic level of the action, the continual testing of the principal characters, the quest as the basic plot structure, which closed upon the attainment of a goal or the achievement of a precious object that is worthy of sacrifice. The end closed the structure in an act of union and reintegration. It is appropriate, therefore, to refer to the structure of romance as one that promises an affirmative conclusion. Incorporated within the world of Christian ideology shared by writers and readers, romance reaffirms its project as a fiction of providence. The hero (and the heroine) have faith in the goodness of the outcome and trust that divine powers will not let their exemplary virtue go unrewarded. Cervantes' *Trabajos de Persiles y Sigismunda* is an outstanding example of the type, and so, on a smaller scale, are some of the "romantic" stories in the collection of *Novelas ejemplares*: *La Gitanilla, La fuerza de la sangre, El amante liberal, La española inglesa.*[14] All of these stories have a closure that is the consummation of the noblest desires and a restoration of harmony in the social and domestic orders. Cervantes also gives us a negative version of this romance formula. The light-fingered boys Rinconete and Cortadillo head for Seville in search of a life of easy pickings, and are drawn into the underworld of thieves and hit men. They are aimless; the plot is appropriately open and inconclusive.

The *novela cortesana*, as the prevailing type of fiction has come to be known, is suggestive both of the novel's predominantly urban setting and of the upper-class characters whose dramas it portrays.[15] "Drama" is an appropriate term here because, as more than one critic has noted, there is a marked resemblance between these stories and the cape-and-sword comedies that filled the theaters for nearly half a century.[16] These plots of love, jealousy, honor,

14. Observe, for example, how frequently Dorotea, in *Don Quixote*, pt. I, appeals to and expresses her trust in heaven for a just resolution of her plight. For the operation of providence in Cervantes' plots, see John J. Allen, "The Providential World of Cervantes' Fiction," *Thought* 55 (1980): 184–95.

15. E. B. Place, *Manual elemental de novelística española* (Madrid: V. Suárez, 1926); Caroline B. Bourland, *The Short Story in Spain in the Seventeenth Century* (Northampton, Mass.: Smith College, 1927); Agustín González de Amezúa y Mayo, *Formación y elementos de la novela cortesana* (Madrid: Real Academia Española, 1929), and *Cervantes, creador de la novela corta española*, 2 vols. (Madrid: CSIC, 1956,1958); Walter Pabst, *La novela corta en la teoría y en la creación literaria* (Madrid: Gredos, 1972), trans. of *Novellentheorie und Novellendichtung: Zur Geschichte ihrer Antinomie in den romanischen Literaturen* (Heidelberg: Winter Universitätsverlag, 1967); Wolfram Krömer, *Formas de la narración breve en las literaturas románicas hasta 1700* (Madrid: Gredos, 1979); Palomo 1976.

16. Marcos Morínigo, "El teatro como sustituto de la novela en el Siglo de

and revenge may reach greater heights of cruelty in the stories than in the drama: murders instigated on the false testimony of a jilted lover or a servant who has been punished; husbands who mistakenly slaughter innocent wives. The plots almost always involve men of title, jealous of their womenfolk and of their reputation, unable to give way on a narrow street, quick to draw their swords. In essence they are stories of upper-class sex and violence in which the sex is merely inferred through passionate declarations of love or through its consequences: the small bundle hastily smuggled out of the house, the brother or the despised rival thirsting for revenge. If matters turn out badly, corpses will litter the pages and the lover will flee into exile or join the army and rush blindly into battle, or the lady will mourn her lost love (or her lost virtue) in a convent for the rest of her days. These are the generic plots. The stories are organized in one of two ways. They may exist as collections of short stories, usually with a frame narrative that creates a situation in which a group of people exchange stories. Or they may be organized as a long novel in which the protagonist is typically fleeing from some unstated danger when he meets somebody who is in distress, but not so deeply distressed as to be unable to start telling his or her life story. This story is interrupted by further events and encounters. These long novels still bear the marks of the Greek tradition: they begin *in medias res*, and suspense mounts as mystery piles upon mystery before the first can be completely resolved.

The principal character has a double function. First, he is the protagonist in his own action, which is a forward motion toward a goal, usually marriage, to be achieved after some obstacle is removed. Second, he is the center, adventures crowd in upon him, and he will be privileged to listen to the story of every newcomer to the scene. The titles of such romances tell the reader ahead of time who is the primary hero (or perhaps couple) of the narrative; Alonso Núñez de Reinoso, *Historia de los amores de Clareo y Florisea*; Gonzalo de Céspedes y Meneses, *Poema trágico del Español Gerardo*

Oro," *Revista de la Universidad de Buenos Aires* 5th ser. 2 (1957): 41–61; Florence L. Yudin, "Theory and Practice of the *novela comediesca*," *Romanische Forschungen* 81 (1969): 585–94; C. Alan Soons, *Ficción y comedia en el Siglo de Oro* (Madrid: Estudios de Literatura Española, 1966).

CARL A. RUDISILL LIBRARY LENOIR-RHYNE COLLEGE

and *Varia fortuna del soldado Píndaro*; Cervantes, *Trabajos de Persiles y Sigismunda*; Castillo Solórzano, *Lisardo enamorado*; Eurique Suárez de Mendoza, *Eustorgio y Clorilene*; Juan Enríquez de Zúñiga, *Historia de las fortunas de Semprilis y Genorodano*. This is a necessary piece of information when the reader may not be immediately able to judge that one fugitive lover, pursued by misfortune and narrowly escaping death, is to be privileged over another in the episodic structure of the whole, and singled out by authorial providence for special protection. The interlacing of stories, the use of movement, of travel as the device for making one character meet another by chance, the shifting function of the protagonist—now actor, now listener—are constant features of the romance tradition from the Greek prototypes via the books of chivalry to *Lazarillo*, *Don Quixote*, and the relatively realistic long novels of the seventeenth century. The setting of the action in real urban landscapes, on roads or in seaports that existed on maps and in the experiences of readers, would demand of the authors a new subtlety in the representation of the providential configuration of the plot.

Shorter novellas gathered into collections titled *Fiestas*, *Jornadas*, *Días*, and so forth have also been placed in the class of *novela cortesana*. We have noted similarities: structurally, the long narratives such as Castillo's *Lisardo enamorado* and Céspedes' *Español Gerardo* are anthologies of interwoven novellas, with each story being related in the first person, as the speaker's own experience. The stories, many of which were adapted from the Italian collections of Giovanni Boccaccio, Matteo Bandello, Cinzio (or Cinthio) Giovanni Battista Giraldi), Giovanni Francesco Straparola, and others, repeat the basic situations and conflicts of the cape-and-sword comedy, no matter how they are organized, and we may suppose that the same readers read both kinds. To the enthusiastic reader the principal differences would have been, first, the greater degree of emotional participation in the long novels, where first-person narratives give opportunities for pathos that other forms lack, and, second, the suspense created by delays and interruptions, as the various speakers appear, disappear, and await the outcomes of their several dramas. Aware of these advantages in the longer form, Castillo Solórzano, María de Zayas, and other writers complicate the short individual *novelas* in their collections so that the double plot and the telling of a story within the story become commonplace in short fiction from about 1630. Fiction is dominated by formula, as the long novels resemble aggregates of stories told in the first person, and as the short ones increasingly divide attention between a pair of characters who come together by chance and discover some common origin, bond, interest, or destination. These different modes of organizing fictional material had consequences for both writers and readers, however, and they have a bearing upon the picaresque works that appear contemporaneously with these widely read literary entertainments.

Beginning from about 1620 the collections of short novels greatly outnumber the long "Byzantine" narratives. Francisco Lugo y Dávila, Juan de Piña, Alonso de Castillo Solórzano, Diego de Agreda y Vargas, José Camerino, and María de Zayas are some of the writers of *novelas cortas* who flourished between 1620 and 1650 and provided a growing reading public with abundant amusement. Each of these collections may contain from three or four up to a dozen separate stories. They are linked by neither theme nor form, though in most cases a fictional frame holds them together. In Castillo Solórzano's *Tardes entretenidas* (1625) two noble families spend the month of May in a country house on the banks of the Manzanares in order to escape the noise and confusion of the capital. The house, the gardens, and the company are all elegantly symmetrical. There are two widows, each with two daughters, and they agree to tell one story each evening. The entertainment is rounded out by some comic verses composed by a professional buffoon, some songs and riddles. In the same author's *Jornadas alegres* (1626) the five stories are told to enliven the five stages of a long journey by coach. In 1606 Gaspar Lucas Hidalgo had already used this kind of containing structure in his *Diálogos de apacible entretenimiento*, in which neighboring families forgather at carnival time in Burgos to exchange anecdotes, jests, gossip, and satirical comment. These *Diálogos* are the familiar entertaining miscellany but are set in a rudimentary dramatic frame that gives them a social context that the reader would accept as being most likely to generate such a text. The collections of *novelas*, however, have a more restricted relation to the frame, and it would scarcely matter if the stories of one collection were shuffled with those of another. In María de Zayas' novelistic frames, too, the people are all superlatively clever, witty, beautiful, and rich.

As we read these descriptions and note the expensive decor that is flaunted in their world, we may easily forget the matter of "profit and pleasure," *enseñar deleitando*. The joys of wealth, social position, power—even of being a voyeur of such good things—seem to fill these writers with exaltation at a time in Castilian history when poverty was never more abject and wealth never more shamelessly displayed.

These prefaces make quite clear to the reader that pleasure rather than instruction in any form is the goal shared by writer and reader. The speakers tell the individual stories simply to entertain, for that is what they are called upon to do. The purpose of these stories is self-evident, and the third-person presentation, though it does not necessarily produce an ethically neutral stance in the narrator, makes "simple telling" easier than it would be if the story were told in the first person. The framework informs the reader that stories will be told as part of a social ritual, and the lavish attention to the setting and the overwhelming respect paid to wealth and titles and great family names taken all together define the kind of society and its rituals of self-celebration. The social setting that has become almost inevitable for these collections of stories is in the tradition of Baldassare Castiglione's *Courtier*, though so vulgarized as to be hardly recognizable as such. The telling of stories as a manifestation of sociability, of refinement, of wit and delicate judgment is given great consideration in that work, as it is in the later *Galateo español* of Lucas Gracián Dantisco (1582). The component of *enseñar* in this exercise was social rather than moral: to tell stories is to use language in nonutilitarian and noncoercive forms and to create a nonpragmatic ground of common discourse. The civility of the procedure in which a speaker conveys a message that has no practical truth or moral authority, while others nevertheless grant him or her an uninterrupted silence, is itself exemplary of a set of social values. María del Pilar Palomo (1976) writes, "The social practice of polite conversation was depicted in literature where it taught a social group that was a symbol of an ideal of living" (54).

While the collections of short *novelas* under their guise of *Días*, *Jornadas*, *Fiestas*, and so on became more and more common, the long novels of interwoven stories became less frequent. Those that were written (Enrique Suárez de Mendoza, *Eustorgio y Clorilene*

[Madrid, 1629]; José Zatrilla, *Engaños y desengaños del amor profano* [Naples, 1687]; Juan Fernández y Peralta, *Para sí* [Zaragoza, 1661]) are scarcely popular fiction, but heavily didactic and stylistically pretentious. Baltasar Gracían's *Criticon* (1651–1657), a great work of the moral imagination, belongs to the tradition of romance by virtue of the structure on which its allegory is framed and the underlying metaphor of the journey as a commentary on the world.

Thus fiction written for the mass market moved away from exemplification in response to the preference for collections of short narratives. Although short fiction abandoned exemplification and the power of the romance structure as signifier declined from the high point set by *Guzmán de Alfarache*, the long adventure plot retained a residual providential message. The framed collection, on the contrary, has no such message. Individual narratives may confirm the expectations aroused by their sententious titles (*No hay mal que no venga por bien* [There is no evil that doesn't bring good]; *La dicha merecida* [Good fortune deserved]; *El buen celo premiado* [Devotion rewarded]; *El castigo de la miseria* [The penalty for avarice]; *Al fin se paga todo* [You'll be called to account]) and achieve closure by means of some not too subtle poetic justice. But the effect of the frame has nothing to do with providence, unless it be that God's bounty is manifested in all these rich, beautiful, witty, proud, and ineffably aristocratic people whom the authors (mostly fortune seekers at court) praise so assiduously. "The triumph of the most conventional social opinion must be assured, and here the universal solvent—bearing away all vestiges of grief and shame—is affluence and the possibility of ostentation" (Soons 1978:68).

Guzmán de Alfarache involves the reader as a moral being because the protagonist, both as actor in the past and as narrator in the present, remains aware of his betrayals and of the depths of his self-delusion, even when he is convinced of the futility of resisting his inclinations and has reconciled himself to the enjoyment of his rapacity. Alemán's novel has no successor on this level. The "sermons"—passionate meditations that delighted earlier readers, Catholic and Protestant, throughout Europe[17]—were Guzmán's attempt to understand and explain himself from inside,

---

17. Peter Russell 1953:72 notes that Guzmán was cited in a tract in defense of Protestantism.

and also to place this understanding within the framework of
Christian redemptive theology—the most humane and universal
framework that was available to him. By contrast, the commentaries and helpful hints that appear in later works, the *aprovechamientos* and *avisos* that offer a moral in a capsule, are crude and
perfunctory. Such detachable moralities were already satirized in
La pícara Justina, where the "lesson" appended to each chapter is
comically inappropriate, but such satire did not deter later writers
from continuing the practice. Francisco Lugo y Dávila, Alonso de
Castillo Solórzano, María de Zayas, and others adopt either the
prefatory or epilogal summary of the story's profit for the reader;
alternatively, they round out the final sentence in such a way as to
leave the reader with the sense that all is well with the world:
"Don Juan and Cardona learned from this tragic example to such
effect that they were worthy of imitation for the rest of their
lives."[18]

The "lessons" are usually trite and solemn exhortations, such as
to choose one's friends carefully, or not to put one's reputation in
the hands of untrustworthy servants. In the third book of his *Escarmientos de amor moralizados*, Castillo Solórzano advised the
reader: "As for Doña Andrea's decision to leave home with her
lover, all women who may think of doing likewise are warned that
such decisions seldom turn out well." Better not to elope, because
things usually go wrong! But then we discover that the elopement
is providentially foiled when Doña Andrea's note falls into the
hands of her lover's rival. A new commentary is now called for:
"In the maidservant's mistake in giving the note to Don Carlos
instead of to Don Gutierre we see how important it is not to en-
trust our frailties to persons of poor judgment."[19] Evidently, if the

18. Miguel Moreno, *El cuerdo amante*, in *Colección selecta de antiguas novelas
españolas*, ed. Emilio Cotarelo y Mori (Madrid: Vinda de Rico, 1906), 4:148.
19. Alonso de Castillo Solórzano, *Escarmientos de amor moralizados* (Seville,
1628), fol. 72r. This work was reprinted the following year, slightly altered,
under a new title, *Lisardo enamorado* (Valencia, 1629). The most interesting
change is that the moralizations were all omitted—the first instance, to my
knowledge, when such respectable (though silly) material was removed rather
than reinforced. In the modern edition of Eduardo Juliá Martínez, in Biblioteca
Selecta de Clásicos Españoles, ser. 2 (Madrid: RAE, 1947), the "Moralidades y
aprovechamientos" excised from *Escarmientos* appears as an appendix. The sen-
tences cited are on p. 325 of his edition.

maidservant had had her wits about her, providence would have had to work harder—or maybe the lesson would have been different. When two men compete for one woman, some ugly trait in the loser will make it right for him to lose. Avarice and haughtiness (toward persons of his own class, not toward inferiors) are the sins most frequently punished.

Castillo Solórzano, the most prolific of these writers, practically abandoned the moralistic labeling of his stories after 1628. His later, picaresque works (*La niña de los embustes, Teresa de Manzanares* [1632]; *Aventuras del bachiller Trapaza* [1637]; *La garduña de Sevilla* [1642]) bear only the most shadowy resemblance to *Guzmán*; their episodes form an empty shell uninhabited by a conscious self.[20] The providential structure of romance is rapidly debased as the fiction of the 1620s and 1630s merely exploits commercially successful formulas. Many writers of novels, long and short, moralize the misfortunes that befall their characters with the conventional pieties: "These things are sent to try us"; "Such are the means that God employs to punish us." Abrupt coincidences, unlikely meetings and denouements that enable the story to end can be attributed to "the inscrutable design of God," or to "heaven, which by its incomprehensible secret judgments of mortals permitted that . . ." But heaven is less inscrutable if we accept its designs as being like those of a novelist desperate to bring his plot to a neat conclusion in a world where class, honor, and pride of blood are the mirror in which readers can reinforce their self-perceptions. As in *El buscón*, the fictional world is encoded according to much narrower prescriptions than the actual world of the reader.

In addition to this literature of aristocratic pretension and self-righteousness, there is another that preserves the structures of romance more unequivocally, if somewhat crudely. This is the story of wandering and adventure, pursuit and shipwreck, with no mythic overtones and no drift toward allegory (unlike Cervantes' *Persiles*), but with attention given to the local world of bad roads, storm, famine, plague, vermin, rural superstition. Such works as

20. Alan Soons observes of Castillo's characters: "It is extremely hard to describe them apart from the moral atmosphere they have their being in, since they are so little more than embodiments of the omnipresent prejudices of an author of 'purveyed literature'" (1978:66).

Gonzalo de Céspedes y Meneses' two long novels are of this kind. Some of the persons encountered in them are typical of the cloak-and-sword narratives and they tell similar stories about themselves, but there are moments of mild gothic horror, days spent in jail, petty thefts, and other signs of a concern to represent a world that is less haughty in its relation to the actual world of its readers. The principal narrator of 'the *Soldado Píndaro* ran away from home as a boy of twelve and was involved in various pranks; the vicissitudes of travel on the road are described; a sequel is promised. Parts of it remind the reader of *Guzmán de Alfarache*, but the whole does not, since there are too many other storytellers. It is neither wholly *cortesana* nor substantially picaresque, though the drift is antiheroic.

The effects of *Guzmán de Alfarache* on later writers were ambiguous. It produced no significant following: Martí, though parasitic, had his own agendas; *La pícara Justina* is an irreverent spoof; Quevedo's *Buscón* is a violent travesty that skews the codes and delivers a very different social and political message. But if it remained inimitable, it did give new energy to the antiheroic impulse in literature, embodied in *Lazarillo de Tormes*, in *La Celestina* and its various sequels, in *La lozana andaluza*, and in the depiction of such trickster figures as Pedro de Urdemalas. One may find this impulse collaterally in the vogue for *bodegones* (Spanish genre paintings) and in the extinction of romances of chivalry. To this extent *Guzmán*, *Marcos de Obregón* (the story of a mild and decent man), and *El donado hablador* (the memoir of a garrulous wanderer turned lay brother) share common ground. So do *Guzmán* and all the sensational *novelas* in which men of violent passions end by becoming hermits, though the ground is obviously different.

Céspedes' *Soldado Píndaro* and other works of the same kind share in this trend. They are often said to be influenced by the picaresque novels, but that is not an adequate account of the matter. Although Píndaro has run away from home, his boyish pranks are of no consequence, except for a brief association with the *germanía* in Seville (1: chap. 14), and he is more a listener to the stories of others than a teller of his own.[21] The narrator moralizes on

21. I cite the modern edition, *La varia fortuna del soldado Píndaro*, ed. Arsenio Pacheco, 2 vols. (Madrid: Espasa-Calpe, 1975).

the role of parents and about the passionate and treacherous nature of women, and is grateful to the Inquisition for keeping witches in check. He assures us that people get what they deserve, but in his world "divine mercy" may be spectacularly indulgent. His preferences are unambiguously aristocratic; men are instantly reassured as they recognize quality and breeding in each other by the cut of the cloth or the trappings of a horse (1:92). When Don Gutierre puts on the disguise of a builder's laborer in order to visit his lady, the narrator exclaims at the power of love to produce such a lamentable transformation; once the lady has recovered her speech, she bids him cast off that base apparel and display his noble self (1:117). The possibility that social boundaries may be transgressed arouses a revulsion of tribal intensity. So, on friendship, we read: "It looks disgusting when an old man and a youth, or a noble and an artisan, or a rich man and a pauper go about as friends; where there is inequality there can be no constancy" (1:27). Within his limitations, which are fairly obvious, Céspedes cultivates the variety that Cervantes' canon claimed was one of the attractions of romance. Céspedes' *Soldado Píndaro* contains a description of the explosion of a munitions store at Malines in 1546, a "notable event" presented, Ripley fashion, in strange and gruesome detail; eulogies of members of the powerful Guzmán family; a *novela sentimental* with its exchange of letters. His allusions to real events and personages, and especially to defeats in war ("God uses the Ottoman Turks to punish us for our sins" [1:61]), allow him to underwrite the poetic justice of his fictional episodes with a widely accepted pious philosophy of history.[22] In accord with the rudimentary conception of his genre, he declares that it is a delightful occupation to write things worthy to be read and to know things that are not unworthy to be written (2:171). After the excursus upon the explosion at Malines he declares that variety is his principal object in writing, and that such intentions may lead to

22. This view of history as a system of divine rewards for the defenders of the true faith and punishments for their lapses persists through the seventeenth century as an incontestable intellectual position; e.g., Fray Benito de Peñalosa, *Libro de las cinco excelencias de los españoles* (1629), and Padre Eusebio Nieremberg, *Causa y remedio de los males públicos* (1642); Céspedes was also author of a deliberately nationalistic *Historia del Rey D. Felipe el IV, Rey de las Españas* (Barcelona, 1634).

good learning (2:205). Finally he looks in two directions at once, promising to bring out a continuation, as Alemán's Guzmán and Quevedo's Pablos had done, and affirming that in it Píndaro will appear like another Theagenes or another Clitophon (2:231).

It is not fair to compare *La varia fortuna del soldado Píndaro* with *Guzmán de Alfarache*. Céspedes' conventional moralities cannot stand beside the powerful eloquence of Alemán, which has the power and urgent rhythms of John Donne and the personal inwardness of Thomas Traherne. The resemblances and the presumed influences are not significant; the differences are nevertheless instructive. Céspedes' adulation of the rich and powerful (he was a seeker after court favor), his trite morality, his confusion of authorial and narrative voice and discourse, his combination of artistically unmotivated patriotic sentiment and attention to insignificant realistic details set him far apart from Alemán. With respect to compositional rigor, social attitudes, and ethical sensitivity they have nothing in common. They share a density of reference to the conditions of material life in the seventeenth century, but this characteristic is not specifically "picaresque." The comparison is instructive, though, in showing how impossible it is to separate a history of the "picaresque novel" from the literary history of narrative fiction in this period.[23] I return to this history in Chapter 8.

---

23. Barry Ife (1985) proposed the interesting thesis that the writers of picaresque narrative were responding to the Platonists' objections to works of imaginative literature; namely, their power to move and persuade readers by affecting their emotions and desires. Authors of picaresque fiction, he suggests, "might be said to have tried in their work consciously or unconsciously to make a proper response to [Plato's] contention—repeated time and again by Spanish Golden-Age critics of fiction—that there is something about the very nature of art that makes it inevitably harmful" (23). Ife finds that "the practice of falsehood becomes one of the major thematic considerations" in these novels (172). Each text compels the reader to take a critical and self-critical posture in relation to it. The moral, aesthetic, and metaphysical objections to fiction, which Ife efficiently summarizes, did not in fact stem the spate of fiction in the seventeenth century, as we' have seen. The academic strictures could be ignored. The censors, royal and ecclesiastical, were predictable and the writers knew very well the mechanical formulas of rectitude. The serious intentions of Alemán are plain, but there is no evidence to suggest that either *Lazarillo*'s unknown author or Quevedo was thinking of how to make a "proper response" to the Platonist argument.

PART TWO

FICTIVE WORLDS

4

Other Worlds

Possible Worlds

It has long been a commonplace of Spanish literary history that society is criticized through the acerbic vision of the picaresque narrator. But there is no single, unified "picaresque" viewpoint. The world of Lázaro de Tormes and his sense of his place in it is not replicated in *Guzmán de Alfarache*. There are questions whose significance varies with the work to which they are addressed, whether to *Lazarillo* or to any of its successors: the reciprocal play of cause and effect that informs the relation between the protagonist and his world; his view of his responsibility to his world, and for its being as it is; and conversely, his view of its responsibilities to him.

We may start from the obvious: the works of fiction under discussion portray events in worlds that conform to the physical laws of the actual world. In this respect they differ from romances of chivalry, in which the physical laws governing the location and motion of solid bodies may be suspended, where the properties of materials may differ from those of the everyday world, and where creatures unknown in our experience not only exist but play important roles in the events and in the building of the suspense that leads from one event to the next. The coherence criteria that govern the romances of chivalry as a genre are not totally different from those we encounter in the actual world (both are cause-and-effect worlds in time and space), but they differ in ways that are important enough so that we would not normally mistake the one for the other. Unlike Don Quixote, we do not expect the real world to conform to the characteristics of the magical world of high romance. Indeed, Don Quixote would not intrigue us if he mistook like for like, and there would be no dialectical tension to suspend us between comedy and pathos. Romances of chivalry are also distinguished from the actual world by their claim to occupy a remote and vague place in the historical record. By the criteria of its pastoral genre, Jorge de Montemayor's *Diana* was closer than the chivalric romances to the world of its readers. It did not normally deviate from the actual world's physical laws, though it did diverge from this world's biological laws, in assuming bonds of sympathy between creatures that do not normally respond to one another: humans, sheep, trees, birds, running brooks. The generic criteria or conventions of the "natural" world of pastoral romance enlist only a small range of phenomena: spring or summer season, poetical shepherds and shepherdesses, a stream, trees, nonspecific rural locations, and no serious occupation to compete with the complaints of love and jealousy. The interactions of people, surroundings, animals, and location could not be extrapolated from our actual experience of them. We can account for them only by inferring a symbolic or tropological relation among them, and between them and our experiences of the real world. The objects in the pastoral world are immediately recognizable, but their cause-effect relations and the symbolic power that they are invested with differentiate them from their counterparts in the world of everyday. In sum, the romances of chivalry and the pastoral romances (both of which were more real to Don Quixote than historical narrative) diverge from the actual world in two ways: by not observing all of its natural laws and by contravening some of its psychological laws.

If we put this discussion into the frame of what modal logicians have called "possible worlds," we have to say that the world we actually do inhabit is but one of an infinite number of possible worlds. Some of them are physically impossible, because their physical laws do not correspond to the ones we live with, but they can still be imagined as possible. Others are physically possible but are impossible for some other reason, psychological or social perhaps, or because they contradict history. If we concede that a world that is impossible physically (that is, at variance with the physical laws of the world we know) might nevertheless have existed in theory (is not logically absurd or self-contradictory), then we see that the range of hypothetical worlds that could be imagined is limitless.

Philosophers construct possible worlds for a variety of purposes; to work out the conditions under which a given proposition or set of propositions might hold, for example, or to observe the process of hypothesis-making, or to understand better the process by which we decide among various more or less plausible explanations of the data of sense experience. This process involves the use of the imagination and the capacity to establish criteria of plausibility. Such possible worlds are designed for a purpose and their purpose necessarily delimits their content. When we attempt, for example, to address the problem "Under what conditions should we feel compelled to say that there are *two* items rather than just one?" (Bradley/Swartz 1979:39) or "Could Socrates have been an alligator?" (Plantinga, 1974:65), the possible worlds that constitute these conditions will be deficient in geography, and probably in history also. Their reason for being has to do with criteria of consistency, not variety or multidimensionality, and even the most complex of them must lack anything superfluous or intriguing for its own sake. But the writer of fiction or the teller of stories may be regarded as a creator of possible worlds of greater complexity. The more propositional the stories are in their intention (parables, for example), the simpler are their worlds; such hypothetical worlds are intelligible as coherent, consistent, but limited totalities rather than replete with objects or developing states of affairs. A novel is a vastly more complicated world than a parable, but writers of the most elaborate novels have had to try out their stories in various directions, adjusting the choices and the outcomes until the novel achieves a satisfactory coherence. Reading, likewise, is an uninterrupted flow of hypotheses that are continually tested against such aspects of the actual world as may be relevant (in the judgment of the reader) to the interpretation of the fictional state of affairs. But fictional worlds can never match the actual world's potential to reveal new information about itself. The products of the most exuberant imagination remain thin by contrast with the endless disorderly abundance of the world available to perception.

Because of the thinness of the fictional world, we may import into it, consciously or unconsciously, items or states of affairs or even whole belief systems from the actual world, in order to give it the coherence, the depth, and the consistency that we seek as the conditions of its intelligibility. Reading has traditionally involved such attempts to naturalize the text, to accommodate it to our understanding of the real world.[1] It is not possible, for example, *merely* to read the poets of *fin' amors*; their discourse has been referred at various times to social practices at the French court, to Sufi mysticism, and to other factors cited from the historical record. Aspects of the relationships in Stendhal's *Le Rouge et le noir* may be referred for elucidation to paternal and institutional authority in France in the nineteenth century (Brooks 1984: chap. 3). The theory of possible worlds could provide a model and a context for reader response criticism on the one hand and for the logic of interpretation on the other.

The fact that modal logicians habitually devise hypothetical situations (possible worlds) in order to test propositions about the real world or their perceptions of some aspect of it can tell us something about fictions and the use we make of them. Participation in states of affairs, events, states of consciousness of which we have no direct experience can be enthralling and for many readers it will never be more than that. But it may cause us to reflect upon our experience of the actual world, to see it as different, to gain a new awareness of what is possible in it (Maitre 1983: 16, 118). An imagined world differs from the actual world in the thinness of its phenomena; however fully documented it may be, it can never approach our experience of the actual world in range and density. The other side of the coin is that our experience of the real world cannot match the coherence of the fictional world

1. The notion that authors and readers share a recognition of this lack, and of what might be called upon to fill it, lies behind Wolfgang Iser's concept of "the repertoire" (1974) and Umberto Eco's "encylopedia" (1979).

and the expectedness (seen in retrospect) of its outcomes. No person's experience can replicate another's, and our own experiences are so varied and occur on so many levels that no individual can derive a principle of structure for the world from them. If some people claim to understand how the world "works" and assert that their lives are lived in total conformity with its principles, the rest of us find such perception elusive if not illusory. Any coherence we find is achieved at the cost of rigorous selection, subordination, and suppression—fictionalization—among the limitless variety of our impressions.

All possible worlds have their respective criteria of coherence; if a narrative is set moving in such a world, these criteria impose constraints on what is possible. They constitute its verisimilitude.[2] Roland Barthes (1980) has noted that description cannot ensure the effect of reality in fiction. Medieval writers who filled in their imagined northern landscapes with Mediterranean scenery were faithful to the requirements of the genre, not to the real world beyond the text. At the other extreme is the case of the barometer in *Un Coeur simple*; a barometer was a familiar object in the actual world, but is seemingly without purpose in Flaubert's narrative (Barthes 1980:81–83). Like the description of Rouen in *Madame Bovary*, it exemplifies the prevailing cultural practice of literature (and its dependence on painting) rather than any necessity of the structure: "It depends on conformity, not to the model but to the cultural rules of representation" (85). It is not that realism has destroyed verisimilitude but rather that one form of verisimilitude (the "classical") has given way to another (the "realist"): "A new verisimilitude is born, which is realism (by that we mean all discourse that accepts the enunciations validated by the sole referent)" (88)—a new verisimilitude, we might add, going beyond Barthes, in which the "useless detail" is, paradoxically, essential to the whole; one in which superfluity, overproduction, is a necessary part of the economy of nineteenth-century narrative.

It is easy to say that picaresque fiction moves a step toward modern realist fiction, but it is important not to let the implied teleology get in the way of our perception of the differences between the two. Narrative discourse in the Golden Age does not

---

2. The classic illustration of this principle is Edwin A. Abbott, *Flatland* (Boston: Roberts Bros., n.d. [1883?]), frequently reprinted.

describe. It has a narrow range of stylized epithets for natural phenomena: "copudos árboles" (thick-topped trees), "ásperas mon-
tañas" (rugged mountains), "caudalosos ríos" (full-flowing rivers),
and so on, the anterior position of the adjective stressing generality, not particularity. Nothing is noted unless it advances the
story or makes an event appear plausible; in this narrative economy, reference is utilitarian. Cities are large and crowded, and so
give opportunity for small cheats; they house rich people, so ingenious swindles can be engineered; noble families have town
houses, so affairs of honor can take place in these winding streets.
Few details are provided to differentiate one city from another;
perhaps an allusion to the Plaza Mayor or to some churches in
Madrid, or to the Gradas of Seville, or to the Zocodóvar of Toledo,
or to the country houses that dotted the outlying areas: a reference
to a *cigarral* tells us that we are near Toledo. As the seventeenth
century advances and fiction becomes more strictly designed for
consumption by the urban aristocracy and their lesser imitators,
cities are identified by the noble families that adorn them and give
them luster. Such phenomena as weather, changing light, the dust
and the smell—all the details of circumstance and atmosphere that
would fill the pages of nineteenth-century novelists and *cos-
tumbrista* journalists have no place in these novels.

Francisco Rico claims that picaresque literature followed
painters in their exploitation of perspective, by fixing the narrative
in the point of view of the subject (1984:15–16). But the development of pictorial perspective not only fixes the scene "from a particular point of view at a particular moment" (16, citing Erwin Pa-
nofsky); it opens up space in all directions and allows, or rather
requires, modeling of individual figures, granting to each its volume, its depth, its space before and behind. Surfaces that would
previously have been devoted to symbolic and hierarchical orders
have increasingly become places of human activity, or portraits of
people, or of objects arranged on tables by people as evidence of
their activity. The viewpoint allowed the spectator to look
"through" the frame into a world that opened out beyond and
behind the wall on which it was placed.[3] Reading a fictional world

3. For the relation of picture to wall, see Rudolph Arnheim, *Art and Visual
Perception*, rev. ed. (Berkeley: University of California Press, 1974), 239–40.

is also a way of reading one's own world; Boccaccio, Chaucer, and Don Juan Manuel in their various ways had explored the power of words not only to show the operation of divine providence or heroic virtue but to create order in the unruly world of human action. A first-person narrator has his viewpoint, indeed, which is to say that through his experience the story opens onto a familiar world of place and time. Yet this place and this time are strictly limited. Lázaro mentions a shortage of food in Toledo and the fact that the laws against beggars were being enforced, but not the content of those laws. The mention only heightens the fact that there are charitable women who help him out. *Guzmán* makes only such reference to bad weather as the story requires, but none to the disastrous plagues that cost perhaps a half-million lives (Kamen 1978:35, 1981:183; Casey 1985:211) or to the terrible freezes and floods that afflicted the final decade of the century (Clark 1985:8); none of those scandalous trials and theatrical executions that led to public disorder, and that fill the pages of Fray Juan de Pinedo's notebooks. Or the coastal raids by Barbary pirates at Sanlúcar and elsewhere. In other words, the "external world" of these novels is no more than is required to confer upon the action a sense of geographical and social extension. The "thinness" of it in comparison with the actual world is easily demonstrated. In this respect, nonpicaresque works may be more "realistic" than the picaresque: Cervantes' *Persiles y Sigismunda*, Vicente Martínez Espinel's *Marcos de Obregón*, and the novels of Céspedes y Meneses.

The social world constructed by these texts manifests some constants from one novel to the next. Honor is problematized in all of them. As the exclusive property of a class of persons to whom it is transmitted by birth, it is transhistorical, an ascribed status within a system of rights, duties, and exemptions that make up the ideology of "blood." When Sancho Panza divided the world into the haves and the have-nots ("dos linajes . . . . el tener y el no tener": *DQ*, ii.20), he conflated property (*tener*) and inherited status (*linaje*), whose corresponding verb is *ser*, to be.[4] At issue here is the

---

4. The discourse of honor turns on this verb, as is seen in such common expressions as "¡Por vida de quien soy!' and the declaration that a person is incapable of some ignoble act "por ser quien es." See Leo Spitzer, "Soy quien soy," *NRFH* 1 (1947): 113–27.

predominance of ascribed over achieved status, for increasingly during the sixteenth and early seventeenth centuries the relation of status to property became confused and reversed. The ownership of land continued to be the sign of nobility, on which honor was predicated, but from the 1520s the sale of *hidalguías* (titles of nobility) by the crown to raise money (a practice begun by Ferdinand and Isabella, the "Catholic monarchs") was increasingly resorted to.[5] Hence, as men became wealthy from manufacturing or commerce or administration, they could acquire noble status and then pass on achieved status as ascribed status to their successors by acquiring land. The class structure was penetrable by the "haves," those with money, though, as usually happens, the *nouveaux-arrivés* did not welcome the next climber. The older nobility, in turn, responded by seeking more exclusive distinctions: *hábitos* (knighthoods in the military orders), membership in closed corporations, preferment at court. Lázaro, seen from this perspective, is the least speck on the upward current of social aspiration. His *Vida* is a testament of self-congratulation on having "arrived," on having a finger in every pie ("throughout the city, anyone who is about to sell wine or something, if Lázaro de Tormes isn't involved in it, they know they won't succeed" [*Lazarillo*, 77]), and on having achieved public office. But his dependence on the archpriest's patronage and the dishonor of his public "honor" (as town crier he would assist at public executions, tarring and feathering, and similar acts of exposure to public shame) marks him as the last in the series of examples of a social order whose every constituent authority is a negation of itself. Lázaro's world is a parodic representation of the real world, reduced to the system of its hierarchies.

Lazarillo has been marginalized by poverty, and by dependence on others who are themselves marginal in their respective classes. His father, a miller, was inevitably a thief. Guzmán's father, vaguely denominated a "Levantine," could have originated from as far east as Syria or as near as Italy, or even Valencia. (We cannot tell, because "picaresque realism" is deaf: all characters speak the same language, undifferentiated by accent.) We are free to see in him a shady generic Levantine or Italian financial manipulator.

5. Elliott 1963:104, 305. But the consequences were less than has been supposed: see Thompson 1979.

He operated at the margins of the Christian world and played at the margins of religious orthodoxy: captured by Turks, he converted to Islam; repatriated, he reconverted to Christianity. Pablos' father was a "barber," also a byword for "thief," and his mother a witch; "she was not an Old Christian," according to the local gossip. In a genre that is often presented as a sort of trope for *converso* marginality, the only explicit converso is Pablos, and since he is designed to embody all of Quevedo's phobias—literary, social, political—he can scarcely be considered representative.

Picaros, being the kind of people they are, cannot remain long in one place. Guzmán is again the exception; his seven years in Italy include lengthy residences with the cardinal and with the French ambassador. These periods, and especially the seven years spent at the university, display the desire for stability that underlies his restlessness. It is not surprising that inns, roads, mule trains, and groups of travelers figure in the stories, or that the protagonists make for the large cities, where the opportunities for exercising their tricky skills are greatest. Poverty, stressed by generations of commentators in search of social documentation, is less evident in these novels than was supposed. Lazarillo struggles through poverty, and in Martí's *Segunda Parte de la vida del pícaro Guzmán de Alfarache* the wandering beggars swap stories of the hard times they have endured (II.3–4). Some of these stories, such as the account of children deliberately blinded and crippled so as to excite compassion and generosity in the people they meet, are shocking. To what end Martí included such details is unclear; perhaps it was merely for the sake of sensation or to arouse sentiment. The larger context of the novel provides no suggestion of political criticism. On the contrary, the space devoted to the pageantry and glitter of the royal wedding suggests that local misery is of little account so long as the court can impress with magnificent display. In any case, the rarity of such cases in the literature shows that the social fact of poverty was not on the agenda of these writers. They focus on the trickery, whether it is provoked by poverty or by some other motive. The single exception is Alemán, whose concern is more with the social arrangements and the attitudes that sustain them and that inhibit productivity than he is with poverty itself, as we shall see.

There are no starved corpses in these novels, although the

1590s were years of famine and plague, and represented a historic low point in the living standards of the mass of the European population (Souden 1985, Davies 1985). Instead, there is much ingenuity. The attention given to the tricks and to the fraternities of beggars indicates that the writers distinguished, as did the theologians and reformers and legislators, between beggars on their home turf and vagrants, and between "honest poor" and "tricky idlers." *Guzmán de Alfarache* is an exception insofar as it exposes a society where leisure with honor rather than work with dignity and financial speculation rather than industry and investment have distorted the social fabric (Cavillac 1983). For the most part, though, the novels exploited these aspects of the low life, as other forms of literature did, in Spain as elsewhere. As Harry Sieber remarks: "The 'literature of roguery' has always been of interest to literate society but it reached the proportion of an international obsession precisely at the end of the sixteenth century" (1977:9). We shall look more closely at this phenomenon later.

Our reading of the world of the picaresque has noted, first, that it is functional and consequently it varies from novel to novel, since the novels do not all tell the same story, and the characters and situations are not interchangeable. In this respect picaresque differs from pastoral, which creates a world in which lovers can be released from the contingencies of everyday social and family living, and from the chivalresque, which is a world that constitutes heroes. The function of the setting is not only to create, through discourse, a world in which the story can plausibly take place; it is more fundamentally to create one in which the hero (or antihero) may be constituted as subject. In the case of the picaresque, the world presented is realistic in the sense that its data refer to recognizable locations and to the time of the writing. The very contemporaneity of the fiction is an essential part of this hypothetical world, and is easily overlooked precisely because we do not expect actuality to be proposed as hypothetical.

The novelist's world, like a philosopher's possible world, is an attempt to pose as concretely as possible a question or set of questions of the kind "What if . . . ?" and to develop the consequences of the initial premises. An implicit question characteristic of much fiction and drama of this period is, again, characteristic of romance: What if the dynamic of desire were shown in action? What if the adjudication of rewards and punishments, of redemption and reprobation, were not deferred to another existence but manifested in this one?

The possible worlds of fiction, although they are more elaborate than those of logical propositions, set firm boundaries for themselves, and set the establishment and maintenance of consistency criteria above the illusion of seamless continuity with the actual world. Traditional novelists, like prosecuting attorneys, are ruled not by the tyranny of facts but by the compulsion to make the facts "fit," "hang together," "add up," "be convincing." The etymological relation between "convincing" and the conviction that may result from the labors of the prosecutor is clear. Storytellers may be interested in acts and their consequences, in cause and effect, but not until recent times do they seek to explore the causes of actions in other than the most general terms. Verisimilitude is a function of the representation of both outer and inner worlds; that is to say, of the items and states of affairs that surround the actors in the plot and also the inner states that lead to, accompany, or result from their acts. The latter aspect of verisimilitude will be taken up in a separate chapter.

If we turn to the representation of time, we find little that relates these narratives explicitly to the new Renaissance modes of experience of time that spread from Italy: devouring time, against which one has to make war so as to leave one's trace in this world; or the element that can be mastered and effectively managed and made to contribute to the "arsenal of human possibility."[6] The mechanical clock, which had appeared late in the thirteenth century, was adopted in the principal commercial centers of western Europe in the following century, and as a sign of the new commercial spirit, the monastic canonical hours of matins, prime, terce, and so on were displaced by the finer divisions of the municipal clock. In the world of commerce, time is a commodity to be used: "In this new society time, motion, and money were intrinsic, all evidencing the greater need for man to achieve mastery and control over

6. I borrow this phrase from Ricardo Quinones 1972:16. See also Francis C. Haber, "The Darwinian Revolution in the Concept of Time," in *The Study of Time*, ed. J. T. Frazer, F. C. Haber, and G. H. Müller (New York: Springer-Verlag, 1972), 383–401.

more aspects of his life" (Quinones 1972:7). The traditional views of time are too common to need repetition: the large unchanging rhythms of nature, the succession of generations, on the level of anthropology and the culture; a reminder of the futility of human endeavor, of the vanity of ambition, and so forth, on the level of ideology and individual conduct. Otis H. Green could find only one literary example in Spain's Golden Age of time as something to be seized and turned to account, in Gracián's *Criticón* (Green 1966:36); and Quinones (1972:500) repeats Green's judgment that the "transition from a sacramental to a secular view of nature and of events was not accomplished in Spain during our period" (Green 1966:9). This is no doubt true on the whole, and yet there are other, symbolic ways of representing time as a value. The *comedia*, which is a race against time made into an art form if ever there was one, deserves study from this perspective. In narrative, the deliberate intervention of the protagonist in the shaping of his destiny and the rupture of the traditional cyclical narrative order (not a return but a new beginning) may acquire immense importance and signal a new sense of worth. Once again, we shall discover that *Lazarillo* and *Guzmán de Alfarache* broach new paths, each in its own way making problematic the traditional indifference to time.

It remains to note the shaping influence of history upon the possible world of the fiction. The Renaissance was not merely a fortuitous moment of immense artistic creativity. It was a crisis, a shift in the relation of words to things, of form to substance, of image to truth, which released creativity, shook religions, and changed the map of the universe. One of the profound consequences of this crisis has been, in the words of William J. Bouwsma, "the recognition that culture is a product of the creative adjustment of the human race to its varying historical circumstances rather than a function of universal and changing nature. . . . This insight of the Renaissance suggested that mankind, by its own initiatives, could, for better or worse, shape its own earthly condition" (1979:12). The investigation and recovery of antiquity by Renaissance scholars led to their discovery of its difference from their own world, and thence to the historical contingency of their own cultural formation.

"Realism" may be said to denote any fiction that, in the consensual judgment of its readers, corresponds to the "realities" of human behavior in a possible world made up of significant items and states of affairs recognizable from their actual world, and having a coherence that is consistent with their perception of their world. It is told in the language of a factual report on the actual world. Reading usually involves an attempt to naturalize the text, to accommodate it to our understanding of the real world. Texts that are regarded as realistic are ones that are constructed so as not to resist this reception by the reader; if they do resist, they do so in subtle and unobtrusive ways.

The Outer World of *Lazarillo de Tormes*

Early readers were not cautious in ascribing a referential realism to *Lazarillo de Tormes*. The earliest translator of *Lazarillo*, David Rowland of Anglesey, commended the work, for "besides much mirth, here is also a true description of the nature and disposition of sundrie Spaniards. So that by reading hereof, such as have not travailed Spaine, may as well discerne much of the maners and customs of that countrey, as those that have there long time continued" (1586/1924:3). George Ticknor (1849), writing of the "tales in the *gusto picaresco*," as he called them, proclaimed: "Their origin is obvious. . . . They sprang directly from the condition of some portions of society in Spain when they appeared," and makes the reader "notice the peculiar circumstances of the country, and the peculiar state of manners that gave them birth" (3:55). It was a commonplace of literary history in the nineteenth century that this mode of fiction arose out of, sprang from, or was a product of the social conditions of its time.[7] The nineteenth-century taste for descriptions of the "manners" of divers times and places and the concomitant assumption by writers of the role of observer and recorder of the life around them, riding on the wave of the observational sciences, set the tone and language of critical writing. At the end of the century, Frank Wadleigh Chandler devoted the whole

7. See Simonde de Sismondi 1813, Dunlop 1814, Hallam 1837.

of the first chapter of his powerful book *Romances of Roguery* to the documentary nature of picaresque writing:

> A study of actual life was thus [the picaro's] aim, observation the method, and the most striking things of everyday experience the subject, as those of imaginary experience had been the matter of antecedent types. Blatant sounds, pungent odors, what was crude to the touch and strong to the sight, appealed to him. No refinements could be expected from his story, nothing but a scrutiny through eager senses of what best would give them immediate satisfaction. The picaresque novel was thus grossly real and usual; more than that, it emphasized and made prominent in all ways the lower elements of reality. (15)

While literary historians were making the too easy assumption that picaresque novels were literal transcriptions from reality, practitioners of the young science of sociology were using the literature of the past to reconstruct the mores and way of life it was thought to reflect.[8] Not surprisingly, the observations of the sociologizing literary historians and the literarily inclined sociologists tend to confirm each other, and to reinforce the unfortunate prejudice that literary composition is the "product" of whichever social fact or set of facts the commentator finds most suitable to the case.

Wolfram Krömer (1984) has put the question of how far these novels were conceived to be "a reproduction of reality" and has adopted a fairly simple procedure for answering it. He points to the disjunction between style and language and the world depicted in *Lazarillo*, *Rinconete y Cortadillo*, and *Guzmán*. In each case, the novel is "stylistically superior" to the world it describes; the narrator does not speak the language of that world. In Cervantes' story, the boy Rinconete and the narrator both use language that puts distance between them and the world they present to us. Quevedo also stylistically asserts his disconformity with that world, hence his picaresque fiction is not an imitation of that reality. In each case, the author feigns a world without idealism rather

---

8. The classic example is Rafael Salillas, *El delincuente español: Hampa (Antropología española)* (Madrid: Suárez, 1898). The risky practice of deriving social generalities from literature has continued into recent times in the works of Ricardo del Arco, and José Deleito y Piñuela, and José María Diez-Borque.

than represents an actual state of affairs. These novels moralize; "tienden a la parodia o bien a la alegoría." The real world is not replicated but rather turned upside down and made profoundly unreal ("de un mundo invertido y, por ello, irreal en su más profunda sustancia" (138). Krömer's argument is a reminder that "realism" and descriptions of low life are rhetorical procedures as much as any other modes of narration are, and therefore must be related to the generally propositional and sententious nature of sixteenth- and seventeenth-century literature. On the other hand, it elides the possibility that picaresque narrative may assume a complicity between a critical author and a discriminating reader in rejecting an accurately described "low" world, precisely because for them that everyday world was unworthy. In Krömer's argument, the writer could achieve the inversion of values represented by the picaresque world rhetorically by depicting in realistic terms a world whose previous association with fabliaux, farces, low comedy, and satire would mark it as trivial.

Picaresque works, unlike the *romances noticieros*, are not "abstracts and brief chronicles of the time," nor are they, in the wanderings of their protagonists, gazeteers to the geography of Spain or guides to the underworld. Their geography is symbolic, or synecdochic. The small world of Lazarillo extends only from Salamanca to Toledo, but we are not told how the boy and his blind master could have walked the dreadful journey through the Sierra de Gredos to Almorox and Escalona. What is important in the structure of the narrative is that Lazarillo emerges from the back of beyond to approach the climax of his career "in this illustrious city of Toledo" (*Lazarillo*, 42). Later the emperor Charles V makes *his* triumphal entry into "this illustrious city of Toledo," to hold Cortes, at the moment when Lázaro is, as he says, at the peak of his good fortune (80). Commentators have wondered to which of the convocations of Cortes Lázaro refers (April 1525 or 1538–39?).[9] It is more important to note the duplication of the formula of praise for the imperial city, and how Lázaro's career travesties the characteristic climactic scene of chivalric romance: a questing knight received at the court of a distant emperor. Lázaro has ar-

9. Rico briefly summarizes the debate, with bibliography, in *Guzmán*, xi–xiii.

rived physically and, by his own estimate, socially: "I was a success and at the height of all good fortune" are his parting words to the reader. When the emperor arrives in "this illustrious city," Lázaro is already enthroned there upon the height of his good fortune. It is left to the reader not just to figure out which Cortes and which date are referred to but what manner of city, what manner of empire are represented by a Toledo where Lázaro and his cozy connections epitomize success.

If geography is symbolic, so too is economics. The century-long attempt to relate the depiction of society with economic conditions, trade cycles, the situation of the bourgeoisie, and so forth has led nowhere. The period 1530–1620 is one of both economic expansions and contractions, of gains and losses in population, of overabundance of labor here and shortage there. Against the easy assumption that these narratives mirror economic decline, one interpreter has suggested that *Lazarillo* should be viewed as a protest against the slowness of the rise in standard of living during a period of economic boom (Lomax 1973). All such explanations fail because they mistakenly seek a mimetic source.

In the discussion of verisimilitude in Alonso López Pinciano's *Philosophia antigua poética*, Ugo grants Vergil's license to change history as it suits him. Any resemblance between the world of a picaresque fiction and the actual world was evidently not of decisive importance in defining the kind of truth that fiction conveys. In another passage of the *Philosophia antigua poética*, Ugo asserts the need for the poet to arouse wonder by imitating a surprising action. Fadrique disagrees: seeing a man frying doughnuts in the street is not interesting, but if on stage an actor were to set up his grate and frying pan and knead the dough and toss it into the pan, then sell some doughnuts and eat some himself—if he were to do all this, "could you refrain from laughing?" Ugo replies that in this case the very imitation of such material is enough to arouse surprise and so cause amusement (II.56–57), though the idea of wonder (*admiración*) really does not refer to cases like this. "I am talking not only about this kind of wonder but about a different kind caused by some new and strange happening; . . . if it is something never before seen or heard, it amazes and delights the more" (II.57–58). The ordinary and commonplace excite no interest in themselves, but arouse amused surprise *in their imitation,* whereas great and moving events excite the emotions proper to epic and tragedy. It appears that the faithful rendering of commonplace, everyday, nonheroic events could be a source of amusement, but not of edification.

A street, an inn, a cellar, the entrance to a merchant's store, a bedroom with two entrances, these have always been the locations of farce, low comedy, fabliaux. Boccaccio added monks' cells and confessionals, but the monastic settings made the stories neither more nor less realistic, except to the extent, already noted, that the desire for verisimilitude draws upon the local world shared by the author and the public. And the shared world was also literary. William Nelson has observed that "there was little agreement among Renaissance theorists as to what the Aristotelian term [verisimilitude] implied, what kind of truth a fiction should be like, and what was meant by its likeness to truth" (1973:50). Moreover, the concept of decorum that hedged Renaissance theories of representation, and that purportedly mediated in a rule-governed, rational way between nature and art, collapses when pressed into something like "taste," an elite social regulator of art masquerading as "natural."[10]

An important feature of that shared literary world is the hierarchy of genres, a hierarchy that could be both observed and breached, so that transgression creates new effects by the mixing and combining of existing forms. The familiar praise of epic as a "learned" poetry benefited kinds of literature that were learned, epideictic, in other ways.[11] Collections of learned sayings and speculations on the origins of things were increasing independently of fiction, with frequent reprints and translations of Pliny, Polydore Vergil, Bartholomaeus Anglicus, and Giambattista della Porta, as well as the native products of Antonio López de Vega, Cristóbal Suárez de Figueroa, Antonio de Torquemada, and others of lesser note. Picaresque novels are hybrids, and such literary facts put constraints upon the empirical value that we ascribe to the fictional

10. Attridge 1988: chap. 2: "Nature, Art, and the Supplement in Renaissance Literary Theory: Puttenham's Poetics of Decorum," a slightly revised version of "Puttenham's Perplexity: Nature, Art, and the Supplement in Renaissance Poetic Theory," in Parker/Quint 1986: chap. 12.

11. See Rosalie Colie 1973: chap. 3, on such writers as Sir Richard Burton, Sir Thomas Browne, and Rabelais and their classical precedents.

world.[12] We have noted the importance of facetiae in the immediate ancestry of *Lazarillo*, and we could mention also the tradition of the "character," whose origin in Theophrastus was obscured by a vigorous medieval tradition of satire. We have noted also the literary epistle, in its enormous variety of subject matter, the *relación* and the autobiography, and the precedent set by Apuleius, recently translated into Spanish. The motif "life as a journey" and its related thematics suggest that such narratives are normative rather than realistic fictions. They owe part of their fascinating ambiguity to the multivalence of this topic. Questing knights, religious pilgrims, wandering lovers, all predate *Lazarillo*; does it parody any or all of them? J. B. Avalle-Arce has suggested that Lazarillo is a secularized pilgrim, engaged in a *peregrinatio famis*.[13] These questions remain as open for us as they probably did for readers around the years 1600–1620, when writers pushed intergeneric discourse farther than they had done before. Literary history is too complex for picaresque narratives to be thought of as something apart from the rest.

How can we tell what importance and value readers placed on the allusions to the current reality of passing events in *Lazarillo*? To the fact that the antibegging laws were being enforced in Toledo, for example? What do the physical conditions of Lazarillo's life mean to the reader? Was the unknown author deliberately pointing through *Lazarillo* at public policy, through his novel at "the system" and its treatment of the poor? At one extreme, L. J. Woodward (1965) and George Shipley have seen in the adult Lázaro a self-exonerating hypocrite telling his story in so artful a way as to excite the sympathy of the reader, assembling "a pastiche of experience and invention that well might gain for him the re-integration and renewed social security he desires, if the common denominator of likeness he claims to share with his *conciudadanos* is anywhere near as base as he . . . depicts it to be" (Shipley 1983:

12. Nelson (1973:65) notes that "Renaissance stories are typically stuffed with speeches, letters, descriptions, and similar matter. . . . The story may even be dispensed with altogether as in the very popular 'treasuries' of speeches, letters, and harangues gathered out of such stories as *Amadís of Gaul* and Belleforest's version of Bandello."

13. Lope de Vega, *El peregrino en su patria*, ed. Juan Bautista Avalle-Arce (Madrid: Castalia, 1973), 31, 32.

106).[14] When we read the book from this perspective, it scarcely matters whether Lázaro exaggerates his past hardships or not, or whether he is true to fact in describing what he escaped from. He takes pride, both as person and as author, in his escape, and in capturing the reader's benevolence. At the opposite extreme from what we might call the "tough" readings of Shipley, Woodward, and others are the "soft" readings that present Lázaro as victim, forced to accept society's degrading terms if he is to survive. The judgment that "he had no alternative" consorts well, though not exclusively, with Marxist and Freudian readings.[15] The interpretation that goes farthest in proclaiming Lázaro's status as victim, impugning society and its structures of power, is that of Javier Herrero (1979). His article is an effort to make the history of the European novel accept *Lazarillo* into its tradition of realistic social criticism. It is also written with the heat of moral indignation. Herrero quotes Spanish writers on poverty—Juan Luis Vives, Fray Domingo de Soto, Juan de Robles (Medina), Miguel Giginta—to show the extent of poverty and the draconian nature of the poor laws. Conditions varied from place to place and from year to year, however, and so did the laws, the provisions for relief, and their application. The most severe laws were against vagrancy: reformers and the better-off municipalities attempted to support their own poor in various ways while avoiding becoming magnets to the poor of other localities.[16] Herrero assigns the role of villain to the Comendador de la Magdalena, who destroys Lazarillo's family through his "soulless steward" and his "thugs" (881a) (not men-

14. See also Shipley 1982.
15. According to Manuel Ferrer-Chivité, "Lázaro de Tormes: Personaje anónimo (una aproximación psico-sociológica)," *Actas del VI Congreso de la Asociación Internacional de Hispanistas* (Toronto: University of Toronto Press, 1980), society molds Lazarillo through (1) hunger and (2) material well-being: "ese grupo que le va modelando a su antojo" (235). Again, "Society compels people to engage in endless self-deception and compromises if they desire to survive and prosper" (Bjornson 1977:98). Similar statements are found in: Jenaro Taléns, *Novela picaresca y práctica de la transgresión* (Madrid: Júcar, 1975); Monika Walter, "¿Existe un realismo picaresco?" *Actas del VI Congreso,* 773–75; Oldrich Bélic, "La novela picaresca española y el realismo," *Romanistica Pragensia* 2 (1961):5–15; Tierno Galván 1974; and many others.
16. The fullest account of this complex subject, with regard to the arguments of churchmen and lawyers, and to the operation of the poor relief at various times and places, is Martz 1983.

tioned in the novel). But when he mentions the boy's father ("who works in the mill"), he avoids calling him a miller, so suppressing a comic stereotype. Millers are thieves, as readers of Chaucer and Boccaccio and folk tales know, and this is but one stereotype among others in this book. Herrero, however, rewrites *Lazarillo* as the social melodrama of a starving family, as if it were composed by Eugène Sue; so the father is recast as the first of the victims, not as a stereotypical cheat.

Lázaro's career spans the distance from Tejares, "a hamlet near Salamanca," to "this illustrious city of Toledo," a distance that is as much experiential as it is topographical, a journey with more than one plane of significance, with a vertical as well as a horizontal axis. The outer world is a map of the inner world. And since the journey is achieved in time, time itself becomes revalued by being the mediator between the subject and the world it has appropriated. Claudio Guillén observed many years ago that "time is there, but to be overcome, just as social or moral reality is there to be subdued by the hero's will" (1957:279). However much of an assemblage of bits and pieces *Lazarillo* may have been, it achieves its *finished* quality with and in time; an important part of its meaning is that it looks triumphantly back, and it does so both in the Prólogo and at the end, so that we will not miss the point. It has reached its end not like a chronicle, and not by simply stringing episodes together around a preformed subject, as in a chivalric romance; not by letting time pass, but by profiting from it. The fact that the outcome is ironic makes no difference. What is significant is that the unknown author has represented a possible world in which the new entrepreneurial sense of time is acknowledged and given play. Lazarillo's meeting with the squire is crucial to this representation, but its importance has not been properly understood. As the boy and his new master walk the streets, time passes and the clock strikes the hours. Guillén notes: "At no other moment are content and discontent, hunger and hope, expectation and delay so closely linked. The hours follow each other with exasperating slowness" (1957: 275). The striking hours measure the passage from hope to disillusion, and more. This is the midpoint in the narrative, and it is the only mention of a clock striking. Indeed, it is one of the very few such mentions in Castilian literature of that period. And it is significant that the sound of the public clock, the mechanical symbol of the trading community, for whom time is money, pursues this pair as they walk the streets of Toledo. The striking of the hours not only measures the boy's loss of hope, it mocks the hidalgo's pride with its call to *use* the time, and it mocks the boy's trust in the hidalgo and his world. It is *negotium* mocking *otium*. Lazarillo, without realizing, will heed its message. From this point he can only rise.

The relation of *Lazarillo* to contemporary discussions of poverty, vagrancy, and poor relief was discussed at the symposium Picaresque Européenne in 1978.[17] Edmond Cros set the ambivalent epithets applied to the blind master against earlier representations of the pair blind man/guide boy and noted a process of "satanization of the poor."[18] The man who offers to be the boy's "second father" is a master of deceit. Both the blind man and his servant lead and are led (both are subjects of the same verb, *adestrar*), and each deceives the other, and others. *Lazarillo* is inscribed in a moment of equilibrium, of "reversibility of concepts," for the pair blind man/servant is equivalent to God/Devil—or Devil/God (18). In reality, the poor were expected to find work, not to become vagrants. On this basis (as Michel Cavillac points out in his paper at this symposium) Medina distinguished "Christ's poor" from "Satan's poor." There is general agreement among the contributors that the novel does not reflect the polemic between Soto and Medina over government intervention versus private charity for the relief of the poor, and that sixteenth-century readers would not have read it in a tragic light. The view of poverty changes from God's poor, whom others must support, to the idle, who should be put to work or expelled; idleness rises in the hierarchy of sins (73) and the picaro becomes its personification. Giginta's desire to suppress begging is consonant with the novel (79). *Lazarillo de Tormes* comes into existence before this semantic expansion of *pícaro*: the poor are not yet resented for rejecting the social structure that keeps them in place.[19] The most extensive and informed dis-

17. Papers were delivered by Edmond Cros, Michel Cavillac, Jacques Soubeyroux, Horst Baader, and Alain Thomas. Additional participants included Francisco Rico, Alberto Blecua, Maurice Molho, and Noël Salomon.

18. Edmond Cros, "Le Folklore dans le *Lazarillo de Tormes*: Nouvel examen, problèmes méthodologiques," in *Actes: Picaresque européenne*, 9–24.

19. "Le pauvre n'est pas encore ressenti comme quelqu'un qui refuse délib-

cussion of the relation of *Lazarillo* to the actual world of poverty leaves undisturbed the prevailing response of generations of readers, that this is a comic story, not a tragic one.[20]

The violence of this novel, its crashing blows on the head and the face, do not amuse modern readers. But before we reach that point, we have already negotiated two discourses of duplicity: first the insolence of the Prologue, then the ironic euphemisms of justice/punishment applied to the narrative of the father: thieving as cure ("certain bloodlettings of the flour sacks"), martyrdom ("he suffered persecution for justice"), shame as blessedness ("the Gospel calls them [the persecuted] blessed"). Within this frame the humor of fear and violence is insulated from its literal referent, even as the narrative traces its uneasy line between survival and destruction. Here is matter for laughter in its therapeutic, antiseptic function, as a means of fending off the insistent brutality of everyday life. But there is also in much of Lazarillo's activity a pursuit of ingenuity, a wit expressed in action. The wit makes his tricks amusing for the reader, rather than just harshly practical. Survival becomes a game, an art, to the extent that the means used for survival exceed the material goal and become gratuitous play. We still laugh when puppets bash one another, when clowns knock each other down or have doors pushed in their faces. Our laughter tells of our need for aesthetic distance, as well as about the reciprocal traces of *entremés* and *commedia dell'arte* and popular narrative. Readers in 1554 were not serious about fiction in the same way that we often are; the readerly codes that command sustained emotional sympathy for and identification with fictional characters are an invention of the nineteenth-century masters.

The Outer World of *Guzmán de Alfarache*

When Enrique Moreno Báez (1948) attempted to rehabilitate *Guzmán de Alfarache* by taking seriously Alemán's instruction to

---

érement une certaine structure dans laquelle il se trouve enfermé": Michel Cavillac, in *Actes: Picaresque européenne* (discussion), 66.

20. "Il est évident que l'interprétation prédominante a été une interprétation comique, pas une interprétation tragique": Francisco Rico, in ibid., 41.

look to the *consejo* rather than the *conseja*, he erected Alemán into a pillar of Counterreformation orthodoxy. In 1948, in postwar Europe, influential voices were urging the need for *littérature engagée*; after the experiences of the 1930s and 1940s, writers were ready to pledge their art to beliefs that could not safely be entrusted to politicians. Jean-Paul Sartre, André Malraux, Bertolt Brecht, Louis Aragon, Paul Eluard, Ignazio Silone, Stephen Spender wrote self-consciously as socialists, while T. S. Eliot, Georges Bernanos, Graham Greene wrote equally self-consciously as conservative Christians. Those who were not politically aligned wrote cautionary stories about the power of the state (George Orwell, Arthur Koestler). "The unknown political prisoner" was not only the subject of an international sculpture competition but the theme of countless plays on the stage and the radio: he was the emblem of a whole generation. At that time it was difficult for art to be politically neutral. Sir Philip Sidney's "the artist nothing affirmeth and therefore never lieth" would have found little sympathetic response at that time, and to many people it would have seemed perverse. Moreno's reading of Alemán was consistent with its times.

Alemán, "a typical figure of his time," made his novel a mirror of the depravity of the human race in order to lead his readers to an understanding of the doctrine of original sin. And if his picaro is no worse than the rest of us, he enjoys no less opportunity for divine grace and salvation (Moreno 1948:56–59). The most powerful phrase then must be the one that makes the promise: "Try to profit from your life [Procura ser usufrutuario de tu vida]; by using it well you can reach salvation in your own station" (*Guzmán*, 275). "It seems as if the author were determined to show that Providence did not neglect Guzmán" (Moreno, 63). The novel, then, must be composed upon an ambiguity or a paradox, for if it is correct to speak of Alemán's pessimism in the depiction of a corrupt world, there is a countertruth: the teleology of the plot emerges from belief in a divine providence and is explained by it. In Alexander Parker's words, "all things are governed by Providence: nothing therefore happens to a man that he cannot utilize for his own good" (1967:39). I shall not repeat what I have written in Chapter 2 concerning the critical responses to Moreno's thesis. It is sufficient to reiterate that the redemptive plot places the novel solidly in the tradition of romance.

Edmond Cros's documentation of Alemán's friendship with a group of highly place lobbyists for reform has been greatly extended by Michel Cavillac (1983). His long, erudite, closely reasoned book shows the moral journey of the picaro to be an allegorical transposition of the life of the whole class of bourgeois merchants, in search of a lost identity. He begins by putting aside the concept of "the picaresque novel," "whose ideological homogeneity is disputable in the extreme" (9), as a reference point for reading *Guzmán*. He also rejects the *converso* mentality as a key to the novel. Rejection of father and home is a basic situation in traditional story, and the large number of editions and translations suggest that it was read enthusiastically by a very wide public. The target public would be, according to Cavillac, the middle class of manufacturers, merchants, and traders who had become marginalized in the late sixteenth century in Spain (40). They were marginalized not because they were *conversos* (many such men were, on the contrary, of "good" families and "clean" lineage) but because of aristocratic prejudice, and because of pressure to make money in finance and banking and to invest it in land.[21] Anticommercial prejudice was not exclusive to Spain, though for various reasons it may have been more extensive there than in France (40). Certainly it was reinforced by the growth of trading in bills rather than production of manufactured goods. The distortions produced in the Castilian economy by the predominance of Genoese bankers who controlled financial operations and the flow of capital, the decline of trade in the adverse political and financial climate after the revolt of the Comunidades in the 1520s, the rise of prices with the arrival of American gold and silver and the loss of native industry to the Netherlands are a few of the more obviously damaging tendencies at work. In the late Middle Ages, Castile was already becoming an exporter of primary products and an importer of manufactured goods, and the conditions that developed in the course of the sixteenth century accentuated this ominous trend. The years 1560–1575 were the period of great failures and bank-

21. Cavillac 1983:40–43; Pike 1972; Richard Konetzke, "Entrepreneurial Activities of Spanish and Portuguese Noblemen in Medieval Times," *Explorations in Entrepreneurial History* 6(1953–54):115–20. Pike documents the involvement of Sevillian clergy in transatlantic trade (71–72).

ruptcies of Castilian merchants as the Italian financiers tightened their hold. By 1573 the crown of Castile owed 37 million ducats to Genoese bankers, and when Philip II suspended payments, the Genoese froze the credit of Spanish merchants, causing many more of them to be ruined. Of those who survived, many became managers and agents for Genoese masters. The way to make money was to manipulate paper, and the most attractive way to use it was to invest in land or in government bonds. Those Spaniards who might have become entrepreneurs and industrialists were more likely to become landowners and rentiers, assimilating themselves to the aristocracy through marriage, the purchase of letters patent (*ejecutorias*), and contempt for commerce. They sent their sons to Jesuit schools where they would be trained for careers in law and administration. This process of ennoblement of the rich had become evident in the mid–sixteenth century, and as economic conditions discouraged commerce and manufacturing, it became increasingly pronounced (Cavillac 1983:150–55).

These processes were not steady and uninterrupted. In fact, there were signs of improvement after the financial crash of 1575. Some merchants began to redeploy their resources and to try to stimulate domestic production and trade. In Segovia cloth production began to rise; Barcelona expanded its port facilities; prosperity increased in Valladolid and Toledo. This slight alleviation was enough to encourage promoters (*arbitristas*) and critics to hope that they could influence the course of events, and to come forward with proposals that would restore the nation to its former glory. The hope persisted until 1599, the first of a series of disastrous years of plague and famine. From about 1600 there is a new sense of crisis: merchants flee to the Indies or to the Netherlands. Between 1599 and 1607 there are two state bankruptcies and an onslaught by the bubonic plague. Castile's world of finance is lost to Amsterdam and its trade to Lisbon. Conditions improve between 1608 and 1625, but then a new decline sets in (Cavillac 1983:161–62).

Alemán was a man deeply involved in the commercial and financial world of his time. Through his mother he was connected to a family of Florentine traders, and a wealthy cousin, Juan Bautista del Rosso (a man of culture as well as of money), helped him out of financial difficulties on several occasions and paid for the

Seville edition of *Guzmán* (1602). Seville, Alemán's birthplace, was a center of international trade and was home to business people of diverse origins. His time was one when commerce, like other activities, was subject to moral judgment and accommodated to the theological categories of nature, justice, ends, means, and use. In an environment where choices are translated into a language system that renders them as *cupiditas*, greed, and where such consequences as failure and loss are rendered as greed punished by divine retribution, choices cannot be simply pragmatic or their consequences merely mechanistic. Alemán was involved as a man of business, active in various enterprises, who knew both success and failure, prosperity and poverty (Cros 1967:442–44; Cavillac 1983:177). More important, he was involved in Philip II's financial bureaucracy as an official of the Contaduría Mayor (government accounting office) for nearly twenty years. On two occasions he was an investigating judge, the second (1593) being an inquiry into how the Fuggers, who operated the mercury mines at Almadén, treated the convicts who worked there. The Fuggers had been granted this concession by Philip II, and it is supposed that the king was hoping to encourage this great German banking family to asume the role of protector of the crown's financial interests, replacing the Genoese, who had become universally hated. Alemán's passionate and vigorous defense of the laborers against the company led to his being relieved of the Fugger file. His interviews with the victims—men crazed and broken by the fumes and the labor—aroused his indignation and brought embarrassment to the monarch. In this position he experienced the economic system as it concerned the exercise of justice in a quite literal sense; he saw that justice was enslaving men to economic interests whose center was not Castile but a foreign nation. His anger is admirable. It is not the sign of a man who wallows in the pessimistic belief that men can do nothing to change their circumstances (Guillén 1960, Bleiberg 1966, Cavillac 1983:175–76).

Equally important are his years of work in the Contaduría, which brought him into communication with members of the Consejo de Hacienda (the Finance Council), where he would make contact with men who influenced royal policy. During his years as an accountant, the bureau also assumed the task of examining the accounts of Genoese doing business in Castile. Other accountants, such as Hernando de Soto and Enrique de Araiz y Verrasoeta, were, like Alemán, members both of the royal bureaucracy and of the larger intellectual community, in which Spain's economic destiny would continually be discussed. Alemán's close friend Cristóbal Pérez de Herrera, author of *Amparo de los legítimos pobres y reformación de los vagabundos* (Protection of the truly poor and reform of vagabonds [1598]) and many other *discursos, cartas, relaciones,* and *respuestas,* was a reformer whose proposals for dealing with the indigent and with vagrancy were widely and enthusiastically adopted by municipalities in various parts of the country.[22] The legal officers of the Cortes championed his plan for organizing shelters for the poor, and support for them went all the way up to the president of the Royal Council and the royal confessor (Martz 1983:88–89). Pérez de Herrera held the post of "first physician" in the royal galleys and was also palace physician to Philip II. Alemán was an activist among activists.

Alemán's novel was evidently not the product of an entirely disinterested imagination. Guzmán became a false cripple and beggar in Rome, and one of Pérez's principal concerns was to discriminate between and give different treatment to the "truly poor" and the able-bodied idlers who ought to have been at work. Guzmán visited his relatives in Genoa and was rejected by them; he was avenged later when he swindled them in a complex fraud. Throughout his career Guzmán has engaged in occupations in which money is made by unscrupulous methods—fraudulent begging, manipulation of bills of exchange, confidence tricks, impersonation, pimping, gambling; by all means except productive work. His play with financial paper recalls the career of his father. His career touches many of the same points, and the mature Guzmán's repressed awareness of this recapitulation emerges in the ambivalence and embarrassment with which he refers to his father at the beginning of his narrative.

Guzmán's turnabout, when it comes, is surrounded and permeated by metaphors that derive from the world of commerce and economy. This is not surprising, since the language of Christian morality has always stressed *accountability* to God and warned of a

22. Cristóbal Pérez de Herrera, *Amparo de pobres,* ed. Michel Cavillac (Madrid: Espasa Calpe, 1975); also Martz 1983:86–89.

day of *reckoning* when a *balance sheet* of sins and virtuous acts would be drawn up and *payment* would be made to "the uttermost farthing" (Matt. 5:26). Folly and prudence have been opposed in parables whose frame of reference is economic: the parables of the talents and of the wise and foolish virgins define the virtue of prudence as productive use, far removed from both foolish squandering and useless hoarding. The idea of Providence itself, as its etymology proclaims, is that of a divine economy that grasps the future, a just balancing of intentions and acts, rewards and punishments, gains and losses. This system of Providence is both rational (conceived by the mind of God) and arbitrary (controlled by the will of God), both severe and generous, since it responds to merit yet leaves room for grace; and since God's resources and his gifts are infinite, it can only be received, never verified by accounting. When Guzmán narrates the moment of his religious experience, he uses the traditional images—climbing the mountain, reaching up, awaking from a dream—that are so frequently encountered in Franciscan and Augustinian spiritual writings.[23] Sisyphus has reached the summit by a road he never expected to take.[24] In addition, he admonishes himself to *invest* the sufferings

23. The significance of the vertical axis and the act of waking from sleep will be evident to every reader of Fray Luis de Léon. Cavillac gives other examples (1983:123).

24. Guzmán compared his laborious rise (he is about to graduate and be ordained) and his sudden fall into love with Gracia to the fate of Sisyphus (II.iii.4, p. 822). Benito Brancaforte, in the Introduction to his edition of the novel (Madrid: Cátedra, 1979), sees this "ritmo de Sísifo" as the rhythmic pattern of the whole book. The rhythm is indeed obvious, but the occasion of the reference to Sisyphus should be noted. It occurs at the end of his longest period of stability: seven years of study, in preparation for a better life. His fall is disastrous, as he acknowledges by his weeping and his prostration (his first tears since the lonely night after he left home). Guzmán has not compared himself to Sisyphus until this moment, and when he does it is, appropriately, "en la cumbre de mis trabajos" (822). We are now approaching the end of the story, on the steep slide from a high point to the lowest. At that low point he will repeat the image of the hill but reverse the sign, as he sees himself at "la cumbre del monte de las miserias" (889). Brancaforte and M. N. Norval (1974) appear to have forgotten that Sysiphus was not the victim of an arbitrary fate. His stone was an eternal punishment for having deceived the gods, especially Zeus; he was known as the greatest of all cheats (Homer, *Iliad*, VI.153; Ovid, *Metamorphoses*, VII.393). At the point where Guzmán applies the figure to himself, he has just cheated God by renouncing his profession (817–18). On reaching the summit, "la cumbre del monte de mis miserias," Guzmán-Sisyphus

caused by his sins: "although it's true that your sins have brought you here, place those punishments where they may yield you some return"; "Get some capital and put it to use; get it now and use it to buy your bliss." All the pain and labor that accrued from serving his masters on the galley, he tells himself, should be "set to God's account . . . to buy grace" (889–90). Shortly before the period of anguish and repentance, he began to prosper through hard work, a desire to please, and the prudent investment of his small resources. The repentance completes an awakening that had already begun.

The languages of theology, of morality, and of commerce are not mutually exclusive, and not only because of the economic metaphors encapsulated in theological discourse to express humankind's *indebtedness* to God. Economics, statecraft, law, justice, history, and anthropology were all understood as dependent upon God's will, his bounty, and his plan of creation, redemption, and ultimate judgment; their logic was teleological, the logic of final causes; their discourse was encoded in the language of theology and morality. The world could be understood only as a sign within the great system of signs which it was the business of theology both to constitute as discourse and to explicate. Within this universe of discourse, humankind's dependence on Providence was most naturally expressed in the language of feudal structures. Here the relation of God to man was expressed by means of the

---

may be said to have finally achieved his goal and possible liberation from his repeated punishment.

Sisyphus endures in the late Middle Ages as a negative exemplar: "Sunt et hic multi qui montem ascensi diuiciarum nil actum putant, et relapsum in avaricie uallem animum reuocare conantur ad montem adhuc ulteriorem; . . . Cor illud bene comparatum saxo Sisiphi . . .": Walter Map (d. 1209?), "De Sisypho," in *De nugis curialium*. And Erasmus stresses the story's value as moral allegory (*Enchiridion* [1518], cited in Seznec, 1961:99n). Of special interest here is part of the *aplicación* supplied by Juan Pérez de Moya in his retelling of the Sisyphus story: "La piedra . . . aplican algunos al estudio de los hombres; y el monte alto, el curso de la vida del estudiante; la cumbre donde Sísifo procura subir la piedra es el sosiego y descanso del ánimo. Sísifo es el ánima, porque como el alma, según el parecer del los pitagóricos, haya sido enviada divinalmente del cielo a estos cuerpos, la cual fue sabidora de todos los secretos divinos, procura con todas sus fuerzas llegar a la felicidad y descanso de la vida, que es el saber, la cual otros pusieron en amontonar riquezas o en larga vida": *Philosophía secreta* (1585; Madrid: Los Clásicos Olvidados, 1928), 2:244–45.

metaphor of the contract between a just lord and a free servant; Satan, by contrast, is represented as a deceitful tyrant who enslaves human souls. The language of these relationships—debt, service, rewards, favors, judgment, sentence, and so forth—contains the manifold aspects of the feudal lord as master, protector, and judge; the reciprocity of these terms is made more complete by the language of feudal ceremonies of allegiance and medieval jurisprudence. This reciprocity is homologous with other reciprocities: of the discourse of passionate veneration of the Virgin Mary, the erotic language of mysticism, and the religious vocabulary and rhetoric in the discourse of courtly love. In *Guzmán de Alfarache*, Alemán appropriates the traditional discourse of feudal relations and inserts it, together with a hortatory rhetoric, into a postfeudal world of entrepreneurial activity.

It is important to realize what "conversion" does *not* mean in this novel. Guzmán does *not* renounce worldly goods; he turns away from greedy acquisitiveness, from usury and gambling, and shows himself to be ready for productive work. The various objects that were stolen or hidden away in the days before the attempted mutiny are brought forth, returned to their owners, restored to circulation. It was customary for those who had escaped death or disaster to make a vow, to visit the shrine of a saint, to have masses said, or to go on a pilgrimage. Many real as well as fictional persons whose lives were profoundly changed by suffering or loss declared their intention to join a religious order or to become hermits as proof of *desengaño*, disillusion with the world and discovery of spiritual truth. Guzmán does none of these things. His is *not* the way of disillusion. Readers may fail to note that his experience of renewal, unaccompanied by any ritual separation and without special ceremonies to mark it, is extraordinary, if not unique. It is one of many features that suggest that the work owes more to the sixteenth-century tradition of Christian humanism than to the Council of Trent.[25] Guzmán's "conversion" is confirmed not by religious ceremonial or public vows but by a *civic* act: the saving of the ship from the conspiracy to mutiny. This is not just any private ship, but a galley of the royal Spanish navy, so

25. See Cavillac 1983:33–37, 87–88, 211–15, 293–99, 344–46 for discussion of the traces of Erasmian thought and expression in Alemán.

that to kill its commander and deliver it to the Turkish enemy would have been to commit the worst treason, and the heinousness of the crime is reflected in the way the conspirators are punished. At this point in a narrative already loaded with symbolism, that of the galley as the "ship of state" is almost painfully obvious.

The career of Guzmán has to be seen within its real-world context of public debate on such urgent matters of policy as financial reform, rural poverty and migration, vagrancy, gambling, idleness. These issues, resulting from the social changes of the early modern period, had frequently come before the Castilian Cortes since 1518, and provoked numerous treatises and proposals for reform (Martz 1983:14). These questions of poverty and vagrancy were perceived as being implicated in those problems of foreign debt, decline of industry and trade, and so forth, and Mateo Alemán as writer, intellectual, bureaucrat, and man of business was inevitably involved in debates on these pressing issues. The Italian translator Barezzo Barezzi showed that he understood this significance of the book, for in the preface to his version he praised it for its "admirable arguments, *economic and political* cautions" (Cros 1967:14; my emphasis).

Alemán's achievement is made to appear too narrow if it is circumscribed by the doctrinal politics of the Council of Trent. The language of theology, I repeat, is a universalizing discourse. Guzmán cannot be understood as the Everyman his author claimed he was if his *general confesión* is limited to communication by an errant individual to an individual reader. The specifically legal and commercial term *usufrutuario* (with its Augustinian echo)—one who has the legal use and enjoyment of something—is not to be found in the original Pauline admonition "Unusquisque in qua vocatione vocatus est, in ea permaneat" (Let every man abide in the same calling wherein he was called: 1 Cor. 7:20). The word pertains to the Christian doctrine that one's life, talents, and goods are not one's own property but are given in trust by God, to be returned and accounted for at death, the most celebrated literary representation of this doctrine being Pedro Calderón de la Barca's sacramental drama *El gran teatro del mundo*. "Usufruct" as a legal term does, however, denote the right of the holder to the complete enjoyment of the property and of all profits that may be got from it. This is not the tone of Paul's instruction that the converted be content with their social condition, whether slave or free. If the picaro in his place can attain salvation, then so can the merchant in his, and the camel may pass through the eye of the needle: such is the force of the generalized *tú*, "thou." The narrator is address-ing himself, and if he addresses us also as picaro to picaro, then all of society is implicated in the picaro's vices of self-indulgence, gambling, speculation, and fraud, of evasion of work and respon-sibility, of erecting unproductiveness into an affair of honor, of putting the blame upon others, upon one's stars, one's parents, one's blood.

At the beginning of his narrative, Guzmán understandably pre-varicates when he mentions his father, uncertain of how much he can or ought to reveal. Where is the line between evasiveness and a modest decency, between honest disclosure and indecent exhibi-tion, between explaining and condoning, between censure of the father and exoneration of himself? If the pleasure garden of San Juan de Alfarache had been Guzmán's childhood paradise of pam-pered innocence, his going forth sets him Adam-like on a hard road of humiliation, equivocation, and regret. There will be no re-turn to the dead father, but he confronts him symbolically in Soto. Had he joined the mutineers' conspiracy to sell the royal galley to the Turks and renounced his religion to save himself, he would have repeated his father's career of betrayal. By betraying the be-trayer, he lays the ghost of his father and is free to enter into new relations with the figures of legitimate authority.

Alemán's place in the international business community, the acute sense of wasted energies implicit in his desire to emigrate, his long association with mercantilist circles at the highest levels of government make untenable Moreno's conclusion that "he looked on society with the eyes of a philosopher, not of a politician or reformer" (1948:137). So, too, does the emblematic portrait that prefaces the first edition of *Guzmán*, where the author is seen hold-ing in his left hand a book bearing the letters COR. TA. This in-scription has been shown to be an abbreviation of the name Cor-nelius Tacitus,[26] and is a clue to Alemán's intellectual orientation, for it ranges him on the side of the *tacitistas* or proponents of active intervention and reform (Cavillac 1983:60, 290, 302). Martín

26. Foulché-Delbosc 1918:554–56, Cros 1967:174.

González de Cellorigo's *Memorial* (1600) diagnosed Spain's sickness as wealth that consisted not in production but "in papers and contracts, annuities and bills of exchange, currency, silver, and gold, instead of in goods that make profit and attract wealth from outside to sustain the wealth within. So the lack of money, gold, and silver in Spain is the result of having them, and we are poor because we are rich."[27] But decades before that Alemán had been filled with righteous fury at the spectacle of Spaniards forced to work the mines for the benefit of German bankers who would exploit Spain's wealth in succession to the Genoese. Cavillac (1980) has shown that Alemán's *Ortografía castellana* contains numerous favorable observations and comments on new processes, discoveries, inventions, scientific and technical advances. These judgments belie the image, fostered by writers such as Moreno Báez, Américo Castro (1967:44–50), and Carlos Blanco Aguinaga (1957) of Alemán as a conservative doctrinaire ideologue. The *Ortografía* supplies one of the earliest uses of the word *novedad* in a positive sense instead of the normally current one of "bad news," "turn for the worse" (as in *no hay novedad*, all quiet, nothing terrible has happened), or "frivolous novelty." Guzmán should be rescued from the same stereotype—the assumption that because humanity is heir to sin and evil, nothing can be made better. We should note that in Part II of *Guzmán de Alfarache* the protagonist returns to Madrid after an interval of years. The passage of time serves to indicate change and loss, to create a mood of instability, but this is not the only lesson that is conveyed. Recall the passage cited in Chapter 3: "Everything was much changed from when I left. There was no longer a grocer, or any memory of him. The fields had been built on . . . squares had become streets and streets were much changed, *with great improvement everywhere*" (756). The ambivalence is easily missed in a work on the scale of this novel. Time carries us toward decline and death; that is the universal experience. But an individual perception flashes at that moment across the generalized image of transience: "*con mucha mejoría en*

27. ". . . en papeles y contratos, censos y letras de cambio, en la moneda, en la plata y el oro; y no en bienes que fructifican y atrahen a sí como más dignos las riquezas de afuera, sustentando las de dentro. Y ansí el no aver dinero, oro ni plata en España es por averlo, y el no ser rica es por serlo" (cited in Cavillac 1983:264).

todo." That, too, is a lesson Guzmán learned from the passage of time: everything was much improved. It has taken his long absence from Madrid to make this change visible, through the operation of time and active memory. Here, on the level of history and culture, is a correlative to the experience of Guzmán as an individual. The effects of change may pass unnoticed in reality unless we remove ourselves from the scene and return after a long interval. The changes in a city or in a society happen whether we attend to them or not. But here a crucial distinction is implied: we can do nothing to arrest time, decay, and death, but we can assist the processes of social change. The natural inborn desire to improve, which has never left Guzmán in spite of his depravities, sees itself mirrored, magnified, and objectified in a sign of universal promise. Once he has made the discovery that improvement is possible, he can eventually become a participant in the process (as Alemán advocated by associating with the economic *arbitristas*), not only an observer of it. Once more, the teaching and mediating functions of memory will be crucial.

Alemán has given to the world of *Guzmán* an ideological density that may easily confuse the modern reader, because it brings into view the structures of contradiction and paradox that underlie the Christian view of nature and of history. Every attempt to order, classify, evaluate, and hierarchize our experience of the world inevitably reveals unnoticed paradoxes and begets new ones. Literature is irresistibly drawn into the field of paradox and incongruity, the more profound works being those that incorporate the oppositions at all levels of symbolization and discourse. Both *Don Quixote* and *Guzmán de Alfarache*, starting from their different premises, do so, whereas most of the fiction that comes after fudges and obscures these deep paradoxes and masks them with ready-made melodramas of love, honor, and family pride.

Guzmán de Alfarache not only incorporates the paradoxes that exist within Christianity (humanity's fallen nature/belief in salvation, etc.) but also embodies the tension between the Christian sense of time and the modern, secular sense of time. The feudal world did not know clock time; its cycle of the seasons and its succession of generations within a sacramental universe that will "in the fullness of time" return to its beginnings endorse fictions that enact the return of the hero or the recovery of a primordial realm or sacred object. The continuity of romance from ancient through Renaissance times is underwitten by this relatively unchanging experience of time and its place in the self-consciousness of the culture. The plots depend not on the heroes' mastery of time but on their mastery of symbols and of the self. But Guzmán de Alfarache does not return in splendid triumph, nor is narrative closure sealed by reintegration with his family. On the contrary, Alemán has disrupted the cyclical structure of romance on both of its traditional levels, individual destiny and group affirmation.

In his *Guzmán*, Alemán has preserved the scale, the range of movement, the abundance, and the master tropes of romance: life as a journey; the quest as image of a destiny that seeks an end that will confirm the origin. But he has also transformed this "prose epic," and not only in such obvious and radical ways as replacing hero with antihero and the fantastic nowhere of romance with a plausible here and now. Just as important, he has negated the conventional ceremonial closure and created new and fascinating paradoxes in doing so. The recovery of the source is not symbolized in an emblematic object or by entry into an ancestral place; such negations inscribe Alemán's narrative in a time that moves uncertainly forward. But because this time is uncertain, open, and nonritualistic, it is a field for change, full of the germs of opportunity rather than the emblems of permanence and repetition. Guzmán is homeless, motherless, fatherless, and childless. His story ends while he is at sea, in the middle of nowhere. But the sea is many things: it is the most unstable and dangerously unpredictable of the elements, but it is also the most life-giving and fruitful. Okeanos, the father of gods, embraces the world; his waters undergird the earth and flow through the region of forgetting, and there they are renewed and flow back to the center. Sea and ships had figured in poetry from Horace to Luis de León as emblems expressing Stoic disapproval of commerce and risk, a disapproval that is not shared by Alemán or Guzmán. The final image of Guzmán at sea in the royal galley awaiting pardon is therefore open. This sea is not a nowhere but a realm of infinite potentiality. Insofar as it washes away the past, and insofar as it is a metaphor of a home that is the whole world, it is so for us readers as well as for Guzmán. Time is redeemed, not lost; Guzmán seizes the experiences that are buried in the past and reinscribes them in a narra-

tive discourse that rejects circularity. He revalues them by project-
ing them upon an open future. Guzmán has rewritten the Horatian *carpe diem* so that nothing will be lost.

Alemán negates the traditional narrative's return upon itself.
He breaks open the structure and leaves the plot indeterminate at
the very moment when romance traditionally demands arrival and
closure. Heroes of romance come ready-made, bearing their destiny blazoned on their shields and inscribed in the family name;
they need only tempering and polishing. But in *Guzmán*, as in *Lazarillo*, the imagined world is not designed to test and confirm a
hero, nor is time the sequential aspect of a testing narrative. Time
has come into its own and is, at last, vitally active in the structure
of the possible world within which the subject is constituted.

Alemán has so often been called a pessimist that the judgment
must be addressed. The case for declaring him a pessimist usually
begins with a passage of generalization that will be cited again
when we discuss the inner world. "There's no way out, no
cure. . . . Everything is, was, and will be the same. The first father
was perfidious, the first mother a liar, the first son a thief and a
fratricide. What is there now that wasn't so before? What can you
expect of the future?" (355). The human story is all one. It may be
objected that this view leaves the *ley de gracia* out of the reckoning,
the redemption that, for believing Christians, has altered the equation. In nonchristian terms, the basic stuff of human nature does
not determine the destiny of the individual. But this argument
overlooks the context of the declaration, which is a discourse upon
wealth: everyone desires it; people flatter the rich and insult the
poor; poverty is esteemed the greatest dishonor (354–55). This is
not a moralist's tirade against money as such but an objection to
its unequal distribution, and to the attitudes toward rich and poor
that result from that distribution. There is nothing wrong with
money or with the desire for it: "Money warms and quickens the
blood; anyone who lacks money is a walking corpse among the
living. Without it, nothing can be done when the time is right, no
pleasure or desire can be satisfied" (355). As Alemán makes no
moralizing assault on money, so he offers no sanctimonious praise
of poverty.

The paradoxes that not only underlie but animate a culture that
we no longer recognize as ours may be pejoratively misread as

contradictions that the author has failed to take note of, eliminate, or harmonize to our satisfaction. They may also be ascribed to an inner tension or conflict within the author. It is less arduous to speculate about the author's psyche than to investigate the cultural correlatives of his work. A simplistic "*converso* mentality" has been invoked to explain the generalized "pessimism" of his work and the failure of the protagonist to act upon his better (Christian) judgment. One of the paradoxes that literature and moral philosophy have quarried endlessly is the fact that we can know what is good but fail to act upon that knowledge—*video meliora proboque, deteriora sequor*, in Ovid's neat formulation. At the metaphysical level, a God who is defined as omnipotent and who grants his creatures free will is bound to create trouble for theologians, with the result that every formulation of doctrine will be unstable. These paradoxes may be translated into a related one that is germane to Alemán's enterprise: the dignity and the wretchedness of the human condition. For each side of this paradox Alemán and his readers had powerful emblematic texts.

Giovanni Pico della Mirandola's *Oration on the Dignity of Man* (1486) proclaims man's unique capacity to become whatever he will. His God addresses Adam: "The nature of all other beings is limited and constrained within the bounds of laws prescribed by Us. Thou, constrained by no limits, in accordance with thine own free will, in whose hand We have placed thee, shalt ordain for thyself the limits of thy nature. . . . Thou shalt have the power to degenerate into the lower forms of life, which are brutish. Thou shalt have the power, out of thy soul's judgment, to be reborn into the higher forms, which are divine."[28] This oration echoes through Fernán Pérez de Oliva's *Diálogo del la dignidad del hombre* (posthumous ed., 1546), through Hamlet's "What a piece of work is man," and through countless other expressions of wonderment at human capacities. Thus it is not unique, nor is it the antimedieval piece of Renaissance optimism that it is sometimes taken for. On the contrary, it is simply the best-known work in a long tradition,

28. Giovanni Pico della Mirandola, *Oration on the Dignity of Man*, trans. Elizabeth Livermore Forbes, in *The Renaissance Philosophy of Man*, ed. Ernst Cassirer, Paul Oskar Kristeller, and John Herman Randall, Jr. (Chicago: University of Chicago Press, 1948), 225.

and Pico himself defended the scholastic philosophy that the humanists are commonly thought to have rejected.[29] In fact, the twelfth-century author of our second text, *On the Misery of the Human Condition*, intended to write a companion treatise on human nobility, but never did so.

I shall devote more attention to the second text because modern readers are surprised by the strength of the "pessimistic" argument in *Guzmán* and are often unaware that it, too, belongs to a long tradition of orthodox thought. This is the tradition of *de contemptu mundi*, which found its classic expression in the little treatise *De miseria humanae conditionis* (1195?) by Lotario di Segni, who became Pope Innocent III. Both the treatise and the tradition of which it is so perfectly representative have been overlooked in previous studies of *Guzmán*, so far as I am aware.

De miseria expounds every aspect of human wretchedness, from conception to death and the final despair of the damned in hell. Its three books elaborate upon the natural life of the body, the sins and temptations, death and judgment. The first section of Book I begins aptly with a quotation from Jeremiah: "Why did I come out of my mother's womb to see labor and sorrow, and that my days should be spent in confusion?" (Jer. 20:18) and proceeds with similarly woeful expressions taken from Job and Isaiah. The plan of the book is explained: "Wherefore with tears in my eyes I shall take up first, what a man is made of; second, what a man does; and finally, what a man is to be. For surely man was formed out of earth, conceived in guilt, born to punishment. . . . He will become fuel for the eternal fires, food for worms, a mass of rottenness."[30] In Book 1, Chapter 3, he declares that the act of conception through the lust of the flesh causes the soul's natural powers (the rational, to know good from evil; the irascible, to resist evil; the appetitive, to desire the good) to be corrupted, and exclaims, "O

29. See the essay on Pico by Paul Oskar Kristeller in his *Eight Philosophers of the Italian Renaissance* (Stanford: Stanford University Press, 1964), 54–71.

30. "Consideravi ergo cum lacrymis de quo factus sit homo, quid faciat homo, qui facturus sit homo. Sane formatus de terra, conceptus in culpa, natus ad poenam . . . fiet cibus ignis, esca vermis, massa putredinis": *Innocentii III Romani Pontificis Opera Omnia*, in *PL*, 217:702b. There is a modern edition: *Lotharii Cardinalis (Innocentii III) De miseria humanae conditionis* (Lugano: Thesaurus Mundi, 1955); and a convenient translation: *On the Misery of the Human Condition*, trans. Margaret Mary Dietz, ed. Donald R. Howard (Indianapolis: Bobbs-Merrill, 1969).

heavy necessity, O unhappy condition! Before we sin we are already chained to sin; before we are guilty, we are guilt's prisoner."[31] These passages on the inescapable sinfulness of human nature establish the fatalistic frame and apocalyptic tone in which the argument is conducted. For five centuries this work was read as a classic, and as late as 1624 the Latin text was reprinted at Salamanca.[32]

This treatise, one of the best-known works of the later Middle Ages, was certainly one of the most widely copied, imitated, translated, and paraphrased. More than six hundred manuscript copies survive in European libraries.[33] It was imitated in about three hundred works in prose and perhaps two hundred more in verse by, among other authors, Chaucer, Langland, Dante, Erasmus.[34] It did not cease to be read with the end of the Middle Ages (an example of how limited is the usefulness of such historical periodization). The print revolution may have made scribal copying obsolete (though much literature still circulated in manuscript in the sixteenth century)[35] but it did not sweep aside those works that the manuscript tradition had preserved and transmitted. On the contrary, as Elizabeth Eisenstein's admirable book (1979) demonstrates again and again, the printing press served to disseminate medieval and ancient works, encouraged translators, and made such works available to a wider public. Spanish and German Jesuits made *De miseria* required reading in their schools.[36]

Rhetorical onslaughts against human vanity, power, and pride, with reminders of the miseries of the human condition, existed before the time of Innocent III, notably in works by Anselm of Canterbury, Bernard de Morval, St. Bernard of Clairvaux. In them one can find abundant expressions of the corruption of the natural

31. "O gravis necessitas et infelix conditio. Antequam peccemus, peccato constringimur; et antequam delinquamus, delictu tenemur": *PL*, 217:704b.

32. *De contemptu mundi, sive de miseria conditionis humanae* (Salamanca, 1624). Palau y Dulcet, in his *Manual del librero hispanoamericano* (Barcelona: Palau, 1954), vol. 7, counted 75 editions in Castilian between 1488 and 1600. Many of them attributed the original to Thomas a Kempis.

33. "Innocent III," in *Dictionary of the Middle Ages*, vol. 6 (New York: Scribner's, 1985).

34. Donald R. Howard, Introduction to Segni 1969:xiv–xv.

35. Antonio Rodríguez-Moñino, *Construcción crítica y realidad histórica en la poesía española de los siglos XVI y XVII* (Madrid: Castalia, 1968); Whinnom 1967.

36. Howard, Introduction to Segni 1969:xv.

order, the vanity of all earthly things, and the evil of the social order. "Why, then, are you proud, you dust and ashes! conceived in guilt, born to misery, living in punishment, dying in anguish?"[37]

The two views of human life represented by *De dignitate* and *De miseria* were really not meant to be taken separately, much less as antagonistic to each other. It would be erroneous to call one "medieval" and the other "Renaissance," and just as wrong to put them together as an instance of "baroque contrast." Each of the two judgments on life was true, but the reader, whether of the thirteenth or the seventeenth century, would have been aware that it was only half of a global truth about the human condition. It was true only insofar as it took account of the other, its complement. So long as they are matched, then, both positions are orthodox, for there is nothing surprising in a declaration to the effect that humankind is capable of the best and the worst, of rising to heights of spirituality and sinking to depths of depravity, of performing acts of selfless generosity and of violent greed. Taken together, both positions were part of the larger concept of man as microcosm, containing within himself the "chain of being."[38] This traditional frame shows man partaking of the nature of all levels of creation (the insentient being of rocks; the vegetative soul of plants, the locomotive power of animals, the intelligence of angels); emphasis on dignity or misery is but one way of representing the whole field of possibility. "Mankind was created as it were so as to be lower than the angel, higher than the ass, and so has something in common with the highest and something in common with the lowest."[39]

If man is a microcosm, he must be understood with reference to the macrocosm, which is structured upon the conjoining of opposites: moist/dry, hot/cold at the elemental level, up through the various transformations of the spiritual/material and the divine economy of sin/redemption, with their associated imagery of light/dark, rising/falling, and so forth, to the ultimate opposition, di-

37. Bernard of Clairvaux, quoted in ibid., xxix.
38. See the classic essay by Arthur O. Lovejoy, *The Great Chain of Being* (Cambridge: Harvard University Press, 1936; New York: Harper & Row, 1960). For more specific reference to man as microcosm, Rico 1970; also Paul Oskar Kristeller, "General Introduction" to Cassirer et al., *Renaissance Philosophy of Man*.
39. Gregory the Great, *Dialogi*, in *PL*, vol. 77; cited in Rico 1970:39.

vine/satanic. "Our subject is bipolar, even though tradition has stressed the more reassuring side, just as the Christian idea of man as flesh and spirit, fallen nature and redeemed nature, is bipolar" (Rico 1970:150).[40] "Man as microcosm" is a concept that affirms participation in all levels of being, from highest to lowest, and provides reference points at every level, with the potential to become the best or the worst of creatures, the most fortunate or the most wretched. So Juan de Zabaleta, in the *Vida del conde de Matisio*, moves without transition from the celebration of human life to cries of woe: "This life . . . is all suffering, all hardship, all danger, all misfortune. . . . O wretched human condition!" Rico observes: "There is no contradiction, nor is it a case of the so-called baroque taste for contrasts: we face one of the constants of Christian anthropology" (1970:151). That is also the view from Alemán's "watchtower on human life."

The long survival of this model is evidence of its success as a cultural diagram. Innumerable clusters of oppositions, paradox upon paradox, could be generated within its system of correspondences; a single paradox, or even one of the elements in a paradox, could serve to recall the whole system. The pessimism of *De miseria* is easily moralized, as is the dark night in Fray Luis de León's Augustinian discourse, but its primordial purpose was not to moralize. Every image, every representation becomes a synecdoche in a world where the whole may be elicited by any part, or even by a part of a part, the *concordia oppositorum* by one of its extremes. This synecdoche is formally embodied in *Guzmán de Alfarache*. This book, like the microcosm itself, is not a simple dialectical opposition. In it, as in *La ortografía castellana*, Alemán demonstrates that one can intervene in one's destiny and, by doing so, can change the value sign that accompanies it.

The Outer World of *El buscón*

Frank Chandler's declaration that "the society . . . . which the picaro traverses is the main thing" (1899:60) never appears to be

40. "Disémico es, pues, nuestro tema, aunque la tradición prefiriera insistir en su más consolador sentido, como disémica es en el cristianismo la noción del hombre, carne y espíritu, naturaleza caída y naturaleza redimida."

more questionable than when it is applied to *El buscón*. In the first place, *El buscón* is very much of a piece with Quevedo's other satires, such as the *Sueños*, where ridicule is directed against persons either as individuals or as types. In his world, people are victims of one another, of their vices or their deformities. Second, Pablos is the child of parents who are grossly untypical: a thieving barber who is later executed and a mother who is a whore and a witch and is later to be burned. His uncle is his father's executioner. Not surprisingly (in a realistic view), he would like to renounce his heritage, but his wish to rise socially by means of trickery is foredoomed. It has been argued that his downfall at the hands of Don Diego is not coincidence, but is a symbolic representation of society's impermeability to aspirants from the lower ranks, that Don Diego embodies a repressive culture's pride of class and rejection of the lower orders (Spitzer 1927, Zahareas 1988). This is an attractive view, but matters are not that simple, as we shall see. On the other hand, the core of Parker's argument is that Pablos' posture toward life is self-defeating regardless of the circumstances (Parker 1947, 1967:68–70). The next step in the moralistic argument is to say that *because* Pablos makes cunning and fraud his instruments, he is plunged into the society of criminals, drunkards, imposters, and reprobates. He finds himself where he does as a result of his false analysis of the world; the squalid society depicted by Quevedo is the only possible one for his protagonist, and it is not a statement about good and evil or the decadence of the actual world. Each of these views makes a sort of sense, but none of them makes sense of the *Buscón*.

Satire, as a recognized but not always tolerated literary form, necessarily singles out whatever the writer judges to be deserving of attack, and its range of representation is limited by the genre that it adopts. In the prologue to the *Sueño* of *Las zahurdas de Plutón*, Quevedo denied that he was attacking authorities or the institutions of society: "I respect persons and I censure only vices; I denounce the negligence and insolence of some officials without impugning the excellence of their office." He will preserve *both* respect for persons *and* "la pureza de los oficios"! But judges and notaries depend upon the existence of criminals and cheats, and the symbiosis is often cozy. Quevedo's self-exculpating phrase is full of disingenuous innuendo. The world of *El buscón* is like that of the *Sueños* in being composed of types made recognizable by their frequent repetition. In this *Buscón-Sueño* world the only criteria of plausibility are that whatever we may think of as justice will not be done in it and whatever we may define as virtue cannot survive in it. Everything else follows: notaries are crooked, judges venal, constables cowardly and brutal, women vain and gaudy schemers, merchants swindlers, mule drivers blaspheming brutes, sailors drunken fools, and so on. That is Quevedo's world, the descendant of the *mundus inmundus* of the goliard poets. In *El buscón* the world is divided between knaves and fools, swindlers and dupes; in addition to these mutually supportive, symbiotic groups are the countless throngs of the self-deceived, bad poets, cracked intellectuals, publicists, crazy armchair reformers, and so forth. The picaro and his society reflect and sustain each other; Pablos adapts himself to the sector of society in which he finds himself, while the society reveals "all kinds of knavery" (*Buscón*, Prólogo). Ronald Paulson (1967) has observed:

> Picaresque novels are built on this shifting relationship between a central character and the many characters he meets. With each encounter the proportion of innocence and guilt shifts into a new ratio. The appearance of either a purely innocent victim or a completely just chastiser is rare. . . . When the picaro is punished he usually has been caught cheating or stealing; when he is a punisher of wickedness it is usually to exploit someone's folly. . . . The Spanish picaresque posits a world in which crime is always being punished, but punishment is based on superior cunning or strength or luck, not on virtue. . . . It is a world with no moral agent to bring retribution, but either a revenger, a prankster, a desperate picaro, or somebody who, by the very act of punishing, succumbs to the degenerate values of this world. (1967:67, 69)

That is an accurate judgment on the worlds lived through and described by Lázaro, by Guzmán, and by Pablos. But it misses Mateo Alemán's determined effort to control our response to the fictional world, to arouse to activity the self-determining agent that he assumes we carry within us.

I referred earlier to *El buscón* as cause for scandal. After the obscene entertainment at Pablos' uncle's house in Segovia, the next most shocking episode is perhaps Pablos' discovery by Don Diego when he is hoping to make a deceitful marriage that will give him the social advancement he has craved. Pablos has cut a ridiculous figure, taking another man's horse in order to pass for a gentleman and then falling off it. Don Diego, who was once his boyhood companion, is struck by the resemblance between Pablos and the newcomer "Don Felipe Tristán," as Pablos wishes to be known: "You won't believe this, but his mother was a witch, his father a thief, and his uncle an executioner. He was the most vile, depraved man in all of God's world" (230). Don Diego had disappeared from the narrative for thirteen chapters; he now comes forth to be the executioner of Pablos, by stealth. He knows that some men are waiting to beat him on account of some wench ("por una mujercilla"), so he exchanges capes with Pablos, who is beaten in his place. Then Pablos is attacked and his face slashed by Don Diego's friends. The parting wound is verbal: "¡Así pagan los pícaros embustidores mal nacidos!" (Take that for being a low-born, lying scoundrel!" [241]). *Mal nacidos*, the words of social rejection, are the last words spoken on behalf of Don Diego, who does not soil his hands by punishing Pablos himself. Earlier, at the university, Don Diego escaped the hazing thanks to the protection of senior students who knew his father (62). The social distance between him and Pablos was measured by the immunity conferred by wealth and rank; now it is measured by the brute force that rank has at its command.

Pablos has hoped for salvation by way of social ascent: when that is denied him and his face is marked forever with the sign of ignominy, his decline is rapid. Don Diego has saved the social situation and maintained intact the barriers of birth and rank. Guzmán accepted the Christian promise of salvation, which is available to all, and chose to abandon the company of reprobates. But the social world's barriers are higher than the spiritual world's, though not as impenetrable as Quevedo would have wished. Here, in the space between the aristocratic world of Don Diego and the sordid world of Pablos, is where he has erected the barrier that cannot be traversed. This is the space where Quevedo's anxieties are most aroused. His satire would not have needed to be so fierce if he had not been aware that the unthinkable transgressions

156

were in fact taking place. The objects of his fear were real enough; upstarts with money did dazzle noble families with marriageable daughters who had no dowry, and did buy land so that their children might acquire rank and a "don" to their names, and they sent those children to be taught by Jesuit teachers to become administrators and lawyers. In all this the old northern aristocrat saw a threat to his class and to the social order. Marcel Bataillon suggested that if there were one thread in the novel that could explain Pablos' career, it would surely be the impossibility of a *pícaro mal nacido*, a scoundrel of ignominious birth, gaining access to the world of respectable people, of "los honrados." "In view of what we know of Quevedo, is it not likely that, in his eyes, this impossibility was no injustice but an imperative of the social order, which had been breached too often already [une exigence de l'ordre sociale, à la quelle il n'y a que trop de dérogations]?" (1967:29).

In *El buscón* we see the would-be transgressor Pablos and a hidden hand that punishes him. The picaro breaks the social taboo, and the author sets up the social reflex that crushes and disfigures him. But it is not a straightforward act of punishment, for, like Fernando in Lope de Vega's tragedy *El castigo sin venganza*, Pablos sees only the hand that wounds him, not the author of the deed. And here Paulson's observation gains special force, that this is "a world in which crime is always being punished, but punishment is based on superior cunning or strength or luck, not on virtue . . . a world with no moral agent." Don Diego defends the respectable upper orders against the scrophulous lower orders, but that does not make him a moral agent. This mediator of authorial justice is a highly ambiguous figure. His family connections saved him from the horrors of student initiation, while he left his protégé to look after himself; now he is involved in a sordid quarrel about a "mujercilla." One might expect Justice to have cleaner hands.

The blood Pablos seeks to deny is not simply plebeian or criminal, it is the blood of his Jewish ancestors. But Don Diego is a *converso*, too. For Pablos, it is one more dishonorable fact to add to the rest. Don Diego's is a very different case. As long ago as 1949, Luis F. de Peñalosa showed that the Coronels of Segovia were all *conversos*, a fact well known in Quevedo's time. The ancestor of this fictional Don Diego, then, was Abraham Seneor, a noble, wealthy, and respected Jew who converted to Christianity and was baptized by Queen Isabella on 15 June 1492. More recently Carroll Johnson (1974) produced evidence to show that in 1589 members of this family went to court to prove that they were legitimate descendants of Abraham Seneor, and so entitled to protection under the royal privilege granted to their illustrious ancestor. Some members of this family were contemporaries of Quevedo at the university. So Don Diego, the mediator of authorial justice, is descended from ancestors who had crossed the invisible boundary from Jew to Christian under the highest patronage and succeeded in changing name, appearance, and identity. He is no longer recognizable to those who, like Pablos, remain outside the favored precinct. Although in the early chapters Don Diego accepts Pablos in a way fitting a servant and companion, there is no sign that either he or anyone in his family accepts Pablos as "one of us."

The Coronels had had the good fortune to be reborn in Spanish society as well as in Christ, and Don Diego's crushing of Pablos is in the vein of Quevedo's blackest humor: "Así pagan los pícaros embusteros mal nacidos" (241). If we look for parallels with *Guzmán de Alfarache*, we have to note that the suffering and rejection that lead to the conversion of the picaro are caused by a companion, a former partner turned enemy, Soto, a ruthless criminal who hides his hand. The definitive crushing and humiliation of Pablos are caused by his former companion and master, who also hides his hand. Accusers who denounced *conversos* suspected of Judaizing could hide theirs too. Quevedo thrusts his readers into one of the most sensitive places in Spanish society. Perhaps the most ghastly moment occurs when Don Diego warns Pablos to watch out: "Pablos, abre el ojo, que asan carne" (keep your eyes open, they're roasting flesh [67]). Of all the phrases Quevedo could have put into the mouth of a *converso* to convey "they're out to get you" or "they're looking for trouble," none could be as grim as the one he chose: "they're roasting flesh." This phrase, in the memory of a person of Jewish origins, could evoke only one image, and it is clearly not there by accident when it is spoken by one *converso* to another. What has broken through to the level of discourse is the voice of generations of *conversos* who know what "roasting flesh" means. Don Diego's command of that phrase reveals his arrogant security and that of his family, who reject Pablos. Anyone who had known the illustrious Abraham Seneor and could now see this scion whoring and frequenting the back streets with other young blades, blending into the vulgar and corrupt urban aristocracy of the reign of Philip III, would catch the full force of Quevedo's sarcasm. Readers would recall, as Quevedo must have heard many times, that the same Abraham Seneor who was honored by Queen Isabella was reviled as a renegade opportunist by those other Jews who remained in their faith. "Abre el ojo" is spoken by a member of a caste (to adopt Américo Castro's term) who often protected themselves by identifying themselves with the persecutor or by merging into the vulgar mass. Here is an irony of competing levels of association: keeping your eyes open meant one thing to Pablos, another to Don Diego, and yet another to Quevedo, arrogant and anxious, the defender of severe traditional values, the implacable scourge of pretension.

If there is one theme that appears and reappears in innumerable forms and insinuations in Quevedo's works, it is an obsession with status and boundaries, a rage for containment. Failure of containment is what *El buscón* is about. Nothing is in its place. The grotesque descriptions (of Dómine Cabra, for example) are composed of things violently torn from their contexts and reassembled into monstrous new forms. When Pablos is a boy, his performance as carnival king turns into a riot when his horse steals a cabbage from a curbside stand. He is pelted with vegetables and the horse throws him into a dungheap. This low comedy works by breaking things loose from their assigned functions and from their links in a rational natural order. The horse is so ravenous it can hardly walk, so it cannot behave as the ceremonial animal it is appointed to be. It steals a cabbage, and upon the loss of this single cabbage the vendors lose their reason and fling all their stock at him. Removed from the normal cycle of production and consumption, the vegetables cease to be food and become projectiles and weapons, then they immediately become garbage in the road. Meanwhile, Pablos is covered with excrement from his fall and imagines himself exchanged for his mother. The carnival itself, whose proper function is to be a therapeutic reversal of order, to relieve tensions and restore harmony through mock violence, becomes a scene of real violence: "the festivity in confusion, people shocked, parents ashamed, my friend's head broken, the horse dead . . ." (30). The hazing by students consists of spitting, fouling of the bed, and so

on. Again the world is a dungheap for Pablos, and it is from experiences of the world and society as excrement that Pablos takes his
lessons. The initiators have to keep a delicate balance between
their ostensible purpose and its violent opposite, which they also
intend. Rites of initiation, of inclusion, are also rites of exclusion;
the lines are reversible, like those of the accommodating violence
of the carnival.

In *El buscón* less than in any other of these works can the external world be read as a literal representation of the actual world. Its
scenes of violence and gross comedy contribute nothing to verisimilitude and everything to a vision of the world as an obscene
body that externalizes the impoverished noble Quevedo's anxieties
of status and hierarchy (Molho 1977).

After *El buscón*

As we look back over *Lazarillo*, *Guzmán*, and *El buscón* it is evident that we cannot reconstruct from these works the everyday
reality of seventeenth-century Spain, as earlier writers hoped to
do. In the words of Lucien Goldmann, "the problem is obviously
complex in that the literary or artistic universe is an imaginary
one, and as such has no direct relation to the real world."[41] Starting
from the text itself, we search for its internal relationships, and
only when we have found them do we look outside for the social
facts that the literature organizes symbolically. By these means we
find that the social facts of poverty, vagrancy, marginality are internalized in the novel, not for the sake of mimetic representation
but for the sake of verisimilitude, which is the price the writer
pays the contemporary reader for his freedom.

The later picaresque works are generally mediocre and escapist.
In the various novels of Alonso de Castillo Solórzano that are
styled "picaresque" it is difficult to find any memory of *El buscón*,
except for some purloined incidents and phrases. The relation of

41. Lucien Goldmann, "Le Structuralisme génétique en sociologie de la littérature," in *Littérature et Société*, Colloque International de Sociologie de la Littérature, 1964 (Brussels: Institut de Sociologie de l'Université Libre de Brux-
elles, 1967), 203.

the narrator to his or her world is completely different. For example, his protagonists succeed in rising socially by means of their ill-gotten wealth. We may wonder whether such transformations based on fraud really took place and, if they did, whether they could become successfully established. By whom would these tricksters be accepted? Surely not by the leading families, whose passion for geneology, a characteristic common to the nobility everywhere, kept them watchful for imposters. This question of how well such dreams—daydreams for Castillo, nightmares for Quevedo—correspond to reality will claim our attention in later chapters. In the meantime, we note that Castillo shares with a generation of writers a desire for honor and social success through writing. He was a secretarial drudge in a politically important aristocratic family. Writing fiction enabled him in fantasy to penetrate invisible barriers and participate more completely in that world where he was a mere servant. At the same time, he could open the same doors of fantasy to a larger public that enjoyed the vicarious participation. Musical soirées, the style of headdress, footwear, plumes and gold braid, carriages and liveried servants: scarcely any facet of that urban opulence is not to be found in Castillo's fiction during these excursions of the picaro into the upper levels of society. Many of his readers must have belonged to that world, others aspired to join it by the purchase of annuities or by marriage, yet others would live in it in fantasy, as people always do. We can find many prejudices that he must have shared with his public: the urban aristocrats appear solid and respectable, and must be protected from the upstart. The peasants and laborers are figures of fun. Such literary categories as the serious and the comic, then, are socially determined, and from this vantage we see that such novels are conformist in ways that the earlier picaresque novels were not.

5

Inner Worlds

Justifying the Self

The inner world (the world of the self, aware of its existence, its nature, its motions and desires, its extension in time, its urge to continue to be, in the face of its own uncertainty) is scarcely represented in fiction before the seventeenth century. Of the characteristic fictions of the Middle Ages—romance, fabliau, and exemplum—the exemplum is given meaning only by its setting, its use to illustrate a proposition or an argument, usually a moral one. The exemplum may originate in fiction or history or anywhere at all so long as its characteristic structure is an act and its consequences; but the corollary is that the consequences should be readable as good or bad, according to criteria enunciated in the frame. Fabliaux are also reducible to act and consequence, though their intent is not normative but comic, naturalistic; the actors are winners and losers, the consequence success or failure. Their field is not bounded by morality, for success most often consists in eluding guardians and figures of authority. Desires that in the exemplum would be thwarted or punished to illustrate the authority vested in the frame are likely to be satisfied by fabliaux to affirm the desires themselves or the ingenuity they promote. The conditions that Ronald Paulson noted in the world of the picaresque— "a world in which . . . punishment is based on superior cunning or strength or luck, not on virtue" (1967:69)—apply to the world of the fabliau.

Romance may appear to offer promise of interiority. An extended narrative in which the protagonist may pass from victory to defeat, from splendor to hardship in pursuit of his goal, and in which the goal at times seems hopeless, could provide spaces for self-questioning. Yet I know of no hero of medieval romance whose self-doubt is more than momentary or whose self-definition is seriously put in question. When Amadís has banished himself to Peña Pobre to pine for the loss of Oriana's love (*Amadís de Gaula*, bk. II), he is simply transformed into a textbook example of dejection. He lets his hair and his nails grow, he refuses to eat, he weeps and sighs and pours out lamentations that conform to the specifications of the manuals of rhetoric. Heroes are men of action, models of how to keep one's eye on the target and not hesitate, but to go from one challenge to the next. On the plots' amorous side, the ladies display more inner life than the knights. They reverse the role of men by waiting rather than doing. In their periods of waiting, they confide their fears or their apprehensions to sisters, companions, and privileged servants, or write letters to complain of neglect or loneliness or to vent jealousy. The sentimental novels of the fifteenth century, followed by the pastoral novels of the sixteenth, also confine the representation of inner states to hopes and fears in matters of love. In the pastoral world of *La Diana* the amorous quests and conflicts and discussions are the plot, and the idyllic external world is a transparent allegory of the ideal relation that ought to hold between human feelings and human society. These romances narrativize the situations that had become traditional in the lyric corpus, the collective text that Paul Zumthor has called the *grand chant courtois*.[1]

The enlargement of the area of the inner world to include feelings other than amorous desire and jealousy comes late in the fifteenth century in Spain, in *La Celestina*. In the person of Calisto,

1. Paul Zumthor, *Essai de poétique médiévale* (Paris: Seuil, 1972).

the alternation of hope and despair, of exaltation and withdrawal, characteristic of the *novela sentimental* is complicated by the presence of old Celestina, because she manipulates his fears and desires to her own professional ends. Upon hearing of her death and the deaths of his servants, Calisto rapidly reconciles himself to their loss: Rojas shows us a man who can trim his conscience to his desires. In Melibea's dialogues with Celestina, we see her becoming aware of her unrecognized love for Calisto; later she listens in anger and embarrassment as her parents talk of finding a husband for their "innocent" little daughter. *La Celestina* is a work that goes much further than anything previously achieved in Spanish in exploring the inner world of feelings, and particularly those feelings that are not already a commonplace of the erotic novel: anger, betrayal, corrupt conscience. A notable example is Celestina's virtuoso performance in Act 7 in corrupting the young servant Pármeno. Equally remarkable, though less obvious, is Pármeno's side of the dialogue. Celestina's pressure gives him little time to reflect, but what he says is enough to show his defenses being undermined, his fiery moral outrage at the shoddiness of the adult world being dampened, his insecurity as an orphan being enlisted to the cause of unity against Calisto. In *La Celestina*, in summary, something new has been achieved beyond the rhetorical projection of states of mind and emotion that was extensively practiced in other fictional forms; it is the representation of *change* in psychic orientation, the *process* of self-persuasion as a manifestation of the economy of desire. *La Celestina* was the first great fictional best-seller in the history of Spanish printing, and it spawned progeny, as such successful works usually do.

There did exist a literature that was devoted specifically to the inner workings of the psyche and encouraged self-examination in its readers. This was not imaginative literature in the usual sense of the term, though some writers exercised extraordinary imaginative power in the creation of possible worlds, hypothetical situations, and in analyzing motives. I refer to the devotional and confessional writings that were abundant and widely read in the sixteenth century and after. They were a mainstay of printers, and in reprints they far outnumbered any genre of literature in that century. When Don Quixote visits the printing shop in Barcelona, he sees a work being corrected in proofs: *Luz del alma cristiana*, by

Fray Felipe de Meneses, first published in Valladolid (1554) and frequently reprinted. Keith Whinnom has drawn our attention to the great difference that exists between the facts of literary history—that is, the history of publication and readership—and our canon of literary preferences. "Despite the success of a limited number of imaginative works, Golden-Age printing in Spanish is dominated by prose non-fiction, by devotional, moralizing, and historical works" (1980:194). In this respect Spain resembled the rest of Europe (Eisenstein 1979:78, 315). The most successful of all Spanish books was Fray Luis de Granada's *Libro de la oración*, with well over a hundred editions between 1554 and 1679. Another book by the same Fray Luis, his *Guía de pecadores*, overshadowed all works of Spanish fiction except *Celestina*. A list of such works would be enormous, far longer than a list of the profane works of the period, and even longer if we include those translated from other languages, such as Thomas a Kempis' *Imitatio Christi*.

These works urge readers to know themselves, to plumb their thoughts to the origin of their desires, to cultivate inner dialogues with themselves and with God. Readers are trained to observe the motions of their passions, to seek peace and harmony by understanding the source of inner violence and turbulence. In Spanish, as in other Romance tongues, one word signifies both "consciousness" and "conscience"; books of devotions and manuals of prayer are not mere exhortations to moral behavior or pious submission, though these results may have been desirable in the minds of their authors, but are incitements to self-awareness. When all the necessary allowances are made for differences of culture, literacy, and social cohesion, they were what the pop psychology and self-help books—how to achieve happiness, success, love, freedom from "codependency," and spiritual adjustment—are for our time. These books, with their aim of cultivating their readers' awareness of the inner life, were perhaps the most powerful examples of the common culture that bound writers and readers in this period. Maxime Chevalier (1976:27–28), discussing the problems of investigating who owned and read which books in Golden Age Spain, notes that the merchants, who were capable of buying and reading books, rarely did so. As in France and elsewhere, these bourgeois owned a few books of devotion, one or two business manuals, an almanac for the dates of fairs, perhaps a travel book. This impression is confirmed by Bartolomé Benassar (1969).[2] A writer who wished to capture the attention of the trading community would have to do so by appealing to their established predilections as readers. It seems that this is what Alemán intended to do, and the phenomenal success of his novel, with many more editions than *Don Quixote* in the first ten years after publication, suggests that he succeeded. In an age when imaginative literature regularly claimed to instruct, Alemán's claim was unusually insistent. He not only declared that he had a didactic purpose but integrated the reflections on the action into the fabric of the novel. Further yet, he aimed not merely to instruct by illustration and example but to force the reader to examine his own motives and conscience at every turn.[3]

Related thematically to the books of prayer and devotion but distinct in genre are the confessions and confessional autobiographies (Gómez-Moriana 1983). The connection has been noted for Italy:

> The close of the Middle Ages in Italy and the beginning of the Renaisssance witnessed a proliferation of these vernacular handbooks of penance both for laymen and priests. . . . As guides to the examination of the individual conscience these penitentials were, in fact, the matrix of early Renaissance autobiography. . . . Whereas early medieval handbooks were legalistic in tenor, the confessional works of popular preachers like Cavalca, Passavanti or San Bernardino were particularly successful in shifting emphasis from the nature of the sin to the conscience of the sinner, their object being to encourage periodic and systematic examination by the layman of his acts and motives. Confessors were instructed to ascertain whether the sinner wished to do what he did or understood what he was doing, and whether he intended to sin without actually carrying out his intentions. . . . Thus during the late Middle Ages and early Renaissance the particular form of self-awareness represented by the practice of confession

2. Benassar also cites Martin 1969:538 and Piere Jeannin, *Les Marchands au XVIe siècle* (Paris: Seuil, 1957), 138–46.

3. The use of the masculine article here is deliberate: I assume that Alemán wrote for a predominantly male readership, especially in view of the reformist program that Cavillac (1983) has demonstrated.

was brought to a high state of development. (Zimmermann 1971:128).

Evidently the process of self-examination and oral confession were given a narrative structure and placed on a temporal continuum; the commission of an act was regarded in relation to its genesis and its consequences, its motives and its attendant circumstances, its completion or noncompletion. Petrarch's *Secretum* can be read as a "self-exploration where the conscience sets about examining the self in the fashion of a Christian confessor with classical sensibilities." Price Zimmermann shows that the attempt to explain himself to the reader forced Petrarch to examine himself by the only systematic practice that was available to him: preparation for confession by identifying sins and errors in thought, word, and deed, failures of obligation to God and one's neighbor, and so on. "Not only did he have sins to confess, not only was the habit of confessing strong, but the preparatory meditation for the confessional was the only form of systematic self-analysis available" (1971:129).

The question whether Augustine's *Confessions* served as a model for *Lazarillo* has been inconclusively argued, but in the case of *Guzmán* the connection is clear.[4] Augustine's double perspective in orienting his discourse to God and his human witnesses is adopted by Alemán for his confessional autobiographical fiction.[5] Moreover, the bitter tone of *Guzmán*, which modern commentators often ascribe to its author and to his pessimistic view of the world, is a generic trait of the confessional autobiography, and derives from a passage in Isaiah 38:15: *Recogitabo tibi omnes annos meos et in amaritudine animae meae* (I shall ponder on all my years in my soul, in bitterness). This phrase, taken up by San Bernardino and by Giovanni da Ravenna, is passed on to the autobiographical and penitential literature. Augustine did not use the full quotation in that

4. Hans Robert Jauss, "Ursprung und Bedeutung der Ich-Form im *Lazarillo de Tormes*," *Romanistisches Jahrbuch* 8 (1957): 290–311; P. Baumans, "Der *Lazarillo de Tormes* eine Travestie der Augustinischen *Confessiones*?" *Romanistisches Jahrbuch* 10 (1959): 285–91; Rico 1984:48.

5. He seeks to do truth "before Thee in confession, and in my writing before many witnesses": *Confessions* x.1. I quote from the translation by F. J. Sheed of bks. i–x (New York: Sheed & Ward, 1942).

form, though he used the phrase *in amaritudine* more than once to characterize the appropriate confessional state of mind (Zimmermann, 1971:140). Added authority and public emphasis were given to the culture of confession by the Council of Trent, with its reaffirmation of the efficacy of confession and of the sacrament of penitence. It is important to note that confession was not confined to the privacy of the confessional, but was part of the spectacle of public executions and autos-da-fe.[6] There inner and outer worlds meet and overlap; more exactly, the inner world of spirituality is projected onto a public stage, given a dramatic role, reminded that it has no claim to autonomy but must be exposed to public scrutiny and even to the public gaze. The self, in its final agonies and its moment of truth, becomes the subject of a performance, an exemplary act played before the theater of the world.

With these paradigms before us we may go on to study the presentation of the narrating self in the principal picaresque fictions. Several preliminary points will already be clear. First, the autobiographical mode was not in itself a means of access to the inner world of the subject. Second, the self was not yet an object of disinterested attention. Those fictions that looked into the inner world of the subject had projected only such contents as could be interpreted as motives for the public world or for the subject's salvation. Third, the discourses of the self that were available had been developed as instruments of spiritual self-preparation, as part of a program of institutional control. It should be no cause for surprise, then, to find that in its use of the discourses of memory, as in other aspects of its textual production, *Lazarillo* is essentially transgressive. Alemán's *Guzmán*, on the other hand, is not simply a text generated in conformity with these norms but a serious rhetorical elaboration of them.

6. See the extraordinary entries in the journal of the Jesuit Father Pedro de León (1545–1632), who ministered to prostitutes and prisoners and, in particular, to condemned criminals in Seville during the lifetime of Alemán; he recorded many of their final declarations from the scaffold: Domínguez Ortiz 1969:13–71. The prominence of the Spaniards in writing and debating on the subject of confession is abundantly documented in Henry Charles Lea, *A History of Auricular Confession and Indulgences in the Latin Church*, 2 vols. (Philadelphia: Lea Bro., 1896).

The Inner World of *Lazarillo de Tormes*

The first-person narration of *Lazarillo de Tormes* seems intended to narrow the focus, to exclude whatever, in a more developed narrative, might have been admitted for the sake of letting the eye and the mind wander over more spacious domains. It confesses very little, being a story rather of "the difficulty and the challenge of self-assertion" (Weinstein, 1981:20). In contrast to the situation in more modern works, or in the English transformations of picaresque nearly two centuries later, the "I" of Lázaro looks out rather than in. A modern reader, expecting to find interiority, might assume that Lazarillo was too busy struggling to survive to be able to afford the luxury of a developed self-consciousness. His reference to his little half brother's scare at seeing his colored father offers less the experience of self-knowledge than a parable of it. The story is marked by moments of revelation and of transformation: the stone bull; the post; the dialogue with the squire; the purchase of clothing, and so forth; and each of these moments presents a new adjustment to someone who may be said to represent metonymically "the world" or some segment of it. At the same time, each one marks a new moment in the history of his ability to cope, and in his awareness of that ability. The self in this work is an operator (in all senses of the word) rather than a consciousness to be explored; each new adjustment is a *prise de position*, not a *prise de conscience*. Arnold Weinstein (1981) declares that "we actually have—almost 300 years before Balzac and Flaubert—the *Urform* of the 'sell-out,' and what is sold goes by various names: soul, consciousness, character" (21); and again, "Lazarillo's virtual disappearance from the narrative, his shift from subject to witness and then false witness, is the fullest embodiment of the novel's meaning" (28). We might rephrase and remetaphorize the idea and say that Lázaro presents himself as a lens through which he makes us view his situation. This is not a purely guileless operation, since the lens composes the image of the situation as he would like us to see it. In other words, this is not a self opened out for the reader to explore but a mechanism that recalls images from the past and persuades the reader that they add up to a sufficient explanation of the situation to which they have led. The designated reader, of course, is Vuestra Merced, and the self that Lázaro composes in his narrative is the creation of the world in which he has grown up and whose characteristic forms of cant and hypocrisy he has internalized. He presents himself, that is, as a quiet triumph of adaptation, in which he and his world are as one.

The anonymous author has Lázaro recreate in his narrative discourse some moments of hardship, hunger, and pain. When, after serving the blind man, he finds that life with the priest is even harder and that he is in real danger of starvation, he comments to himself: "The first had me dying of hunger, then when I left him I chanced upon this one who has brought me to my grave already. So if I leave him and meet another who is even worse, I must surely die. So I didn't dare to budge because I truly believed that each step would be more disastrous, and that if I sank any lower the name of Lázaro would never again be heard in this world" (31–32). Here the mature Lázaro, the writer, recalls his reflection on his situation years earlier, the feeling that he might easily disappear from the world without trace. The precariousness of his existence is the theme of this comment and of others, too, as it is the theme of the whole of the apologia that he addresses to Vuestra Merced. The thought that poor Lázaro might never be heard of again, evoking an elegiac strain, elicits a sentiment rather than a sensation of starvation or the terror of impending death. Hunger plays a large part in *Lazarillo*, but the *experience* of hunger does not. It is the motive for some comic acts at the level of the events, and it is also a metaphor for desire generally. So bread, in the complicated play between him and the squire, is not mere food but part of a transaction; he supports his master materially, and in exchange he has the knowledge that he is needed. Here a new sequence begins. The hunger for food does not cease, but it is transformed into a hunger for security on other levels of existence, for acceptance, for participation, for a secure position. This hunger is at least equal to that for sustenance, and it moves him toward his final contentment as the archpriest's cuckold, comfortable in his respectability and suppressing all contradictions. There is one moment of terror when he meets the funeral procession in *tratado* 3. But this fear is simply the narrative pretext for a verbal conceit, which allows him to modulate into farce as he identifies the squire's lodging with the tomb.

Although the experience of hunger is not represented directly, it is conveyed metonymically through the experience of time. As the boy follows his new master, the squire, around the streets of the city, passing by the food markets in first one quarter, then another, clocks chime, bells toll, the hours pass, but there is no pause to buy provisions. Lazarillo responds to each disappointment with a new hope; they are not stopping to buy because the master is not satisfied with the goods that are on display; or his master must be one of those who buy in bulk. As the clock strikes one, the hour when people eat, he is happy to see his master stop in front of a door and bring out his key. But inside, there is nothing to eat (43). The narrative conveys the anguish of passing time, but modulates again into the mode of comedy: first the comedy of mistaken interpretations as Lazarillo fails to grasp the inevitable but unacceptable reason why his master does not stop to buy food (he is penniless); then the comedy of mutual dissembling (I have a tiny appetite; I don't drink wine, says Lazarillo); then the comedy of inversion as it becomes apparent that the servant will have to sustain the master (44–46).

Lázaro's story gives plentiful opportunity for the narrator to press the button of pathos, to amplify fear, hunger, physical suffering, but he does not do so. In the first two *tratados*, the boy is pushed, prodded, has a pot broken on his face by the blind man, and is severely beaten over the head by the priest and rendered unconscious for three days. Yet he does not mention the pain, and his fears are merely stated. An inner life is scarcely inferred. Nevertheless, the fact that fear has any place in this story is significant. Fear belonged in comic genres, where it was usually exaggerated. Extended narrative in antiquity and the Middle Ages was predominantly heroic, and the protagonists of heroic narrative do not experience fear. "Fear is proof of low birth" (*degeneres animos timor arguit*), wrote Vergil (*Aeneid*, IV.13). The chevalier Bayard was admired because he was both fearless and blameless (*sans paour et sans reproche*). Courage has always been a necessary condition of honor and fear a sign of baseness. In the words of Froissart, "As the log cannot burn without fire, the gentleman cannot achieve perfect honor or worldly glory without proving his valor" (Delumeau, 1978:3). Chronicles repeatedly draw the distinction between the nobleman, moved to battle by desire for honor, displaying courage against all odds, and the common foot soldier, ready to retreat or run away. Even the archers, who could rout an army, need to be kept under supervision by a large number of nobles, according to the testimony of Commynes (Delumeau, 1978:4). The iconography of ruling classes since ancient times was composed of military images, of triumphal arches, fortresses, equestrian statues, literary panegyrics that exalted courage, valor in arms. Such tokens justify the powerful and arrogant in their own eyes: only the fearless deserve to rule, the fearful deserve subjection.

Sixteenth-century humanism denied that the nobility had a monopoly on courage, and the criticism of war and military glory by such writers as Erasmus and Montaigne help to explain the reception of an ironic novel such as *Lazarillo*. In the courage of Don Quixote and the pusillanimity of Sancho Panza, Cervantes characteristically sets up the double stereotype even while he exposes both to ironic reappraisal. The claims of honor upon life and limb are challenged by such powerful imaginative creations as Panurge and Falstaff. "Can honour set-to a leg? No. Or an arm? No. Or take away the grief of a wound? No. Honour hath no skill in surgery, then? No. What is honour? A word. What is that word, honour? Air. A trim reckoning! Who hath it? He that died o' Wednesday" (*Henry IV, Part I*, v.1). Sir John Falstaff, of course, is by no means the moral voice of the age; he repudiates honor when he may have to fight a duel and expose himself to danger. Lázaro's story becomes richer for us if we see in it a reaction not only against chivalric literary conventions but against the chivalric social code.

In two of his essays (xvi, xviii) Montaigne describes the fear that seized the city of Rome during its siege in 1527. Lázaro's story does not describe the fears that he felt, and the reader has to guess that the boy lived in fear and pain. His human adversaries were not military opponents but representatives of his own society and those who wrote and enforced laws against begging. In such works as the *Praise of Folly* and *Colloquies* of Erasmus the literary acknowledgment of fear has its beginnings; fear is shown to be inherent in all forms of subjection, including the most domestic. In this respect, as in others that I have mentioned, the story of the boy is a device for unmasking the scandalousness of the adult world.[7] The process of detaching valor and honor from their monopoly by the noble warrior caste as that caste's specific mode of self-definition makes possible a broader erosion of stereotypes. Cervantes, Lope de Vega, and Calderón illustrate and affirm the valor and the honor of humble folk by various strategies and with various ends in view. A more radical move, though, is the separation of fear from its moral and social nexus of negative concepts: baseness, cowardice, slavery, treachery. The author of *Lazarillo* has taken a step toward claiming the freedom to represent fear as a feeling in its own right, as a response to arbitrary power, unearned authority, or any fate that cannot be explained away as the workings of divine Providence.

Because *Lazarillo* is so short, and because in its little space it spans the years of infancy, youth, and young manhood, and because it is constructed with ready-made anecdotes, we can not expect it to reveal the inner world of the narrator. But it tantalizes us precisely because it appears to promise such self-revelations and then to withhold them. Lázaro is asked to explain "the matter," and he proceeds to explain *himself*, but he does not really do that either. We are left with a double evasion, and that evasiveness, that ability to shift ground, is Lázaro's distinctive trait. This text does not allow us to separate the inner from the outer world because he wants to tell his reader: "See, this is the world that made me what I am." He constructs the kind of world that, when its values and power relations are internalized, can mold a subject such as Lázaro, and he reveals only as much of himself as is intelligible if it is read as a product of such a world. The center of interest in Lázaro's story, that which generates the plot, is not the self as source and motor of actions, nor is it the external world, as determinant of the self and its actions; rather it is the relation between self and world, as Lázaro wishes to fix it. At the level of the discourse, therefore, there is a second center, which is the relation of the self to its text. How *does* Lázaro fix it? How does he sell this package of self and outer world? The answer is that he uses an-

7. The device is taken up and used by Cervantes in *Rinconete y Cortadillo*, and given a new twist in the *Coloquio de los perros*; also by Leo Tolstoy in *Kholstomer*, where the narrator is a horse. See Viktor Shklovsky on "defamiliarization" in "Art and Technique," in Lemon/Reis 1965:3–24.

other text, of his own invention, namely the Prólogo, to mediate the *vida*, the life story, to us. I referred to this transaction briefly in Chapter 2 and at length elsewhere, so I will add only a few words here.

After we have read his prologue, Lázaro's text is no longer a simple response to "Your Honor writes [to say] that I should write." His "trifle" (*nonada*), originally exacted in tribute to the authority of Vuestra Merced, is not to be filed away, but to be brought "to the attention of many" and offered in the marketplace. Lázaro the obedient servant has been transformed, by virtue of his insolent obedience, into an Author. No less an authority than Cicero has underwritten this text, with the dictum "Honor inspires the arts." The act of writing has transformed him, an obscure temporizer in a corrupt domestic and social order, he asserts, into something more illustrious: an Artist. How is this transformation achieved? His lifelong pursuit of security has entailed the acquisition of honor, or at least the trappings of honor. But honor requires that certain things that people say about him, his wife, and the archpriest of San Salvador be suppressed. Now he has to put in writing the shameful circumstances of his existence, and in performing this act of obedience he both demonstrates his subservience and commits to paper what should not even be spoken.

I will say no more about the function of the Prólogo, except that it separates the text from the very subject that it has constituted and makes it into a commodity. There is no self; we are left with only a simulacrum, a collage of superimposed roles, and an authorial voice. The author asserts this voice by displacing Vuestra Merced, ejecting him from the frame and seizing his authority to ascribe value to the text. Two inner processes appear to be at work: memory and the internalization of experience. In fact, memory is here identical to the sum of the story and its discourse (the *récit*), the narrative sequence of the events as they are recalled. Memory is not really *represented*, either as depository or as a process of reconstituting its contents. In the second *apparent* process, the experience of "the other" (particularized as mother, surrogate father, priest, etc., all of them embodying various modes of authority), is interiorized and transformed into an ironic parody of the external world's values. This is essentially a rhetorical construct, metonymy piled upon metonymy. In brief, the subject that is constituted as Lázaro de Tormes is a public image, totally lacking interiority. As we reach the end of his story and circle back through the Prologue, we have to conclude that our search for the self has been a vain pursuit of a false promise. Behind the mask is only another mask. The false promise, mask within mask, is the only self there is in Lázaro's world.

The Inner World of *Guzmán de Alfarache*

Guzmán de Alfarache is the only one of the picaresque novels that resembles a fully autobiographical narrative. *Lazarillo de Tormes* is a story that adopts the strategy of autobiography in order, it appears, to avoid directly answering a question, and Lázaro does not tell what was the "matter" his questioner wants explained. He responds by laying out the trajectory of his career so as to inform, divert, and distract his readers and to justify himself at the same time: "Let those who inherited great fortunes reflect on how little praise is due to them since Fortune was favorable to them, and how much greater is the achievement of those who, with Fortune against them, rowed into a safe harbor by strength and cunning" (7). Guzmán tells his story for totally different motives, unbidden by any external authority. One of Alemán's models of first-person narration was the *Confessions* of Augustine, which are known to have circulated in at least eight editions during the latter half of the sixteenth century. The saint's combination of story, prayer, and self-analysis, and particularly his intense preoccupation with how the mind and the will are continually subverted by desire and by habit, enable us to understand more clearly the kind of book Alemán wanted to write.[8]

Neither Augustine's nor Guzmán's story resembles a conventional rose-colored saint's life. In neither text does the new direction taken by the life offer an easy resolution; rather it offers new uncertainties. I believe, too, that Alemán owes much to Augustine's mode of constructing a self (which has little in common with

8. Cros (1971:140–43) also noted the Augustinian thinking on grace and the will that permeates the novel.

twentieth-century concepts of the self, as any early modern self-representation will show)[9] and especially to his account of the operation of memory in Book x of the *Confessions*. I do not look for parallels between the prayers and meditations in the *Confessions* and those in *Guzmán*. Both works draw freely upon biblical texts, but so do many others that Alemán must have read. The rhetoric and the topics of the homilies and *sententiae* in *Guzmán de Alfarache* are another matter that do not concern us here. One can open Luis de Granada's *Guía de pecadores* at almost any point and encounter rhetorical and topical resemblances. The fascination exerted by the *Confessions* over readers of many generations can be attributed to their human breadth, their ceaseless self-inquiry, and their preservation of the "old" classical, brilliant, philosophically restless self within the discourse of the "new."

Guzmán, like Augustine of Hippo, writes to make an example of himself ("this general confession of mine, this public display of my affairs that I put before you, not for you to imitate, but rather so that, after seeing them, you will amend your own" [484]. His life has been changed by an experience of conversion.[10] But his experience does not repeat that of the saint, who played the *sortes biblicae* by opening Paul's epistles and reading the first words he saw. And unlike Saul's conversion on the road to Damascus, Guzmán's epiphany has no external sign that a witness could have reported. It takes place in his mind, in solitary reflection. The "cumbre del monte de las miserias" (889) from which he can either plunge into damnation or reach up for salvation is not a visionary experience; no angelic voices or celestial "special effects" signal its authenticity. It is simply a way of conceptualizing that crucial moment of understanding, a metaphor that places his life unmistakably on a vertical heaven-hell axis. This *monte* is also a metonym by virtue of the fact that it evokes the whole vertical, ideologically

9. Maurice Molho has aptly commented: "Nothing is more futile (or more anachronistic) than to try to reconstruct the 'psychology' of Alemán's picaro. Guzmán has no personality: he has a soul, like everyone else's, not a distinctive 'I'" (1972:85–86).

10. In the literal sense of the word "conversion": turning around. As Barry Ife has observed, "repentance" describes Guzmán's change of heart better than "conversion" (1985:118). Since Guzmán is no more of a believer than he was before, I mostly prefer to speak of his "lucidity."

loaded perspective on human destiny. The clear up-or-down, salvation-or-damnation message of the trope, with its assurance that he who is an outcast among men may be favored by God, is familiar to both protagonist and reader. The vertical, nontemporal axis with its traditional symbolic concretizations is a cognitive model that forms part of their shared repertory, as does that temporal, horizontal figure of life as a journey, with which it is bonded in an existential paradox.[11] The choices signified in this figure at this moment are no different from those he faced at every stage. Life has continually presented itself to him in images of rising and falling. The difference is that he now "sees" in it the possibility of escaping from the fateful repetitions. The trope *miserias = monte* reflects back to him in spatial terms the figure of his experience. It is either the lowest point on his trajectory or the summit on his road; either way, it is part of *his* road, the road he has made, not a ladder dropped gratuitously and dramatically to him from heaven.

The trouble with any claim to have "seen the light" is that only those who say that they have experienced it know it, but they may be deceived or deluded, so when (or why) should they be believed? In real life, confessors and spiritual directors were trained to make such discriminations (it would be interesting to know their diagnostic success/failure rate). In drama, visual conventions such as those in baroque painting were developed to show the difference between the true and the false, Tirso de Molina's *Condenado por desconfiado* being the best-known example. Adoption of similar means would not have resolved Alemán's difficulty. Once the first-person narration is adopted, the narrator's self-presentation seems to pose an impossible dilemma at precisely this climactic point in the telling: either the narrator must report some divine reassurance, endangering the low mimetic level of discourse, or he must report that he attained a moment of overpowering lucidity in which the imperative of either/or became clear to him. If Alemán were to choose the first, the problem is: Divine assurance of what? since Guzmán has done nothing yet to merit special consideration.

11. Readers of Wolfgang Iser's *Implied Reader* will recall his concept of the "repertoire of the familiar" and how it mobilizes the participation of the reader. The "familiar" must include all such experientially and ideologically loaded tropes; see George Lakoff and Mark Turner, *More than Cool Reason: A Field Guide to Poetic Metaphor* (Chicago: University of Chicago Press, 1989).

Moreover, the possibility of salvation has always been available to him as a Christian. The alternative and more problematic course is for Alemán to present evidence for the inner transformation effected by this moment of lucidity. Here we should note Augustine's concept of confession: "accusation of oneself; praise of God."[12]

By avoiding conventional theatricality (the heavenly voices, the signs of divine approbation), Alemán rejected the available literary means of authenticating the experience. In real life, a penitent could be expected to display a newfound capacity for constancy and fortitude. Indeed, this is the first test that Guzmán faces as he is subjected to humiliations, torture, and isolation far surpassing anything he suffered before. "Truly, I was now so different from what I had been that I would have let myself be cut up into a hundred thousand pieces rather than commit the slightest offense" (900). He is beaten, and salt and vinegar are rubbed into his wounds (900). A few days later: "They raised me up with my wrists tied and kept me hanging in the air for a long time. It was horrible torture, and I thought I'd die" (901). Next he is flogged almost to death. During this torment, he says, his worst pain was having everyone believe he was guilty (901). He does not yield, however: "I remained firmly resolved to do nothing base or unworthy, no matter what benefit I might get from it" (904). Nothing in his previous history would lead us to expect this display of fortitude, since he has always yielded before obstacles.[13]

The confessant should also be a truthteller, with no concern for the prejudices of respectable folk or for the cynicism of skeptics. Guzmán meets this requirement by writing his book, offering his life of cheats and humiliations in a narrative that is an act of self-exposure, a negative example to others. Fortitude, submission to authority, telling it all: these are the only resources that Alemán

12. Sermon 67, cited in Brown, 1967:175. See also *Confessions*, xi.1: "confitendo tibi miserias nostras et misericordias tuas contra nos."

13. Cavillac observes: "Comment imaginer, avec certains commentateurs de l'*Atalaya*, que le héros offre ici une image hypocrite de lui-même, et que sa conversion n'est qu'un simulacre destiné à assurer son élargissement des galères ou à clore artificiellement le récit de ses aventures? Inversement, quel référent, en dehors de la grâce efficace, eût-il pu rendre vraisemblable aux yeux du grand public la transformation radicale qui s'opère dans l'esprit du Gueux?" (1983:106).

can employ, consistent with his chosen level of verisimilitude, to show that Guzmán "means it."[14]

Once self-conscious telling is adopted as a sign of change in the protagonist, choice of the mode of telling is narrowly circumscribed. Regression to the simplicities of the lives of saints was inappropriate, and Alemán could not anticipate a Dostoyevskian psychological realism. It is most probable that, in spite of his promise of a sequel, Alemán did not propose to extend Guzmán's story into the future. The climactic recognition scene was the necessary and unquestioned terminus for a romance. For all these reasons, validation of the narrative had to be provided within the discourse, not in an extension of the action.

For Alemán's contemporaries, a twofold validation of the changed Guzmán was offered by the "truths," the "little sermons." First, considered from the authorial perspective (that of the novel's composition and the response that the composition is designed to evoke), the narrated *Life* is enclosed within these "truths" as in a rhetorical frame. Together, the "Life" and its frame of "truths" carry out the program announced in the prologues. Second, from the narratorial perspective, these "truths" are generated *in the act* of writing. They therefore validate the narrative, since the life and the "truths" that enclose it are generated in the same penitential act. Seventeenth-century readers, brought up in a religious milieu, whether of Catholic Spain or of Protestant England, and for whom manuals of devotion and of the spiritual life were habitual reading, found no difficulty with Alemán's solution. It is we twentieth-century readers, whose concept of verisimilitude is underwritten by radically different terms for truth, who retract authority from Alemán, and who bracket "truths" that earlier readers affirmed as Truth.

14. For the psychic and rhetorical processes involved in "meaning it," see Erik H. Erikson, *Young Man Luther: A Study in Psychoanalysis and History* (New York: Norton, 1962), chap. 6. Zimmermann (1971:132) sees Augustine dealing with the same predicament: ". . . whatever the effects of Christian renewal, he could not jettison the memory of his youth. The same self still linked the mature bishop to the young man. Augustine's response to this predicament was to try to understand the young man in the light of God's purposes. . . . [It] is apparent that Augustine was preoccupied in the same fashion as Luther by what Erikson calls 'meaning it.'"

We may turn to Augustine's *Confessions* as the most powerful model that had moved and continued to influence readers and writers. Augustine's narrative has a clear before and after, marked by his embrace of a faith that he had previously repudiated and the change of life that followed. We never see what Guzmán makes of his life, since the narrative ends before he returns to land.[15] The only "after" that is represented is the writing itself, and the intentionality of that writing. The book is an act of expiation, and its self-accusatory discourse wraps around and seals in the persona of the narrator, thereby putting "realistic" questions about him off limits. Such a book, a chronicle of sordid successes and humiliations, accompanied by a demystifying commentary, was entirely original. Conceived on a massive scale, unprecedented in structure, the work was also Alemán's first attempt at writing. Not surprisingly, it has some rough places and some technical mal-adroitness. Some readers find in these places not the faltering hand of the author but evidence of the narrator's irredeemable rottenness and bad faith. I cannot agree with them.[16]

Finding Guzmán's change of heart questionable, Carroll Johnson has observed that "the longer a behavior pattern is reinforced, the more difficult it is to change" (1978:17). Augustine himself would have agreed, preoccupied as he was in the *Confessions* and in other writings with the fact that we are prisoners of habit (*consuetudo*), the proverbial "second nature." "By reason of 'some mys-

15. There are signs that Alemán did not end Part II as he had expected to do when he wrote the "Declaración" of Part I, and that the ending may have been hastily composed. The contradictions and confusions are summarized by Rico in *Guzmán* (905) and discussed by Ife (1985:118–23). These awkward passages should not be read as if they were deliberate equivocations by Guzmán, a procedure that would have been inconsistent with his whole enterprise.

16. In particular the writings of Benito Brancaforte and his former graduate students at the University of Wisconsin, published by that university's Medieval Seminary. They approach *Guzmán* as if it were a *tranche de vie* and trap the protagonist with behaviorist questions, ignoring the work's structural codes. They condemn Guzmán (for example) for his lack of compassion for Soto: by the same token one should condemn Dante, who, after passing through purgatory and being raised up to paradise by the transfigured Beatrice, treats his contemporaries mercilessly. If he were really purified by those experiences and enjoyed the grace of that beatific vision, one might ask, how could he return to write those indictments in the *Inferno*, and with such evident poetic relish? Is Dante therefore deceiving us? Is Dante's conversion then a "proceso de degradación" (Brancaforte's phrase for the writing of *Guzmán*)?

terious weakness,' the pleasure of every past evil act is amplified and transformed by being remembered and repeated."[17] Even as he writes Book x of his *Confessions*, he describes himself as "in a limitless forest, full of unexpected dangers" (x.35).[18] Books x-xiii are designed to defeat the expectations of pious readers who looked for a conventional story of a successful conversion, dramatic, simple, and leading to a safe haven. Alemán's fictional equivalent of Augustine's "limitless forest" is the limitless ocean, likewise far from a safe haven.[19] "For Augustine, conversion was no longer enough. No such dramatic experience should delude his readers into believing that they could so easily cast off their past identity" (Brown 1967:177). His words, repeated in other texts of the same period ("When you hear a man confessing, you know that he is not yet free") are applicable to Guzmán (Brown 1967: 179). The point would have been obvious to Alemán, who did not write with pious sentimentality, and to his readers. Having recounted in Books i-ix his life of restless wandering, physical, intellectual, and emotional, in Books x-xiii Augustine develops the prayers, reflections upon his life, time, memory, habit, and so forth. *Guzmán* reads as though Augustine had taken the postconversion reflections, broken them up, and made them part of the act of remembering. Working with the model of human nature that was given him, Alemán would not expect his reader to believe that Guzmán immediately became a paragon of virtue. Like Augustine, Saul, long after he became Paul, could still write, "Though the will to do what is good is in me, the performance is not, with the result that instead of doing the good things I want to do, I carry out the sinful things I do not want" (Rom. 7:18–19, Jerusalem Bible).

Carroll Johnson has observed rightly that theological questions are a dead issue to American students and to most of their teachers, "yet they are keenly interested in *Guzmán de Alfarache*, which they find 'relevant' in a profoundly un-Christian and un-seventeenth-century ambience" (1978:8–9). I could reply that it is

17. Brown 1967:149, citing *De sermone Domini in monte*; see also p. 150.
18. "In hac tam immensa silva plena insidiarum et periculorum."
19. An interesting contrast could be drawn between Guzmán, supposedly still exposed to the dangers, physical and figurative, of the turbulent element, and Lázaro, complacently ashore in his "buen puerto."

our business as teachers and critics to historicize both our texts and our twentieth-century selves. If theological questions got into imaginative literature around the year 1600, it was not simply because the reading public was interested in theological matters but because theology provided the common discourse in which questins were formulated and debated on every theoretical level: the destiny of the soul, the individual in society, royal authority, ethical choices, the just price, the power of signs, and the activity of the imagination. It is important not to underestimate the ability of readers of that time to become passionately involved in questions of free will or the conditions for salvation;[20] it is equally important to know that questions of social justice, trade, war and peace, magic, colonial rule, rights of conquest, language, and reason had a theological base and were not viewed as totally distinct fields of activity. We must therefore historicize our own situation as readers. Ethical choice and intellectual argument must *feel* different if the subject believes that salvation or damnation is at stake.

We cannot ask readers around the year 1600 what, for them, would make narrative fiction credible.[21] The evidence of what they read shows that plotting and exemplary action are the primary narrative values. The plots are teleological; volition is therefore the motor. What drives the action to its end are passions, desires, loyalties struggling to control the will. On this basis there is little to choose between *Guzmán de Alfarache*, Cervantes' *Novelas ejemplares*, Céspedes y Meneses' *Español Gerardo*, Italian *novelle*, *novelas cortesanas*, and most of the plays of Lope de Vega. In fiction the presentation of states of mind appears as schematic and superficial as do descriptions of the external world. There is not even the rhetor-

---

20. See Otis H. Green, *Spain and the Western Tradition: The Castilian Mind in Literature from "El Cid" to Calderón*, vol. 4 (Madison: University Wisconsin Press, 1964), chaps. 4–6; Cavillac 1983: chap. 2. Some communities in the United States have retained that passion until the present; likewise, many Welsh coal miners were passionate about dialectical materialism (a more recent theology) in the 1930s and 1940s.

21. The most frequently quoted formula is one attributed to Cicero by Aelius Donatus (fourth century), writing on comedy: "imitatio vitae, speculum consuetudinis, imago veritatis." Donatus' *Ars grammatica* was one of the first books to be printed wherever major presses were set up: in Mainz, in Haarlem (Fèbvre/Martin 1976:53–56), in Florence (Eisenstein 1979:36). It may have been the first book ever printed (Fèbvre/Martin 1976:253). It was also one of the most widely published.

ical or "pathetic" use of scene to define an emotion that we commonly find in verse and drama.

The structure and the function of the self are represented no differently than these other orders of phenomena, which is to say that verisimilitude consists of a high level of generality. These fictional worlds are ruled by a single guiding principle, the providential order. For most popular fiction, this order ensures outcomes that are in conformity with the readers' least complicated understanding of the idea of justice, or with "the inscrutable design of God" (an indispensable escape hatch for authors). In *Lazarillo* the providential order is ironized by that sardonic authorial turn of the screw that makes Lázaro's end mimic his beginning. During his story the self accommodates itself so completely to the generic qualities exemplified in his masters that we finally cannot distinguish between the self and the outer world. In *Guzmán de Alfarache*, the relation between self and society is more variable and discontinuous. Guzmán's roles (servant, porter, beggar, buffoon, soldier, gambler, sham nobleman, businessman, student, estate manager, pimp, convict) exhibit a protean existence that swings erratically from alienation to accommodation, from trickster and jester to professional soldier and student for the priesthood. His studies at the University of Alcalá lasted seven years, but neither these years nor those in the army are made to affect the quality of his feelings, the focus of his perception, or his sense of a self. The plot traces a simple dialectic between his desire to live a good life and the generalized human nature that subverts the good intentions and produces shameful acts. The narrative discourse is full of self-excoriation and reflections upon the nature of humankind that prevents him (and us) from doing what he knows (and we know) is right. The only aspect of the self that Alemán exposes programmatically is, indeed, the capacity for self-knowledge, which is a praxis, not a psychic content of the narrating "I." What, then, does Guzmán discover in himself through the practice of self-knowledge, and how does he do it? What Guzmán recalls is a story, and what he tells us is that story and its significance, this quality of "significance" being, as the Aristotelians would have said, what made it more "philosophical" than a mere sequence of events. He reveals no more than any reader can discover in the action, that he has been a great sinner (his word), deceitful, vengeful, greedy for

money and for celebrity. He progresses from naiveté to worldly
cynicism, deploring the path he takes even as he commits his
frauds. The inner world of Guzmán is a psychomachia where
readers may observe forces in contention that they can find also
within themselves.

Carroll Johnson's Freudian reading is grounded on the claim
that "no character in fiction (as distinguished from allegory and
other unverisimilar forms of literature) can fail to have a psychic
dimension, because the canon of verisimilitude simply demands
it" (1978:55). This claim should be qualified because Guzmán *does*
require us to allegorize his life, to bring it to a level of generality
where we assent to his proposition that whatever makes the world
the ugly, degenerate place it is, is in him and also in us. The allegorical turn is evident, in any case, in the genre of romance, upon
which *Guzmán* is a variation. Second, verisimilitude has varied
with the time and the genre; as part of the generic contract, it
enables the readers or audience to hold on, collectively, to the
reading experience. Verisimilitude may be established by the demonstration that time goes forward (or backward) in a given fictional
world; in any case, it denotes a level of generality that we recognize as being common to both the possible world of the fiction and
the actual world of the audience, or a structural alternative to it.
This "actual world" comprises not only people, objects, and social
and physical phenomena but also existing literature, so that verisimilitude may be established by conformity to generic convention, by allusions, by mythical patterns, and by other intertextual
practices.[22] The question is not only whether inferences about, say,
Guzmán's infantile sexuality can be verified from the text (Johnson
1978: chap. 5) but whether, in Alemán's fictional universe, they
point to an important level of generality on human nature or to a
relatively trivial one. If the level of generality on which an author
formulated his problematic has totally lost meaning for later
readers, they will look for another to explain the work's power to
hold them. I do not believe, however, that Alemán's portrayal of

22. If these genres and practices include the fantastic and are inscribed in a
culture that has divorced teleology from its concept of time, then time may well
go backward and still remain verisimilar. For a recent discussion of verisimilitude as the product of a narrative grammar, a sequence that is fully motivated
and not dependent on the mimesis that is imposed upon it, see Riffaterre 1990.

the tragic split between intention and act, between desire and consequence, between knowledge and will, has ceased to be intelligible and compelling.

Guzmán's preadolescent sexuality does figure in the novel, and it is interesting to note what Alemán does with it. After the death of Guzmán's father, his mother squanders the remains of their fortune. If only he had a sister, he laments, she might have been the "staff of [mother's] old age, pillar of our wretchedness, and safe haven for our disasters" (145). There is no reason why he himself should not become the family support; he praises Seville as the land of opportunity, and claims that he is as smart as anyone. But rather than exploit those opportunities himself, he decides to leave: "The best recourse I could find was to try my hand at escaping from poverty, by leaving my mother and my homeland" (145). The inescapable inference is that the absent sister would have restored their fortunes and embodied those comfortable clichés ("staff of her old age") by following the same career as the mother: speculative whoring in that land of opportunity where "there are dealers in everything." We may well imagine the nature of the "benefits, employments, commissions, and other honorable gains" that would have come the way of young Guzmán, "because the man who has such a piece of goods [*semejante prenda*] to pledge or sell will always find someone to buy it or give him what he needs in return" (145).

The urge to manliness with which he sets out is sharply defined: "Look; wasn't it right for a swaggering boy like me [que ya galleaba], with such fine qualities, to think himself somebody?" (145). *Gallear*, to strut like a rooster; here is the emerging macho eager to make his space in the world. Adoption of the grand name Guzmán de Alfarache and a precocious concern with honor and revenge are all part of this phase of self-identification and assertion. Alemán, like the author of *Lazarillo de Tormes*, has made his protagonist a master of artful prose, who knows how to cover his tracks when he alludes to the depravity of his parents and to the unprincipled opportunism of his father. But neither Guzmán nor the author suggests that any of this requires explanation. The parents are merely an extreme case of a universal phenomenon. Other readers have noted that the country house at San Juan de Alfarache is a sensual and already corrupt Eden from which Guzmán ("Goodman") is sent into the world (San Miguel 1971:43–59). From then on he will, like every other son of Adam, be divided against himself, his human desire for direction and purpose in continual conflict with the inherited human condition.

Guzmán stresses the universal nature of his experience in words that are often quoted as examples of pessimism: "This is the way of the world. . . . As we find it, so we'll leave it. No one should expect better times or suppose that the past was any better. Everything was, is, and will be the same. The first father was pefidious, the first mother a liar, the first son a thief and a fratricide. What is there now that wasn't so before? what can you expect of the future?" (355). That is one side of the dialectic. The other, noted earlier, may be exemplified in that moment of Guz-mán's return to Madrid, where he finds everything altered: "There was no grocer, nor any memory of him. The fields had been built on; infants had become youths, the youths men, the men grown old, the old ones dead; squares were now streets, and streets were much changed, *with great improvement everywhere*" (756; my emphasis).[23] It is exemplified more importantly in Guzmán's climactic effort of self-transformation and in his first public act of testifying to his change: namely, this writing, interpretation, and demystifying of his narrative, for the benefit of readers.

Our search for the inner world of Guzmán brings us once more up against the generality imposed by the conventions of pre-modern fiction. What drove him forward ("ya galleaba . . .") was not a unique urge to restless adventure but the generic teenage itch to go out and prove himself. "A boy like me"; his conduct is referred to a model of what is *typical*. Also, when the narrative reaches his passage to Italy, he recalls his ungovernable self at the age of twenty, observing that "twenty years is a fearful animal" (599). Guzmán is seen responding to motives that are not those of an individual youth in his unique singularity but those of a represen-

---

23. These two passages are not contradictory. Thousands of parallels can be found for the first, which belongs to the tradition of *De miseria humanae conditionis*; the second is more interesting because it does not represent the traditional complementary antithesis, *De dignitate*, which asserted that an individual could draw creatively on his divine nature (Ficino, Pico della Mirandola, Pérez de Oliva). It rather suggests that there is a general meliorative current *in human affairs*.

tative youth who passes through characteristic stages in relation to family, world, and self. It is evident that what is being constituted by Guzmán's retrospective discourse is not the formation of an individual self with its unique, complex interiority but a process of typification. In the possible worlds of traditional fiction, typifications (that is, the ascription of certain restricted roles, characteristics, and performances) are accepted as metonymic substitutions, standing in for the representation of a whole self.[24]

All of this fits the Aristotelian mold. The orthodox position is stated by Ugo, the spokesman in López Pinciano's dialogue: "I say that the poet's obligation is to write not truth but verisimilitude, I mean possibility in the work" (II. 79). Ugo earlier cited Horace on the *decorum* of representation: young boys are playful, and quick to change moods; older boys enjoy riding and other pleasures, are not easily corrigible, are reckless and spendthrift. So the stereotypes follow one another through the ages of man until we reach the old men, who hold on to their wealth and are slow to decide and to act (II.77). El Pinciano objects that not all children are as described, that not all old men are miserly, slow, and indecisive (II.81). Ugo concedes that there are exceptions, but that "by nature and ordinary experience" they are as Horace described. An old man who is resolute, quick to anger, or in love is more appropriate to "joking and burlesque . . . to provoke laughter and add salt to the comedy" (II.82). Such a one would be "true [verisímil] to the individual nature of some old men but not to universal nature" (II.82). Here we see confirmation that verisimilitude is not referable to the infinitely variable particularities of the reader's world; rather it is a function of stereotypes of human behavior which are not limited to the statistically "natural" (nimble children, solemn elders) but are determined by "what is due" to figures of rank and authority (kings to be obeyed, priests to be reverenced). It is also a function of the conventions of literary genre: "the poet should respect [verisimilitude] with respect to kind, age, custom, and rank of the person" (II.83).[25]

24. For the concept "typification," see Berger/Luckmann 1966:30–34, 72–76.

25. El Pinciano seems unaware of the contradiction in ascribing *decoro* to nature. For a brilliant discussion of this point as it is presented in George Puttenham's *Arte of English Poesie*, see Attridge 1988:17–45.

Lazarillo de Tormes and *Guzmán de Alfarache* are both presented as acts of memory. Lázaro's memory has been stirred by the presence of an external authority with its demand for an explanation. The ensuing narrative is less the revelation of a singular being than it is the result of a shadowy game of compliance and noncompliance, for Lázaro slips past that authority while appearing to bend to it. That is the internal transaction, a transaction with a fictitious reader. Between Lázaro and the implied reader there is a further transaction that consists in appropriating and transvaluing his own text by means of the Prologue. It is through this essentially fraudulent transaction that Lázaro's *vida* is mediated to the reader. In the *Guzmán*, the protagonist demands that our writing and reading be truly reciprocal. His *Atalaya* is a heroic feat of memory, self-imposed as a deliberate act of the will. It is composed and written over with commentary; its subtext—sin and the possibility of salvation—is fully exposed. All this is also an act of the understanding, the moral intellect. For Alemán, the three Augustinian faculties of the soul (memory, will, understanding) are enlisted in the practice of representation and must be equally operative in the practice of reading. In this involvement of the reader, Alemán is thoroughly traditional, as the presence of the Augustinian model of the soul indicates.

Guzmán's autobiography is an exercise in self-knowledge initiated at the moment of lucidity in the galley (II.iii.8; p. 889). The writing extends that lucidity over the length of the written life. The events of his life are told as a journey, and the telling is also an inward journey. This romance of a self finding itself,[26] like any romance, conventionally turns upon a moment of discovery. Here the conclusion is precipitated by what we may call the *self*-recognition scene in the galley. From this moment of self-recognition, this pivot in the action, there unwinds the long self-exploration in the narrative discourse. Interestingly, El Pinciano treats of three kinds of recognition attained through the agency of each of the three faculties of the soul: *agnición por el entendimiento* (recognition

26. Cf. Augustine, *Confessions*. III.6, V.2, X.6; in particular the passage made famous by Petrarch, "Et eunt homines admirari alta montium et ingentes fluctus maris et latissimos lapsus fluminum et Oceani ambitum et giros siderum, et relinquunt se ipsos" (X.8). See Courcelle 1963:339–40.

through understanding [II.30–33]), *agnición por memoria* (recognition through memory [II.33–34]), *agnición por medio de la voluntad* (recognition through will [II.34–38]), and gives examples of each, taken from Homer and the Greek tragedians: recognition through memory is declared to be "more delightful than any other" (II.37–38). We must examine further this operation of memory as producer of the narrative, and also the ideology of memory.

It is impossible to talk of memory in historical context without reference to orality. An oral culture's knowledge of the world and of itself are dependent on the accuracy and reliability of human memory. The development in preliterate societies of very specific functions and strategies of memory for the transmission of knowledge, juridical practice, wisdom, rules, and values encoded in symbolic systems of ritual performance, stories, proverbs, and the like is now a familiar field of study.[27] These systems of cultural storage, transmission, and retrieval persist in early modern Europe; the more recent literate practices, which enabled modern organs of administration and government to develop, were islands in a sea of preliterate practices.[28] Within those islands—courts, universities, urban elites—the print revolution of the sixteenth century made much more of the intellectual heritage of classical antiquity and the Middle Ages available to those who could read and were trained to use it. The rapid multiplication of copies; the simultaneous availability of ancient, medieval, and modern works of learning; the use of the printing press for dissemination of information and for the shaping of opinion by governments, by their critics, and by every kind of sectarian interest; all these and other aspects of print culture had profound effects upon the intellectual life of early modern Europe. They also affected reading, the acquisition and storing of knowledge. When students could read and teach themselves, elaborate mnemonic arts such as "memory theaters" became unnecessary; the ease of cross-reference could blur the boundaries of existing disciplines; texts became more stable,

27. Ong 1982 has an extensive bibliography.
28. For the deep and far-ranging effects of the print revolution upon intellectual, artistic, commercial, political, religious, and scientific life, the growth of sects, the instruments of government, and so forth, see Eisenstein 1979; Fèbvre/Martin 1976; Ong 1982; also Carlo Cipolla, *Literacy and Development in the West* (Harmondsworth: Penguin, 1969).

because less subject to scribal misreading, and so did diagrams, maps, illustrations. Many classical and foreign books were made accessible to the unlearned through new translations.

Guzmán retains features of both its literate (romance) and pre-literate (anecdotic) traditions, but beyond this obvious fact is another: that memory and orality are given very specific functions in relation to the author, the narrator, and the reader. Although Alemán's huge novel is written, printed, bound, and destined for reading, it imitates oral discourse on both of its levels, narrative and commentary (as, indeed, *Lazarillo de Tormes* does). The narrative pretends to be a general confession (ii.i.2; p. 484), a form of enunciation that would normally be transmitted orally to a single listener under the seal of secrecy.[29] Alemán preserves the appearance of confidential utterance by addressing the reader in the singular. The semblance of oral immediacy is confirmed by the embarrassed evasions and false starts in Guzmán's address to the reader, even as he appears to be *writing* over his own erasures from his very first sentence: "the desire that I had . . . put me in such haste . . . I forgot to close off" (105). In this first chapter, the relation of the narrator to the reader in the text is uncertain and unsettling.[30] Guzmán is by turns evasive, aggressive, and patronizing, as if carrying on an altercation with a *tú* who intruded upon his monologue with impertinent curiosity. In the following chapters, Alemán has Guzmán drop this querulous tone, which is replaced by his characteristic two levels of discourse, the narrative and the homiletic. The reader is still addressed directly, but less often, and as the attentive object of Guzman's revelations and of his sermons.

Sermons are an oral genre; they follow certain traditional and well-founded rules of rhetorical composition in order both to instruct and to affect listeners, to convince and to transport them. Like the university exercises, public lectures, expositions, and dis-

---

29. In special circumstances, notably in time of plague, a confession might be made openly (Lea, *History of Auricular Confession*, 1:449) or in writing (1:367–69). On the seal, see ibid., chap. 13.

30. This "reader in the text" is not to be identified with an "implied" reader. The ornery and hypercritical fictional reader imagined at the outset by a self-conscious Guzmán writing for the first time cannot be the reader conceived by Alemán.

putations, sermons might be prepared with notes but were presented as if they were extempore feats of memory and improvisation (Martin 1977:590–93, H. O. Smith 1978:31–32). Knowing that sermons were collected and printed, to be read at home (re-oralized aloud, perhaps, to one's family or other small groups) may help us to understand how *Guzmán* could be admired as a model of moral and spiritual eloquence not only in Spain but in Protestant England.[31] At each level of discourse in *Guzmán de Alfarache* (address to a reader who is imagined as answering back; the confessional mode; the sermons) a para-orality asserts itself against the bulk and the density of its written pages. There is a sense, therefore, in which Alemán's novel represents both sides of this crux in European culture, the onrush toward print with its interiorization of discourse and the persistence of a rhetoric that is formulaic, oral, and mnemonic. So, in its very different mode, does *Don Quixote*.

Great as the effects of the print revolution were, and much as they reduced or modified reliance on memory in education and in other formal activities, the traditional place accorded to memory among the faculties and its mode of functioning were not revised until much later. Memory, to be sure, is still the element, the medium in which that *episteme* constructed of similitudes and affinities, described by Foucault, is held in suspension.[32] "Those who work at learning," Hugh of St. Victor tells us, "must be equipped at the same time with aptitude and with memory. . . . Just as aptitude investigates and discovers through analysis, so memory retains through gathering."[33] Hugh of St. Victor, like other medieval writers, did not conceive of learning as an end in itself, or as a means to a secular end. For him, learning and, a fortiori, memory

31. For *Guzmán* as a rhetorical showcase, see Cros 1967; for admiration of its religious eloquence in England, see Russell 1953.

32. Foucault 1970, chaps. 2, 3. Curiously, Foucault gives no attention to the human space in which an *episteme* holds sway. He is unconcerned by how it is conserved, transmitted, and ultimately displaced.

33. Hugh of St. Victor, *Didascalicon*, trans. and ed. Jerome Taylor (New York: Columbia University Press, 1961), 91, 93. On p. 93 he explains that "'gathering' is reducing to a brief and compendious outline things which have been written or discussed at some length" to discover the "principle on which the entire truth of the matter and the force of its thought rest." Original text in *PL*, vol. 176.

were to be directed toward union with divine wisdom and the attainment of salvation. So also medieval mystic writers found in the interrogation and the disciplining of memory an instrument in the ascetic endeavor to experience Christ's mystical presence, as evidenced by Bernard of Clairvaux in his hymn "Jesu dulcis memoria."

Orthodox doctrine on memory had its origin in Augustine, whose *Confessions* are both a theory of memory and and an exemplary demonstration of memory in action. In Book x of the *Confessions* the nature and function of memory are the object of a penetrating inquiry. The memory stores the images collected through the senses, "distinct and in their right categories," ready to be "brought to light when the need arises" (x.8).[34] In memory, Augustine declares, he can produce colors though he is in darkness, and "though my tongue is at rest and my throat silent I can sing as I will." And "in my memory too I meet myself—I recall myself [ibi mihi et ipse occurro meque recolo]. . . . From the same store I can weave into the past endless new likenesses of things either experienced by me or believed on the strength of things experienced. . . . I can picture actions and events and hopes for the future. . . . Great is this power of memory, exceedingly great, O my God, a spreading limitless room within me" (x.8).

Besides the images of things experienced, the memory retains what has been learned: concepts, questions, arguments; in this case, what is held in store is not an image of a thing but the thing itself (x.9). Further, by considering what we have learned and experienced, we bring together and put into order things that were scattered, and others we thought we had lost (x.11). Augustine goes on to note other operations of the memory: we can recall having learned something, or having recalled something; we can even recall having forgotten it, having understood or failed to understand, having had this or that feeling about something that we thought. As he reviews each of these operations, we see that he is proceeding in a meaningful order, starting from the experiences that have come through the material senses and progressing to the "higher" truths of relation, knowledge, principles, and laws, for-

34. "Ibi sunt omnia distincte generatimque servata . . . haec omnia recipit recolenda, cum opus est, et retractanda grandis memoriae recessus."

mulated by the intellect. Memory takes an *active* part in this procedure; it is essential to the construction of a self, and to the ordering activity of the mind.[35]

Memory, then, has the basic threefold meaning that we find in modern usage: the capturing and retention of an experience; the "place" in the mind where the experience is "stored"; the summoning of the experience back to consciousness. Memory contains the potential for future thought and act, and this potentiality requires activity of the judgment and of the will to be exerted upon the recollected images. Augustine makes unavoidable the conclusion that memory and judgment collaborate in the discovery of truth, in its formulation and elaboration. The verb *to cogitate* (*cogitare*) "is named from this drawing together. For *cogito* (I think) has the same relation to *cogo* (I put together) as *agito* to *ago* and *factito* to *facio*. But the mind of man has claimed the word *cogitate* completely for its own: not what is put together anywhere else but only what is put together in the mind is called cogitation" (x.11). Truth is always within our grasp: "thinking, learning and remembering are all one to the soul" (Gilson 1960:75).

Augustine's treatise on memory occupies a large part of Book x of the *Confessions*. The preceding nine books contain his personal and intellectual history, which terminates in its twin peaks, the climax of joy in his reconversion to Christianity and reception into the church and the climax of sorrow in the death of his mother, Monica. The analysis of memory comes at that point in the writing where past and present, narrative and discourse, former self and new consciousness meet. It is thematically pertinent and also rhetorically effective within the structure of the whole, and this is not the least of the ways in which the *Confessions* are relevant to *Guzmán de Alfarache*. Having reached the point in his argument where memory is shown to be inseparable from mind—"when we forget something, we say: 'It was not in my mind' [non fuit in animo] or 'It escaped my mind' [elapsum est animo]" (x.14)—he introduces the problem of forgetting and knowing that we have forgotten.

35. Augustine's grasp of the active wholeness of the self, in which memory is an active and creative remembering as well as an obstinate reinforcer of habit, must appear attractively modern. See Oliver Sacks, "Neurology and the Soul," *New York Review of Books*, 22 November 1990, pp. 44–50, and works cited in notes.

Since memory is not something different from mind, the problem of knowing that we have forgotten something is not fundamentally different from that of knowing that we do not know something. It now emerges that truth is not merely the exact recollection of things but the truth hidden within the soul, which it has "forgotten," in the Platonic sense.[36] At the beginning of Book x, Augustine prays to God, "Let me know Thee who knowest me, *let me know Thee even as I am known* [Cognoscam te, cognitor meus, cognoscam, sicut cognitus sum]" (x.1), and declares his wish to penetrate beyond memory to find him, only to be baffled once more, and finally concludes that God both is above him and resides in his memory (manes in memoria mea, et illic te invenio [x.24]).[37] So the treatise on memory is finally revealed as the story of a quest for God, and it ends, as good quest plots should, in an act of comprehension, of *com-prehending*, seizing the past with its core of meaning for the future. This artful passage of philosophical inquiry into memory leads into a "recognition scene" in which he finds God in his own memory, and recognizes himself anew in making this discovery. In the following three books he turns outward from himself as his confession turns from the past to a confession of faith, a testament to the creativity and power of God. Book xi contains the celebrated discourse on the nature of time, which leads to the question of God's existence before time, so to the meaning of "In the beginning" and of "heaven" and "earth." From the individual memory in which the quester finds God, the source of his own being, we are led to the source of all being, of time, of all that exists. The search for the end and purpose of his existence has led Augustine back to the origin, to the eternal One that joins beginning and end. In the final book he meditates, fittingly, upon Genesis and demonstrates that it contains all that is to come.[38] In the source is the end.

36. Gilson, drawing upon *De Trinitate*, explains: "In St. Augustine [memory] is applied to everything which is present to the soul . . . . without being explicitly known or perceived. The only modern psychological terms equivalent to Augustinian *memoria* are 'unconscious' or 'subconscious,' provided they too are expanded to include the metaphysical presence within the soul of a reality distinct from it and transcendent, such as God" (1960:299).

37. Cf. iii.6: "tu autem eras interior intimo meo et superior summo meo."

38. The three powers or faculties of the soul are reflections of the threefold

The *Confessions* have a shape and a plot, which are those of the literature of quest and discovery. They take their form around Augustine's conception of memory, which is inseparable from the faculty of understanding, of judgment, and which includes a "memory of the present" by which the soul "remembers everything present to it even though unaware of it" (Gilson 1960:102). To Augustine is attributable the extension of the idea of remembering to embrace "being mindful of," which is fundamental for the Christian writers who follow, whether they expound a theory of knowledge or a mystical experience.[39] The devotional literature that so abounds in sixteenth-century Europe is postulated upon this exercise of "present memory."[40] One of the clearest and most explicit expressions of the Christian ideology and practice of memory is found in a sermon by John Donne:

> The art of salvation is but the art of memory. When God gave his people the Law, he proposes nothing to them, but by that way, to their memory. . . . And when we expresse God's mercy to us, we attribute but that faculty to God, that he *remembers* us. . . . *Memorare novissima*, remember the last things, and fear will keep thee from sinning; *Memorare praeterita*, remember the first things, what God hath done for thee, and love . . . will keep thee from sinning. Plato plac'd *all learning* in the memory; wee

nature of God, and are but one example of how, in Augustine's vision of things, the form of the Holy Trinity has impressed itself upon the whole of creation and specifically upon human nature. The argument may be found also in *De quantitate animae* and in *De Trinitate*, particularly pt. II, bk. 14.

39. "The operation of memory is retention and representation, not only of things present, corporeal, and temporal, but also of past and future things, simple and eternal. . . . [It] retains the eternal principles of the sciences and retains them eternally. For it can never so forget them while it uses reason that it will not approve of them when heard and assent to them, not as though it were perceiving them for the first time, but as if it were recognizing them as innate and familiar. . . . And thus, through the operations of the memory, it appears that the soul itself is the image of God and His likeness, so present to itself and having Him present that it receives Him in actuality and is susceptible of receiving Him in potency, and that it can also participate in Him": St. Bonaventura, *Itinerarium mentis ad Deum*, translated as *The Mind's Road to God* by George Boas (Indianapolis: Bobbs-Merrill, 1953), 22–23.

40. Many of the poems of Fray Luis de León are constructed around correlated pairs of opposed concepts, of evident Augustinian inspiration: remembering/forgetting, waking/sleeping, day/night, knowledge/ignorance.

may place *all Religion* in the memory, too: All knowledge, that seems new to day, says *Plato* is but a remembering of *that*, which your soul knew before. All instruction, which we can give you to day, is but the remembering you of the mercies of God. . . . Nay, he that hears no Sermons, he that reads no Scriptures, hath the Bible without book; he hath a *Genesis* in his *memory*; he cannot forget his *Creation*. . . . Let them remember what they will, what they can, let them but remember thoroughly, and then it follows there, *they shall turn unto the Lord*. . . Therefore *David* makes *that* the key into this Psalme; *Psalmus ad Recordationem, A Psalm for Remembrance*. Being lock'd up in a close prison, of multiplied calamities, this turns the Key, this opens the door, this restores him to liberty, if he can remember.[41]

This excursus on memory may help us to see more clearly how Guzmán's autobiography, Alemán's fiction of remembering, is the embodiment of the message. Alemán makes Guzmán remember the events of his past life, which are the story, the *conseja*, in order both to expose his shame and to find the hidden self that the life of habit had occluded. We also see the significance of the adult's insistent recollection of the boy's feelings of shame throughout Part I, as if to confirm a declaration of Donne in that same sermon: "Hee that is past shame of sin, is past recovery from sin."[42] In this (to us) unfamiliar conception of verisimilitude, the commentaries and meditations accompanying the story are anything but digressions. They function first by creating a verisimilar frame in which to recollect those feelings of regret, compunction, or remorse that assailed Guzmán when he was still a boy. At that prereflective stage, evidence of his nature was already manifest in that Augustinian "memory of the present." His "conversion," or emergence into lucidity, releases into present consciousness what was there already, but hidden: the self concealed beyond the self. So it is in his self-awareness as writer of his life that Guzmán achieves the unity of recollection, thought, and act.

41. Sermon 2, preached at Lincoln's Inn, 1618, in *The Sermons of John Donne*, ed. George R. Potter and Evelyn M. Simpson, 10 vols. (Berkeley: University of California Press, 1953-1962), 2:73–74. I owe the reference to this wonderfully apposite text to my colleague Khachig Tölölyan.
42. Ibid., 2:73.

Besides what the writing says, we have to note more particularly what it is and what it does. Renaissance poetics enjoined delight in teaching, and aesthetics still followed Horace in yoking the *dulce* to the *utile*. By emblematizing his work as *atalaya de la vida humana* (watchtower on human life), Alemán declares its public utility; a utility conceived for a known constituency of which author, patrons, writers of encomiastic prefaces and sonnets, and readers are all part, within a shared social situation. After hundreds of pages of revealing cheats, swindles, and acts of every kind of bad faith, his protagonist seeks to be reconciled within himself. But how (to return to the vexing question) is he to show that he "means it" not only in the discursive act but in action? In the galley he is in no position to perform the penitential act of being reconciled to those desperately villainous fellow men who are seeking to destroy him. They cannot stand as a metonym for the community. But beyond one's immediate neighbors, the idea of community could be conceived as the *res publica*, the common weal constituted and bound by the authority of the king, or as Christian *societas* under God. So Guzmán is placed in a position where "meaning it" in advance of the writing requires that he be reconciled at least to these two supreme powers against whose authority he has transgressed, God and king, even if he thereby alienates the secular, antiauthoritarian reader of today. That first act of the will augurs the integration and the unified activity of the soul's (or self's) three faculties in the world.

In the course of sketching a history of reader responses and expectations, Jane Tompkins declares: "The first requirement of a work of art in the twentieth century is that it should *do* nothing" (1980:210). The text of *Guzmán de Alfarache* is not autonomous, nor is the self that it constructs. The resistance of some twentieth-century readers to Guzmán's "conversion" may be seen as a rearguard attempt to retain the text within a modernist mode of reading, a self-contained artifact designed to have no impact upon the world of its readers. Our discussion here and in connection with the "outer world" should leave no doubt that Alemán's novelistic project was addressed to the regeneration of the inner man and that of the social and economic man also. We have learned that in early modern Europe the individual has not an inalienable "self" but a soul, and a social identity that is "granted and guaranteed to

197

him by the laws and authority of his larger community" (Parker/ Quint 1986:8). And yet Alemán belonged to a group of thoughtful and active men who were convinced that it was possible to shape the cultural and material relations in which this identity was produced, that one could redefine *honra* as dignity acquired through action in the world. No other writer attempted that.

The Inner World of *El Buscón*

In the pseudo autobiography of Guzmán, Alemán created a generic cliff-hanger: the last-moment retrieval of romance from destruction in a sordid world of infamy and ignoble desires. The inner world of the hero-antihero is a function of his desire to remake himself, and to do that he must make himself known. The act of making himself known, mediated by the faculty of memory, is at the same time an act of self-recognition. Seen in these terms, *Guzmán de Alfarache* could scarcely be more different from *Lazarillo*. Quevedo's *Buscón*, in turn, derisively negates once again the premises of its vast predecessor.

One way Quevedo derides *Guzmán* is by overriding Alemán's careful distinctions and in particular by collapsing his moral discriminations, and the effect is the more devastating because he preserves a rigorous economy of discourse and a taut structure. In this respect *El buscón* differs notably from that other travesty, *La pícara Justina*, which aims a riposte of endlessly inconsequential episodes, garrulous monologue, and private jokes against Alemán's monumental claim to discursive universality. Guzmán discovers shame very soon after setting out; Quevedo pricks his Pablos with shame from the first; indeed, shame is his mode of self-consciousness, and the swing from shame to shamelessness is his vital trajectory. The disquisition on shame in *Guzmán* II.i.1 distinguishes between a lower, diffuse sense that includes social embarrassment, the fear of being judged by one's peers, refusal to retreat from one's mistakes, suppression of one's better judgment to gain approval, and a higher, morally directed sense of shame as an aversion to doing anything base or unworthy, even when alone.[43] Pablos' shame is the feeling that he has for his impossibly repellent family, and it is also the sense of humiliation that he undergoes when he falls from the horse and when he is subjected to hazing as a new student. Quevedo has him humiliated relentlessly, on one hand by the brazen depravity of his parents and on the other by his own timidity and naiveté in a malicious world. He surmounts this timidity by a conversion that is the opposite of Guzmán's: "I finally determined to be a knave among knaves, and more knavish, if I could, than all of them" (74). He never turns back from this resolution, which is an Augustinian travesty: an act of the will consequent upon a self-evaluation that brings together the contents of memory and the exercise of understanding. In *Guzmán*, consideration of shame is a signal to the reader that, whatever may happen in between, there is continuity between the boy and the writer. The "conversion" will be a convulsion only in relation to the depraved adult, not a rejection of everything he has been. In *El buscón*, shame spurs Pablos to adopt a program that leads to his destruction: to outdo the world in shamelessness.

Parker's psychological study based on the "individual psychology" of Alfred Adler identified the root of Pablos' behavior in his sense of inferiority; the desire to compensate with an impossible ambition leads to his downfall. This analysis proposes an intelligible mechanism for the transformation that we observe in Pablos, but I believe that Quevedo was less concerned to make him intelligible than to make him ridiculous. That a son of such parents might wish to live a different life from theirs is plausible; that he could seriously have ideas of transforming himself into a gentlemen and attempt to realize them is not. That a young man who has harbored such ambitions from his earliest years would waste his time at the university in practical jokes and then make so poor a performance in pursuit of a comfortable marriage—these actions are not consistent either. An intelligible structure of humiliation and compensatory fantasy is translated into a performance of guignolesque extremes, without a center to serve as benchmark. Total shameful humiliation or total nonreflective tricksterism—either one would doom him to annihilation in a world "normal" enough

43. "De ti mesmo es bien que tengas vergüenza, para no hacer, aun a solas, cosa torpe ni afrentosa" (249).

for the postulates of Adlerian psychology to serve as criteria of consistency.

In the world inhabited by Pablos, the outer reality is mediated to the inner predominantly by excrement. At the *rey de gallos* (king of cocks) festivity, which turns into the *batalla nabal* (turnip fight), vegetables become first projectiles, then garbage littering the street; before the occasion is concluded, Pablos has been tossed on a pile of dung. The drunken party at his uncle's is awash in swill and vomit. Each of these episodes ends with his having a momentary apprehension of himself as about to be either ingested or excreted by this world. The freshman initiation at the University of Alcalá comprises two equally repulsive stages, in which Pablos is covered in excrement, the first mucous, the second fecal, and from this experience comes his resolution to outdo the rest in knavery, that is, to be assimilated to the world's nauseous substance.

Quevedo makes no serious attempt to represent self-consciousness. Pablos is aware of himself only as the narrator of his story. Phrases such as "I confess that . . . ," "I resolved to . . ." do not present his experience of self-reflection; such comments as "Being young and foolish, I started to say . . ." (29) and the mock good manners with which he apologizes for mentioning a pig cannot be construed as openings into an inner self. Rather, they are Quevedo's gesture of disdain for both his protagonist and his reader.[44]

44. Harry Sieber (1968) examined a principal device by which the narrator's presence in this work is maintained: the apostrophes to the reader. The continuity they sustain and protect is not that of a subjectivity but that of a narrator addressing his reader.

PART THREE

BEYOND THE CANON

6

Cervantes

In 1925 Américo Castro's influential *Pensamiento de Cervantes* opposed the aesthetic values of Cervantes to those of Alemán, and it has since become a commonplace to contrast Cervantes with the picaresque works of his time, and to interpret the allusions to and reflections of them in his works as expressions of hostility. Much has been written to sharpen the contrast and to present it in terms that are not limited to literary devices, techniques, and characters, but bring out underlying differences of attitudes and human values. *Rinconete y Cortadillo*, the *Coloquio de los perros*, and the conversation between Don Quixote and Ginés de Pasamonte (*DQ*, I.22) have been presented as exercises in parody, or as criticism by example: doing what picaresque writers might have done but failed to do. Walter Reed, referring to Cervantes' writings "of a picaresque sort," says they "function like Quevedo's *El Buscón*, as sophisticated deconstructions of the ongoing novelistic series" (1981:71). These oppositions require closer scrutiny.

The question of the authority of the text may take many forms, and when the text is presented in the first person, the question devolves upon the narrator, whose reliability, powers of recall, trustworthiness, and self-interest become problematic. This concern has exercised critics since Henry James and Percy Lubbock made "point of view" central to the narrative discourse. The proliferation of autobiography, personal memoirs, diaries, and political reminiscences has made us sensitive as never before to the bias of first-person narration, so that it is more difficult for us than for previous generations of readers to accept any first-person fiction as true on its own terms.[1] In our skeptical frame of mind we may fail to grant due attention to the difference between the narrator whose account is complete and reliable within its limited angle of vision (such as Guzmán de Alfarache) and another who fudges the memory of his experiences in order to make a self-serving case (Lázaro). If all such fictional personae arouse our skepticism, we become unreliable readers. The authors and the readers of such works operated within criteria of verisimilitude whose principal question was whether the rhetorical means had been competently and effectively employed. (It is reasonable to ask whether Alemán, writing his first and only novel, was always in control, but that question does not get asked since the "death of the author.") Reading all first-person narrators as unreliable or untrustworthy witnesses rather than as rhetorical means of presentation does not respect differences of expectation; it brings to fiction questions that should properly belong to history, not poetry, at a time when the refinement of the epistemological distinction between history and poetry had acquired the greatest importance.[2]

The encounter between Don Quixote and the convict Ginés de Pasamonte is often said to show Cervantes' rejection of picaresque; in particular, Ginés' inability to finish his book because his life is unfinished is read as a reductio ad absurdum of the autobiographical urge to leave nothing out. Or it is said to be a parody of autobiography's lack of formal control, the lack of such control being the result of another lack, that of an external perspective (Guillén 1971:156, Sieber 1977:25). The lack of an external narrator, however, does not mean that there is no check at all on the narrator's trustworthiness. I am not convinced that the episode of Ginés represents Cervantes' simple disparagement of picaresque. If we

1. The basic discussions: Friedman 1955; Booth 1961: chap. 7 and "Distance and Point of View," *Essays in Criticism* 11 (1961); Scholes/Kellogg 1966; Chatman 1978; Genette 1980.
2. This debate is studied at length in Riley 1964 and Nelson 1973.

set the stories he wrote in a picaresque mode against *Guzmán de Alfarache*, they undoubtedly deviate from it in form, ideology, and discourse; but so do *Lazarillo*, *La pícara Justina*, *El buscón*, and the rest. It may be that Cervantes is more radically opposed, but the case needs to be reexamined. If we detect parody in his pieces, we must remember that parody involves complicity with its object, and evident intertextuality. What is parodied is incorporated, preserved, memorialized in the parody. *Don Quixote* would be impossible without *Amadís de Gaula* and other romances of chivalry; *Rinconete y Cortadillo*, the *Coloquio de los perros*, and *La ilustre fregona* would likewise be impossible without *Lazarillo* and *Guzmán de Alfarache*.

La pícara Justina (traditionally included in the picaresque canon) is an elaborate travesty of *Guzmán*, which it trivializes, replacing the grand design by local forays and the reflections and moralities by relentless prattle and innuendo. Interestingly, Cervantes was more offended by this "anti-*Guzmán*" than he was by the *Guzmán* itself. Whatever his opinion of Alemán, it is obvious that he was stimulated to reflect upon the place that low life might occupy in his own fictional world, and upon the efficacy of the split narrative consciousness as an instrument for representing it. *Justina*, by contrast, appears to have had no such heuristic or even counterexemplary value. In the *Viaje del Parnaso*, López de Ubeda is the "lay chaplain" in the army of the bad poets advancing under the standard of the crow to attack the true poets, who rally under the sign of the swan:

> Haldeando venía y trasudando
> el autor de *La pícara Justina*,
> capellán lego del contrario bando.
> Y, cual si fuera de una culebrina,
> disparó de sus manos un librazo
> que fue de nuestro campo la ruina.
> Al buen Tomás Gracián mancó de un brazo;
> a Medinilla derribó una muela
> y le llevó de un muslo un gran pedazo.

> With skirts flying, sweating profusely, came
> the author of *La pícara Justina*,
> lay chaplain of the opposing faction.

> And as though from a culverin
> shot from his hands a tome
> that was the ruin of our camp.
> It disabled good Tomás Gracián's arm;
> it knocked a molar out of Medinilla's mouth
> and took a big chunk out of his thigh.

López de Ubeda, a physician, hence a depository of secrets, could be tarred with the same scandalous reputation that attached to private chaplains who were often employed "in traffic incompatible with priestly dignity."[3] *Haldeando* alludes to the long gown worn by physicians, but also echoes the use of the same verb by Fernando de Rojas to describe Celestina hurrying to the house of Melibea. Tomás de Gracián was the assessor whose authority López de Ubeda had flouted in printing the *aprobación* to his book (Bataillon 1969:57–61, 1973b:220–21). The cryptic "cutoff verses" that Cervantes appends to *Don Quixote 1* under the name of Urganda "la desconocida" (the unknown), in particular the lines "No indiscretos hieroglí-[ficos] / estampes en el escu-[do]" (No foolish hierogli[phics] do you emboss on the shie[ld]) allude to López de Ubeda's promotion of the upstart favorite Rodrigo Calderón's questionable coat of arms. These and other wounding allusions are deciphered by Marcel Bataillon (1969, 1973c), who notes that Cervantes was probably piqued by López de Ubeda's dismissive placement of *Don Quixote* among other objects of his insolent disrespect: Justina refers to herself as

> Soy la rein- de Picardí-
> más que la rud- conocid-
> más famo- que doña Oli-
> que Don Quijo- y Lazari-
> que Alfarach- y Celesti-　　　　　　　　　　(848)

> I am the quee- of Picard-
> more than the crude nobl-
> more famou- than doña Oli-
> than Don Quixo- and Lazari-
> than Alfarach- and Celisti-

---

3. Noted in Sebastián de Covarrubias, *Tesoro de la lengua castellana o española* (Madrid, 1611), under *capilla*. Recall Lope de Vega's pandering for the Duque de Sessa, even after his ordination.

López de Ubeda appears to have been the inventor of these chopped-off verses, and so Cervantes replies in kind, demonstrating his command of the adversary's weapon.

But Cervantes' antipathy clearly had more substantial bases than these personal slights. *La pícara Justina* trivialized some of the fundamental premises of Cervantes' art, most notably his belief in the responsibility of the writer and the nobility of the poet's vocation. The very idea of poetry as a noble calling, the queen of sciences, expressed by Cervantes throughout his career, and the corresponding effort to sustain a decorum in expression and subject matter are scoffed at in the *Justina*'s scurrilous practice as well as in the solemn mockery of the author's preface. So are the revered classical models, the poetic myths and symbols, and the emblems (*geroglíficos*) derided by Justina as "giroblíficos". *Justina*, a torrent of mordant and impious witticisms, wounding epithets, insolent verses (in fifty-one different verse forms, displays of virtuoso juggling), could not be further from Cervantes' ideal of poetry as a "casta doncella" (modest maid) or from the traditions of Garcilaso and the pastoral to which he adhered. Cervantes wrote of himself in his *Viaje del Parnaso* the well-known lines: "Nunca voló la pluma humilde mía / por la región satírica. . . . . " (My humble quill never flew / through the region at satire). If his sonnets "Al túmulo del Rey Felipe II en Sevilla" (At the tomb of King Philip II in Seville) and the earlier one on the Earl of Essex's raid on Cadiz appear to refute him, we should discriminate modes of satire and refer these verses to the Horatian tradition of satire, which sought to incite the reader to virtue and rational behavior. Cervantes' satire is elegiac, lamenting the passing of true glory, and insists upon due proportion between greatness and rhetoric. López de Ubeda's satire is subversive, attacking the nation's preoccupation with honor and its pride in "blood," in genealogy. Justina characterizes herself as a "pícara montañesa" and "pícara hidalga"; the mountainous north was the part of the nation that prided itself on its purity of blood, so that conjoining "pícara" with either of those epithets was an insolent jibe at a potent cultural myth. Cervantes, on the contrary, never ceased to express his pride in his exploits in the service of his king and his God; acts, that is to say, that show how a man of honor and good breeding should be prepared to give his life (Bataillon 1973b:221). Unlike *Lazarillo* and *Guzmán de Alfarache*, *Justina* leaves no mention and no trace in Cervantes' prose; it is banished to a margin occupied by the shadowy Urganda with her cryptic broken verses.

The relations between *Lazarillo*, *Guzmán*, *Justina*, and *El buscón* are complicated to the point where the disconformity of Cervantes with any of them is not grounds for declaring him to be hostile toward "the picaresque" as a whole (whatever that whole is). The works that we judge most original are antagonistic to their predecessors in the way they make their shared formal elements convey radically different signifieds. Since there is no fixed one-to-one correspondence between formal units and their thematic functions, a writer can as well alter minimally the established conventional units in order to disrupt their referential system as substitute very different formal units in order to enhance or to protect the traditional truth value of the total discourse. Quevedo's *Buscón* is a clear example of picaresque narrative that disconcerts the reader by presenting familiar signifiers (the formal units of autobiography: boy leaves home; ignominious parents; closing the narrative circle) in combination with a different social perspective and in an imperfect series. Carlos Blanco Aguinaga (1957), however, identifies the picaresque completely with Alemán, claiming that he presents the picaresque traits taken to "an absolute extreme" (314). *Guzmán* is put in the peculiar position of being both the most representative picaresque text and also the most extreme.[4] In any case, whatever is true of *Guzmán* is not true of all the rest, for the different texts respond to different projects. Blanco sustains his paradoxical argument at considerable length, and it enables him to oppose Cervantes to picaresque fiction twice over: as the champion of the free creative spirit against the monolithic genre and of the open imagination against the "closed dogmatism" of Alemán. Bataillon (1973b) follows the same path, though less vehemently and with characteristic circumspection. The "bitter vision" (229) that he finds in Alemán echoes Blanco Aguinaga's "dogmatic realism of disillusion" (1957:313). But *Guzmán*, as we have seen, is not the determinist tract that it is often represented to be; the protago-

---

4. "Necesario es advertir por qué, por ahora, bajo el nombre genérico de *picaresca* estudio sólo el *Guzmán* . . . : en esta historia de la vida del pícaro por antonomasia se dan, llevados a un extremo absoluto que facilita la claridad de análisis, los rasgos que en otras picarescas aparecen sólo fragmentariamente" (Blanco 1957:314).

nist's message to bis readers is "If I could break free from my inheritance and my circumstance, so can you."[5] If Cervantes' characters are "open to the future" (Bataillon 1973b:229), we know that a
poetic justice awaits them at the end. Preciosa (*La gitanilla*) is determined in her traits and her accomplishments as much by
"blood" as by the select upbringing given her by the old gypsy, as
much by nature as by nurture; more by nature, in fact, since the
segregated education has reinforced her "blood", giving her some
of the manners of a proper young lady. In the same story, wellborn "Andrés" in the guise of a gypsy kills the soldier whose comment has offended him. His noble blood has rushed to his head;
he is exonerated. Dorotea (*DQ*, 1.28–36), taking her destiny into
her own hands and repeatedly entrusting herself to heaven, pursues the conventional marriage that is her only salvation, in the
literary as well as the social world. In *La fuerza de la sangre*, the rape
is theatricalized, made the point of departure for a quest narrative.
La ilustre fregona appears to support the claim of "openness": Carriazo escapes from his noble family to pursue a picaresque existence in the tuna fisheries, following his free "picaresque inclination." We later learn that Carriazo's father had exercised *his*
inclination in a particularly brutal way when he raped the mother
of Costanza. So when we recall that the narrator presented Carriazo, in the well-known oxymoron, as "a virtuous, clean, well-
bred picaro," we may suspect an anticipatory irony. Cervantes has
us contemplate the possibility that freedom may be limited by an
inherited tendency to deviant behavior, the impulse to break out
("pícaro") pulling against the acquired values of his class, the decorum of a noble upbringing ("limpio, bien criado"). Aesthetically,

5. A notable exception is Luis Rosales, whose *Cervantes y la libertad*, 2 vols.
(Madrid: Gráficas Valera, 1960) does not set up the picaresque as antagonist.
His single and apt quotation from *Guzmán de Alfarache* is the following, in
which Guzmán emphatically declares responsibility for his acts and the resulting misfortune: "No podré decir que mi corta estrella lo causó, sino que mi
larga desvergüenza lo perdió. Las estrellas no fuerzan, aunque inclinan. Algunos ignorantes dicen: '¡Ah, señor!, al fin había de ser y lo que ha de ser
conviene que sea.' Hermano mío, mal sientes de la verdad, que ni ha de ser ni
conviene ser; tú lo haces ser y convenir. Libre albedrío te dieron con que te
gobernases. La estrella no te fuerza ni todo el cielo con cuantas tiene te puede
forzar; tú te fuerzas a dejar lo bueno y te esfuerzas en lo malo, siguiendo tus
deshonestidades, de donde resultan tus calamidades" (2:544; *Guzmán*, 1.iii.10).

Cervantes and Alemán may be far apart; ideologically, the distance is much less. This opposing of Cervantes to a narrow, dogmatic Alemán and a monolithic genre (these two being interchangeable) makes clear that the force of Blanco's argument depends on some rhetorical strategies that we need to examine, in view of the influence that his essay has had on a generation of readers.

At the beginning of his article, Blanco states that *Don Quixote* and the picaresque have been jointly credited with establishing the modern novel, because they break away from the dominant idealizing forms of fiction. He objects to this joining of Cervantes and writers of picaresque on the ground that they are not realist in the same way; rather, their respective realisms are "two contrary ways of conceiving of the novel." These two modes of realism, the *"dogmatic realism"* that he attributes to Alemán and the *"objective realism"* of Cervantes (1957:313; Blanco's italics), are totally irreconcilable. He assures us that this opposition will be demonstrated in the pages to follow. He offers no discussion of realism as such, however, or of the aptness of the term, nor does he relate realism to mimesis, to representation, or to verisimilitude, all of which are crucial concepts for the topic at that period. We are given a sort of perspectivist manifesto that invites us to let go of our discrimination between history and novel, between the world of the fiction and the world of the reader.[6] The "two modes of realism" and the

---

6. "Destruiríamos la complejidad del mundo cervantino si no viéramos como un todo esta superposición y cruce constante—equivalente al del *Quijote* —entre realidad aparente y realidad real, realidad real y crítica, historia y novela, novela y novela, *en que todo está constantemente fluyendo en su aparente contrario y confundiéndose con él, hasta que no es posible deslindar los contrarios y oponerlos, aceptar y rechazar dogmáticamente"* (Blanco 1957:333). Readers of this passage, and especially of the part I have italicized, may recognize that what is here attributed to Cervantes is that supposedly Semitic blurring of boundaries that Américo Castro attributed to the aesthetics of Juan Ruiz (cf. Castro 1966). A particular trait of the master's rhetoric is also evident in the tail of the sentence: the implication that one cannot discriminate without being "dogmatic," so that the reader will be corralled into accepting the proposition rather than face the charge of being "dogmatic." (Blanco himself is nothing if not dogmatic.) But the premise to Cervantes' playful confusion of these planes of reality and representation is surely that we shall be challenged rather than deluded or confused by his games, and will be intelligent and competent enough as readers to separate the planes, and to enjoy doing so. Not to do so is to join with Don Quixote in attacking the puppet show. Cervantes could not foresee that twentieth-century literary historians would find the confusion of distinc-

antagonism between them are not demonstrated, but are given a priori; what was to be demonstrated becomes part of the demonstration. In Blanco's universe of representation, realism is opposed to idealism; within realism, a split between two kinds that are "absolutely antagonistic." This tight, tense conceptual world is, as can be seen, an adversarial one, and it is sustained, first, by assimilation of all picaresque writing to *Guzmán*, and second, by repeated use of dogmatic absolutes: the picaresque world is "*only* vanity and appearance"; it is the "*lowest, most* contrary to the ideal"; picaresque is narrated "*always* in the form of autobiography"; the pícaro is "*always* a vagabond," "*always* alone" (my emphases). The frequency of *always, never, all, absolutely,* and related absolutes is particularly evident, in a procedure of cumulative assertion that precedes and largely displaces the expected demonstration. Curiously, this procedure resembles the method that Blanco attributes to Guzmán and denounces: moving "from the definition to the defined" (316–17), though such is not, in fact, Guzmán's way of storytelling. In short, a world of sharp contrasts, of fixed positions, of adversarial dogmatism underlies the argument and drives it forward. Blanco has interesting things to say about both *Guzmán* and Cervantes, but they subserve a strategy of pitting the "open," "objective" Cervantes against all of the picaresque as represented in the oppressive work supposedly created by Alemán. This scheme is held in place by a system of absolute identities and equally absolute antagonisms.

A systematic deconstruction of Blanco's essay would note his ideological position, his time of writing, and his evident projection of the myth of the "two Spains," in which Alemán is clothed in the uniform of authoritarian Spain ("closed," "dogmatic,") while Cervantes waits with calculated patience and triumphs in posterity. The Spain of the Habsburgs is not only the precursor of the Spain of Franco in the work of such critics and intellectuals as Blanco and Castro, it is a kind of unfolding allegory with such cultural icons as El Greco, Alemán, Cervantes, Calderón playing the parts of historical abstractions. Not surprisingly, Blanco's arguments have received little criticism. Everyone loves Cervantes, and dualistic

---

tions between reality and nonreality to be aesthetically commendable rather than deplorable, or comic, facts of life.

systems exert a powerful attraction. The Manichean image of Cervantes as a champion of light in history's ongoing struggle is an alluring one. But it is unfair to both Alemán and Cervantes. The part played by Alemán at Almadén, in asserting the human rights of condemned criminals against the agents of the monarchy and of foreign capital, is no less admirably quixotic than that of Cervantes in Algiers. And it is better documented. And the ecclesiastical portraits in Alemán's fiction are devastating in their social and institutional implications.

Blanco's ideologically directed literary history is not the only possible construct. The reader of fiction in the period 1600–1610 could have seen Alemán's vast and inescapably serious romance followed by *Lazarillo*, all but forgotten and now revived with great success. Brief, laconic in its irony, it exemplifies a morality of survival by paddling with the current. To those readers who came to it for the first time after encountering Alemán and Martí, it must have seemed more like a torpedo than a precursor. *Lazarillo*, *Justina*, and *El buscón* (circulating in manuscript) can be seen as both subverting and exploiting *Guzmán* in their several ways, as creative parodies, as parasites burrowing into and feeding off its great bulk in order to create something startlingly new, variously skeptical of Alemán's aesthetic and ideological ambition, which had also been daringly new even if the material it recycled was not. But Cervantes goes much further in the creative recycling and transformation of the repertory of devices and motifs that were only recently assembled, and were just as rapidly being dismantled and recombined. If we think autobiography and the single focus are indispensable, here is *Rinconete y Cortadillo*, with two boys presented by a third-person narrator who, moreover, appears occasionally uncertain of his story. The *Coloquio de los perros* restores the autobiographical mode of presentation but abandons the human subject and the credible narrator, thus "making strange," in Viktor Shklovsky's phrase (1965), both the narrative convention and the world it discloses.[7] The process does not end here: Espinel's Marcos is no marauding picaro but a perambulating *honnête homme* demonstrating, with fictionalized snatches of Espinel's own life, that decency can be preserved in adversity.

7. See Lemon/Reis 1965:3–24; Ehrlich 1981:76–78, 176–80.

The encounter between Don Quixote and Ginés de Pasamonte (or Ginesillo de Parapilla, as the guard calls him) is routinely cited as an example of Cervantes' rejection of Alemán's aesthetics. But the relation is more elusive than it may appear. Cervantes' convict on his way to serve in the galleys does indeed remind us of Alemán's, whose narrative begins in a galley, where he has just earned a royal pardon. Both are notorious criminals. Both are writing their life stories. Ginés proudly explains how he has written his life "with these thumbs," and that it is so good that *Lazarillo* and all others like it that were ever written or ever will be written had better watch out; their lies are no match for his truths (*DQ*, I.22).[8] It is not yet finished because his life is not yet finished. Here is an arrogant rogue who wants to leave his mark as a writer, claiming that his truth is better than fiction. In fact, he wants to have it both ways: when he asserts that his "truths" are "pretty" ("lindas"), his no-nonsense claim on behalf of the unvarnished facts over the "lies" of fiction turns into a claim for the *aesthetic* superiority of unvarnished nature. This encounter has been taken to indicate Cervantes' hostility to the picaresque. Ann Wiltrout (1978) asserts that "with Ginés de Pasamonte, the perpetual outsider, Cervantes takes his most conclusive stand against the picaresque novel." Claudio Guillén is more cautious, observing what other commentators have not stopped to consider: Ginés is a reader, and in this episode Cervantes gives us an encounter between two readers (1971:135–58).

Characteristically, Cervantes tantalizes us by leaving unasked and unresolved the questions we would like to ask. One would like to know how Ginés read *Lazarillo de Tormes* and "all the rest of them," including, presumably, *Guzmán*, both its authentic and its spurious parts. What did he mean by calling them "mentiras" (lies)? That he knows they are fictions? Or does he believe them to be real autobiographies, but full of lies? Does "mentiras" have any sharpness of definition at all? Does it refer to tall tales and the like, that the public at large would agree are beyond belief? Or is it merely an arrogant charlatan's way of declaring that everyone

8. "Mal año para *Lazarillo de Tormes* y para todos cuantos de aquel género se han escrito o escribieren . . . trata verdades tan lindas y tan donosas que no puede haber mentiras que se le igualen."

else's writing is rubbish? It is tempting to suppose that he, like the mad hidalgo, has taken fiction for truth, but we cannot assume anything. What does seem clear is that, in the scheme of pairings and balances that Cervantes elaborates within Part I, Ginés de Pasamonte's relation to his chosen reading (picaresque) is homologous with the relation of Cardenio to his (amorous romance). The convict has read *Lazarillo* and the rest as desirable modes of action, as models to be surpassed in the conduct of life. They must, then, have mediated to him a world of possible adventure, rather as amorous fiction had mediated to young Cardenio, through its deceitful tropes, a world of romantic longing and anguished separation by which to conduct his desperate courtship of Luscinda (Girard 1965). Ginés' "truths" become "pretty" insofar as he succeeds in surpassing those models, first in his life and then in his writing. The attractiveness (as he sees it) of his narrative derives from the supposition that there is an exact correspondence between life and narrative, that the story can tell itself, that life can become language as an act of the will. This supposition has its parallel in Don Quixote, who narrated his first setting out (1.2), translating the act into the word, as his words determine his acts.[9] Ginés, like Don Quixote, is both writer and reader of his life; he creates himself, looks upon his work, and sees that it is good. So, in order to become his own ideal reader, he has eliminated the critic that every writer must nurture within himself. And like the knight, he aspires to make his life total discourse, to abolish the difference between story and diegesis, between the teller, the telling, and the told.

Claudio Guillén has argued that Don Quixote's encounter with Ginés represents Cervantes' rejection of first-person narration:

> *La vida de Ginés de Pasamonte* is presented by its author, with the commissary's consent, as a truthful autobiography. Nevertheless, Cervantes stresses most explicitly the problem of narrative structure. A dramatic or epic character possesses, to be sure,

9. "'Apenas había el rubicundo Apolo tendido por la faz de la ancha y espaciosa tierra . . . cuando el famoso caballero Don Quijote de la Mancha, dejando las ociosas plumas, subió sobre su famoso caballo Rocinante, y comenzó a caminar por el antiguo y conocido campo de Montiel.' Y era la verdad que por él caminaba."

some sort of identity; but how does one shape a "life"? The supposed proximity to "life" of the autobiographer is exacted at a very high cost: that of formlessness. Any life that is narrated by its own subject must remain incomplete and fail to achieve artistic unity or, very simply, the status of art. (1971:156)

He goes on to declare that narrative form "demands a 'second' or 'third' person expressing a consciousness that is extrinsic to the events" (156). Esssentially the same argument is made by Harry Sieber, who sees this episode as Cervantes' criticism of of "an open-ended and frameless imitation of experience without the structuring control of art" (1977:25). But the assertion that "autobiography can have no clear resolution and therefore no plot"[10] is overhasty. The mistake is not Alemán's or Guzmán's but Ginés', and his mistake is to believe precisely what Guillén says is true. It is Ginés, not Guzmán, who assumes that his written *vida*, as distinct from his lived life, cannot be terminated, cannot reach a closure that discloses significance, while the subject remains alive. Guzmán believed the exact opposite. Both Guzmán and his great model, Augustine, saw that their lives at a particular point *had* achieved an exemplary unity that confers "shape" and significance on a "Life". In each case there *is* a plot, and that plot is constituted by the act of retrospection, by the climactic point from which that retrospection is performed (Guzmán's *atalaya*), and by the rhetorical construct that declares "this is what my life means."[11]

Ginés' autobiography may be said to parody picaresque fiction only to the extent that it is unfinished, and that the authors of picaresque narratives promise more to come (but so does the author of *Don Quixote* and of *La Galatea*). If it is a parody, it it so by

10. This phrase is Roberto González-Echevarría's (1980:20) summary of Guillén.

11. At a different level of analysis one might argue that Augustine's *Confessions* demonstrate that his subsequent career bears out his claim to have disclosed form in his life, although it is not yet complete, whereas Guzmán's subsequent life is a blank; that Ginés' refusal to terminate his narrative is a vehicle for Cervantes' skepticism toward Alemán's enterprise. This is a different question, and it takes us into the labyrinth of verisimilitude (exemplarity versus the protocols of realism: it is the exemplarity that is Alemán's goal; Guzmán's subsequent life would be unwritable and unreadable). Moreover, it puts Cervantes in the quixotic position of treating Guzmán as a real person; it is not clear that even Ginés does that.

virtue of that fiction's search for a mimetic truth to life that renounces the well-rounded story, the geometrical plot, and the climactic endings of more traditional forms of romance. Whereas Ginés wants, absurdly, to hoard his pages until his dying breath, readers of picaresque know when the story has come to its end, even when more is promised. These endings are not arbitrary. The ending of *Lazarillo* comes where it does because that is where its internal poetics demands that it should be. Once the temporal segment is marked off, the writer is impelled to disclose an artistic necessity structuring it, thus allowing the reader to perceive that what are represented as life's vicissitudes are the field of operation for such forces as heredity, fate, divine providence, will, judgment. Guzmán looks back from his new lucidity and his newly conquered freedom of action and rereads his life as he narrates it, covering it with commentary. So the other viewpoint called for by Guillén is contained within the book as one of the layers of consciousness. In *Lazarillo* it is extrinsic not only to the sequence of events but to the narrator, located in that Vuestra Merced to whose point of view Lázaro continually adjusts his narrative. These procedures are the result of an artful artlessness, quite the opposite of Ginés' naiveté. Alemán organizes his narrative, produces structure, from the Janus-like perspective of a climactic or visionary moment, at which the narrator sees himself as other. Alemán has faced the problems of representing the retrieval of past experience and of justifying the writing; I find it difficult to accept Ginés' *vida* as parody (or willful misrepresentation) of Guzmán's.[12]

Thus far, our examination of Ginés' relation to his acts and his words has revealed analogies with principal figures inside the world of Cervantes' book, rather than patterns from an alien world of fiction. He does not seem to represent an uncomplicated stand by Cervantes against picaresque writing. Perhaps his name can cast some light on the matter. But is he "really" Ginés de Pasamonte, as he insists, or is he Ginesillo de Parapilla, as others declare? This is one more question that Cervantes leaves pending.

---

12. The problem of the credibility of the narrator is not confined to those who relate their own actions and thoughts. Any narrator who is given an identity apart from his discourse creates an unstable relation between reader and narrative, especially if he voices opinions and judgments concerning his story or the people in it, as is the case with Cide Hamete.

There is a resemblance between the names Ginés de Pasamonte and Guzmán de Alfarache: each contains a linking *de*; they are constructed upon the same number of syllables (2 + *de* + 4) and the same pattern of stress; they have the same placement of the vowels *a* and final *e*. Is this a parodic echo of *Guzmán*, and if it is, what can it signify, in the absence of any supporting frame of parody? I suggest that this is the name he has chosen for himself, as being more evocative and more apt for the literary figure he wishes to cut than Ginesillo de Parapilla with its overtones of *el hampa*, the underworld of rogues. He has adopted a name suggestive of the literary picaresque in order to incorporate himself into that world, just as the hidalgo Quixada (or Quesada, or Quexana) named himself Don Quixote so as to pass into the world of chivalry. Adopting a name is an act of identification, and means more than appending an identity tag; it becomes an act of symbolic assimilation of oneself to the idea represented by the name. To change a name is to change more than a label, more even than a status. Change of name is an essential component of rites of passage, and the change signals a transformation, a desire for new ontological definition. Thus, when the hero's *rocín* (nag) becomes Rocinante, the narrator informs us that the new name is "significant [significativo] of what he used to be when he was a nag, before what he was now" (1,90). Similarly, when Aldonza Lorenzo is transformed into Dulcinea del Toboso, the new name is, once more, "musical and unusual [peregrino] and *significant*" (1.91). That is to say that her name is a sign that announces the semiotic system of chivalrous romance, and draws her into it; and since that system is a Platonizing one, the name discloses an essence that she shares with the system, which was latent in her, and which has waited for just those magic syllables to evoke it. The bearer of the name will forever be known for the quality designated by the name, and Don Quixote can sally forth, confidently asserting that things are not what they appear to be, but are what their names (*his* names for them) evoke, which is solidary with that other, more Platonically real world. Ginés de Pasamonte's name is *significativo* in this quixotic sense. Indeed, it is fully quixotic, being not only "significant" but "elevated" and "sonorous" (*alto, sonoro*), like the name Rocinante, or "musical" and "unusual," like Dulcinea del Toboso.

The most we can say about this Ginés, I believe, is that he has to steal the echo of another man's name before he can create a written identity and project himself into literature. As a descriptive name, *Pasa-monte* conveys well the senses of both "marauder, highwayman" and "fugitive outlaw."[13] His given name, Ginés, delivers yet another Cervantine irony. This role-playing convict and future puppeteer bears the name (and therefore evokes the spiritual patronage) of the Roman actor Genesius. Performing the part of a Christian martyr for the entertainment of the emperor Diocletian, Genesius was moved to a true conversion by the role he was playing. In his case the feigned experience became a true one, the fictional role became real, the scoffing actor became Saint Genesius, martyr. (This story is the subject of Lope de Vega's play *Lo fingido verdadero*.) "Ginés" names two referents and points to the ironic distance between them. One is the man who steps through illusion into a transcendent truth when he accepts the given role as a "figure" of his destiny in the theater of the world. The other moves in the contrary direction: a man who descends from his natural freedom to a self mediated by a fiction, and who finally shrinks to being a manipulator of puppets (*DQ* II: chaps. 26–27). All Christian saints are members of the same system of paradigmatic virtues, which the believer is implicated in and called upon to witness by the act of being named. The Christian tradition sees no accident in the fact that one is born on the day of a particular saint and is thereupon destined to adopt his or her name. There is a figural similarity between the pattern of the saint's life and that of Guzmán. But Ginés–Maese Pedro's career reverses and travesties that of his saint as he moves along a trajectory from a teller of vaunted truths to a manipulator of puppets and a fraudulent prophet or soothsayer speaking through the mouth of his monkey.

It is likely that Cervantes found *Guzmán* objectionable for its preaching and for its direct haranguing of the reader, two procedures that he never employed without irony, or without the mediation of a different voice. As a whole, the career of Ginés-Maese

---

13. It is difficult to see how Cervantes' criminal could allude to the soldier Jerónimo de Pasamonte (a fellow captive in Algiers, writer of a *Vida*, and evidently a man of disturbed mind) unless one accepts Riquer's thesis that Pasamonte was also Avellaneda, author of the spurious *Segunda Parte de Don Quixote*: Martín de Riquer, *Cervantes, Passamonte y Avellaneda* (Barcelona: Sirmio, 1988).

Pedro appears to owe as much to Cervantes' fascination with another trickster, Pedro de Urdemalas, who ends as the incarnation of a famous actor, as it does to *Guzmán de Alfarache*. Indeed, to the extent that it looks to *Guzmán*, it does so in order to produce an example of that intertextual richness and complexity in which he is unequaled. The quiet allusions seem to suggest only that Guzmán's literary example will produce charlatans and mountebanks. They also suggest that if Guzmán is to be celebrated as a new Proteus, Pedro de Urdemalas, trickster and folk hero, is the more truly protean figure of the two.[14]

One of the triumphs of Cervantes' art is the play of many voices, a polyphony to which the voice of the narrator is subtly responsive, varying its own tone and distance. With his vocation for theater, Cervantes was not inclined to allow a single voice either to define the imagined world or to hold uncontested sway over it. It is perhaps no surprise that he did not follow *Lazarillo de Tormes* and *Guzmán de Alfarache* in adopting the first-person narration throughout; to have done so would have deprived him of the opportunity for multiple perspectives and narratorial comment. He did not write first-person narrative except within a third-person frame. But without *Lazarillo* and *Guzmán* he could not have written *Rinconete y Cortadillo* or the *Coloquio de los perros* or *La ilustre fregona*. In Joaquín Casalduero's phrase, "Cervantes skirts the picaresque without wanting to plunge right in" (1962:44). It remains to approach more closely and analytically the subject of this phrase.

Our contemporary critical engagement with language, and in particular with writing as a social practice, has led to the perception of picaresque as a testimonial of a crucial moment in the formation of self-consciousness (Gaède 1983:119–33). In his *Language and Society in "La Vida de Lazarillo de Tormes"* (1978) Harry Sieber reads *Lazarillo* as a linguistic performance: the protagonist acquires and becomes proficient in a series of discursive practices that enable him both to adopt and to manipulate the roles necessary for survival. Sieber seeks to trace the "the individualizing acts of language through which [Lázaro's] experience takes form" (x): the object of his inquiry and the theme of the book is Lázaro's initiation into the complexities of the linguistic codes of his society. La-

14. For the reputation of Guzmán as a Proteus figure, see Cros 1967:88–94.

zarillo's relationship with each of his masters is an apprenticeship in a new discourse, and his accumulated experience brings a final mastery of a whole hierarchy of discourses. Lázaro is thus able to exist ironically, to subvert while conforming, to be honorably dishonored, to live at the center but write from the margin. Roberto González-Echevarría in his 1980 article (which is only partly a review of Sieber's book) epitomizes the major preoccupation in picaresque novels as the emergence of writing and its ambivalent relation to authority (18). This judgment is appropriate to *Lazarillo* but less so in the case of *Guzmán*; here the discourse that enmeshes and is internalized by the emerging self is neither subversive of nor subverted by the codes of authority. Rather, it unambiguously *is* the discourse of Authority, ratified by reason, which excoriates the shams of society, and it has been learned not in adversarial psychodramas (as in Lázaro's case) but at the university, the place of Authority and reason. In *Guzmán* it is turned against the self, that part of the self that had embraced too easily the prevailing codes of honor, of success, of revenge, of conformity to the norms of the *vulgo*.

As González-Echevarría notes, Cervantes also makes his quasi-picaresque narratives foreground the question of language. It is important to realize how they do so, how different the presentation is from that in *Don Quixote*; how radical is the shift in Cervantes' attention from the practice to the sources of language. This is a shift that would be inconceivable without the provocative mediation of *Lazarillo* and *Guzmán*, whatever his opinion of Alemán or of "the naked realism of the picaresque model" (Bataillon 1973b:230) may have been. In *Don Quixote* the knight himself is the creation of a certain fictive writing, the language of romantic desire. Language has become action, in the expectation that it will become writing again by the operation of the magic of an unseen enchanter. This chain is unending, and we watch the effects of language proliferate, awakening desire, provoking violence, creating illusion, dissolving reality, and precipitating it into potentially endless text. The phantom author and his surrogates write, or wonder what to write, and are troubled by doubts about the text that is given them. Readers, both inside and outside the text, are baffled by the various authors' doubts, concealments, and evasions. There are two points to note here: first, that the operation is *playful*, its confusions are comic; second, that the confusion and violence, the mystifications and equivocations, the proliferating textuality and the polyphony of voices are *consequences* of chivalric texts and of romantic discourses that are culturally and historically given. Their origin is not obscure, the story may be comically strange and incredible, but it is not mysterious. With *Rinconete y Cortadillo* and even more in *El casamiento engañoso* and *El coloquio de los perros*, all that is changed. *Don Quixote* begins with the hidalgo Quejada's reading and ends with Alonso Quijano's denunciation of it as lies; *how* he read and *what* he read there, its ultimate source, its origin in desire, are left unquestioned. That mysterious terrain is precisely where Cervantes locates the last of his *Novelas ejemplares*.

But first we turn to *Rinconete y Cortadillo* and its codes. Here he performs some very witty intertextual games. He splits the tricky protagonist into the two boys Diego Cortado and Pedro del Rincón; he shrinks the autobiographical mode to a few lines of self-presentation at the outset, embedded in the third-person narration; and he leaves the conclusion open-ended to an unprecedented degree. The conclusions of *Lazarillo* and *Guzmán de Alfarache* rehearse, each in its own way, the circularity of romance, compelling us to review the beginning, to see the end as a transfiguration of the moment of origin. No such structural coordinates are offered to the reader of Cervantes' story. The origins of the boys are related with brevity, flippancy, and detachment, thrown away by the speakers (though nothing is thrown away by Cervantes). The plotting of the narrative also is untypical of its predecessors in that it does not present either of these lives from beginning to end but encloses their beginnings in a brief parenthesis. The whole action is almost unbelievably short as well as inconsequential: a few trivial anecdotes strung out and lasting no more than a few days.

Cervantes' ambivalent relation to his predecessors is apparent. If he has overcome their tyranny by incorporation and inversion (that is to say, by an act of parody), the effort has left no signs of strain in the text. It would seem that influence was never less anxiously felt, or if there was anxiety it was never so wittily sublimated, with the exception of the more astonishing *Coloquio de los perros*. The flouting of expectations in *Rinconete* goes even so far as to allow readers to ask a question that sixteenth- and seventeenth-century fiction did not normally allow to be asked: "Where's the story?" The temptation to ask this question becomes more pressing as we notice that this novella is preceded and followed by others that have notably strong plots: *La gitanilla, El amante liberal, La española inglesa*. If we shift our attention outward from structure and plot to the discourse, we find something else that is highly unusual: *Rinconete y Cortadillo* contains more voices, more different registers than any narrative work of comparable length at that time, more listeners who make judgments (practical and moral) on the basis of what they *hear* being said. But before we pursue this matter, let us first observe the who and the where of the discourse.

The first segment occupies a very few pages, yet it runs through the modes of narration, exchanged monologues, and dialogue; it presents description, speech, and action. The story begins unmistakably on a road, and moreover at a midpoint: "En la venta del Molinillo, que está puesta en los fines de los famosos campos de Alcudia, como vamos de Castilla a la Andalucía . . ." The narrator gives first place in his narrative to this location, which is explicitly set between Castile and Andalusia, on the way from the one to the other, at an inn, a staging post, a boundary that is about to be crossed. Here are two boys from distant places in Old Castile. What the two boys, as yet unnamed, tell each other in that location, on that threshold on which they find themselves and each other, is that they both have run away from their homes, have no attachment to the past, no identification with a place, and no sense of a destination. "Mi tierra . . . no la sé, ni para dónde camino, tampoco" (I don't know where I'm from, or where I'm going either) says one of them, and his interlocutor comments that "éste no es lugar para hacer asiento en él, que por fuerza ha de pasar adelante" (this is no place to settle down, there's nothing to do but go on). The other, who will soon be identified as Diego Cortado, alludes to his alienation from his family and repeats that he has no place: "mi tierra no es mía." It is here that these two boys enter into partnership and declare their new and everlasting friendship, sealing it with an embrace. Already a transition has been made, a boundary crossed, a transformation effected, a new situation created, and they enter upon a new stage in their existence. They now have a destination, and it is Seville, the great center of commerce, of wealth, of confusion, and of crime, the city that occupied a position in Spanish popular mythology of the seventeenth century like that of Chicago in the United States in the first half of the twentieth. They are about to remake themselves, they believe; but the rite of passage will be performed by Monipodio, according to his protocols.

The spatiotemporal structure of the piece, fragmentary as it is, is still recognizably characteristic of romance: the hero leaves home and passes through a succession of adventures before being reunited with his people and claiming his reward. A descent to the lower regions may be either a test or an epiphany, or both at once. The identity of the protagonist is affirmed by the passing of time rather than changed by it. Mikhail Bakhtin, noting the absence of profound changes in the experience of romance, adds: "And yet people and things have gone *through* something, something that did not, indeed, change them, but that did (in a manner of speaking) affirm what they, and precisely they, were as individuals, something that did verify and establish their identity, their durability and continuity. The hammer of events shatters nothing and forges nothing—it merely tries the durability of an already finished product. And the product passes the test."[15]

Cervantes condenses this spatiotemporal configuration into the reduced scale of the *novela*, most obviously in *La gitanilla*, but by no means exclusively in that work. The author of *Lazarillo de Tormes* parodies it with the appearance of completion by closing the circle, of returning to the source by matching a new ménage à trois with the original one, and by keeping before the reader a few key axiological phrases, such as *arrimarse a los buenos*. Apuleius' *Golden Ass* began the movement toward the modern novel by introducing transformation as both a structural and an ideological element: Lucius' transformation into an ass is the consequence of foolish curiosity; his restoration is simultaneous with his purification and enlightenment. In between, his life is, indeed, continual movement along life's road. Here the part stands for the whole in the sense that the protagonist's life as an ass and his restoration to human shape do mark a true beginning and end although there is living both before and after—a point missed by Ginés.

Rinconete y Cortadillo presents only a brief stage on the journey.

15. Mikhail Bakhtin, *The Dialogic Imagination: Four Essays*, ed. Michael Holquist (Austin: University of Texas Press, 1981), 106–7.

The past is folded into the narrative present by means of the boys' laconic summaries of their lives, and there is no conclusion, no definitive arrival. The reader cannot tell whether the boys' identities are firmly established or not, or what it might mean either way. The moment at which the lives are thrust in a new direction—a meeting on a road—is the usual one of romance. Other meetings follow, notably with Monipodio's young scout in Seville and then with Monipodio himself, but it seems impossible at that point to decide whether these encounters establish in the *novela* a system of chance or a system of causality and consequence. It is plausible that, given the boys' inclinations and the pragmatics of the narrative, the road to Seville will eventually lead, through their flirtation with the picaresque life, to the center of the underworld and its presiding spirit of evil. Will they lose their independence of judgment and be absorbed into the underworld, as (conversely) Preciosa loses her voice and her wit on being absorbed into the world of respect and gentility? These questions remain open for the reader so long as the reading that is being practiced is a literal and realistic reading. But once we recognize the master trope of the journey and the road, and the fact that the plot of *Rinconete y Cortadillo* embodies only a fragment of that master trope, there is little room for doubt. This trope, we have observed, informs the plot of romance, the quest with its episodes of separation and reunion, of ordeals passed, of misunderstandings and chance encounters revealed as the operations of a higher purpose. The part of this master plot to which *Rinconete y Cortadillo* corresponds is the descent into the underworld, in which horror of the ordeal should become the catalytic agent of self-knowledge and -discovery. In this case the road leads down, but not up again; it takes them into a world of self-loss, of identities surrendered, of names changed, a world with a system of language that erases the values of the upper world.

In summary: two boys have met by chance at an inn, the embodiment of transience, on a road at a place that is neither here nor there, but in between; they are of an in-between age, neither boys nor men. Their reception into the circle of Monipodio will be a rite of passage into a world where adult rights and responsibilities will be conferred on them, but as members of a closed society of criminals, not as free citizens. The quest for picaresque freedom leads to the negation of freedom: *facilis descensus Averni*. Both Bataillon (1973b:229–30) and Casalduero (1962) stress the festive character of the scene in Monipodio's house (Casalduero has a section headed "Alegría de *Rinconete*"). But if the narrator's quiet smile invites our participation in his *alegría*, he can only mask the violence, not erase it, and our smile becomes complicity in a world too much like our own. The *hampa* of Seville is less a travesty of the respectable world than an extension of it, like the road that leads from the open skies of Castile to the sunless hub of the underworld.[16] Cervantes' polyphony of voices has become a cacophony. But the theme of language as deception was announced at the start.

What the boys reveal of themselves in their opening dialogue is conveyed in stolen speech, a sociolect that is put on as a disguise. In order to meet and converse and, in particular, to perform the ambiguous function of concealing their past in the verbal act of revealing it, they trespass upon a linguistic field that is not properly theirs, adopting formulas of politeness, dressing their speech with the curlicues of respect. They perform highly self-conscious speech acts designed to declare "I am not what I appear to be," but each recognizes that the physical appearance of the other *is* the

16. The British journalist Claud Cockburn (1957) describes his interview with Al Capone: "'Don't get the idea that I'm knocking the American system. The American system . . .' As though an invisible chairman had called upon him for a few words, he broke into an oration upon the theme. He praised freedom, enterprise, and the pioneers. He spoke of 'our heritage'. He referred with contemptuous disgust to Socialism and Anarchism. 'My rackets, he repeated several times, are run on strictly American lines, and they're going to stay that way. . . . This American system of ours', he shouted, 'call it Americanism, call it capitalism, call it what you like, gives to each and every one of us a great opportunity, if we only seize it with both hands and make the most of it.'" On being asked later why he had not written up this interview for *The Times*, Cockburn replied: "When I came to put my notes together, I saw that most of what Capone had said was in essence identical with what was being said in the leading articles of *The Times*, and I doubted whether this paper would be best pleased to find itself seeing eye to eye with the most notorious gangster in Chicago" (190–92). Readers of Mafia trials over the years will recognize a familiar phenomenon: the neighbors and other witnesses who testify that the defendants are loving parents, fine neighbors, good citizens, pious Christians, etc. Rinconete's observation at the end, that justice was lax in Seville, should have come as no surprise to anyone, least of all to him, who had chosen that city for his destination.

reality, and that the message must be rewritten: "I *am* what I appear to be; it's my *words* that are not to be trusted." The innkeeper's wife, who only hears their words, believes that they are well-bred youths and is surprised to find that they can cheat at cards. The question of the social authority and power of certain modes and levels of discourse is presented from the outset, as well as the ease with which they can be counterfeited.

An opportunity is offered the reader here to be deceived, the depth or intensity of the deception being dependent on the strength of the reader's intertextual desire. When each boy begins his narration, he does so in a euphemistic style that recalls *Lazarillo* and *Guzmán de Alfarache*. Given these precedents, the reader's expectation is aroused that one or the other of the boys will become the writer of his life. To expect this outcome is to be deceived, as the inkeeper's wife is deceived, when the narration continues in its serene third person. Lazarillo edged Vuestra Merced out of his story and claimed the authority to tell it for himself, as an artist, and hoped by doing so to expel Vuestra Merced from his life. Rincón and Cortado do not write but tell, and they do so for no stronger motive or better reason than that each is in the presence of the other, without pressure of power or authority, and each sees himself reflected in the other. Whereas *Guzmán de Alfarache* involves the reader in a grandiose drama of self-accusation and self-knowledge, *Rinconete y Cortadillo* arouses the reader's self-awareness quietly, at the edge of farce. The mode of play involves us less directly as moral beings, but rather as social and language-using beings.

Rinconete y Cortadillo, then, is composed of two modes of discourse: first, the narrative mode in which the narrator recounts events objectively, with some hesitations and uncertainties, but without moral posturing, so that readers are persuaded of the narrator's good faith; second, the dialogic mode, which is modulated in a number of ways, the most obvious being that with which the two youths begin addressing each other, the parody of respectable speech: "señor gentilhombre," "señor caballero," their pursuit of the well-turned phrase, the disdainful reference to *el vulgo*. Together they mimic the public voice, the phrases that invite public trust and confidence in the speaker. Among the thieves the discourse of dialogue is more violently modulated, with the total erasure of words and phrases by which the world of respectable people judges them. The words for punishment, for thief, for galleys and torture and gallows are among those lexical items that have been eliminated and replaced by the thieves' own slang. This common dialect or code expresses solidarity, of course, but it also splits off the community of thieves and enables them to reject the world that rejects them. The thieves' community with its brotherhood, its year of novitiate, its sharing of goods, its renunciation of the world outside, its code of loyalty enjoining the members to martyrdom for the good of the whole, its authority vested in a superior who is adressed as "father," all this is a mirror image or parody of the "upper" world in the underworld.

The language of the boys is, initially, no more than a rhetorical gambit, a *captatio benevolentiae* that they practice upon each other, but it is revealed before long as their attempt to wield the verbal forms of respect and authority. Later the hierarchical and functional orders of the underworld community come into focus: we have been taken from the semiotics of the verbal expressions of respect, authority, and power to the semiotics of the social forms of those same relations. The licit and the illicit forms of power relation mirror each other; the illicit is distinguished by its seizure and appropriation of such concepts as honor, service, loyalty. Thieves steal "to serve God". As we hear the familiar moral platitudes roll off the tongues of Monipodio and his acolytes, we recognize in our own world the indeterminacy of words and their reversibility; and not only of words, but of the gestures and the forms of our most cherished pieties. The malapropisms and solecisms committed by Monipodio and the members of his company are not merely comical; since they originate in legal and religious discourses (*pompa y solemnidad; per via sufragii*) they are signs of distortions in the system that produces the language. Rinconete's final reflections on what he has seen and heard are evidence that the language of the *novela* cannot be read unless we read the social text of which it is merely one manifestation.

In *Rinconete y Cortadillo* we follow a narrative that commences with some high-spirited and amateurish exercise in linguistic deceit and leads ultimately to a linguistic system that encodes a society that exists solely for purposes of fraud. Rinconete's last comments on the matter are ambiguous because the indirect discourse in which they are expressed blends the voices of the boy and the narrator.[17] Does the narrator endorse Rinconete's comments? If we assume that he does, must we assume that the boys do emerge from that underworld? We remember that they robbed the riders who gave them hospitality on the road, without qualms. Between the logic of the *novela*'s construction and the narrator's promise of a sequel that will relate "the life, *death*, and miracles of both, with that of *their master Monipodio*" (my emphases), there seems little room for doubt.

In most of the *Novelas ejemplares* and also in important episodes of *Don Quixote* and *Persiles y Sigismunda*, desire is mediated and entangled in words; many episodes in the longer works turn upon acts symbolized in words or upon fulfillment of a pledged word: the final matching of word and desire and social norm. Seductions are as much social as they are sexual; that is to say, the seduction releases a desire for identity with an institution—marriage, a noble family, honorable blood—as much as with a person. In *Rinconete y Cortadillo* this desire, this verbal net, finds its antiheroic mode. It is within such constraints as these—linguistic and social codes, generic typology, and the intertextuality of the historical moment— that as readers we struggle for our freedom; even within such constraints we may encounter a truth that we have not expected to find.

It has been said that Cervantes rejects autobiographical narration because it lacks the control of a third person, a consciousness beyond the events, and because it forecloses a living process that, by its nature, must remain open. We now see that Cervantes stands the argument on its head in *Rinconete*; his third-person narrator leaves the story truncated, and the outcome is as unresolved as in any first-person fiction. Indeed, his fiction increasingly problematized questions of authority and validation, no matter what the voice in which he delivered it. But nowhere does he make so

17. "Admirábase también de la obediencia que todos tenían a Monipodio, siendo un hombre tan rústico y desalmado. Sacábalo de su juicio lo que en el libro de caxa había leído, y los exercicios en que todos se ocupaban, y sobreexageraba quán poca o ninguna justicia había en aquella ciudad, pues quasi públicamente vivía en ella y se conservaba gente de tan contrario trato a la naturaleza humana: y propuso en sí de aconsejar a su compañero no durase mucho en aquella vida tan perdida, peligrosa y disoluta."

radical a move as he does in *El casamiento engañoso* and *El coloquio de los perros* (The deceitful marriage and The colloquy of the dogs), where he suspends these questions entirely from the authorial discourse. The author removes himself from his narration and leaves his characters to worry about the authenticity and the truth value of their narratives, which they do, continually.

The problems of origin, of truth value, and their effect on the reader's commitment to the act of reading are explicitly raised for *El coloquio de los perros* by the Licenciado Peralta, who reads the manuscript. Campuzano, its author, claims that the dialogue, as he reports it, was truly spoken by the dogs at the foot of his hospital bed. This is one obvious example of the novel's foregrounding its relation with the reader and its thematizing of the problem of the truth of fictions. The question of origins is insistently present: we need only note how often we are made to *begin* reading in this work. We begin at the beginning of the narrator's discourse: a limping soldier emerges from the Hospital de la Resurrección, in Valladolid, outside the Campo gate. This beginning is located with documentary precision. Within a couple of pages we begin reading *El casamiento engañoso*, and from the end of this story we move quickly through a brief dialogue between the Licenciado and Alférez Campuzano to the beginning of the *Coloquio*. This is not all: the opening of the narrative presents the meeting of two former friends in a new relationship that has to take account of the drastically changed condition of one of them. At the same time, this encounter of friends points to the past, to a friendship whose origin is hidden from us. And if the narrative denies us knowledge of the beginning of the friendship, the story of the deceitful marriage denies us knowledge, in any deep sense, of the origin of Campuzano's desire for Estefanía. In this composite and complex work, margins become centers, genres call each other into question by their contiguity and their supplementarity. The picaresque life of Berganza is believable in its referentiality and consistent with convention in its mode of presentation, but unbelievable in its canine speaker.

Our expectation that we begin at the beginning is led off on branching tracks. If we disentangle the temporal sequence that Cervantes has deliberately raveled up, we find that he begins the telling almost at the end of the sequence, just when two friends are united, to their mutual surprise. Everything else that is to be told has already happened. Not until we have read the *Casamiento* and the *Coloquio* and have reflected on the last words of the whole, "'Let's go . . . .' and with that, they went," do we perceive that this insignificant event has been the climax, the recognition scene of the untold story. What the telling of the *Casamiento* and the *Coloquio* does for the speakers is to transform their narration of experience into a significant event. Between the beginning and the end, the matter is conveyed in flashbacks; unusual flashbacks, because they do not bear the usual causal relation to the narrative that contains them. They neither develop a situation nor create suspense in the principal narrative (the friendship story), but rather displace it and even efface it from the attention of the reader. This is one of a number of ways in which Cervantes defeats the reader's expectations concerning structure, temporal sequence, and causality.

If the friendship of the two men is not accounted for, and acounts for nothing but the telling, the infatuation of Campuzano for Estefanía is another beginning that is simply there, but resonates through all that happens to the Alférez thereafter. The manner in which these two play out their unconvincing drama of desire suggests possession by fantasies that have little in common with mature passion. His pursuit of his shabby femme fatale, Estefanía's simulation of the reformed wanton—these postures reveal them acting out the scripts of debased cultural codes, courtly and domestic. The mystery is the deceit, which is blind to both its origins and its effects. Neither he nor she stands to gain anything by it. Not only their marriage but their narrative is a deception. The story becomes a beautiful example of mimetic form, deceiving the reader by its seeming simplicity, its easy symmetries, the Petrarchan epigram tacked on at the end. It demands to be complemented by the *Coloquio* because it is too neat; its compactness, its symmetries and repetitions are evidences of the repression that has made its composition possible, and that will be challenged by the dialogue of the dogs.

If his story exemplifies anything at all to the speaker of it, it is not the neat poetic justice of deceivers being deceived, but rather the mystery of desire. Desire is misled as to its ostensible source, which in this case is his brief glimpse of Estefanía's little white hand. Unable to determine its true origin, desire compulsively transforms itself into narrative. At a deeper, subtextual level, Campuzano and the dog Berganza share the same desire and tell the same story. Berganza's story is really Campuzano's story, the one Campuzano was unable to tell.

The unknown author of *Lazarillo* and Alemán, in their different ways, question and thematize the desire to tell and to write. Lázaro's insolent duplicity is contested by Guzmán's urge to confess, and by the troubled gaze he turns upon his failures and his unreachable motives. Cervantes, in this last of the *Novelas ejemplares*, has made each member of his cast, both as speaker and as listener, reach back for an occluded past, search compulsively to explain who he is, why he should be believed. Their compulsions feed our desire for the knowledge of origins as we try to explain to ourselves where the story *really* begins, and also our desire for (and fear of) closure. Within his frame, Cervantes has made friendship partially motivate the desire to tell and to listen, to read and to understand. But that is only a start, for beyond that he tantalizes us with mysteries of origins, of the relation between desire and narrativity. He symbolically displaces the origins of his characters' experiences and makes a playful mystery of the ability of the dogs to discourse in human language (Berganza is convinced that he was born human but was changed by witchcraft). The intimate implication of beginning and ending that we have noted in *Lazarillo* and in *Guzmán* is here given unprecedented complexity, with recognition within recognition, epiphany within epiphany. And the reader is implicated both in Berganza's picaresque, dog's-eye view of the world and in what Alban Forcione (1970) has called Cervantes' "humanist vision." Like Peralta, the reader in the text, we have to find the truth in fiction for ourselves, then close the book and go out to look anew at the world: to "renew the body's eyes," having already "renewed those of our understanding," in Peralta's words. We, the readers of the whole, cannot fail to be influenced by a strategy of closure in which the characters, in true readerly fashion, have already restructured the provisional meanings of the partial texts of their lives. The end is a new beginning.

7

Rogue Females

The word *pícara* appeared in writing for the first time, as far as I am aware, with *La pícara Justina* (1605), by Francisco López de Ubeda. This is the first of a number of novels by various authors with female protagonists. It marks a new departure, but the newness is to be found not only in the fact that the principal figure is a woman but also in its literary relations, in where it comes from and where it is going. Also, Justina is no more typical of the antiheroines who come after her than Lazarillo was typical of later picaros. Neither of them imposes a fictional stereotype. But the very fact of being female imposed new roles and eliminated others from the narrative; a *pícara* is not, and could not be, simply a female *pícaro*.

La pícara Justina was licensed for publication in the year that Alemán's Part II of *Guzmán de Alfarache* appeared in print (1604) and the two works are peculiarly linked, as much by their differences as by their few similarities. Guzmán's telling of his life is fully motivated, whereas Justina's has no justification; in Rico's words, it is "an absurd sham" (1984:73). *Guzmán* is serious; *Justina* is frivolous from start to finish. Guzmán's reflections upon his life are inseparable from his narrative of it; the little moralities (*aprovechamientos*) that the author puts into Justina's story are placed at the ends of chapters so the reader can easily skip past them. They interrupt the narrative by being where they are, and they always draw attention to the fact that the narrator and the implied author are not the same, because the text of the female narrator is presented by an unidentified and implicitly male commentator. The unity of consciousness that Alemán strives to represent across a lapse of time and a change of heart has been replaced by a split into two quite separate personae. Moreover, this woman, this incorrigible trickster, far from repenting, has just made her third marriage—to Guzmán de Alfarache! *Justina*, then, contests Alemán's project in every respect: significant structure, didacticism, discursive level, unity of voice, gender.

That *La pícara Justina* is a riposte to Alemán's project may be inferred from the protagonist's parting words ("being married to don Pícaro Guzmán de Alfarache, my lord" [Valbuena, 884–85]), in which she promises a continuation. The sequel will contain an account of her life with her husbands Lozano and Santolaja and, finally, with Guzmán, "in whose marital company I am now the most celebrated woman at any court in matters of games and harmless pastimes, pursuits, activities, displays, fashions, fancy dress, farces, singing, repartee, and other pleasant things" (885).[1] Some of the Spanish words in this list carry overtones that were not entirely innocent. It would be difficult to imagine a future for Guzmán that was more remote from Alemán's mind than an alliance with this flighty, vain, verbose, showy, luxury-loving moll. Difficult, too, to conceive of a relation with the reader that was further from Alemán's prescriptive either/or (you will be *vulgo* or *discreto lector* according as you attend to the *conseja* or to the *consejo*): "Libros son de poco gasto y mucho gusto. . . . Dios nos dé salud a todos, a los lectores para que sean paganos, digo para que los paguen, y a mí para que cobre, y no en cobre" (Books cost little and comfort much. . . . God grant us all good health, so that readers will be pagans, I mean payers, and so I can collect, but not

---

1. ". . . en cuya maridable compañía soy en la era de ahora la más célebre mujer que hay en corte alguna en trazas, en entretenimientos, sin ofensa de nadie, en ejercicios, maestrías, composturas, invenciones de trajes, galas y atavíos, entremeses, cantares, dichos y otras cosas de gusto."

in copper coin [885]). The facetious and punning style is established from the start: *gasto/gusto* (expense/pleasure); *paganos/paguen*
(pagans/payers); *cobre/no cobre* (collect/ not in copper coin). López
de Ubeda states in his "Prologue to the reader" that he decided to
publish his playful book ("este juguete") because nobody reads
books of devotion or lives of saints, and that he had written it
while he was a student at Alcalá, in his idle moments, "though it
grew a bit after that book about the Picaro came out and made
such a stir" (707). It would be interesting to know how much truth
there is in this declaration: whether he had really begun the book
before the publication of *Guzmán*, Part I; if so, how his reading of
Guzmán had influenced his conception of his own work. How did
the students he mixed with in Alcalá (if indeed he was a student
there) receive *Guzmán*? With sardonic laughter, perhaps? Or is his
claim to have composed it as a student rather a deliberate intertextual echo of Rojas' account of how he wrote *Celestina*? The ancestry
of *Justina* can be traced both to *Celestina* and to *La lozana andaluza* as
well as to the immediate presence of *Guzmán de Alfarache*, although
nothing in *Justina* could excite the most prurient of readers.

López de Ubeda, a physician, appears to have been closely connected with the court of King Philip III. He dedicated his book to
the royal favorite, Rodrigo Calderón, but we cannot say what favors, benefits, or protection, if any, he hoped to achieve by doing
so. Like the famous Dr. Villalobos of the previous century, he
seems to have combined the functions of physician and court
joker, and to have used his position to make many in-jokes.

We observed with what awkward defensiveness Guzmán took
his stance at the scene of writing; uncertain of what and how
much to reveal of his disreputable parents, caught between
shame, a residual piety, and the desire to reveal everything; making a preemptive strike against the logic-choppers over his shoulder. Justina, too, prevaricates, though her parents are not so
deeply corrupt as his were: they have the stereotypical dishonesty
of their trade, and her hesitations and false starts seem to be mere
caprice. But López de Ubeda addresses the moment of writing in a
manner that problematizes it and trivializes it in the same gesture;
he makes a travesty not only of Guzmán's embarrassment but also
of Cervantes' mock self-portrait of a writer who is unable to get

started on his prologue to *Don Quixote*.[2] She addresses her pen, but not as an honored friend or trusted servant, as was usual, for this friend has betrayed her: there is a hair on the quill, which smudges and spoils whatever she writes.[3] The quill came from a duck; real pens were cut from goose quills, and the idea of a duck quill is ridiculous. Duck (*pato*) and hair (*pelo*) generate more untranslatable wordplay.[4] The hair on her pen gives rise to a seemingly endless flow of puns on every conceivable sense and the remotest connotations of the word *pelo*. The proverbial phrase "no tener pelos en la lengua" (to have no hairs on the tongue), meaning to be free with one's tongue, applies truly to her: the flow of verbosity is unquenchable. The hair (*pelo*) on her pen draws attention to her loss of hair (*pelada*), which readers would recognize as a symptom of syphilis: there is more hair on her pen than on her head. The smudges (*manchas*) produced by the hair on the page besmirch what is already written, but cannot entirely conceal it, and at the same time they draw attention to themselves. The pun on *mancha* (stain, defect, ignominy, dishonor) is crucial:

¿Ofrecéisme ese pelo para que cubra las manchas de mi vida, o decísme a lo socarrón, que a mis manchas nunca las cubrirá pelo? . . . Mas entended que no pretendo, como otros historiadores, manchar el papel con borrones de mentiras, para por ese camino cubrir las manchas de mi linaje y persona. (711)

Do you offer me the hair to cover the stains on my life, or are you slyly insinuating that there's no hair that can cover my shame? . . . Unlike other chroniclers, I don't intend to stain the

2. On López de Ubeda's familiarity with *Don Quixote* before the 1605 publication date, see Bataillon 1969, 1973c.

3. "Un pelo tiene esta mi negra pluma. Åy pluma mía, pluma mía! ¡Cuán mala sois para amiga, pues mientras más os trato, más a pique estáis de prender en un pelo y borrarlo todo! . . . En fin, señor pelo, no me dejáis escribir" (710).

4. "No sé si dé rienda al enojo o si saboree el freno a la gana de reirme, viendo que se ha empatado la corriente de la historia y que todo pende en el pelo de una pluma de pato. Mas no hay para qué empatarme; antes os confieso, pluma mía, que casi me viene a pelo el gustar del que tenéis, porque imagino que con él me decís mil verdades de un golpe y un golpe de mil verdades" (710). (*Pato*, duck; *empatar*, to tie (as a score), to check, to stymie; *viene a pelo*, fits the case).

paper with lying smears so as to cover up the stains on my person and my family.

The seemingly chaotic stream of associations started up by the hair on the pen reveals the ravages of age and sex, and she angrily accuses it of causing her to reveal what she did not intend. What *is* revealed is not chaotic; it is the result of a deliberate play of signifiers: the hair spoils the writing, but were it not for that *pelo*, causing the smear, dragging the ink, staining her dress, releasing a runaway chain of signifieds, this chapter could not exist. The *pelo* and the *mancha* are both totalizing tropes and yet they also deconstruct the text before our eyes. They upset the normal logical hierarchies of cause and effect, of event and consequence. This writing is the consequence of the inability to write. Both the writing and the stain that mars it strive to realize self-presence in the text and also to efface it. The hair is a material thing that interferes with the flow of writing; it is also the sign of the repressed at the very point of origin that returns to disrupt the intentionality of writing; as a trope it is produced by the very discourse that it has set moving. As Justina says: "colijo para conmigo que mi pluma ha tomado lengua aunque de borra, *para hablarme*" (my pen has found a tongue, I guess if only of lint, to speak to me) (711; my emphasis). The hair, the tongue on her pen, speaks to her, but more exactly, it speaks her. As Barbara Johnson has noted: "When one writes, one writes more than (or less than, or other than) one thinks" (1990:42). This double fiction played upon the reader, the pretense that the hair prevents her from writing even as she writes her unstoppable flood of words and the contrary pretense that it has caused her to write *more* than she intended are signs that López de Ubeda's project has nothing in common with Alemán's.

La pícara Justina is a *jeu d'esprit*, at the far extreme from Alemán's claim to linguistic responsibility. In his Prólogo, López de Ubeda lamented the quantity of profane literature; people watch plays that are full of deplorable examples, and nobody reads edifying books. If he were to write the kind of book that the times need, it would not be read, so he has composed this frivolous entertainment full of salutary warnings (*desengaños*) (707–8); that is to say, he does what other writers do, with the difference that his "warnings" are so conspicuously tagged that they are easily avoided.

Any reader who does linger over them will be amused by their comically solemn ineptness. It is, of course, untrue that no one read edifying books. These prefatory chapters also evoke the stereotype of women in general (not only Justina) as garrulous and self-contradictory. The question of female stereotypes inscribed in the female rogue literature will be considered later.

Typically, Justina is prefigured in her ancestry. But whereas Guzmán squirms in his writing as he brings out his parents' history, Justina's prose leaps and pirouettes as she recalls four generations of merry fellows, all of them performers who had the gift of gab. Even their deaths provided entertainment, as in the example of a tamborine maker who was attacked by a man who had a grudge against him as he was playing his pipe in a procession:

> He gave him a great punch on the end of his flute and stuffed it down his gullet. . . . It wouldn't budge until a tavernkeeper got it out with a great heave as if getting a pipe out of that body were a matter of getting a funnel out of a pitch-coated wineskin. . . . In short, with that tug the pipe came forth, and with it out flew the leaping, hustling, prancing, dancing, jigging little soul, just like quicksilver. (736)[5]

Passages like that one reveal the kind of book it is. It has no narrative structure worth mentioning, it is not a life with a trajectory that can be assigned to a typology, and its discourse does not fit into any of the categories that other picaresque works have adopted. It is sui generis.

5. ". . . le dio una gran puñada en la hondonada de la flauta y atestósela en el garguero. . . . [Y] nunca quiso salir, hasta que de un estirijón se la sacó del cuerpo un tabernero, pareciéndole que lo mismo era sacar una gaita de aquel cuerpo que sacar un embudo de un cuero empegado. . . . En fin, de aquel envión salió la gaita, y junto a ella revuelta, aquella animita saltadera, brincadera, bailadera, sotadera, que parecía un azogue." The last phrase, with its diminutives, recalls the emperor Hadrian's poetic farewell to his soul, "animula vagula blandula, / hospes comesque corporis, / quae nunc abibis in loca, / pallidula, rigida, nudula, / nec ut soles dabis iocosi," and the similar verses dictated by Ronsard on his deathbed: "Amelette Ronsardelette, / mignonelette doucelette, / très chère hostesse de mon corps, / tu descens là bas foiblette, / pasle, maigrelette, seulette, / dans le froid Royaulme des mors" (A son âme, 27 December 1585) (both in Familiar Quotations, ed. John Bartlett, 15th ed. [Boston: Little, Brown, 1980], 123).

Beyond the Canon

The insistent presentation of death as farce transgresses every reader's expectations of such scenes, and has no equal, except perhaps in Quevedo, in Valle-Inclán, and in Monte Python. Her father, an innkeeper, is killed by a blow from a customer as he is about to adulterate the horse's feed. At least, says Justina, he died without leaving medical bills. The body is left overnight in the bakehouse, with a dog as guard. The dog smells the wedding feast:

> . . . when the cursed little dog sniffed the stew and the meat, it began to bark to get out, and finding that we didn't open up, it went to complain to its master, who was stretched out on the floor. When it saw that he didn't get up to open the door, and supposing that he hadn't heard, it went to shout in his ear. When it seemed that he wasn't taking any notice, it took offense, and to get revenge it grabbed him by the ear; seeing that he remained obstinate, it tore off the ear, roots and all, and dispatched it to its stomach. Then in case he'd been deaf in that ear, it went to the other one, remembering the wise saying: "If one door doesn't open, try the other." So it went and harangued the other ear, with the same result. The dog must have figured: "This guy is *really* dead, but my mistresses are alive; I'm starving and they're celebrating. They're celebrating the wedding without me? All right, I'll have my own celebration. . . ."

When Justina returns, her dead father is unrecognizable.

> When I saw the dog had filled up on innkeeper flesh, and found my father's face disfigured and his body dog-eared, I felt sorry for him. I might even have believed my mother did too, if I hadn't heard her say, "Hell, what am I going to do with all that carcass? Where's the needle and thread to stitch him up?" (745–46).[6]

6. ". . . el diablo del perrillo como olió olla y carne, comenzó a ladrar por salir, y viendo que no le abríamos, fuese a quejar a su amo, que estaba tendido en el duro suelo. Y como vio que tampoco él se levantaba a abrir la puerta, pensando que era por falta de ser oído, determinó de decírselo al oído. Y como le pareció que no hacía caso de él ni de cuanto le decía, afrentóse, y en venganza le asió de una oreja; y viendo que perseveraba en su obstinación, sacóla con raíces y todo, y trasplantóla en el estómago. Con todo eso, por si era sordo

They make frenzied attempts to patch up the corpse with butcher's meat; and so it goes on. This scene cannot be explained by any of the conventionally accepted touchstones of picaresque. It has no obvious connection with the possibility that the author may have been a *converso*; if he brutally assaulted conventional pieties, so did the pure-blooded conservative Quevedo. The illusion of a documentable narrative realism is no part of this author's project. The absent Justina "knows" exactly what events took place in the locked bakehouse, and in what order, and she can tell us what passed through the mind of the dog, even though she is not cast in the role of omniscient third-person narrator. The logic of the dog, its dynamic of affront and revenge, its recourse to proverbs to clarify a situation simply stress the author's indifference to consistency of voice, point of view, and similar notions. Or rather, his comic world depends precisely on a verbal structure in which human and animal, animate and inanimate displace each other, where the logic of the joke prevails over all literary and social proprieties, over *decoro*, verisimilitude, proportion. The dead father becomes food for a dog; the mother dies eating.

The dog devours the father out of human feelings of rancor, and the mother is overwhelmed by what she tries to conceal. The death of Justina's mother occurs when a butcher has left a string of sausages mounted on the spit over the fire in the inn kitchen. The mother plays the part of an officer of the law, and orders the sausages to dismount along with their companions, some legs of lamb. They refuse, and appeal to their absent master. This scene is played out in legal jargon as a burlesque of a police confrontation and interrogation; the sausages are arrested and confined to the prison of her stomach. When the butcher arrives to rescue his

de aquel oído, acudió al otro, acordándose que suele ser respuesta de discretos: 'A esotra puerta, que ésta no se abre.' En fin, acudió a la otra oreja, hizo su arenga y la misma diligencia. El perro debió de hacer su cuenta: 'Este está muy muerto, y mis amas muy vivas: yo muerto de hambre, y ellas de boda. ¿Así que sin mí hacen boda? Pues yo haré la mía sin ellas. . . .' Cuando . . . vi al perro harto de carne de mesonero, y la cara de mi padre tan descarada, y el cuerpo tan emperrado, dióme lástima. Y aun yo creyera que la tenía mi madre, si no la oyera decir: —¡Valga el diablo tanto muerto! ¿Dónde tengo yo ahora hilo y aguja para andar a coser muertos?"

"men," she hastily stuffs the rest of them into her mouth where they are packed so tight that they can neither advance nor retreat.

> The butcher demanded an explanation. . . . And the best part of it was that besides having her throat crammed, there was a length of sausage sticking out of her mouth, so that some said she looked like a dragon on a coat of arms, with its tongue out, others said she was like a woman who had been hanged, to some she resembled a wineskin with its spigot, and to others a windpipe with a loose end, to others a newborn monster with its cord not cut; to some she seemed to be a magician with festoons coming from his mouth, and to others a snake in the entrance to a burrow. But to the butcher she appeared as an ambush full of enemies, a den of thieves, and in short, the tomb of his sausages.[7]

Narrative logic is suppressed (who were the "some" and "the others," when did they say what they said, and to whom, and to what effect?). The consistency of the scene depends solely on Justina's aesthetic of verbalized comic surprise: *lo lindo* (the funny part). The mother dies when the bystanders fail to extract the sausage, leaving Justina astonished that her soul could escape through that crammed gullet.

Rather than write a "picaresque novel," López de Ubeda plundered recent fiction for his own comic and satiric purposes. His readers could see how he was fooling with earlier fictional motifs and situations, flouting expectations, or wildly exceeding them. Justina's parents, as innkeepers, are stereotypically dishonest, as was Lazarillo's father, the miller. Lázaro and Guzmán reveal themselves through their parents; but Justina goes back four generations. And they are trivial cheats, figures of farce. Her acts are insignificant, provoked by neither pride nor shame; they are not stages in a process of socialization, nor do they give significant shape to a life of cumulative experience. The narrative is inter-

---

7. "Entró el tocinero, y pedíale razón de sí y de su gente. . . . Y lo lindo era que demás de estar relleno el gaznate, le sobraba fuera de la boca un pedazo de longaniza, que a unos parecía sierpe de armas con la lengua fuera, a otros ahorcada, a otros bota con llave, a otros garguelo con cabo, a otros que era boca recién nacida con ombligo cortado, a otros tropelista con trenzas en la boca, a otros culebra a boca de vivar."

rupted, its sequence broken by bizarre juxtapositions whenever the narrator follows random associations, allusions, and the possibilities of polysemy. Adventures boldly announced by the narrator turn out to be trivial cheats, or misadventures, or pranks, or displays of verbal ingenuity.

It may be impossible ever to discover to what extent *La pícara Justina* is a deliberate travesty of *Lazarillo* and *Guzmán*. Their normative pattern of journey and quest, marking an ultimate desire for acceptance, has left no trace here. Justina's journeys are undertaken mostly for fun, or to get back at persons who have made her look foolish. They do not, taken as a whole, "imitate the rhythm of a life."[8] Justina faces no hardship and little danger. Rather than travesty the episodic structure of *Lazarillo* and *Guzmán*, Justina exploits the same vast repertory of facetiae, *chascarillos* (wisecracks), and *burlas* (practical jokes) that they had incorporated into the architecture of their plots. It has much in common with the poem *La vida del pícaro* (c. 1600), which is a joyous celebration of a life of freedom. This poem, which praises the life enjoyed by wandering students and beggars for its freedom from ties to one place, to work, to routine, to authority, could be described as "urban pastoral" insofar as it is anticommercial and anti-industrial, and it takes no account of the floods, the plagues, the miseries of winter, the hostility of sedentary citizens. It offers to the fantasy a release from both society and its demands, and also from nature with its rigors and constraints. Marcel Bataillon has said that *La pícara Justina* offers a new concept of *la picaresca*, namely, a picaresque way of life. That is true so long as we recognize that the "picaresque way of life" is opposed to the picaresque novels: it is a life of release, not of struggle, a praise of poverty, not a desire to escape from it, an almost evangelical "take no thought for the morrow." It looks back to the goliardic tradition of tavern humor. This attitude reappears in Cervantes' *Ilustre fregona*, where the wellborn youth Diego de Carriazo runs away from home to the picaresque life among tuna fishers for no cause other than his own high spirits. A long chapter in *Justina* (II.i.1) is devoted to just such praise of singing, dancing, fun.

Bataillon has shown that this book is full of in-jokes, that many

8. Bataillon's phrase (1969:44–45).

of the ridiculous figures in it allude to real people, objects of the author's mockery of the power elite. Justina's journey to and sojourn in León alludes to a recent visit of the royal court in February 1602 (Bataillon 1969:35). As capital of the early Christian kingdom where memory of the Romano-Gothic ancestry and resistance to the Moors remained strong, León was a symbol of Old Christian pride. The episodes in this section of the book can be read as part of López de Ubeda's assault on the manifestations of this pride and exclusiveness, and on the obsession with "purity of blood." There are jokes about genealogies, about the vast quantities of paper consumed in proving one's ancestry, and even a kind of surrealistic transcription of inquisitorial investigations into family history (Bataillon 1969:40). Justina herself repeatedly returns to the subject of her ancestry, in ways that would confuse and provoke the reader. She flaunts her "impure" (non-Christian) blood in those diehard regions. She travesties the protracted investigations into the ancestry of applicants for honors and titles—*desenterrando los difuntos* (disinterring the dead), in the common parlance of the time. Justina even claims to be the heir of a wealthy dead *morisca* who was a notorious hater of Christians (III.4.861–63). She is a deliberate affront to *honra* as it was lived in that Spain obsessed by purity of blood (Bataillon 1969:196).

López de Ubeda's verbal art is an art of mockery, of double entendre, of euphemisms and allusions, of *motes* and *apodos* (epithets and nicknames), an art at which Spaniards reputedly excelled, in the estimation of foreign observers (Bataillon 1969:42; Joly 1986:5). Employing the double mask of a trickster and a woman, the doctor López de Ubeda, like the doctor Villalobos and the jester Francesillo de Zúñiga before him, goads and taunts his place-seeking fellow courtiers with transparent (but to us obscure) social allegories. His book would have been read as burlesque rather than as novel, as political satire and skit: calypso for an upper-class audience. Like all literature that is relevant to a particular public at a particular moment, it is almost meaningless to another audience and another time without the aid of an interpreter.

Being the kind of book it is, *Justina* tells us virtually nothing about the voice or the subjectivity of real women. It draws upon the perennial male stereotype of the garrulous woman, whose chatter follows a hopelessly irrational impulse. The characteristics that typify the *pícara*—deceitfulness, greed, inconstancy, and so forth—are precisely the ones that had always been attributed to women in the classical and medieval tradition of rhetoric (Schwartz-Lerner 1989). It is possible that some of the authors who worked this stereotype of garrulous womankind may have done so because of the opportunites it offered for a show of linguistic virtuosity rather than because they wished to affirm the gendered ideology that supported it or to make a statement about women's irrationality. Even in the Arcipreste de Talavera's *Corbacho*, which is truly in the medieval tradition of misogyny, the famous set pieces in which he mimics a woman distracted by the loss of an egg and then by the loss of a hen (ii.1), are showpieces of comic rhetorical invention. In the late fifteenth and sixteenth centuries, a great impetus is given to the literary representation of unconventional, nonliterary discourse. The *Celestina* and its many sequels are the most obvious examples, with their bawdyhouse and tavern talk, their gossiping servants and bragging soldiers. But these works are innovative also in introducing baby talk, or the pitiful attempts of a beaten child to speak through his sobs (Sancho de Muñón, *Tragicomedia de Lisandro y Roselia*, 1542). It may be the case, as Royston Jones claimed, that these works satisfied a need for greater realism, and that they "manifest an interest in human variety for its own sake" (1971:64–65). They also should be seen in relation to contemporary debates on language, its resources, and the meaning of change. These writers are aware of being involved with language as something *made*, fascinated by the madeness of *parole* as against the givenness of *langue*. So *La pícara Justina* illustrates the paradox that established stereotypes and caricatures may provoke vigorous originality. But Quevedo, picking up the latest *pliego de cordel*, and the writers who frequented fin-de-siècle vaudevilles and music halls would not have found that paradox surprising.[9]

9. In *The Antiheroine's Voice* (1987), a kind of Hegelian history of the will-to-be of the female voice in Hispanic fiction, Edward Friedman continually refers to Justina as if she were not the author's invention but a real being with an existence beyond the text. This treatment is curious because it contradicts not only the rhetorical theory and practice of the Golden Age but Friedman's own theoretical assumptions. For example, the declaration that Justina "resists self-examination" (94); but self-examination, it should be clear, is never a possi-

Female protagonists, by the very fact of being female, impose new roles and therefore changes of design. In the novels that followed, little girls were not put out to serve masters, as Lazarillo was. Girls did not leave home on foot in search of a fortune, or go to universities, or walk the streets looking for an employer. All of these acts, plausible for the young male, were implausible for the young female of the seventeenth century. On the other hand, Alonso de Salas Barbadillo's Elena is the only protagonist, male or female, to be executed (in the third person, naturally) for participating in a murder. Later female rogues are more deliberately criminal than Justina, and the differences between her and Salas Barbadillo's *Ingeniosa Elena, hija de Celestina* (1612, 1624) or Alonso de Castillo Solórzano's Rufina in *La garduña de Sevilla* (1642) are as great as any in this problematic genre. In the novels of Castillo, the financial swindles and confidence tricks of the protagonists enable them to move and to be accepted in circles of high aristocratic opulence. Did this mobility correspond to the facts of life in the second quarter of the seventeenth century? Did the great cities of Spain encourage upstarts to falsify a name and an inheritance in the hope of making a prestigious marriage, and female tricksters to lodge themselves in the expensive demimonde? Our knowledge of people and big cities tells us that the answer must be yes in each case.[10] Castillo, a humble secretary to politically important aristocrats, did not so much explore the social construction as exploit his own preferences and his social definition of his public. For as long as the protagonist succeeds in his or her deception, the author can exploit the kind of formula he worked successfully in his *novelas cortesanas*: love and intrigue in plush surroundings, with aristocratic name-dropping and much of the realistic paraphernalia of the urban nobility.

---

bility or an option in this work. One must suppose that it is required to be an option by Friedman's project: to plot the emergence and the vindication of a feminine voice and discourse. Here is a curious example of a generic determinism (though a different one from that which is the subject of this book) skewing the reading of an individual text.

10. José Antonio Maravall (1986:644–47) presents evidence to suggest that women became more demanding of jewelry and similar luxuries ("son las mujeres costosísimas de sustentar" was a typical complaint [647]), and that bejeweled women were items of male ostentation. Reality evidently kept pace with the rhetoric.

Justina's first-person narration is a joke. All subsequent female narratives are in the third person, except Castillo's *Niña de los embustes, Teresa de Manzanares*, where the mode of autobiography is unmotivated and nonfunctional. None of these authors shows any interest in the layered temporal aspects of experience that gave the first novels their profound originality: incorporation of past experience into the self and the social perspective of the narrator; recovery of the past in the present moment and situation of writing. Their adventures are connected by nothing more than an overlapping cast of characters, and they turn predominantly upon the sexual baiting of men. The one constant narrative unit is the confidence trick, with a degree of theatricality not found in the earlier works, except for the episode of the pardoner in *Lazarillo de Tormes*. Castillo's *Garduña de Sevilla y anzuelo de las bolsas* (1642) provides a sample. Rufina and her partner, Garay, overhear some robbers talking about their leader, Crispín, who has evaded detection by posing as a pious hermit and keeps the loot in his hut. Rufina decides to play the damsel in distress, and for this purpose she has Garay tie her to a tree within earshot of Crispín's hut. She does not simply scream "Help!" but declaims: "Will no one come to the aid of an unfortunate woman who is about to lose her life? Heaven have pity on me and avenge this affront to my innocence!" Garay takes the role of the heartless attacker: "It's useless to cry out to someone who's not going to free you! Commend yourself to God in the little time you have left to live; as soon as I have you tied to this tree, I'm going to stab you to death!" (Valbuena, 1574b).[11] As they had hoped, Crispín rushes out to the rescue, entertains her in his hut, and falls in love with her. She learns of his plans for new assaults and is able, through Garay, to betray the whole band into the hands of the law. The robbers are hanged; Rufina and Garay keep the loot. After some more expedient betrayals and executions, Rufina sets up shop with a handsome young lover and they sell silks.

Castillo pushes all his plots, picaresque and nonpicaresque, in

---

11. "'¿No hay quien favorezca a una desdichada mujer que la quieren quitar la vida? ¡Cielos, doléos de mí y vengad el agravio que se le hace a mi inocencia!' . . . '¡No tienes que dar voces a quien no te ha de remediar! ¡Encomiéndate a Dios el poco tiempo que te queda de vida, que luego que seas atada a este árbol te he de sacar el alma a puñaladas!'"

the direction of the prevailing *novela cortesana*, the novel of love and adventure. Were he a wittier writer, passages like the one just cited could be mistaken for pastiche of bad melodrama. Rufina is made to look less like a criminal than like a heroine of romance because she is set up against men who are more violently criminal than she is, because she is a woman, and because beauty, in the simplistic moral and chivalrous world of Castillo and his readers, has its prerogatives. As soon as she begins scheming to betray the bandits who have sheltered her, all right-thinking readers know whom to cheer; it may not be cricket to abuse hospitality and hide the loot, but what could be worse than cloaking crime in false piety? When Crispín escapes and seeks revenge, she becomes the heroine and co-opts the reader's sympathy, not by heroic virtue but by opposition to the vengeful male monster. Once the heroic mantle has descended adventitiously upon her, it is too late to protest when she reaps every reward a true bourgeois heroine could pray for: marriage, wealth, and a good business. This denouement does not quite achieve the propriety of a *novela cortesana*, since the couple have had to flee to Zaragoza to escape their latest victims. And we can be reassured that the two worlds (of romance by birthright and romance by fraud) are not really interchangeable when the couple set themselves up in the retail trade. That is something the best people would not do. So the bourgeois happy ending contains an unresolved ambivalence that would be felt differently by different publics: crime (ingenious fraud, not brutality) does pay; but blueblooded readers looking down from their comfortable height could view the successful accommodation with amused disdain. Those readers who had made it into the urban respectable middle class or lower aristocracy might feel less comfortable in their disdain. To those who were sliding into poverty, clinging heroically or pathetically to their *hidalguía* and their *honra*, such fictions were very possibly a too vivid representation of what their world was coming to.

The sensibilities of Castillo's world are peculiar, and they must remain incomprehensible to modern readers unless we take account of the fact that his novels have reverted to the tradition of facetiae and practical jokes that antedates *Lazarillo de Tormes*. Almost any act, however monstrous, is presented as a joke, and any person may be the object of one. Rufina's robberies are jokes, and so are Teresa's brutal acts of revenge. In *La niña de los embustes*, a young man is in love with a girl who does not respond because she is infatuated with a choirboy, who is a castrato (*capón*). In the literature of this period castrati, hunchbacks, dwarfs, nearsighted persons, cripples—in sum, anyone who falls short of a Hollywood standard of physique—may fairly be the object of ridicule, so Teresa sees fit to play a "joke" on the singer by claiming to have invented a lotion that will promote the growth of a manly beard. The promised remedy is a bottle of acid, which will leave him disfigured for the rest of his life. Knowing a good thing when he has one, Castillo recycles this joke and another ingenious little piece of cruelty directed against quack doctors into short dramatic farces and inserts them into the text. Each of Rufina's depredations in *La garduña* is presented as a joke and made acceptable by some moral or physical shortcoming in the victim. An example of this moral compensation (so to speak) of the immoral act can be seen in the authorial treatment of Marquina, a miserly old man who has nonetheless lodged Rufina lavishly in his sumptuous house and fallen in love with her. She ransacks his house and decamps. Usually the narrator pays no further attention to the victim, but in this case we are told, with some complacency, that the loss of his property and of his hopes of gaining Rufina drove him crazy and that, because he was stingy, there was rejoicing in Seville at his "punishment."[12] The jokes, tricks, and swindles in *Lazarillo* and in *Guzmán* form part of the representation of a cumulative experience; they are fragments of an internal mirror in which the writing consciousness reviews the processes of its formation. They and Quevedo's *Buscón* did not bring to an end the independent literature of facetiae; they may rather have fostered it. Works such as Melchor de Santa Cruz's *Floresta Española* (1574, 1592), Gaspar Lucas Hidalgo's *Diálogos de apacible entretenimiento* (1606), Cristóbal Suárez de Figueroa's *Pasajero* (1613), Sebastián Mey's *Fabulario* (1613), and others testify to the continuing vigor of this tradition. Salas Barbadillo

12. ". . . en Sevilla fue celebrado el hurto, holgándose muchos de que fuese así castigado quien tan pocas amistades sabía hacer con lo que sobraba" (1550a).

and Castillo Solórzano exploit it in a sense totally different from Alemán's—an escapist, cynical sense—while keeping up a pretense of moralizing.[13]

What the *pícaras* have in common is rejection of both of the traditional roles of the female protagonist: the wife (submissive or faithless) and the mistress (inspiring or merciless). These traditional roles either support or threaten the male whose acts and choices are the real matter of the narrative. The female rogue, by contrast, may entice male victims, but she is independent of their social roles. Indeed, since she is most typically a confidence trickster, she operates by exploiting automatic masculine expectations concerning her sexuality, her need for male protection, and so forth and then frustrating them. It is because these expectations pass unquestioned in traditional cultures that she can exploit them; it is important to note that though the men are fooled, the social roles and practices on which their expectations rest are not exposed as folly, however arbitrary they may now appear. Sometimes she is caught; it then becomes clear that her exemplary punishment is more than the wages of theft and deceit: it is the consequence of upsetting the assumed "natural" order of things, the price of abandoning the roles programmed for her in the system of the culture.

Although these stories are cruder and less provocative than *Lazarillo* and the other exemplars, they reveal something about the limited conditions within which the individual self may escape from the prescribed social roles. These conditions are clearly negative ones for the female protagonists; they always require some level of criminality, and all the *pícaras* resort to masks, disguises, denial of identity in the ingenious swindles they bait with sex in order to contend with the world of male authority and inherited wealth. These lives of adventure usually terminate in marriage

13. See the comments of Pablo Jauralde on the moral drawn at the end of each section of *Las harpías en Madrid*: ". . . tan traída por los pelos y en evidente contradicción con el texto anterior. Porque, en definitiva, lo que el libro enseña y sus primeros lectores aprenderían es aquello que decíamos del triunfo de la astucia y la malicia—escudadas en las apariencias—sobre el poder y el dinero valiéndose de las convenciones y falsos valores de la época. Para mostrarlo se emplea la perspectiva picaresca y femenina, en doble degradación": "Introducción" to *Las harpías en Madrid*, ed. Pablo Jauralde (Madrid: Castalia, 1985), 30.

with a man of the same social class and qualities; less frequent is capture and punishment by the law. It is notable that the sex that functions as a lure is never more than a lure. There are some brief male-female partnerships in crime, but the norm is that a man falls in love with the *pícara* only to be fleeced. Even as she escapes from the institutional order into her role as parasite, the picaresque anti-heroine confirms the authority of that order in fundamental ways. She has no sexual role except one that is legitimized by the institutional order.

It is useless to look for any trace of authentic feminine discourse in these narratives. The question of gender is occluded; it is absent as a discursive category. This is not surprising when we observe that the very few women writers, except María de Zayas, strive to write stories that are virtually identical to those of male novelists, except for some very occasional remarks on male tyranny by a female character. Although the construction of the female self in these fictions departs from the positive models of wife and mistress, it is still tied to a powerful traditional conception, or set of conceptions, of the feminine. These conceptions are, of course, masculine in origin and transmission; they are continuous with ancient medical notions, they perpetuate long-standing misogynistic attitudes, and they are sustained by a rhetoric that also can be traced from classical through medieval literature (Schwartz-Lerner 1989). In particular, they portray women as irrational, unpredictable, and unstable. These conceptions are appropriate for underwriting the role of woman as trickster: less amenable to reason and morality than men, women are consequently more inventive and better liars, have a livelier fantasy, and can pull off frauds more convincingly. They are ruled by their desires, and in this kind of fiction the desire is for wealth—jewelry, sumptuous apartments, carriages, the conspicuous wealth of the times. A *pícara* is a comic mask by means of which a male author can impersonate the prevailing conceptions, and thus validate them in a tight little loop of demonstration. The feminine is a traditional male-generated category that has been activated to provide entertaining adventures of a uniformly unscrupulous kind. It does not open a way into the margins of the society, and it cannot call into question the way that the female gender is appropriated by the male narrator.

Identity, the reality of the self, is grounded in the everyday life of the society. As Peter Berger and Thomas Luckmann express it, "the individual can live in society with some assurance that he *really* is what he considers himself to be as he plays his routine social roles, in broad daylight, and under the eyes of significant others" (1966:101). Given that the everyday life of a society is validated in turn by the symbolic universe that envelopes it, the phenomenon of the rogue female is interesting in a very particular way. She is both something more and something less than an ingenious literary twist applied to the already popular male pícaro. She pursues money and ostentation for the pleasure of it, whereas the male protagonist may hope to rise socially. Thus, in spite of all her evasions, her masks and disguises, invented identities, acquisition of riches and other external keys to status—silks, jewelry, carriages, servants—the *pícara* is not transformed, but diminished. Her sexuality is flaunted, not enjoyed. She is a machine, a device invented by the author for conceiving entertaining swindles and bringing them to birth. My metaphor of conception and birth makes clear the sexual displacement and sterilization that occur in these novels. There is a great distance between such a literary creature and the intellectual female adventurer of eighteenth-century France, who finds her sex of value in her efforts to transform her social role. The *pícara*'s liaisons are business partnerships, or masks with which to gain mobility. Teresa, in Castillo Solórzano's *Niña de los embustes* (1632), marries a merchant, an occupation with a very ungentlemanly smell to it in seventeenth-century Spain. That was the end of her story—one of profounder poetic justice than Castillo may have suspected.[14]

However we look at these females, we find that they have, in effect, been neutered by their separation from a society that is both patrilineal and matrifocal. Power and creativity (intellectual, cultural, economic) are ascribed to the male, veneration to the chaste

14. In a neat formulation, Marcia Welles writes that the "trials and tribulations of these *pícaras* as they seek a *buen puerto* prove both the 'vanity of virtue' and the 'virtue of vanity'" (1986:68). This phrase, however, like the article of which it is a part, loses sight of the fact that these *pícaras* are creatures of male fantasy created for purposes of entertainment. Their victims never enjoy authorial respect. The paradox that their depredations are eventually accommodated, if at all, within a bourgeois setting is really no paradox, given the prejudices of these writers.

(including the dedicatedly reproductive) female. The symbolic universe or functioning world view that validates self and society and orders their mutual relations, assigns values, and justifies institutions was of such a kind in seventeenth-century Spain that no creative transformation of the traditional roles of the fictional heroine was possible except simple inversion.

8

Dissemination and Dissolution

Juan Martí: *Segunda Parte de "Guzmán de Alfarache"*

Juan Martí's spurious Second Part of *Guzmán de Alfarache* (1602) is easily dismissed as tedious, poorly constructed, inconsistent with Alemán's original.[1] This is all true; but the work is not merely inferior, it is different.

Martí's continuation is grafted minimally onto Alemán's Part I. Guzmán leaves the French ambassador; he also refers back to earlier events from time to time, as some new situation recalls an experience narrated by Alemán. The desire to change his ways, though captive to his accustomed picaresque life, is stated at intervals, but it lacks the tense dialectic between past and present selves that Alemán was able to create.[2]

---

1. Parker 1967:45, Rico 1984:37–38. The *Segunda parte de la vida del pícaro Guzmán de Alfarache, compuesta por Matheo Luxán de Sayauedra, natural vecino de Seuilla* was published in Valencia in 1602. The identity of Juan Martí behind this "Luján de Sayavedra" was evidently known to Alemán; see Alemán's revenge in his own *Segunda Parte* (1604), II.ii.4., where a false friend of Guzmán named Sayavedra goes mad and drowns himself.

2. "Dejar yo de tomar o poco o mucho era imposible, que se me había

Martí's digressions are of a different order. Like Alemán's, they fall into two temporal and discursive categories: those that were part of the action and those that occur to the narrator as he writes; but the difference is that, on the level of the narrated action, Martí's digressions are not acts of self-examination. In a moment of crisis, Guzmán sits and reels off a traditional commonplace on the wretchedness of human existence (i.2) or the blindness of love (i.6). Asked by the Italian cleric to whom he has attached himself for some information about Spain, he delivers a long and vibrant eulogy on his country, its cities, its noble families, its conquests, and so forth (i.3). Other speeches and monologues are reported; for example, the curious quarrel between two members of the Pignatello family, in which the one who had been accused of having a servant insult the other refused to appear and defend himself in battle, but kept insisting that the accusation be documented. This clash between the systems of honor and jurisprudence would be of interest to the jurist Martí, and to present-day cultural historians, but it has no relevance to the novel's action or to the narrative constitution of a picaro's self. In a lengthy disquisition a Basque "proves" historically and juridically that all those of his nation are by birth hidalgos (ii.9–10). Moralistic reflections (in praise of poverty, on sensuality, on impatience in the young, on the wiles of women, etc.) alternate with random observations (on astrology, on how clothes confer authority, on dreaming, on the various categories of notaries, etc.). When Guzmán wolfs his food at great speed, onlookers annotate the event with references to great eaters in history and legend, citing appropriate authorities (i.3). Imagine what Sancho Panza's response might have been to this extraordinary pedantry, had it been served to him by Basilio's cousin (in *DQ*, ii.22)! These trivia are not redeemed by being presented in the form of paradox; indeed, their triviality is made more conspicuous and their truth put in question. We are informed, for example, that the Flemings are great locksmiths, although people in Flanders are respectful of property; in Spain, where thieving is rife, the locks do not work (i.1). In the same paragraph we learn

---

convertido en naturaleza" (ii.1); "Así yo . . . perseverara en el buen camino comenzado: pero era mi natural seguir mis apetitos, que eran bien desordenados" (ii.6).

that stairs are steep and unsafe in Flanders, though the people frequently get drunk; in Spain, where heavy drinking is frowned upon, the stairs are broad and safe.

The one extended passage of didactic address which is structurally important to the novel occurs in Book ii, Chapter 4. As Guzmán and his traveling companions are resting at Montserrat, they talk of their lives as beggars, the tricks and deceptions they practice, the sham cripples they have known, the stolen infants they have used. This conversation is overheard by a hermit, who comes forth from behind a rock, sits with them, and delivers a homily on true and false mendicancy, advising them of the spiritual danger in which they are placing themselves, as well as depriving the genuine poor of what is due to them. Guzmán, who begins by listening unwillingly, ends by resolving to leave this way of life and make good his intention to study at the university and to "follow the path of virtue and religion" (Valbuena, 625b). The reason for this clumsy transition is that Alemán has explained in his preliminaries that Guzmán studied and became "a very good student in Latin, rhetoric, and Greek," and that he wrote his life after being sentenced to serve in the galleys. Martí, then, had to get Guzmán into the university, and to connect this move with awareness of the spiritual self within the man of appetite and of habit, as it was established by Alemán.

In order to profit from Alemán's success, Martí needed to do two things: to continue Guzmán's life of trickery while incorporating the future events that Alemán had made public, and to sustain the dialectic between past and present, intention and act, narrator and narratee. Neither of these desiderata is competently achieved, and we may ask what Martí could have done; what conventions of composition and narrative structure would have supported him? An author who successfully continues the work of another has not only to imitate the other's specific traits but to have mastered the devices it shares with the type. The existence of the spurious Part II of *Guzmán de Alfarache* raises the question what could have been the characteristics of the type.

There really was neither a concept nor a stable practice of "picaresque writing" for Martí to assimilate. Apart from continuing the story, he was either unable or unwilling to structure his narrative around the picaro's bad conscience, as Alemán had done. He observes the requirement to have Guzmán educated and to terminate his career as a galley slave, but his learning is accessory and anecdotal. The digressions bear no organic relation to the whole, but are trivia gathered from such widely used handbooks as Pedro Mexía's *Silva de varia lección* and the *Officina* of Ravisius Textor (Jean Teissier, sieur de Ravis).[3] The defense of the nobility of the Basques is lifted from Juan Gutiérrez, *Practicarum quaestionum*. Moreover, he has a more pressing agenda of his own: to take Guzmán to Valencia to witness the wedding of King Philip III. This goal is announced in Book ii, Chapter 7, we are reminded of it at intervals, and it determines the rest of Guzmán's itinerary until he finally arrives in that city, in the book's penultimate chapter (iii.10). The series of events is then described in abundant detail: the arrival by sea of Margaret of Austria at the port of Vinaroz in a fleet of forty-one galleys on the 28 March 1599; the grandees and ecclesiastical dignitaries who received her; the comings and goings of the archduke Albert; the cavalcades into the city of Valencia on Sunday, 18 April; the processions into the cathedral; who preceded, who accompanied, and who followed; all the great names, with their silks and finery and jewels. The marriage ceremony is transcribed verbatim, in Latin. Then follow the feasting and the dancing, the public illuminations, the fireworks and salutes of artillery.

> And to conclude, with the quality and quantity of persons, the grandees and great titles alone numbering more than seventy, with the richness and beauty of the clothing, the grandeur and abundance of liveries, the beauty and bearing of the horses, the decorations and finery along the streets and squares, and with

3. Other identified works plundered by Martí include Alejo Venegas' *Agonía del tránsito de la muerte*, Alonso de Cabrera's *Sermones*, Alonso López Pinciano's *Philosophia antigua poética*, and Cristóbal Pérez de Herrera's *Discurso del amparo de los legítimos pobres y reducción de los fingidos*. See Américo Castro, "Una nota al *Guzmán* de Mateo Luján de Sayavedra," *RFE* 17 (1930):285–86; Miguel Herrero García, "Nueva interpretación de la novela picaresca," *RFE* 24 (1937):343–62; Enriqueta Terzano and José F. Gatti, "Mateo Luján de Sayavedra y Alejo Venegas," *REH* 5 (1943):251–63; Donald McGrady, "Mateo Luján de Sayavedra y López Pinciano," *Thesaurus* 21 (1966):331–40; Bernadette Labourdique and Michel Cavillac, "Quelques sources du *Guzmán* apocryphes de Mateo Luján," *BHi* 71 (1969):191–217.

countless other things that were put together for this triumphal occasion, it does not seem possible that there will ever be seen in any other place, any other time, or any other occasion a more solemn, more opulent, or more joyous spectacle. (696b)

On the following days there are more processions and banners, daily jousting, an oration at the university, more finery, ceaseless aristocratic glitter; all the great names are admired for their lineage, their courtesy, their opulent display.

In the following and final chapter, Guzmán plays his last anticlimactic tricks, is arrested, tried, and sent to serve his sentence. It is evident that Martí, in completing what Alemán began, complies with the minimal postulates of the existing story, and does so in the most mechanical way. He has no concept of a generic picaresque matrix within which to develop his narrative, but this is not surprising, because there was no such generic matrix. This manner of ending, however, reveals Martí's own project in completing the *Guzmán*. These triumphal scenes occupy the whole of the last chapter but one, and this is by far the longest chapter of the book, more than twice as long as the others. This placement of an actual historical event witnessed, perhaps, by the author and the monumental space given to it are significant.[4] Martí makes

4. We cannot assume that Martí personally witnessed everything he describes. Even if he was able to witness it all, he did not need to rely on his own memory or notes in order to incorporate it in his novel, since contemporary *relaciones*, or news sheets, had given minutely detailed accounts of each stage of the royal progress, beginning with the betrothal of the archduchess Margaret by proxy in Ferrara, 13 November 1598. See Mercedes Agulló y Cobo, *Relaciones de sucesos*, vol. 1: *Años 1477–1619* (Madrid: CSIC, 1966), items 307, 311–14, 320–25, 328–30, 332-35, 338, 342. Of these eighteen *relaciones*, all but three relate the ceremonies and festivities in Valencia. Item 330 (in verse) claims that "por extenso se relata todo el acompañamiento que se le hizo [al rey], con los nombres de todos los Grandes y Titulados, y muchos Cavalleros, con las diferencias de las Libreas que cada uno traía, y los aparatos, y regocijos que hizo la Ciudad en la dicha Entrada." Item 338 relates the solemn oath taking at the ceremony on the first Sunday in Lent, "y los personajes que le besaron la mano, y las fiestas que uvo en la dicha Ciudad, y los Arcos Triunfales que auia, y de que estauan entapiçadas las calles. Y como en el vn Arco estaua una bola y della salio vn Angel, y San Vicente Ferrer, y en otro auia otra, a modo de Granada, de la qual salio vn niño, y le dio una Clauellina á su Magestad, y otras cosas que salieron de la dicha bola." In fact, Martí could easily have narrated it all without having been there, everything was so well documented. It

clear by such means that this chronicle of the royal entry, nuptials, and festivities is no mere "digression," like the observations upon the impatience of youth, the truth and the dangers of astrology, or the benefits of sleep—digressions that every extensive narrative employed to achieve variety and to acquire authority and truthfulness. Rather, this passage recalls that exalted praise of Spain and everything Spanish that occurs near the beginning (i.3). Here we have to recognize that Martí has his own agenda, which is to contrast the deceits and petty criminality of the protagonist and his associates with the splendors of imperial Spain, and especially the triumph of that Spain as it affirms, once again, its Habsburg destiny in a dynastic marriage celebrated in his own city, Valencia. It is clear that Martí made his text permeable to versions of reality that Alemán had excluded: a world of exalted ceremony and noble personages in which his readers could take patriotic pride. Alemán's anger is comprehensible, but it is impossible to imagine him trimming his *Segunda Parte* to Martí's pedantic and sycophantic model.

The patriotic sentiment, the desire to clear the authorial voice, to distinguish it from that of the narrator and align it with imperial attitudes and with the interests of the great noble families, is a characteristic to be found in almost all the seventeenth-century novels that have been called picaresque, and especially in those that abandon the first-person mode of presentation. Later we shall note another text, Luis Vélez de Guevara's *Diablo cojuelo*, where the climax of the tour of the cities of Spain is the scene of the evening *paseo* along Madrid's Calle Mayor, where all the titled personages and their splendid retinues parade in a glittering array of gilded coaches, culminating in the royal couple and the Holy Roman emperor, Ferdinand, with his empress, to the admiration and applause of even the humblest *mulata*. Satire has its limits, and they are tightly bounded by social class and national sentiment.

---

is evident, too, that he was not alone in wishing to transmute a public event into literature. Apart from the anonymous verse-narrative cited above, we find the following (item 339): "Romance a las venturosas bodas que se celebraron en la Insigne Ciudad de Valencia. Va nombrando todos los Grandes que se hallaron en ella debaio de nombres Pastoriles. Compuesto por Lope de Vega."

All the novels of low-life adventure written after Cervantes' *Novelas ejemplares* are drawn into the orbit of the *novela cortesana*.

Vicente Espinel: *Marcos de Obregón*

In 1618 the poet and musician Vicente Espinel published his *Relaciones de la vida del escudero Marcos de Obregón*. This work had a quick success, being printed in Madrid and also in Barcelona (twice, by different printers in this city) in the same year.[5] This is the novel that yielded most material to Alain René Lesage for his *Gil Blas de Santillane* and consequently it has a certain importance in the history of the novel in France and, more widely, in Europe. It helped to form Europe's idea of what a Spanish picaresque novel is and gave a firm direction to the development of indigenous picaresque literature, but it is not easily recognizable as picaresque now. Its place in the canon of *la novela picaresca* has long been in dispute.

Frank Chandler made no distinction between this and other picaresque works, but Francisco Rico declares that *Marcos* is "obviously not a picaresque novel" (1984:124). Angel Valbuena Prat included it in his anthology, but Alberto del Monte objected that it is rather an adventure novel or an autobiographical novel (1971:108–9), a judgment repeated by Alexander Parker (1967:54–55), among others. Marcel Bataillon's characterization of the protagonist as an "antipicaro" is taken up by Del Monte and by Harry Sieber (1977:35).[6] How can the conformism and the humanistic outlook of this work be considered picaresque? asks Del Monte.[7] Parker and Richard Bjornson (1977:70) speak not of a break with tradition or

5. Madrid: Juan de la Cuesta; Barcelona: Sebastián de Cormellas and Gerónimo Margarit. The Consejo Real had given its permission in October of the previous year.

6. "*Marcos de Obregón* constituye, en efecto, una verdadera humanización y rehabilitación de la honra 'escuderil.' Marcos encarna todas las virtudes del buen escudero; perfecto servidor de los nobles, se inspira en su orgullo matizándolo de filosofía, sin excederse del lugar que le corresponde en la jerarquía de las personas *honradas*. Casi nos atreveríamos a decir de él que es el perfecto anti-pícaro" (Bataillon 1969:209).

7. "Marcos ha sido definido precisamente como el antipícaro, en cuanto es la encarnación del honor, que supera la honra externa y se basa en la virtud" (Del Monte, 1971:109).

an antipicaresque novel but rather of a new direction taken by the genre. Espinel evidently did mean to write something different: the title, *Relación de la vida . . .* , puts it, formally, in the same drawer with other first-person memoirs, and Espinel blended his own life and experience into his fiction (Haley 1959).

Calling it a *novela de aventuras* does not help us out of the difficulty; in a broad sense all picaresque novels can be classed as adventure novels, along with chivalric romances and the newer long fictions by such authors as Céspedes y Meneses and, later, Castillo Solórzano. *Don Quixote*, parody and satire that it is, is obviously an adventure novel also. Sieber points out traits that would put *Marcos* in the category of romance, but we have already noted that *Guzmán* and all other long fictions that are picaresque in parts (and others not picaresque at all) can be categorized as romances. If, indeed, this novel was located at some boundary, this fact will be of interest for both our concept of picaresque and our understanding of literary history.

Marcos' story is told in stages to a listener (a hermit) and only later is it supposedly written down. The motive for writing is "the instruction of youth" (Valbuena, 925b), though Espinel does nothing to make this motive believable. The story is marked off formally from the earlier works by the order of telling. It begins not with the narrator's parents, home, and childhood but with his recollection of his service as "squire" (*escudero*) in the house of one Dr. Sagrado and his wife, and some of the adventures in which he became involved there. The term *escudero* no longer denotes one who serves a knight and carries his arms, or the kind of famished squire we find in *Lazarillo*, the fly-by-night master who lives (he says) for honor. These negations are instructive. Marcos is a worthy individual, not a hero in shining armor or an empty shell but a man who is usefully occupied in a world where heroics are repeatedly made to look ridiculous and dangerous.

The oral narrative is addressed to the hermit who occupies a shrine beyond the Puente de Segovia on the outskirts of Madrid, and is in two parts (II and III) separated by the interval of a night. Part I is a reminiscence that appears to be addressed to the reader. It is not clear how these parts fit chronologically, and they cannot be forced into a neat sequence. The story as told orally begins with Marcos' boyhood in Ronda (Espinel's own native city) and ends with his decision, as an old man, to retire into solitude to prepare himself for death. The course of his life has taken him to many parts of Spain as well as to Italy and to captivity in Algiers. Formally and conceptually, Espinel's novel is far from Alemán's. Marcos has served a number of masters, including members of the high Spanish nobility. He has served them well and not engaged in swindles. He has been a student at the University of Salamanca. Now an old man, he is retiring from the world. By the time he writes up his story and adds Part I, he is an elderly inmate of the charity hospital of Santa Catalina. His break with the past is not abrupt or dramatic, so his relation with the reader is less urgent than Guzmán's. The many anecdotes, reflections, and commentaries are relaxed in tone. There is no sudden moment of truth, so Marcos does not rewrite his personal history as an exemplary fable, nor does he force the reader to make reading a matter of personal salvation. The story's movement through journeys, shipwrecks, and lucky escapes fits no symbolic pattern.

Marcos' relation with his world does not correspond to that of any picaro. He is not an outcast, not alienated, not a victim. He is not tempted to blame the world for what he is. He is an honest man with no ambition and no desire to make mischief. His few practical jokes are committed in self-defense or are designed to avoid direct and violent confrontation; they have a heuristic value that is uniform with the whole thrust and intention of the book.

The order of the telling—the long episode of his service in the house of Dr. Sagrado, followed by his life since childhood—appears arbitrary, and might be taken as deliberate deviation from picaresque works. This period of service, taken out of the temporal sequence, has its own unity and is also a paradigm of the whole narrative. Dr. Sagrado, a man of quick temper and great vanity, has a wife, Mergelina, of similar condition. In the house there are no books, but there are a large mirror and an imposing collection of swords, daggers, and bucklers mounted on a wall, items that are clearly metonymic. Mergelina is a proud beauty who falls for a young barber's assistant. Marcos' principal duty as *escudero* is to chaperon the wife, so he has to perform the part of a discreet retainer, rescuing her from the consequences of her own impetuosity, hiding the gallant when her husband returns unexpectedly. He even stage-manages the husband's unexpected return as a prudent warning to them. By the time he leaves their service the couple has learned some caution and the would-be lover has withdrawn from the scene. So, by his calm control and his ingenuity, this servant of mature years has contrived to preserve life and honor in situations of danger and defended the cast of characters from the consequences of their actions.

At the opening of his narrative, Marcos tells of an incident that took place only a few days ago. He is laying hands on a sick person and reciting the prayer to perform a cure when a passer-by remarks on the "frauds of those imposters" (926b). His companion draws his attention to the remark, and Marcos' reply is: "He was not talking to me, and I am not obliged to resent or to pay attention to anything not addressed to me." To take offense at remarks that the speaker lacks the courage to address to him directly is "great stupidity" propounded by men who wear their honor on their sleeves. One should not take offense unless the case is patently obvious, and even then it is best to avoid confrontation if possible (927a). These prefatory pages announce the book's thematic core or subtext: "to set one's face against the perils of time and fortune and so to preserve honorably the precious gift of life that the Divine Magesty has bestowed on us" (925a-b). The dangers to which this "precious gift of life" are exposed include all forms of irascibility and especially those that are socially sanctioned: revenge, a bridling sense of honor that is always alert to occasions to take offense. This theme is worked out through a dialectic of impatience, anger, and frustration on the one side and patience, compromise, and ingenuity on the other (A. M. García in *Picaresca*, 609–18). A man spends time, energy, and application learning how to wield a sword and become expert at it, but with less time and effort could become expert in wielding the weapon of patience; that is, learning to control the "bestial impulses" of rage. Patience demonstrates strength of mind and will, not to be confused with ignoble submission or laziness, as they say in Italy: patience, as Marcos understands it, polishes and refines the virtues, producing peace of mind and body (927b).

In *Marcos* 1.21 we see this program in action. Marcos enlists as a soldier in the fleet that is being assembled at Santander. The admiral takes a liking to him and makes him an *alférez* (ensign), and this favor arouses the envy of a presumptuous young hidalgo (*un hidalguete*), who enlists his companions in an effort to dislodge

Marcos from his position. Marcos ignores all provocations until the other man calls him a liar in the presence of his companions. Marcos can no longer fail to respond, but if he hits the man, his companions will cut him to pieces, so he embraces him and leaps overboard, knowing that his enemy cannot swim. The drama turns to comedy as the hidalgo struggles and hangs on to Marcos, who can punish him with impunity, while the companions on deck are reduced to laughter (989b–990a). Marcos tells us that at that time he was choleric by nature, so the incident is to be read as a lesson in self-conquest as well as a comedy of table-turning and a shaming of the insolent.

Just before meeting the hermit, Marcos is engaged in conversation with a gentleman, an hidalgo, who would like to hire him as tutor for his son. The conversation, a dialogue on the education of a gentleman, suddenly turns into the introduction to a burlesque comedy as a herd of cattle is driven onto the bridge. Marcos prudently gets off while the hidalgo stands his ground, attempts to fend them off with his sword, and is unceremoniously butted aside. The incident is glossed by A. M. García: "The use of the sword and the whole sociomoral ethos embodied in it put life and reputation in danger, while Marcos preserves both from his peaceable corner" (*Picaresca*, 611).

This resilience in the presence of inevitable violence is the larger message of the book. It manifests itself as patience and wit in action when the violence is irrational, as in the case of animals, thunderstorms, and men who cannot control their arrogance and rage, or are too stupid to be aware of what they are doing. It has a subversive edge, as García's words indicate, precisely because the goal here is not to survive in the face of hunger, callous masters, and cruel exploiters but in despite of cultural codes that sanction haughtiness, petulance, and use of the sword. Beyond survival, it is to enjoy relaxed and rational discourse. This claim may appear to be contradicted by the urgings of Marcos to respect and show reverence for the bearers of authority. In Salamanca, for example, he and fellow students find their lodgings uninhabitable, and are questioned by the Corregidor for being on the street after dark (1.12). The others look surly, but Marcos takes off his hat and bows low before answering; by his courteous response he induces the Corregidor to feed them, and they enjoy his favor from then on.

Although the city authorities do not have undisputed jurisdiction over students, Marcos rebukes his companions: persons of duly constituted authority are entitled to our respect and courtesy, whether or not they are our superiors, and not only because they have a right to it (God has created distinctions of rank and degree) but because they can do us greater hurt than we can do to them (965b).

That was, fortunately, an instance of authority vested in a man who knew both his power and his responsibilities and showed compassion. On a later occasion (1.14) Marcos is waylaid by men posing as game hunters who are really highway robbers. He maintains a cheerful countenance, and when his captors realize that he is traveling alone and penniless, they take him to their hut and debate whether or not to kill him. Marcos entertains them with stories, pretends to praise their way of life, and finds some quality to praise in each one (973b). Later, when Marcos and his companions are on the island of Cabrera, they are surprised by Turkish marauders. Marcos dissuades his friends from trying to defend themselves against impossible odds: Why invite annihilation? He ingratiates himself with his captors, addressing their interpreter as "noble gentleman," pretending to have known him, and proffering similar "vanities," as he calls them (1014b).

Very near the end, the narrator meets his former master Dr. Sagrado, who escaped from captivity by a race of barbarous giants: he, too, has saved his life and those of his comrades by exercising patience and ingenuity and eschewing useless heroics. The episode of the giants in the cave (III.19–22) recalls the story of Ulysses and Polyphemus and underscores the parallel that Espinel intends to establish between his concept of heroism and Homer's: that of Ulysses, not that of Achilles. For Marcos de Obregón, patience creates the space in which ingenuity and resourcefulness can go to work. It must be active on behalf of the self and others, and only then is it a virtue. Without this intelligent activity, patience is sterile and indistinguishable from servility or faintheartedness.

The narrative is cyclical, since the narrator disrupts the linear autobiography in order to begin and end with Dr. Sagrado. Following the example of his wise and resourceful retainer, the irascible doctor and his provocative wife have learned how to cope with adversity and come through with dignity. The novel, then, is a demonstration of its own heuristic assumptions as the lessons of patience, reflection, affability, and resourcefulness under duress are learned, applied in new situations, shared with comrades in adversity, and passed on. Dr. Sagrado, the reluctant neophyte, has become a seasoned practitioner of the art of patience, has triumphantly survived his own adventures, has a story worth the telling, and has earned the right to be his own exemplary narrator. At the point where Marcos concludes his repetition of Sagrado's story, he also concludes his own. Sagrado has graduated, the cycle is complete, the moment for Marcos to retire from the world and make himself ready to face death is at hand.

Espinel disappoints modern readers who look for ugly realities, pessimism, and bitterness. This book requires different reading strategies and expectations. Marcos avoids confrontation by observing the forms of order and authority. He earns acceptance; he is listened to; he gains a foothold in the territory of the other, where the power is. We see him acting out his theory of patience in the face of at least three modes of power: the duly constituted power of a judge; the violent, arbitrary power of highway robbers; the violent but customary traffic of war and piracy. He would not try to stand in the way of a stampede of cattle, nor does he attempt to defy a thunderstorm, but takes refuge with the hermit in his shrine, the appropriately named *humilladero*, a place of humility.

So rather than read Marcos as "submissive" or as accepting the "norms and values of a society which Alemán regarded as irrevocably corrupt" (Bjornson 1977:72), we should see him judiciously picking his way in a dangerous world, a rigid and vindictive culture ceremonious in its forms, but also—and here is the key—one that values courtesy. In even the grimmest society a key is available to the person endowed with patience and ingenuity. It is misleading to say that Marcos accepts a world that Alemán did not, because they do not register different responses to the same "possible world." The two protagonists face different realities.

With the literary tradition of romance Marcos' outer world shares soldiering, voyaging, shipwreck. The conventional world of comedy (lovers hiding in closets) is also present. There are many references to the actual world: the plague in Seville (II.6); a description of how a ship breaks up in a storm (II.7); life in a newly established village (1.14). There are conversations in a wide variety of settings, particularly in inns and on the road. Many of them consist of stories exchanged by travelers, stories of human folly or credulity. Marcos tells how he was taken for a necromancer and a small man came and begged him to use his powers to make him taller. A discussion on bringing up children is devoted partly to refuting foolish expectations and widely held fallacies. There are curious digressions on great feats of memory, on teaching music to children, on the water in Italy compared to that in Castile, on the prevalence of fog at Turin, on ghosts and apparitions that are really vapors, or human contrivance. Marcos' world is peopled by credulous and superstitious individuals, but more important, it is inhabited by others with whom Marcos can converse rationally. Repeatedly he finds himself in the company of thoughtful, speculative minds, and he sets down in his narrative the conversations that have passed between them. He assumes that his readers are rational people, and therefore he depicts a possible world in which irrational fears and superstitions may be dispelled in talk and laughter among men who have achieved the patience to discriminate. Fear and superstition belong to the same order of aberration as irascible or hasty judgment and impetuous action.

Bjornson observes that after *Guzmán de Alfarache* Spanish fiction "in the picaresque tradition" splits into four categories: those like Martí's spurious *Guzmán* Part II, *Marcos de Obregón*, and Jerónimo Alcalá Yáñez' *Donado hablador Alonso, mozo de muchos amos*, which "retain the morally serious tone, encyclopedic tendency and autobiographical perspective"; parodies of Guzmán, such as *La pícara Justina* and *El buscón*; picaresque adventure stories by Castillo Solórzano and Salas Barbadillo; and the "socially critical novels" of the exiles Juan de Luna and Carlos García. This observation has the merit of recognizing that after *Guzmán* there is no unified, coherent picaresque genre, but does so without noticing, apparently, that the "picaresque tradition" is thus rendered moot (1977:72).[8]

Espinel's novel of an aging penitent owes little to *Guzmán*. Marcos' career does not resemble Guzmán's, his determination to withdraw from the world is simply the final stage in a life characterized by mental clarity. His relation of aging mentor to the

8. Rico is fully aware of this state of affairs (1984:81–90).

young Dr. Sagrado follows a much older tradition than picaresque. Marcos is in the line of descent from the medieval figure of Good Counsel, and his ancestor in Spain is the Patronio of Don Juan Manuel's *Conde Lucanor*, who was also a mature man who wisely tutored his master. Before ending his days in the company of a hermit, however, Marcos the counselor has traveled the world; his life has been a pilgrimage. As pilgrimages go, this one has been as entertaining as it is instructive. He has survived by talking until his captors either forgot their intention to kill him or relented— here is a reflection of Scheherazade and other fabulous talkers. If *Guzmán de Alfarache* recalls the *Odyssey* in its pattern of travel and return and in its dependence on the sea for the return to the lost self, Marcos recalls the same work in the figure of the hero himself; the wily figure of admirable resourcefulness, always afloat in a world of tempest, violence, and malicious cunning. *Marcos de Obregón* is more complex than it appears at first glance, combining in itself more literary perspectives than one might suppose. And since the protagonist is an *escudero*, we should not forget the most recent literary example of that honorable profession, one who also has served an irascible master who becomes chastened by his experiences on land and water: Sancho Panza, loyal *escudero*, man of patience, avoider of unnecessary conflict.

Guzmán exerted a field of force, but as one work among others that played variations on the genre of romance, and Espinel set his *Marcos* in a new and unique relation with them all. *Lazarillo, Guzmán de Alfarache*, Lope's *Peregrino en su patria*, and the works of Cervantes represent a great reservoir of possible forms, themes, and motifs that could be broken down and reassembled as usable parts. Espinel experimented in his own way with autobiographical narrative, flashback, and an episodic life as a means for representing a cumulative experience and for testing the premises for living. As A. M. García says, *Marcos de Obregón* offers a new order of values in fiction, where patience is heroic and heroics are ridiculous.[9] It could not have been written without the example of *Don Quixote* or the very different *Guzmán de Alfarache*.

9. García claims that, by virtue of Espinel's admitted quickness to anger, "la novela es la confesión de un arrepentido" (*Picaresca*, 618). I am not concerned here with the author's possible self-projection, interesting as it may be.

Dr. Carlos García: *La desordenada codicia de los bienes ajenos*

Another interesting work with a marginal status in histories of the picaresque novel is *La desordenada codicia de los bienes ajenos* (The disorderly greed for other people's riches; abbreviated hereinafter as *Codicia*), published in Paris in 1619. Its author, Dr. Carlos García, was a Spaniard living in Paris. The story of Andrés, a famous thief, occupies the major part of the book, though not the whole. The work departs from what we expect of picaresque fiction in a number of ways, particularly in not showing the subject as having arrived at a new awareness of himself and in lacking any interaction with parents and other persons who embody the practices, values, and lines of power that operate in society.

La desordenada codicia opens with reflections upon the experience of imprisonment by a narrator who does not identify himself: the reader assumes that he speaks with the voice of the author. He relates that, being in jail, he came upon a prisoner with strange speech and manners, who promised to tell his personal story. This prisoner is Andrés, who begins his story in Chapter 3 and continues speaking for the remainder of the book's thirteen chapters. The original narrator (the implied author of Chapters 1 and 2) is the listener or narratee in the rest of the book. He does not speak again, even to resume his presence as implied author or reporter. The book has no formal closure: it ends when Andrés stops talking, as he does quite unexpectedly while reciting the constitution and rules that govern the thieves' community. The speaker stops speaking, but the frame is not closed; that is all.

In addition to problems of narrative coherence, stability of voice, and continuity of the relation of narrator and reader, there are others. Andrés' narration encompasses childhood memories and adult swindles, as one might expect, but it also contains a classification of thieves and thieving and other extensive nonnarrative sections. All of these elements are contained in Andrés' monologue. By normal standards of verisimilitude, they are misplaced. *Guzmán* and *El buscón* have burlesque ordinances, constitutions, and edicts, which are read aloud from documents. In *Codicia*, the final chapter consists of Andrés' exposition of the "statutes and laws of thieves," spoken extempore, although it has the features of a written text in bureaucratic style. Formal precedents for this kind of exposition exist in works by Cervantes. In *Rinconete y Cortadillo* the scout who takes the boys to Monipodio's headquarters explains the organization of the gang "family." But that is an exposition, not a recital verbatim. In *La gitanilla*, an old gypsy expounds to the young hero the structure of gypsy society with its rights and duties. The fact that the speaker is an elder of a community based on oral custom permits a lengthy exposition of this sort. He embodies its authority, and his seniority gives plausibility to his complete rhetorical control of his information. Carlos García's thief Andrés has no such authority; we did not even know him to be a member of an organization of thieves until this moment. Again we encounter a Vuestra Merced of problematic status and function, because the primary narrator/implied author/observer is also the Vuestra Merced to whom Andrés' picaresque narrative is addressed. His presence seems to need no explanation other than that he is reporting to us about this extraordinary fellow whom he met in the prison. But we are not prepared for his total effacement, for the fact that when Andrés stops addressing him as "Vuesa Merced," there will be nobody there.

Let us delve more deeply into the book, and then see how three readers, all writing at about the same time, arrive at three quite different interpretations.

The narrator begins by comparing the miseries of imprisonment with the pains of hell: privation of liberty for the prisoner is comparable to privation of God for the damned. Both reduce the sufferers to a less than human condition. Prisoners are denied hope, lose their true nature, are reduced to envying animals their freedom. This comparison is ingeniously amplified to include the darkness, the physical horror and confusion, and also the hierarchy of prison functionaries, analogous to the ranks of devils who minister in hell. The narrator does not say why he is in the prison, but he is no common criminal. He has money and he uses it to ingratiate himself with those who have none. He is the one to whom all turn to confide their troubles and to seek a sympathetic ear. He tells us nothing of himself; no name, place of birth, family, or age. We are not told where the prison is located, though at the end of his story we learn that his latest robbery and arrest occurred in Paris. The headings of the first two chapters name the first narrator as author; I shall therefore refer to him as Autor.[10]

On his first appearance, Andrés behaves so strangely that Autor thinks he must be drunk or crazy. He fears he is about to be sent to the galleys in Marseille and implores help in a strange, punning language so as to frustrate eavesdroppers. He is a witty fellow, as his career and his narration of it show. He possesses, he says, the elixir of life and the philosopher's stone; namely, the art of thieving. He is the son of thieving parents, so his origins and childhood resemble those of other picaros.

His father having been executed, he was apprenticed to a cobbler, but ran away because of "noble impulses that urged me toward a higher and grander calling than making shoes" ("ciertos ímpetus de nobleza que me inclinaban a cosas más altas y grandiosas que hacer zapatos"). The consequences are very different from those that befall Pablos el buscón as the result of his "noble impulses." Pablos falls into criminality, but Andrés purposefully adopts thieving as a noble and ancient profession. The first thief was Lucifer, who tried to steal God's knowledge and wisdom, a desire he passed on to humankind. All human history since Cain's attempt to steal God's favor from Abel, Jacob's hoodwinking of his father to cheat Esau of his birthright, David's murderous manipulations to steal Uriah's wife, and so forth, up through the exploits of the Greeks and their heroes, is the history of theft. This glorious art of thievery, invented in heaven, was passed down to the most noble earth dwellers, but it could not long remain the preserve of an elite, so it descended to the common people, and now there is no beggar who does not imitate his betters in this matter of thieving.[11] In order to recover from this general debasement and not to appear as a vice, it dressed itself in the forms of all the respectable trades and professions, forms that were invented for the purpose. Thieving is therefore both noble and universal; lengthy examples from history are then given. After this lively satirical *jeu d'esprit*, Andrés informs his listeners of the various kinds of thieves, then

10. i: "En el cual compara el autor la miseria de la prisión a las penas del infierno"; ii: "De un gracioso coloquio que tuvo el autor en la prisión con un famosísimo ladrón."

11. "No había remendón ni ganapán que no quisiese imitar la nobleza en ser ladrones" (Valbuena, 1174a).

recounts examples of ingenious robberies, including those in which he was caught. The book ends with the description of the *república* of thievery.

Charles V. Aubrun and Ricardo Senabre have offered interpretations of this work that are almost diametrically opposed. Aubrun sees *La desordenada codicia* as an ambiguous work that conceals its intention but reveals it by indirection. Greed that is *desordenada* (the unchecked aggressive appetite of the new bourgeois for property and position) calls forth its opposite, the orderly, more modest acquisitiveness of the traditional aristocracy and the peasants. The book shows the lines drawn for the class war as it reveals the current mentality. Aubrun also points out the book's many faults, its inconsistencies, its lack of continuity. He has a poor opinion of it and of its author.[12] Senabre, on the contrary, not only finds it to be a logical development within the parameters of the picaresque,[13] which had been broadened by Quevedo and Espinel, but claims for it formal balance and orderly progression (633). The life is structured on a pattern of repetitions (640) and is told from a moment of crisis, as the thief is about to be taken off to the galleys. The work starts from a vision of disorder and chaos and ends with the harmonious "republic" of the thieves' "model society," based on liberty, free from strife and injustice.[14] The paradoxes suggested by this reading give us pause. Are they really the deep structure that generates the work? This vision of a free and just society comes not from Autor but from the satirical Andrés. We know that criminal organizations resemble well-ordered societies, with family loyalties and so forth. If Autor

12. With such phrases as "Carlos Garcia está dispuesto a vender su pluma, su puñal y su honor [to his noble patron]"; "el pobre plumífero no se da cuenta de lo que va en el juego"; "sepultada quede en el olvido *La desordenada codicia*" (*Picaresca*, 629).

13. ". . . la autobiografía de un ser marginado, que ha heredado la vileza de los padres y cuenta su vida desde un estado de infortunio al que le han conducido sus bellaquerías" (*Picaresca*, 637).

14. ". . . la falta de libertad provocada por la acción de la justicia conduce al desorden; por el contrario, el orden y el buen gobierno son patrimonio de la libertad. . . . Apoyada en estas ideas el doctor Carlos García construye una novela en la que se exalta como modelo de buen gobierno una sociedad de ladrones basada en la libertad; una sociedad casi platónica en suma, donde los agravios, rencillas e injusticias han desaparecido por completo" (*Picaresca*, 644–45).

were to sponsor such a model, he would have to do so in the spirit of Voltaire, and Senabre makes no such claim. Andrés and Autor agree that prison is like hell; but the punishments meted out in both places are explained on a higher plane of justice and rational order. Or does Autor speak with the experience of Dr. Carlos García in the Paris prison of Fort-l'Evêque? If that is the case, Andrés' sarcasm is underscored by the writer's sense of grievance, *injustice*, revenge, and arbitrariness. Believers in divine justice must presume that hell is run on higher principles than those.

Andrés' world reminds us once more of that orderly society of Monipodio in *Rinconete y Cortadillo*, "good and holy," "to serve God and good people." Both are *rational* societies, admirably adapted to the world they prey upon. The society of thieves has attained a level of distributive justice, or equity, but only by insulating itself from the world where ethical values are worked out. If we read this final section as satire, the satire must cut both ways. The criminal society perfectly serves its ends, but within that society these ends are not to be critically examined or referred to any criteria beyond themselves. It is self-sufficient, administratively efficient, with an esprit de corps sustained by ceremonies. The outer world, the world of families and churches and schools, where values are formed, tested, and reinforced, is incapable of sustaining a society based upon rational order, of giving people what is their due, or of keeping innocent persons out of prison.

Aubrun sees *Codicia* as the work of a rather inept writer, who was attacking the bourgeois in servile submission to his patron's social class and unaware of what he was doing. Senabre is more concerned with vindicating *Codicia* as worthy of a place in the history of the picaresque novel. A large part of his emphasis falls on the autobiography of Andrés as the principal structure in the book, and on the claim that the genre has undergone important transformation while remaining true to its tradition.[15] This statement begs the question whether a tradition of picaresque fiction exists.

We noted earlier the anomalous role of Vuestra Merced in *Co-*

---

15. "El género ha asistido a transformaciones notables, provocadas por unos autores que desean innovar sin desarraigarse por completo de la tradición picaresca" (*Picaresca*, 633).

dicia. It is he, not the picaro, who writes, but he gives no motive for writing, and he does not conclude his book. And yet Senabre stresses the author's "avidity for verisimilitude." As earlier readers observed, Andrés' story is unlike a picaresque *vida* in important respects: he did not write it; it is a sequence of thieves' tricks, some of them not his own; he does not reveal his formation, the internalizing of experience and the construction of a complex response to the world, as do Lázaro and Guzmán. He prefaces his recollections with the view of human history as the history of thieving, and ends them with his account of the utopian thieves' community where individuals are assigned tasks according to their talents and capacities. Presumably these are his last words before he is shipped off to do his service as a convict. There are anecdotes, some simple, some incredible: he fools the captain of the galleys into believing he can make a woman love him by magic, and leaves him and his similarly lovesick majordomo tied up naked in the forest. Thieves are usually caught. These stories, framed by a diachronic vision of thieving as the characteristic human (and superhuman) activity and a static synchronic vision of the thieves' guild as microcosm, are part of a witty satire, more Gallic than Spanish. The activities described by Andrés resemble the beggar books or "anatomies" of thieving that were popular in England and France.

All in all, *La desordenada codicia de los bienes ajenos* is an interesting example of intercultural intertextuality. Spanish picaresque fiction was in vogue in France (Chartier 1987). But García did not write a short Spanish novel in the mold of *Lazarillo* or *El buscón*. He chose, while writing in Spanish, to display his mastery of the preferred French forms: episodes of trickery, formally balanced descriptions that embody social and moral paradoxes, like a *moraliste*. What is picaresque is denatured, stripped of significance for the narrative. If there is an urge to self-vindication, it comes not from the fictional picaro but from the real author, formerly inmate of the prison of Fort-l'Evêque, suspected of dabbling in magic and of trying to procure a magician for a companion's noble client. The fact that magic in this novel is always exposed as a hoax may be seen as part of Dr. García's plea of not guilty.

In various ways the text of *Codicia* demonstrates how an individual may merge into the dominant culture. The times were difficult for the Hispanic (Spanish and Portuguese) and Jewish communities in France. The royal Spanish marriages had been delayed until 1615, and each rapprochement between France and Spain spelled anxiety for the expatriates, many of whom were Jewish, others of whom were comrades of Antonio Pérez. García, like Pérez, was not Castilian but Aragonese. The classic picaresque works are a Castilian phenomenon, and Aragon produced writers who were disruptive of the dominant literary models, Alonso Fernández de Avellaneda (the author of the spurious Part II of *Don Quixote*) being the best-known example.

In 1617 García published, in a bilingual edition, a curious work titled *Oposición y conjunción de las dos grandes luminares de la tierra. Obra apazible y curiosa en la qual se trata de la dichosa Aliança de Francia y España: con la Antipathia de Españoles y Franceses*. This treatise uses astrology to create a celestial model of international politics. Spain and France being the "two great luminaries" that outshine all others in that firmament, their "conjunction" in the marriages of Louis XIII with Anne of Austria and of Elizabeth of France with Spain's Prince Philip promises an era of peace; their "opposition," when it happens, must make for the most malign horoscope for the destiny of Europe. He stresses the value that both nations set upon courage and honor and comments sharply on their differences in manners. But the differences are secondary to those values of courage and honor in the two Catholic kingdoms. The work has come to be known misleadingly by the short title *Antipatía*, but García was clearly concerned to ingratiate himself with the French court at the same time that he affirmed his loyalty to the pro-Spanish faction in that court.

It is a mistake to regard *La desordenada codicia* as one more Spanish picaresque novel. The reading strategies that such an assumption imposes prevent the reader from evaluating what is discordant in it. García has turned the picaresque inside out by making Vuestra Merced the primary narrator as well as the author; the picaro and his story are mediated through him to us. The pretext is this narrator's curiosity in the fellow's career, but the picaro has the secondary role of oral informant. His picaresque traits are empty of significance; he does not look upon the life that he has made and see that it is good; he does not write his text, nor does he ever read it, so it cannot be for him the mirror that it is for

Lázaro, Guzmán, or Pablos. His jokes are intellectual jokes, and he is unconcerned with honor. The author has clearly aimed to shape the products of a Spanish literary fashion to a different literary culture, to perform an act of conciliation on the order of what he had done in his more overtly political *Antipatía*. With such a project, it is understandable that those structural items and narrative codes that were most potent in a Spanish setting are neutralized and incorporated into a text for French persons who liked to read Spanish, and for Spanish expatriates aware of their alienation from their original culture.

Antonio Liñán y Verdugo: *Guía y avisos de forasteros que vienen a la Corte de Madrid*

The *Guía y avisos de forasteros que vienen a la Corte de Madrid*, by Antonio Liñán y Verdugo (1620), is, as its title states, a book of advice for out-of-towners who come to the capital. It is not a guide for tourists, but a manual for those—men, of course—who have to spend time there on business. The business of these men is not commerce but legal or administrative affairs, lawsuits and claims. These are *pretendientes*, agents for the lords of country estates or for provincial towns, claimants and litigants who have to spend unpredictable amounts of time making the rounds of the royal bureaucracy. Their traffic is not in goods but in favors, titles, and rights.

In its general structure, this guide belongs to the venerable and distinguished genre of the colloquy. Two men of experience and gravity, Don Antonio and the Maestro (this Master of Laws is never named) meet a new arrival in the capital, Don Diego, and are later joined by another recently arrived companion in the same lodgings, Don Leonardo. The two older men advise Don Diego on the matters that any newcomer to Madrid would have to consider, beginning with how to choose one's lodging and continuing with such topics as neighbors, friends, the dangers of the streets, the prevalence of confidence tricksters and hangers-on, wasteful entertainments to be avoided. Each of these topics is illustrated more or less pertinently by one or more stories told by one or another of the gentlemen present. Although it has the formal outline of the colloquy, the *Guía* is far from being a distinguished example of the type. The agility of mind, the intimate drama of intensely felt ideas, the interpenetration of the great philosophical questions and the little vexing ones, the subtle and fascinating shifts from profundity to surface—these and other such qualities that we find in the conversations imagined by Erasmus, Andrés Laguna, and other masters of the sixteenth century are almost entirely absent. Some pretenses are made at keeping the feeling of a conversation—one of the cast of characters will ask another to repeat something he said the other day for the benefit of a newcomer, for example—but these are technical tricks, and fairly elementary ones. Instead of the ease and the artful drift of a good simulated dialogue, we have a tendency for the speaker to harangue and to lecture the listener, and through him the reader.

The practical aims of the *Guía* are very imperfectly realized; Liñán was no more capable of writing an objective how-to book concerning human choice and behavior than were his contemporaries. He could not fail to moralize, to generalize where we would expect him to be specific, to amass learned sources where experience might speak more aptly and briefly. In the first conversation, on choosing a good place to stay, Leonardo makes the obvious point that you cannot tell what people are like from appearances, and supports the assertion with reference to Plutarch's *Life of Alexander*. In response, the Maestro declares that virtue will not forever remain concealed, appealing to St. John Chrysostom and Aristotle, and that one can find out about the character of lodging-house owners by studying their neighbors—see Plautus, Vergil, Themistocles, Ovid, Cicero, and other authors both ancient and modern on the subject of good and bad neighbors (35). We may doubt the utility of this advice for the puzzled newcomer to the big city. But moral reflection is the preferred mode of instruction, augmented and illustrated in traditional fashion by stories that show the pitfalls that lie in the path of the unwary. If these stories enhance the utility of the book for the visitor, they do so by revealing some forms of trickery, fraud, and deception that he should expect to encounter. Some are of literary origin, others may be based on real experiences. Taken altogether, they create an image of a world governed by deceit and illusion, of men and women living by their wits, sometimes amassing great wealth in doing so (*aviso* 5, *novela* 8), sometimes ending in the galleys (*aviso* 4, *novela* 7). There are anecdotes about pickpockets, and about men who pose as acquaintances in order to have the protection of a respectable man while carrying on a life of crime (*aviso* 2, *novela* 2). There are stories about simpletons being fleeced and there is a long narrative about a man who schemes to trap his unwary young lodger into marriage with his daughter. The young man flees and eventually dies, and his servants are tortured as part of the judicial inquiry. The girl also dies, and the old man marries the duenna who was his accomplice in setting the trap. So those who have a true sense of honor die of grief while those who have none live on in comfort. The picture is more desolate than is usual in the imaginative literature of the time.

The practical goal of this book is satisfied less in the advice it gives the stranger on how to find his way and survive than in the examples of fraud that he needs to avoid. The four speakers represent a little island of civility and rectitude from which the great sea of confusion and delinquency can be surveyed. They maintain a high moral tone and sustain an image of ineffable respectability and self-importance,[16] but they can laugh at the stories and at themselves as victims of pickpockets and tricksters. As a collection of stories set within the frame of the dialogue it also forms part of the literature of entertainment. Some of the stories seem likely to have been based on the careers of real criminals, while others have a literary origin, so that the boundaries between invention and reality, fiction and fact, are blurred; all the stories are presented as factual within a portrait of Madrid which is claimed to be true. This portrait or general image of the capital is the one that characteristically serves to set the tone of many picaresque fictions and to set up the expectations of the reader for that type of narrative: in this Babylon, this confusion, you cannot believe half of what you hear.[17] A long harangue by the Maestro on this topic is, in turn,

16. ". . . si estuviera bien a mi edad y hábito deciros cosas que he experimentado . . . en esta Corte" (79); ". . . os contaré lo que me sucedió a mí propio con toda mi autoridad" (*Guía*, 229–30).

17. ". . . en esta Babilonia de la confusión de la vida de Corte, de cuatro cosas que se ven, no se han de creer las dos. . . . Todas son apariencias fabulosas, maravillas soñadas . . ." (*Guía*, 78).

part of a conversation on the difference between the country or small town from which most visitors come and the great city.

Villages are praised, because there things are what they seem, but in this Babylon, all are creating false appearances, spending what they do not have.[18] This description is not quite the traditional praise of country life and dispraise of the city. It is preceded by references to the precariousness of life on the land, to illustrate the incompleteness of the proverb "Ara bien y cogerás pan" (Plow well and you will gather bread). Moreover, there is no idealizing of the relations between people or between people and natural things in a bucolic setting. It is simply a question of scale and therefore of familiarity. Everybody knows whether he who claims to be a *señor*, with a title, really is one or not. In the great city all is fluid and precarious, and newcomers are deceived. Titled gentlemen, away from their provincial estates, are taken in by smooth rogues with courtly manners, some feathers and gold braid. Nobility is known by its external signs; everyone puts on a display appropriate to his or her patron's rank; an imposter can impress by riding a borrowed horse, by name-dropping, by being seen embracing the right people though he has never spoken to them before. Roles are assumed, images created, ostentation and theatricality the norm.

Liñán has here characterized the milieu in which rogues of all kinds flourish, a world in which the outward trappings are read as signs of the essence. The genuinely wellborn adopt the codes of dress, of courtesy, of extravagance, but so do the cheats and upstarts. Liñán is representing the world in which *el buscón*, Elena, Trapaza, Teresa de Manzanares are nourished, make fortunes, play upon the stage of illusions, and (perhaps) are unmasked. If his declared object, to instruct the newly arrived on how to survive in Madrid, is to be believed, we must assume that his assem-

18. ". . . esta vida, que es vida de tanta paz y quietud, adonde se vive tan de espacio y con tanto desengaño, teniendo cada cosa por lo que es . . ." (*Guía*, 77–78). "¡Qué de galas sin poder traerse; qué de gastos sin poder sustentarse; qué de ostentaciones de casa y criados sin que se sepa dónde se cría, ni a qué árbol se disfruta aquello que allí se consume; qué de opinión de hombres ricos más por opinión que por renta; qué de rentas sin opinión y qué de opiniones sin probabilidad! Todas son apariencias fabulosas, maravillas soñadas, tesoros de duendes, figuras de representantes en comedia . . ." (*Guía*, 78).

277

bled vignettes, anecdotes, and picaresque episodes are true to the world as he and his readers perceived it. The construction of a whole picaresque life in the form of a confession evidently no longer has the imaginative force that it once did. The lives of Lazarillo de Tormes and of Guzmán de Alfarache are singular enough in their symbolic power that they can transcend their world. They go even further: they make it strange by their unique presence in it and passage through it. These later figures, like those of Liñán's anecdotes and reminiscences, do the opposite: by being fully adapted to an environment that assigns a range of possible roles, they familiarize the bizarre actions of everyday.

Agustín de Rojas Villandrando: *El viaje entretenido*

Agustín de Rojas Villandrando, the author of *El viaje entretenido* (The entertaining journey), was a writer seeking a stable position and a respectable public. In his life he practiced the few desirable options available to Spaniards of his time. After a youth spent as a page in the service of a socially superior family, he had a mediocre career as a soldier. Personal service and military service were the two honorable roads to merit, if one did not have a university education. Having made no progress in them, he turned to the theater, with little better result. The book that he wrote as a consequence of his experiences on the road with the traveling companies of the actors Angulo el Malo and Ríos brought him renown. Amusingly written, it provoked the curiosity of the public about these scandalous people while relating very little that was truly scandalous. This relative success did not encourage Rojas to become more adventurous as a writer; the effect was the very opposite. He made a comfortable and respectable marriage, bought his way into both the royal and the ecclesiastical bureaucracy (*Viaje*, 19), and diligently set out in pursuit of his long-term objective: to acquire noble status. His next book was *El buen república* (1611). This is another miscellany, but here we find no entertaining journey with its narrative structure, its conversations, jocularity, and dramatic monologues. These elements are replaced by stories narrated with evident care for their elegance of style and by erudite expositions of various matters, including his reflections on political philosophy, from which the book derives its title. Here a writer who has achieved some success in his writing uses that success to consolidate his position in society. As he does so, he composes a new book, one that is consistent with his more elevated social station and with the more solid company he now keeps. Complementarily, he identifies himself with a public that needs the kind of writing he is able to provide, in order more adequately to define itself as cultured. This is a particularly persuasive example of a writer finding his public, both of them joined in a common need, a reciprocal definition of respectability.

Luis Vélez de Guevara: *El diablo cojuelo*

In this elastic zone other works of indeterminate genre may be most appropriately housed. A relevant case is that of *El diablo cojuelo* (The limping little devil, 1641), by Luis Vélez de Guevara, a prose fantasy that some literary historians have classified as picaresque. This is a fiction that has been labeled in a different way by almost every critic who has attempted to discuss it. I limit my examples to those who have mentioned it in the context of a discussion of the picaresque. Angel Valbuena Prat included it in his anthology, although he was far from certain about what to call it: "social and picaresque satire" and "novel of fantasy" (32); "picarescosocial novel" (72); "this novel fits a satiricosocial genre better than the picaresque" (1639). Chandler stopped short of calling it picaresque, but discussed it even so in his *Romances of Roguery* (1899:380–81). Bjornson calls it, awkwardly, "picaresquelike" (1977:127), and even claims to find in it the story of Don Cleofás' progress toward a higher level of consciousness (129). Del Monte sees nothing picaresque in it (1971:149). Rico (1984) passes over it in silence. It is worthwhile, however, to ask where on the literary map it belongs.

This book has not one but two central actors: Don Cleofás, a student who is running from justice across the roof tiles of Madrid, and the little demon whom he frees from a bottle in the attic of an astrologer-magician. The little demon first reveals to Don

279

Cleofás what is taking place in the houses of the capital at 1 A.M by lifting the roofs, then helps him to escape in difficult situations as they travel about together. The traits that this story shares with earlier picaresque novels are the changes of location during an escape from some danger or comic pursuit and a milieu where deceit and fraud are commonplace. Don Cleofás is a student, and students in literature are hungry, they live by their wits and engage constantly in trickery. The deceiver in numberless *entremeses* is a student; Pablos, *el buscón*, becomes a picaro while he is a student at Alcalá. Evidently there is some overlap with picaresque literature. The facetious style reminds one of *El buscón* or of *La pícara Justina*, but such facetiousness is not a necessary characteristic of picaresque. These traits, however, are all superficial ones. The companions move in great leaps from one chapter to the next (each chapter is called a *tranco* a stride), but there is no necessary connection between these episodes. There is a gallery of comic figures who are already familiar to us from Quevedo's *Sueños* and other satirical pieces. These resemblances to picaresque literature, however, are incidental. Don Cleofás, the student, is running away from his mistress, Doña Tomasa, who is attempting to force him to marry her while (as the limping demon reveals) she is preparing to elope with another lover. Apart from this entanglement, we know nothing about him or his circumstances. He has no past, and so this is no picaresque biography. Not only has he no past, but the events that are presented do not cohere into the representation of an existence; there is no self to which they can become assimilated. Though this narrative has two central characters, together they make less than one.

Structurally, *El diablo cojuelo* is a series of set pieces of various kinds. In the second *tranco* is the vision of Madrid as a monstrous pie with the crust lifted off; the next section animates another culinary metaphor—the "puchero humano" (human stewpot)—portraying a confused mass of follies and vanities and ostentation, people with coaches that they cannot afford, cheating in order to acquire a *don* to their names, and so forth. There is a duel between a "scientific" fencer and an opponent who relies on brute strength; a quarrel with foreigners who do not confess the superiority of the king of Spain over all other monarchs; a description, seen in a magic mirror, of all the titled personages as they parade along

Madrid's Calle Mayor (a catalogue of adulation); a meeting of a literary *academia* in Seville. The whole piece ends when the devil is overtaken by the officers who have been sent from hell to apprehend him and, after the climactic scene of confusion, Don Cleofás renounces the faithless woman and decides to resume his studies. The ending could not be more perfunctory. To conclude, as Bjornson does, that Cleofás "ultimately attains a heightened awareness of himself, his world, and the genuine noble principles according to which he should act" (1977:128) and that "his picaresque journey is a maturation experience which allows him to perceive realities behind a world of illusory experiences" (132), one must be very eager indeed to reinstate Alemán's redemptive structure, which Vélez has so breezily dismissed.

Vélez de Guevara's own designation of his work betrays his uncertainty concerning its generic status. On the title page it appears as "Novela de la otra vida" (Novel of the other life), a curiously inaccurate description, since the action all occurs in this world, not the next. In the Dedicatoria he refers to it as "this volume" and "this novel"; in the Prólogo it is "this discourse," a term that he uses again in the jocular "Carta de recomendación al cándido o moreno lector" (Letter of recommendation to the simple [or white] or dark reader). If any conclusion can be drawn from this vacillation, it is that the term *novela* has, by the year 1641, come to be less restricted in meaning, since it can designate a work composed of equal proportions of satire and sycophancy, with almost no narrative interest. In the first *tranco*, the little demon promises the student that what he is about to reveal will outdo Lucian's Menippus (Valbuena 1643b). It is a matter of argument whether the whole work is to be read as a Menippean satire, or only the particular set piece that follows. The phrase "Menippus had better watch out" ("malaño para Menipo en los diálogos de Luciano, te he de enseñar") restricts the Lucianic model to what is about to be displayed and avoids using the term "satire," which appears nowhere in the book, although *El diablo cojuelo* could be called one. Perhaps it does not matter; the term *novela* had become so loose that its boundary with *discurso* had virtually disappeared.

This work, like *El viaje entretenido*, is located in a zone between didactic colloquy and exemplary fiction. (I discuss this development more fully at the end of this chapter.) It offers the writer some freedom of invention while imposing social and ideological constraints, but *El diablo cojuelo* fails to exploit this freedom. Gonzalo Torrente Ballester (1979) lamented Vélez' failure to convey by means of the devices of the pie and the magic mirror the experience of reality in his time, the vast areas of personal and social life as yet untouched by Spanish writers.[19] Like Quevedo in the *Sueños*, Vélez satirizes classes of people, professions, activities. Some of the techniques of representation used by the two writers are similar. The portrait of the repulsive imp released from the bottle is composed of vegetables and other objects, after the manner of the Milanese painter Giuseppe Arcimboldo. The little devil finishes up inside the body of a notary, also in imitation of Quevedo (*El alguacil alguacilado*). More important here is the coincidence in the range of the reality presented, the depth of that reality, and the prejudices that are encoded in it. The objects of satire are all egregiously familiar: promoters portrayed as madmen; cuckolded husbands; extravagances of dress; foreigners; old men who try to look young; duennas; crazy poets; people with carriages; venal constables and clerks, and so on. The presentations are underscored by the demon's solemn comments. Of a singer who will not stop singing except when he is asked to sing, and then has to be insistently pressed to do so: "That's the peevishness of everyone in that profession" (1649b). Promoters "are the most pernicious madmen in the republic" (1649a). The satirical discourse continually leads into such generalities and reaches its extreme in an allegory of Fortune (*tranco* VII). The satire is aimed at easy targets that are already conventional: harmless foibles; examples of vanity or presumption in the lower or middle class; examples of bribery and corruption, in the lower ranks again; ostentation in those who do not have grand titles. But there is boundless praise of royalty and titles. The mild satire assails nothing that could make us uneasy, and seeks only our amused superiority. Deviations from social norms are made laughable, while the established embodiments of those norms, no matter how crass, are venerated. The satire evidently serves the purposes of a powerfully sustained

19. "No se le ocurrió que con la tapa del pastel en una mano y el espejo mágico en la otra, pudo habernos dado una versión directa, real y, al mismo tiempo, fantástica de la sociedad española de entonces" (Torrente 1979:440).

conformity, entered into by readers and writers alike. A measure of the complacency can be seen in two contemptuously flippant passing references to the new astronomy. In the first, Don Cleofás (this student sports the noble *don*) finds himself in the attic of the astrologer, "leafing through the notes of Euclid and the frauds of Copernicus" (1642a). In the second, the devil makes punning reference to the "antojos" (eyeglasses; also whims) of Galileo.[20]

There is no *Lazarillo*, no Alemán, no Cervantes in these decades, or if there were, none found a voice. What is certain is that the narrative forms the earlier writers used to open up a problematic reality, to question relations of power, to ironize the *doxa* of their world, had been rendered impotent. The frivolous picaresque lives invented by Castillo Solórzano, the hundreds of upper-class *novelas* that claimed to be exemplary, the fact-and-fiction miscellanies, the satirical fantasies, all serve the interests, promote the fantasies, and flatter the prejudices of the same homogenized public. In the hands of their place-seeking authors, they become effective instruments in the process of homogenization.

La vida y hechos de Estebanillo González

At this point the reader may suspect that most of the works that are commonly classified as picaresque novels are so called to swell the genre to a respectable size, to give it some critical mass. *La vida y hechos de Estebanillo González, hombre de buen humor. Compuesto por el mismo* (1646) is one more case in point. The royal copyright (*privilegio*) names Estebanillo González as the sole grantee, and the dramatist Pedro Calderón de la Barca, who wrote the censor's certificate (*aprobación*), names Estebanillo González as the author. Moreover, Estebanillo González has put his name on the dedication to the famous general Ottavio Piccolomini, Duke of Amalfi. A work that has been given a place in histories of the novel is evidently not a fictional work but a memoir (which is not to say that all its tall stories are true). Until recently there appeared to be no

20. See also "la óptica de estos señores antojadizos que han descubierto al Sol un lunar en el lado izquierdo, y en la Luna han linceado motes y valles, y han visto a Venus *cornuta*" (1661a).

record of any such person, but the latest edition, by Antonio Carreira and Jesús Antonio Cid gives documentary evidence of an Es-
teban González in the household accounts of Prince Emmanuele
Filiberto of Savoy, as well as a Stefaniglio, or Stefanillo, in the
records of the Duke of Amalfi. The editors also provide persuasive
evidence in support of their contention that the *Vida y hechos* was
written by a Spanish poet and chronicler living in Flanders, Gab-
riel de la Vega. Could this be an early example of a modern phenomenon, an autobiography written "with" a professional writer?

This work has been described as the quintessential picaresque
novel,[21] and it would be difficult to be more mistaken. The narrator's parents are not shameful; on the contrary, unlike Guzmán
and Pablos, Estebanillo embarrasses his father, an hidalgo, by his
scandalous pranks.[22] The parents are of no particular importance in
the story; when Estebanillo runs away, it is not in order to leave
home, but to escape an enraged customer in the barbershop,
whose aggressively macho whiskers he has destroyed. His life is
in no sense exemplary, either as a model of what not to be or as a
sardonic example of how to succeed against the odds. There is no
return to an originary place or state of affairs; the story is one of
constant movement, but the well-modeled trajectory of fictional
lives is altogether absent. This adventurous life is played for two
kinds of effect: comedy, and the proximity to great events and
great actors on the stage of Europe during the Thirty Years' War.
The comedy is in two principal modes. The first is the farcical,
slapstick comedy of incompetence. Twice in his youth he is apprenticed to a barber, and on each occasion he has to flee an enraged victim of his red-hot curling iron or his misdirected scissors.
In Naples he reads some manuals of surgery and is accepted as
assistant to a surgeon; here the victims would not have appreci-
ated the comedy. With this combination of effrontery and the capacity to present his incompetence as comic, it is no surprise that
he eventually becomes a buffoon. The other mode of comedy is

21. Nicholas Spadaccini, "*Estebanillo González* and the Nature of Picaresque
'Lives,'" *CL* 30 (1978):209–22. See p. 210 for Estebanillo's "ignoble birth."

22. Carreira and Cid have also brought together the documentation concerning a Lorenzo González, presumably Estebanillo's father, in the records of
the St. Luke Academy of painting in Rome (*Estebanillo González*, Introducción,
lx–lxvi).

the entertaining journey, a mode that picaresque narrative incorporates and with which it is often mistakenly identified, as we noted in the example of *Marcos de Obregón*; *El donado hablador* is another moralized journey told by an aged penitent. Since people traveled in groups, the travelogue gives abundant scope for meeting bizarre types, gambling, cheating, and deception, as well as small plots of chance and mischance.

Estebanillo's proximity to great events and personages does not diminish the opportunities for buffoonery; rather it renders them grotesque. The central chapters (6 and 7) give a reluctant soldier's view of a small segment of the military campaign, in which his accident-proneness, his barefaced cowardice, and his effrontery give an unprecedented representation of the stupidity of war. He is terrified. "Thinking that all Sweden was coming against me, and that I would lose an ear at the very least," he hides in a ditch, where he has a corpse's-eye view of the action. Also in the ditch is the stinking carcass of a nag, and he gets under it for protection. He escapes, pretends to be wounded, and when it is safe goes out and brandishes his sword "to give it some air," yelling, "Saint James for Spain! Charge! At them! At them! Charge!" (1.314). The enemy is routed and the field is full of corpses, so he determines to show his courage; desperately crossing himself and trembling, he furiously attacks the dead and the dying, "slashing guts, opening bellies, and slicing gullets. . . . I wrought such havoc that I paused to consider that no man is more cruel than a chicken that finds itself at an advantage or more brave than an honest man when he fights with cause." One of his victims groans, so he flees. His commanding officer, mortally wounded, asks him angrily why he failed to carry out orders; his insolent reply is "Sir, so as not to be like you are now."[23] The officer is carried into the village, "where he gave up the ghost because he was not as smart as I was." From this account one would not suppose that here was the great victory of Nördlingen, where imperial armies finally destroyed the Swedish power.

These excerpts show Estebanillo's relentless facetiousness, a quality found in the protagonists of Quevedo, Castillo Solórzano,

---

23. ". . . después de encomendarme a Dios y hacerme mil centenares de cruces, temblándome los brazos y azogándoseme las piernas . . ." (1.317).

and others. But however debased these others may be, their patriotism is never in question. Estebanillo declares that for a good meal he would serve the Turk, a comment that Guzmán could never have made (Guzmán recalls with shame his father's shifts to the Turk and back). No picaro would fail at least to cover his shame from the public gaze. No picaro changes allegiance so easily, deserts so frequently, or is so disinclined to denounce the enemies of his king and his faith. Even so, Estebanillo rises to positions of trust in the imperial headquarters in Brussels, and has words of consummate flattery for Piccolomini, and remembers the personal kindness of the king and queen of Poland when he served as courier for the imperial court. This book is basically autobiography, written with conflicting political and personal motives that make it fascinating. He is proud of the high circles that he has reached, but can shamelessly tell how he threw away his trust by getting drunk while carrying imperial mail to Brussels. As buffoon and self-conscious scapegoat, he surrenders all dignity, fawns, and accepts the status of a pet animal: well fed, threatened, beaten, and rewarded. He casts his sardonic eye over the world of artifice, ceremony, vanity, and honor, being estranged from all such concerns. There is a moment of terror when his patron the Cardinal-Infante dies and he is left completely alone, and no one wants to know him (chap. 9). Such moments may explain (but not excuse) the painful anti-Jewish practical jokes. Estebanillo could not fail to exploit the vulnerability of persons whose social respect was less than his own, and evidently could not resist the temptation to unload the burden of self-mockery onto another, universally available scapegoat.

Blurring and Merging of Genres

From the late 1620s on, such writers as Alonso de Castillo Solórzano, Matías de los Reyes, Juan de Piña, Bartolomé Mateo Velázquez, Alonso Jerónimo de Salas Barbadillo, and many others purveyed fiction shaped to formulas that offered a predictable range of situations. This is a literature of consumption, whose prevailing form is the novella, of a length that is appropriate to an evening's reading in a household where the presence of servants made hours of relaxation regularly available. Their collections almost invariably present adventure, escapes, and amorous involvements in the lives of persons with titles, and are written in a style with some pretensions to elegance. In addition, the reader commonly finds one or two stories of picaresque chicanery or of some ignoble quality punished, centered upon humble characters, and written in a facetious style. The literate fiction-reading public could thus define itself socially; the majority of the published *novelas* presented the adventures of persons at or somewhat above readers' own social class, and a few enabled them to look down upon the unprincipled acts of characters who were socially and morally inferior. The romantic stories of love and heroism reinforce their messages by the use of a generalizing, sententious, and moralizing discourse. The cheats and tricksters and ridiculous misers have their stories told in a manner that dissociates them from serious ethical or social discernment and presents them as comic stereotypes.

The possible world offered by this kind of fiction is a complacently edited view of the actual world, with such values as purity of blood, aristocratic breeding, unquestioned patriotism, the providential inevitability of the existing political and social arrangements clearly affirmed. The alternative to acceptance of this simplistic image of the world is not rejection of it but withdrawal from its imperfections in pursuit of a higher good: *desengaño del mundo*. At this period it is almost impossible to find extended narrative of any originality. Writers displayed originality by writing whole stories with one of the vowels omitted, or by setting the story in a remote land with strange customs, or by cultivating a bizarre, idiosyncratic style. The first person as narrative mode, with its potential for representing the flow of experience, the texture of existence, the direct encounter with otherness, has all but disappeared from Castilian fiction.

With fiction safely in the hands of bureaucratic functionaries, fortune-hunters, secretaries and majordomos in noble households, new canons of literature emerge. They include new ways of bringing together fiction and nonfiction, as in Rojas Villandrando's *Viaje entretenido*. Learned miscellanies already had a small continuing vogue; their contents and their earnest prologues imply a group of readers who were convinced that one gained intellectual status by possessing facts and conjectures about the natural world, history (biblical, ancient, and modern), moral philosophy, and mythology, with extensive reference to Pliny, Plutarch, and other ancient and medieval authorities. Such works continue to be constructed on the plan of the humanistic dialogues and colloquies familiar to us in the works of Erasmus, Alfonso de Valdés, Andrés Laguna, and even the *Philosophia antigua poética* of Alonso López (El Pinciano); namely, a conversation between a pair or a group of friends. From the early years of the seventeenth century, the range of such works is enlarged. The same plan, a group of friends meeting for sociable talk, accommodates works whose object is more obviously to entertain than to stimulate thought (Rojas, *El viaje entretenido*; Gaspar Lucas Hidalgo, *Diálogos de apacible entretenimiento*, 1606). These works, and others like them, are miscellanies of conversation, local and national gossip, news, travelers' tales, and stories told to friends. Rojas' *Viaje* is the pretext for the author to include a number of his *loas* (dramatic curtain raisers). The journey narrative informs the reader about a real traveling theater company, but it also contains episodes that are clearly fictional. Then again, like other journey narratives, it presents information about people and places. This kind of writing does not conform to any well-defined or recognized genre, though it may be derived formally from the more philosophical and didactic colloquies of the preceding century. It occupies a space between the colloquy and the framed collection of *novelas*, and is infinitely adaptable. The proportions of fiction and fact can be varied, and so can the means that are employed to present them; structure may be looser or tighter; stories may be anecdotic in their brevity, or they may be artistically developed; the instructional side of the formula *enseñar deleitando* may be achieved through learned disquisition or through snippets of information derived from bookish tradition, or from popular medicine, or from hearsay; the possibilities are endless. This variety is not separable into subgenres. Rather, these works occupy a continuum that extends from the truly philosophical dialogue at one end to the collections of fiction at the other. Moreover, the boundaries are blurred, because the *novelas* themselves are routinely sententious, and the long adventurous romances are deliberately made the vehicles for information about people, places, and events, or political discussion between the characters (as we saw in chap. 3).

This indeterminate space between the deliberately didactic and the specifically fictional shares their blurred and porous boundaries, and so is hospitable to some limited literary novelty. The extent of the innovation is bounded not by the discursive space itself but by the social and ideological constraints of the actual world of Spain upon writers and readers. This is an area where thought should be free to experiment and to take on new imaginative forms. The freedom for thought to find new modes of expression, however, was limited by the topoi within which thought had become encapsulated since the middle years of the previous century, as well as by the consensus of writers and readers concerning the instrumentality of literature. Here it may be relatively easy to perceive on what terms that public was prepared to devote itself to reading, and what benefits it expected to derive from the outlay of its time and money.

The constraints within which the mentality of literate Castilians was formed in the early and middle years of the seventeenth century have been alluded to in other parts of this book, and have been amply documented by Jose Antonio Maravall, Pierre Vilar, Michel Cavillac, Noël Salomon, and others. Few writers could exist without aristocratic patronage or ecclesiastical benefice. The relative isolation of Spain, and particularly of Castile, from the intellectual currents of the rest of Europe helped to reinforce and was in turn reinforced by the intense chauvinism and the heavily institutionalized forms of religious belief and practice. The experience of commercial and industrial recession, the control of Spanish finances and commerce by foreigners, the impoverishment of the countryside, the many deterrents to enterprise and innovation contributed to the formation of a public that sought stability and the continuity of what was familiar. A literate public that was largely dependent for its income upon investment in government annuities rather than in commercial or industrial enterprise or in the development of agriculture, that was intensely suspicious of foreigners and novelty, having a collective image formed by a peculiar sense of honor based on purity of blood (an image validated by the past rather than open to the future); a public so constituted could hardly be responsive to intellectual risk or be expected to welcome verbal probing of what lay behind the many masks of authority, and behind acceptance of authority. On the side of the writers, few could work independently of noble patronage or an official post in the legal or administrative bureaucracy.

9

Picaresque as Cultural Text

It is difficult, often impossible, to determine what kind of public or publics would have read a given work, and to conjecture how it was read by its various publics. Fictions enable us to enter imaginatively into situations and participate in experiences different from our own, and the participation necessarily varies, not only from individual to individual but also between classes of readers. To take an obvious example, experts may read differently from nonexperts. Science fiction can elicit objections from technical readers that "it couldn't work that way," while historians are shy about reading historical novels and complain that "it didn't happen that way." Wise experts, however, will respond like Cervantes' Licenciado Peralta: "I understand the artifice . . . and invention, and that's enough." It is safe to assume that the same detective story will be read differently by a policeman, by a criminal, and by a priest. Two readers, one an enthusiastic fisherman and the other not a fisherman but aware of the patterns of myth, are unlikely to give similar readings of Ernest Hemingway's *Old Man and the Sea*. Ideological orientation also affects us as readers; Salman Rushdie's *Satanic Verses* is an obvious if extreme case.

Thomas Pavel, investigating the ontology of the imaginary, affirms as the basis for reference in fictional works two fundamental principles that

> have for a long time constituted the privileged core of the fictional order: the *principle of distance* and the *principle of relevance*. Creation of distance could well be assumed to be the most general aim of imaginary activity: the journey epitomizes the basic operation of the imagination, be it realized as dreams, . . . imaginary worlds, or merely the confrontation of the unusual and the memorable. Scandal, the unheard-of, the unbearable tensions of everyday social and personal life, are expelled from the intimacy of the collective experience and set up at a distance, clearly visible, their virulence exorcized by exposure to the public eye, by the safety net of exemplary distance. . . . Symbolic distance is meant to heal wounds carved with equal strength by unbearable splendor and monstrosity in the social tissue. But the cure cannot work unless it is somehow shown to pertain to actuality. Symbolic distance must be complemented by a principle of relevance. (1986:145)

"Relevance" may be conceived in any way that will "vividly bear upon the beholder's world"; whether it sustain that world's logical consistency, ideological presumptions, ethical judgments, or density of documentation of a familiar or a technical sort is not of crucial importance. Distance and relevance are mutually dependent, and the balance between them constantly changes. "Romance versus epos and tragedy, fantastic literature versus realism, these were and still are cyclical fights between two projects. . . . Thus *Quixote* could have appealed to a period overfed with fantasy, whereas *Master and Margarita* exploded in a context in which realism was the sternly enforced obligation" (147).

Cervantes and Alemán were evidently aiming at the same public, and each was making his own adjustment of distance and relevance, each claiming to have overmastered romance and incorporated it into a plausible representation of a world known to a broad spread of readers. What each of them distanced is radically different: in *Don Quixote* it is the hypnotic and destructive power of the Same, endlessly reflected in fantasy through mediated desire;[1] in *Guzmán* it is the threat of the Other, fear of the loss of self. In *Don Quixote*, selves (Quixote, Cardenio, Grisóstomo, Lotario) are hostages to desire mediated by a web of inherited romantic myths; in *Guzmán*, the tyranny of the past is centered in the parents, and through them in the myth of the fall of humanity's first parents. In each case, the tyranny is finally overcome, exorcized in a moment of trauma that becomes a moment of truth, a new lucidity.[2] We may suppose that most readers read both of these extraordinary works; the two projects are radically different in conceptual terms, but not "totally antagonistic," as Carlos Blanco Aguinaga (1957) asserted. They are both necessary, both true (see chap. 6 above).

Modern societies contain a variety of publics, and any reader may belong to more than one of them; so a text may have different relevances for different readers, as I suggested in relation to Castillo Solórzano's *Garduña de Sevilla*, ranging from amused and disdainful recognition to a high level of anxiety about "what the world is coming to." It is not difficult to understand the great success of *Guzmán de Alfarache* when we recognize the range of its relevance. It gave pledges of a happy outcome, not of the romantic kind, but one consonant with the religiosity of the age, while for more inquiring and sophisticated readers it left room for debate over what still had to happen for those pledges to be redeemed. In spite of its massive frame and huge bulk, it belongs recognizably to the medieval tradition of the exemplum in both its negative ("if you live thus, these are the miseries that may await you") and its

1. Foucault 1970: chap. 3.i; Cesáreo Bandera, *Mímesis conflictiva: Ficción literaria y violencia en Cervantes y Calderón* (Madrid: Gredos, 1975).

2. Both works also end with open questions. However deep Guzmán's inner transformation may be, his future in society remains problematic. Quixote recovers his sanity, but his name has changed again: not Quejana, but "Alonso Quijano, a quien mis costumbres me dieron renombre de *Bueno*" (*DQ*, II.74). Not only does Quijano not correspond to any of the versions of his original name (i.1), but he has just this instant invented the unearned sobriquet *el Bueno* (the Good), on the basis of "costumbres" for which there is no evidence. A *Bueno* after the name, like the *Don* before it, cannot be legitimately applied to oneself. A title to virtue, like a title to knighthood, has to be bestowed by external authority. So he can still not face death without an assumed persona. Deep questions remain, bearing upon T. S. Eliot's much-quoted line "Human kind cannot bear very much reality."

positive ("if I could finally get off that treadmill to safer ground, so can you") applications. It offered something to those who looked for salvation of souls, and also for those with Alemán's reformist impulse, who looked for economic salvation to schemers with influence in the government. It triumphantly appropriated for fiction that homiletic discourse of pastoral theology and spirituality that moved readers everywhere and was on everyone's shelf. At the same time, its relevance was given exemplary distance by means of the structures that it incorporated: the mythic journey over land and sea, the mistaken quest for self (mistaken because it sought everywhere but within), with a last-minute reversal, and all this in a surprising adaptation of the Byzantine novel. And, of course, the peculiar fascination with urban low life, a matter I shall return to shortly. Like all great art, *Guzmán* allowed its public to have a many-layered cake, and to eat it. The later works, including the novels of *pícaras*, purvey fantasy under the guise of relevance: the fantasy that a marauding and parasitic "freedom" can be enjoyed at the small cost of some little advertisements for morality (as if tobacco companies were left to write their own health warnings).

If we bear in mind the claim that has frequently been made, that picaresque novels present a critique of social institutions or of social structures, it is instructive to note how little and how conventional is the implied criticism that they contain. *Lazarillo de Tormes*, the earliest, remains the most mysterious. It alone makes us stare at poverty. In others the protagonist may lose at cards or be robbed, or fall into penury through some other cause, but these cases are the characteristic vagaries of fortune. The picaro is particularly subject to such falls since his life makes him an archetypical hostage to the goddess Fortuna, and in the moralizing world of classical fiction the point would not be allowed to escape the attention of readers. In *Lazarillo*, however, poverty is a condition of the world. Its setting is predominantly the provinces, where poverty is a part of the history, but it also presents poverty that is self-imposed, as a part of the actor's reading of his social role. Thus we are shown the skinflint poverty of the priest ("I don't know if it was his own or if it came with his priestly garb"), and the poverty that is endured in the pursuit of a perverse code of respectability, "for the trifle that they call honor."[3] I said that *Lazarillo* "makes us stare at" rather than "raises the issue of" poverty, because I find no sign there that poverty is made an issue. Rather, in its various manifestations, poverty is the ground from which the protagonist, his need to keep moving, and his urge to achieve independence have sprung. In spite of what many other readers have written, I cannot see this representation of poverty as being ideologically conceived. Words and phrases recur, creating isotopies that signal progress, upward movement, self-improvement. In doing so, they link the end to the beginning in a spiral of irony and moral ambiguity which effectively blocks the emergence of a political discourse. Readers in our time tend to identify and to privilege whatever may appear to sanction a political discourse. It is more disconcerting for us than it was for earlier readers to have the conditions of poverty presented as objective facts of life, making the truth that "the poor are always with us" into a guarantee of the narrative's verisimilitude. It is disquieting to find the grim precariousness of life given simply as a truth of history (even when our twentieth-century meliorist expectations are pulverized every hour by the shocking images on our television screens); that a crafty pleader in his own cause can use it to validate his dubious triumph, to congratulate himself upon his integration into the lowest level of the religious-administrative complex.

As we contemplate this process of social integration and moral abdication, we have to practice a peculiar form of abstinence, which consists of not supposing that those men who have the power to palliate those miserable conditions, through the exercise of charity or other available means, also have the power to change them. In each of Lazarillo's first three masters we may see emblematically portrayed not only members of the three estates but the condition of dereliction and the breach of trust that direct their words and their acts. In this travesty of the ideal structure—*bellatores, aratores, oratores*—are we meant to understand that they (like all sublunary things) have declined from a better state? Or that this social trinity was always characterized by bad faith and mocked by the reality on the ground? Or that it was never any-

3. See Maravall 1986:237; Domínguez Ortiz 1969.

thing more than a game of rhetoric and numerology ? There is no
sure answer. The homology *ciego-clérigo-escudero* and Lázaro–Arcipreste–Vuestra Merced suggests that each representative of the
social structure is implicated as both exploiter and victim, not exclusively as one or the other. And if Lázaro is, as he claims, the
broker, the operator through whose fingers trade in Toledo now
has to pass, what does this fact say about "This illustrious city of
Toledo," the imperial city where Charles held court? Such poly-
morphous satire as this will not reappear in later works.

Francisco Márquez-Villanueva (1975:229) (among others) has
noted how detached the *Quixote* is from the events, pressures, and
crises of the real world. It may come as a surprise to discover how
inattentive are these other, supposedly realistic novels to the harsh
determining conditions of everyday life: plague, famine, flood, as
well as less spectacular but more constant assaults on the lives of
people.[4] And just as these fictions barely mention the natural disasters, so they bear little witness to those manmade catastrophes,
poverty and war. As *Lazarillo de Tormes*, which many critics have
excluded from the canon of truly picaresque works, is the only one
that attempts to represent the experience of poverty, so the *Vida de
Estebanillo González*, at the opposite end of the historical time span,
and whose status as fiction is questionable, is the only one that
presents the experience of war. *Guzmán de Alfarache* creates a different novelistic world from *Lazarillo*, though both represent the
play of personal responsibility in the social nexus; the one employing ironic understatement and euphemism, the other wielding
overwhelming confessional oratory. Even the most literal-minded
readers of *Guzmán* must be aware of themselves as spectators at a
drama of conscience; the ideal reader of *Lazarillo* has to respond to
the protagonists' conscience as a lack, an absence.

La pícara Justina proceeds gleefully from trick to trick, from
swindle to swindle, in a world of gullible merchants, lecherous

---

4. Exceptions are a brief mention in Alemán's *Guzmán*: "Dábase muy poca
limosna y no era maravilla, que en general fue el año estéril y, si estaba mala la
Andalucía, peor cuanto más adentro del reino de Toledo y mucha más nec-
esidad había de los puertos adentro. Entonces oí decir: 'Líbrete Dios de la en-
fermedad que baja de Castilla y de hambre que sube del Andalucía'" (I.ii.2),
and the experiences related by beggars in Martí's *Segunda parte*, noted in chap.
8, above.

hermits, and unscrupulous vagrants. A world where there are good pickings for the ingenious *pícara* is one where poverty has little place; indeed, this is a carnival world of well-stocked larders and roistering students. There is incidental satire, especially of the forms of popular religious piety, in contrast with the more inclusive, emblematic social satire of *Lazarillo*. Moreover, the techniques employed by López de Ubeda are ridicule and parody, a large part of whose function is to sustain a nonserious discourse of quips and puns and continuous surprise, as part of the author's deliberate program of opposing the massive structure and the aesthetic didacticism of *Guzmán*. The *pícara* faces in two directions: her dialogues and her endless prattle look toward the colloquy, in a comic mode, while her actions as protagonist establish a new space that will be exploited by Castillo Solórzano with his Teresa, his Trapaza, and his Rufina. The complexity of *Justina* is not repeatable, but it is the antecedent of the uncomplicated, swashbuckling, cheerful liars and swindlers whose careers are uninterrupted sequences of thefts and confidence tricks, unclouded by scruples on the part of the character or of the narrator. Thus it forms a link with that literature of vicarious gratification which becomes so abundant from the 1620s.

In the satirical writings of Quevedo and of Salas Barbadillo, the objects of the satire are classes of people, trades, professions, vices, not institutions. Quevedo's satire is brilliant and ruthless, but it offers no threat to established powers or privilege. It is morally stern and occasionally points the finger at individuals, but essentially it is conservative, aristocratic, truculently nationalistic, intolerant of any behavior or belief that deviates from his own fiercely asserted norms. The *Vida del buscón* represents the closing of the ranks by an embattled nobility of pure blood. The bitterness of the work, however, derives not only from the beating down of a vulgar swindler by his former noble protector. We can now see what Quevedo signaled to his knowing readers, that Don Diego, the defender of the nobles' purity of blood, is himself a carrier of "tainted" blood. He successfully shields his family from a shameful marriage with the upstart mongrel Pablos, but he himself, being of *converso* descent, is evidence that the closed ranks have the enemy already within them. The message encoded in the act of violence is one of sardonic desperation, for not only can the racial integrity of the nobility not be saved but the necessity of defending it is both compelling and absurd.

For Alexander Parker, the subject matter of the picaresque is delinquency, and delinquency is a way of asserting freedom. By making delinquency the mode of life of the protagonist, the writer points to "the difference between the responsible freedom that chooses discipline and the licence that rejects it" (1967:118). The pursuit of an unacceptable freedom becomes a kind of enslavement; that is the lesson to be found in morality literature everywhere, and not only in the Christian tradition. The value of this material for Alemán was the opportunity it gave him for "an intelligent and earnest attempt to investigate the nature of moral evil" (45). In other words, delinquency as a subject can lead us to consider the paradoxical nature of freedom. This is not the only angle from which the paradox of freedom may be viewed; for the moment, however, let us merely note that literature seeks out those areas of experience that are perceived as containing tension and that may be conceptualized in terms of paradox. If evil (moral or any other kind) is interesting and not merely grim or repulsive, it is because we are fascinated by examples in which somebody finds it desirable, or believes that it is good, or in which it is the tragic outcome of acts that were not inherently evil. Alemán's project was and remains interesting for readers precisely because on some level of consciousness Guzmán is always aware of the initial paradox, even when the evil can offer no more reward than the consolation of its own continuity.

Lazarillo de Tormes, brief as it is, is thematically too complex to be described as an exploration of moral evil, and Quevedo's *Buscón* is too much of a caricature and too intemperate to be a vehicle for exploration. Besides, delinquency is too narrow a concept to contain this literature. The idea of a delinquent, as we understand it, is of a person "whose entire pattern of life has taken an aberrant course,"[5] a case history for whose understanding everything is relevant: biography, biology, sociology, and more. In Alemán's view, Guzmán is not a case of an aberrant individual but rather an individual example of the *typical* human process of the loss of freedom in the pursuit of desire. A "case" is understood within a natural

5. Clifford Geertz, in *New York Review of Books*, 26 January 1978.

world and a system of rational norms, but Guzmán also represents himself as a sinner; for Alemán and his readers, the world is not exhausted by natural laws and rational norms. The referential world shared by the protagonist and the reader was one in which norms were divinely ordained. This is not the case with the other novels that we accept as picaresque.

A generic distinction is usually made between picaresque novels and those in which some part of the action takes place in a low-life setting that may be seen as a threat, in some sense, to the principal characters. This distinction may be necessary to protect the picaresque as a novelistic genre, but when the existence of such a genre is in doubt, it is a hindrance to an understanding of the field of narrative fiction. Isolating a small group of novels and seeing them as governed by the desire to explore moral evil (Parker) or alienation (Guillén) not only create the kinds of distortions that we have observed but render us blind to a significant historical fact: the quantity of fiction whose action is set, either wholly or partially, in the lower levels of society, among beggars and thieves, in inns and gambling houses, with traveling mule trains or in crowded squares. It would be difficult to find any long work of fiction, from *Don Quixote* and *El peregrino en su patria* to *El criticón*, in which there is not an encounter with cheats and swindlers, or any collection of *novelas* that does not contain one or more stories of a picaresque sort. In *Don Quixote*, in addition to Ginés de Pasamonte, there is young Andrés, who packs his bundle and heads for Seville, cured of his naive faith in chivalry.

Novels that are wholly picaresque are distinguished from those that are so only incidentally by the protagonist's social origins and, of course, by the degree of commitment to or involvement in that way of life. But even Guzmán, the picaro par excellence, harbors a deep existential refusal that eventually prevails. Pablos' *picardía* is a means rather than an end in itself. None of the canonical picaros can be said to prosper or to free himself from his social origins, except the sardonic Lázaro. To the prosperous and socially respectable world on which they prey they remain parasites. Neither the picaresque novel nor the novel of travel and romance shows the established social fabric being seriously penetrated by ambitious outsiders. We cannot doubt that unscrupulous upstarts were perceived to be a threat to the traditional order, but the literature, no matter whether it adopts the point of view of the picaro or that of the embattled nobility and gentry, grants them no entry, allows them no symbolic victory. The message in either case is the same reassuring one: we may be swindled (our sense of honor requires that we show trust and that we be magnanimous, for in this way we show our superiority) but the upstart will be unmasked. The picaresque literature is as far from being socially subversive as is the *novela cortesana*, into which the picaresque world intrudes. In fact they are complementary in their rejection of the picaro. The difference is that one of them presents the impulse to lawlessness as if seen from within the offender whereas the other shows it merely as a troublesome fact of life.

A functionalist view of fiction would force us to conclude that there is no sociocultural difference between the several forms of narrative that we have been discussing, or between them and the amorphous, intermediate forms of miscellany, dialogue, mixed entertainment, and satire. The great disturbers of the reader's peace, *Lazarillo*, Cervantes, Alemán, have no worthy successors outside the theater, and even on the stage the audience is far more often flattered than challenged, its social prejudices confirmed but seldom scrutinized.[6] Thomas Pavel notes that "fictional space can accommodate almost any ontological construction" (1986:143); the surprising fact about Spanish, or at least Castilian, literature in this period is the proliferation of narrative forms, ranging from some very fixed and predictable *novelas cortas* to forms that feign an ad hoc improvisation, but all bearing the same ontological construction. Alienation is denied except when it is the consequence of moral error or spiritual arrogance. Both the narrative and dramatic literature, particularly the latter, are replete with individuals whose unhappy fate is inexorably tied to an error that is presented by means of explicitly religious imagery. But the most curious and spectacular examples of this ontological construction are to be found in the dramas of banditry, in which an apparently normal or even virtuous person becomes an outlaw as the result of some

6. José Antonio Maravall, *Teatro y literatura en la sociedad barroca* (Madrid: Seminarios y Ediciones, 1972); José María Díez-Borque, *Sociología de la comedia española del siglo XVII* (Madrid: Cátedra, 1976); Melveena McKendrick, *Theatre in Spain, 1490–1700* (Cambridge: Cambridge University Press, 1990).

frustration or disappointment or misunderstanding.[7] The bandit's gesture of separation, the language of insurrection against all forms of authority, the renunciation of pity for humankind, all to be found in these dramas, clearly conflate the social and the divine realms. The outlaw bandit is simply an extreme case of the displaced individual, and by that very fact the audience is persuaded that the two realms are circles having a common center; to err in one is to earn condemnation in both.

Simplistic interpretations that explain the picaro and his world as a transcription of social conditions or as an expression of protest against those conditions are always with us. More sophisticated studies retrieve social and ideological subtexts from historical sources, in the expectation that we will be able to share with the original readers those contents of their referential world that meshed with the world of the text. Maravall's last book (1986) is a huge labor along these lines, recreating the "mental texture" of the culture from which these writings emerged.[8] Some of the constituent parts of this texture are the degeneration of the vagabond into the picaro and the social responses elicited by it and such crucial binary structures as the oppositions rich/poor, integrated/marginal, static/upwardly mobile, country/city, money/power of rank, master/servant, male/female, to name the most obvious. The segmentation of time into units of value permits the traditional elitist opposition *otium/negotium* to escape from the favored precincts and to become generalized and, in so doing, to assume new forms and meanings. Leisure is no longer the privilege of rank but may be bought with money, and it is all the same whether the money be earned or stolen. The impersonal relations created by money also have their symbolic equivalent in the anomie of the picaro, whose characteristic habitat, when he is not traveling, is the crowd.

---

7. Alexander A. Parker, "Bandits and Saints in the Spanish Drama of the Golden Age," in *Critical Studies of Calderón's Comedias*, ed. J. E. Varey, vol. 19 of *The Comedias of Calderón*, ed. D. W. Cruickshank and J. E. Varey (London: Gregg International, 1973); published originally as "Santos y bandoleros en el teatro español del siglo de oro," *Arbor*, nos. 43–44 (July–August 1949): 395–416.

8. See also Cavillac (1983); Chevalier (1968); Noël Salomon, "Algunos problemas de sociología de las literaturas de lengua española," in *Creación y público en la literatura española*, ed. J.-F. Botrel and S. Salaün (Madrid: Castalia, 1974), 15–39; and *Actes: Picaresque espagnole* and *Picaresque européenne*.

When picaros praise their life of idleness and freedom (as in the long festive poem *La vida del pícaro*) they can claim to be the enlightened few who understand the new equation of time, money, and freedom. Money makes the difference between freedom and servitude; it also makes the difference between freedom and punishment. The power to influence the course of justice had been the traditional prerogative of social rank and authority, but bribery democratizes that power. These few examples of the greatly expanded importance of money in the urban economy show how the literature of picaros marks important shifts in the history of society's structures and value systems. Such information, patiently assembled, scrupulously analyzed and interpreted, serves two functions. It can help us to reconstruct imaginatively some segments of the mental horizon of the readers of these novels and of other related works, and it may enable us to judge more accurately how far the literary picaro may be used as an implement for deconstructing some central myths of Spanish society and its official rhetoric.

Let us suspend, if only momentarily, the distinction between picaresque novel and other kinds of low-life portrayal, in the interest of making a brief and provisional anthropology of this field of fiction. I do not know of any quantitative survey of *poesía germanesca, rufianesca, jácaras,* and so forth, but I would expect them to surpass picaresque fiction in total volume. Like the picaresque fiction, the literature of *la mala vida*, the underworld, was not consumed by its real-life counterparts. Much of it was published in anonymous broadsides, but much was also written by such well-known poets as Quevedo, or written for inclusion in a stage performance. This kind of literature, much of which persisted in the oral tradition, along with *romances*, ballads narrating crimes, executions, miracles, shipwrecks, and the like, uses thieves' cant and underworld jargon to an extent unknown in the picaresque novels. It presents in picturesque, joking, truculent language the violent activities and adventures of cutthroats, pimps, thieves, and other fearsome denizens of *el hampa*. Although this is still literature, it is closer to the reality of the city, its crime and its dangers, than the novels of Castillo Solórzano, with their ingenious and well-plotted swindles, their huge fortunes stolen and then gambled away, recounted with pretensions to style and elegance. The presentation in verse, in the traditional *romance* form, gives to the *poesía germanesca* and its related kinds a double perspective, for *romance* is the form for giving deeds a heroic tone, a public voice, but it has also become the vehicle for burlesque, for the mock-heroic posture.

Picaresque narrative, *poesía germanesca*, *rufianesca*, and so on are all ways of creating an imaginatively tolerable world that incorporates an intolerable reality: the violent and deceitful reality of urban life. This reality menaced the nobles and the bourgeois, but in different ways. For the aristocrats in their town houses, the menace was scarcely more than physical, a matter of maintaining law and order in the streets, of keeping the rabble at bay. For the bourgeois, the threat was of a different order. The merchants, traders, financial agents, lawyers, and other functionaries, many of whom were of humble origin, were the obvious victims of frauds and swindles. They were less removed from that obscure reservoir of violence, more precarious in their own social place. They lacked appropriate class definition, recognition, authority. Unlike the nobles, they did not have the protection afforded by an aristocratic caste system, the firm texture of family, genealogy, name, conspicuous livery, recognition by the right people in the right places, exemptions, privileges, deference from those who were below them. Below the bourgeois were the artisans, the laboring poor, the apprentices, and, too close for comfort, the unruly mob of vagrants and picaros. But there were no marked boundaries between them; only such moral boundaries as they might project upon their world. The traders, physicians, and other citizens of means and social ambition aspired to the prestige and ultimate security of noble status, and this status had become possible through the government sale of annuities and of patents of nobility, and the entailing of estates as rural land prices slumped. There was, then, in the early decades of the seventeenth century, an institutional route for the ennobling of those commoners who were financially successful, provided that they could prove (or forge) evidence of *hidalguía* and of purity of blood. Literature, drama, comic satire, and the historical archives provide ample evidence that this route was well traveled, and, as was to be expected, those who arrived by it were resented by the established nobility. The dominant thrust in the social structure, then, was this limited and controlled upward mobility of wealthy commoners, constrained by ideological tests (genealogy is ideological) and resisted by the traditional nobility, of whom Quevedo was one. A picaro ruthlessly clawing his way up from obscure poverty to fraudulent riches and (ultimate horror!) fraudulent nobility was a possibility too ugly to be contemplated. Quevedo deals with his *buscón* Pablos with condign ferocity when he attempts to marry into a respectable family.[9]

The literature of picaros after *Guzmán de Alfarache*, and with the exception of Alcalá Yáñez's *Donado hablador Alonso, mozo de muchos amos*, tends toward swindles for the sake of the story, told in a bright, facetious style. Such works could easily be consumed by readers who felt distanced enough from the dangerous world of picaros to be entertained by a facetious distortion of it. Thus it is not surprising that Castillo Solórzano purveyed both his short *novelas* of aristocratic love, adventure, treachery, and surprising encounters and also his picaresque frivolities, which, on examination, turn out to be traditional tales of feminine wiles in a new guise. They achieved success because they could appeal to the class to which his aristocratic employers belonged, and also to the nouveaux riches, who by the 1630s and 1640s were striving to merge into the urban nobility.

Looking back at *Guzmán*, we might wonder where would be the readers for a story that is also a meditation on evil. Maxime Chevalier (1976), Keith Whinnom (1980), and others have partially answered that question by pointing to devotional literature as the most widely bought, and the most usually found in the personal possession of merchants and traders. If Cavillac's (1983) mercantile thesis is correct, one might conjecture that Alemán had discovered an infallible formula for capturing the attention of men of affairs at all levels of activity. I observed earlier that bourgeois traders, financiers, lawyers, petty officials were protected by no class iden-

---

9. I know of only one example in literature of an upstart who marries into a higher status by wearing a badge of knighthood to which he is not entitled. The narrator, however, expects that the fraud will be exposed before long. In the meantime, the woman's family is to be blamed for being so dazzled by the match that they did not investigate the young man. Significantly, the bride is the daughter of a rich merchant, not of a hereditary nobleman. See José Camerino, *El pícaro amante*, in *Novelas amorosas* (Madrid, 1624), reprinted in *Novelas amorosas de diversos ingenios del siglo XVII*, ed. Evangelina Rodríguez (Madrid: Castalia, 1986).

tity, no symbolic boundaries, from the turbulent lower depths of urban life, but only by such moral boundaries as they set up for themselves. Having only recently, like Lazarillo, "made it to port," they could not be practitioners of that aesthetic distance that would have enabled them to see a challenge to their security as comic. The combination of realism in the telling and the moralizing discourse would both confirm the threat and frame it in familiar and acceptable terms. This is the only novel for which the case can be made that it represents the frustrated desires of a marginalized group to rise and prosper—not because Alemán himself failed to win prestige (he occupied important positions in the government bureaucracy) but because his business failures, like those of other merchants and manufacturers, could be blamed on bad economic and fiscal policies. Cavillac has demonstrated the novel's economic thesis, but it is a unique case. The weakness of a naive reading of marginality into these texts is easily disposed of: readers who paid for these books would not identify their frustrations with the disreputable characters in them. We saw in the case of the *pícaras* how the question of marginalized gender was elided. What is conveyed and released in these texts is exactly the reverse: not the anxiety of the marginal but the *anxiety of others toward* the marginal; the anxiety of the Lázaros for the security that, once it is won, may be lost to others. Landless hidalgos, rentiers, traders, merchants, public officials, all are insecure, *conversos* and old Christians alike; they all fear the beggars, vagrants, insolent rabble, whose very abundance reveals their instability, as emblems of what they could become.

The French parallel may prove instructive. The French public shared with the rest of Europe the interest in the lawless strata of sociey; "strata" is not an apt word here, since what distinguished them, both as groups and as individuals, was their mobility, their capacity to disperse through a city, or to coalesce into roving bands. In particular, French translations of *Lazarillo*, *Guzmán de Alfarache*, Quevedo's *Buscón* and *Sueños*, Cervantes' *Novelas ejemplares*, *Marcos de Obregón*, and *La desordenada codicia de los bienes ajenos* went through many editions (Chartier 1987:293). *Lazarillo* and *El Buscón* enjoyed special favor: the former's autobiographical mode provided a structural model for *La vie généreuse des mercelots, gueuz et boémiens* (Lyon, 1596), which enabled the narrator to reveal the oaths, rites, and ceremonies, the argot, and so forth, of the guilds of beggars, vagrants, and petty criminals in the course of unfolding his own story. *El buscón* had the distinction of being translated, mistranslated, bowdlerized, expurgated, and finally enshrined in the Bibliothèque Bleue, a library of popular fiction that continued to be published into the nineteenth century. The excisions carried out by the ecclesiastical censors (far more severe than those in Spain) and by the publishers left a text lacking in much of the facetious wordplay but kept two levels of reading clearly in view: the "scatologic tradition of Carnival culture on the one hand and the parodic and grotesque forms of burlesque literature on the other" (Chartier 1987:294). Presumably what became visible to French readers only after a troublesome linguistic surface was scoured away would have been evident to Spanish readers at all levels of the text (Cros 1975). Carnival can be risky in the way it serves both distance and relevance: it enables the violence on which the structures of everyday life depend to be projected in grotesque form, distanced by inversion, but also to recoil dangerously against the reality whose tensions it was supposed to release safely.[10] This collapse of the distance between reality and representation, which art has traditionally claimed to prevent, when it does happen does not always produce violence (as it does in *Don Quixote*, 11.26, at the puppet show). It more often, and more insidiously, mediates and shapes readers' perception of the reality that was to be distanced. Roger Chartier observes this process when he notes that the literature of the subculture of vagrants and beggars "embodies an ambiguity . . . since the literature of those descriptions claimed to be based on observations of reality, yet, conversely, the fictional portrayals of such people became proof of an incontestable and disquieting reality" (1987:275).

Part of the difficulty we have had in agreeing about picaresque is due to the position of the picaro himself, that singular subject who has his own road to follow, but also enters and leaves those unruly communities. He is not entirely of them, but neither does he wholly dissociate himself. Interposed between them and us and speaking in a voice that has already become familiar to us, he

10. Emmanuel Le Roy Ladurie, *Carnival in Romans* (New York: Braziller, 1979).

makes them familiar through his mediation at the same time that he distances them by his commentary and his foreordained detachment from them. Cervantes seized on this ambiguity, pushing it to extremes in presenting Carriazo oxymoronically as "a virtuous, clean, well-bred picaro" (*La ilustre fregona*), and again in the unresolved distance at the end of *Rinconete y Cortadillo*, a conclusion "that concludes nothing," to borrow a phrase from Cervantes in another place. But this ambiguity is not sustained after Quevedo's *Buscón*: then we are to be entertained by unmitigated swindles and crude humiliations of whoever may be the designated victim.

The literature of low life in the Spain of the Habsburgs is important to literary history, for its abundance and its persistence. We have shaped that history by privileging the more concentratedly narrative part of its low-life material. However finely we discriminate among the various kinds of literature that portray *la mala vida—picaresca, rufianesca, germanesca, celestinesca*, and so forth—together they represent an important part of the cultural experience of that epoch. Just how important it is can be seen in the eight hundred pages of José Antonio Maravall's (1986) book on the relation between picaresque literature and the "mentalities" of Habsburg Spain. I wish to close, however, by suggesting an anthropological perspective rather than a sociological one.

Literature stimulates and also attempts to satisfy our desire to be other, or elsewhere, and incidentally to be free from the constraints of the here and now. As they live out the consequences of leaving familiar ties and taking to the road, picaros demonstrate the paradox that freedom from constraints becomes loss of freedom. We learn this through the irony of Lázaro's praise of his situation, through Guzmán's meditations on the topic, through watching Pablos' downward spiral, through Marcos' cautionary anecdotes. The individual picaro speaking from within his experience is an effective conveyor of this truth, more certain and effective than are the deviant communities that he encounters. Those communities believe in the freedom that the picaro is designed to expose. For them there is a more powerful paradox than the picaro's deconstructive one, which is that *their* solidarity conceives a higher liberation. This sense of liberation into a higher unity has been dubbed *communitas* by the late anthropologist Victor Turner.

Turner started from Arnold van Gennep's classic *Rites de passage* (1909), which identified the three essential stages in such rites as initiation and childbirth ceremonies: (1) separation or detachment from the social structure that the subject has occupied, (2) transition, and (3) incorporation into the new structure, or reaggregation into the former structure but with a new status. The initiand in the passage from boy to adult hunter, for example, is removed from his group, and in stage 2 he is kept apart from them while new, sacred knowledge is imparted, new experiences are imposed by means of ordeals or challenges or encounters with the spirits of the dead. Turner was the first to investigate the full richness of the intermediate "liminal" phase (van Gennep's term), and to perceive that it not only is a stage in which certain acts are carried out but that it has its own peculiar dynamism, and that it restructures the consciousness of the reintegrated subject, which is, quite literally, transformed.[11] For the person involved, this is a stage of betwixt and between, as Turner says, of being neither one thing nor the other. But it is precisely in this state of liminality that consciousness is released from a previous identity and status (a minor, say, or a pregnant woman) and heightened, and may expand to include experiences of the "other world." The ceremonies of transition open up a space in which freedom from the normal limits of social and familial structure permits an awareness of the cosmic powers that give meaning and identity to the culture.

> Liminal entities, such as neophytes in initiation or puberty rites, may be represented as possessing nothing. They may be disguised as monsters, wear only a strip of clothing, or even go naked, to demonstrate that as liminal beings they have no status, property, insignia . . . in short, nothing that may distinguish them from their fellow neophytes or initiands. . . . [T]hey must obey their instructors implicitly and accept punishment without complaint. (Turner 1969:95)

Turner remarks that this process is "as if they were being ground down to a uniform condition to be fashioned anew," but he also notes that in group ceremonies, "among themselves, neophytes

11. We are, unfortunately, familiar with the disorientation induced by isolation, from the techniques of interrogation and brainwashing.

tend to develop an intense comradeship and egalitarianism." This superior sense of belonging together is what Turner has named "communitas," or antistructure; the Latin word serves to bring out the transcendent nature of the experience, to differentiate it from the visible community, from which the initiands are now separated, and from the "community sense" that shapes everyday living. A comparable phenomenon can be observed in the collective life of a community, with its public ceremonies marking the passage from season to season, year to year, peace to war, and the reverse. On such occasions, the liminal phase is that in which the society as a whole is liberated from the usual constraints—in carnival, mock usurpations of authority, ceremonial games, and so forth.

Turning his attention from the Ndembu people to more complex societies, Turner noticed that whole groups exist in a "betwixt and between" condition, without moving on to a new level of incorporation. Some of these groups have detached themselves and live in a more or less permanent state of liminality, resisting reintegration; others separate themselves for a limited time and for a specific purpose. Of the latter, the bands of pilgrims that took to the roads for a long journey with a spiritual goal offer a notable example (Turner 1974). Marchers for a cause, hunger strikers, civil disobedience groups, all assume a cohesive antistructure, and all are sustained by their communitas, that sense of an overriding community with higher obligations and allegiance to some more compelling ethos than the laws and conventions that normally bind them to their fellow citizens. Those that live in a state of permanent liminality are all who choose to occupy a place apart, in observance of other rules and "alternative lifestyles," in the current jargon, religious orders being the clearest example. Then, as these orders become institutionalized and their religion established, new liminal space is claimed by friars, fratelli, apocalyptics, Joachites, and so on, who reject possessions and existing authority, as well as by individual hermits, mystics, and the like. This state of permanent liminality that lacks transitive function Turner called "liminoid." Such groups find their cohesion in a collective identity and an ethos that override societal expectations. In this respect, if in no other, the troops of vagabonds, guilds of beggars, bands of gypsies, covens of witches, companies of thieves are likewise sodalities bound together by common aims that exploit, negate, and travesty the established order. Their communitas crystallizes into notions of freedom, mutual help, common service, sealed by a private language; they see themselves as persecuted, and pride themselves on their spirit in the face of persecution and their silence under torture, "as if *no* had more letters than *sí!*" (*Rinconete y Cortadillo*). As we observe these groups occupying the interstices of the society and replicating its structure of authority (the underworld in *Rinconete y Cortadillo*, the gypsies in *La gitanilla*), it becomes clear that they are more accurately categorized in anthropological terms as liminoid rather than in the less precise and less dynamic sociological term "marginal."

From this excursus we can understand why these groups were so feared, what made them so dangerous, and why they could not be permitted to figure more prominently in literature. They all asserted a seductive concept of freedom that was at odds with the established order, and in many cases they enjoyed a mobility that was perceived as a threat to person and property as well as a denial of the very concept of order. In *Don Quixote* it is the morisco Ricote who speaks for the band of German "pilgrims" who make money by doing the rounds of the shrines ("which for them were their Indies"), who are well dressed under their pilgrim garb and carry caviar to arouse their thirst for wine. There is evident a sardonic ambivalence toward the German "liberty of conscience"; a freedom that a morisco, tragically liminal, would yearn for, but that was also license to exploit Spain's holy places (*DQ*, 11.54).[12] Andrés' praise of thieving as the ideal way of life (*La desordenada codicia de los bienes ajenos*) has to be read as sardonic in the same sense.

When a picaro falls in with a gang of thieves or swindlers, the association does not last; he tricks them when he can, and besides, he has his own agenda. Consequently, in scenes or sequences of action involving *el hampa* or migrant bands of thieves, the presence of the picaro serves in some cases to make them appear vulnerable or foolish, and in others to reveal a chaos at the center of their order. A Guzmán or a Pablos who enters their company and

12. This episode is much more complex than I have suggested. The political implications are thoroughly explored by Marquez-Villanueva 1975:229–329.

leaves it by his wits stands between them and us and reserves his claim on our attention. He can reveal their incompetence or reduce them to an amusing bag of tricks, making the reader forget their formidable solidarity, the communitas that is at once enviable and frightening. A picaro, especially a repentant one, is more acceptable than the bands of starving beggars, mutinous soldiers, and marauding gypsies that peopled the real landscape. It is notable that Cervantes did not shirk the dangerous fascination, the allure of freedom projected by gypsies, criminal societies, and other traveling charlatans.

Marcel Bataillon (1969) raised an interesting question when he noted the bounds of violence within which picaresque fiction operates: it presents all forms of theft except armed robbery; picaros do not spill blood, and they are not bandits.[13] Part of the answer to this question is already given, I think. The picaro is designed not to bring violence closer to the reader but the reverse: to contain it within traditional comic forms—fights in the dark, foolish lovers beaten, falls into latrines, drunken brawls. It is as if the whole culture of early modern Spain were in a condition of betwixt and between, a liminal phase of emergence from long-established social and mental structures and conceptions of relevance in literary representation (our current use of the term "early modern" implies as much). Reference is contemporary and urban; but death is still heroic or tragic or exemplary, in literature as in painting. If there is truth in the hypothesis propounded a century ago by Enrico Ferri, a sociologist of crime, we may have another piece of the answer to Bataillon's query: "Every phase of civilization has its peculiar criminality which corresponds to it. As there was a criminality of violence and bloodshed in feudal society, and a criminality of robbery and fraud in bourgeoise society, so the criminality of the future will have its own appropriate character. . . . [N]atural crime passes more and more from the material forms of violence into the intellectual forms of cunning and fraud."[14] This postulated shift

13. "Merecería consideración el cómo y porqué son tan inherentes a la materia picaresca española todas las modalidades del arte de robar menos el robo a mano armada. No son materia picaresca los delitos de sangre. En otros términos, ningún pícaro literario es un bandido" (Bataillon 1969:14).

14. Enrico Ferri, *Criminal Sociology* (Boston: Little, Brown, 1917), 179. The first Italian edition, of 160 pages, appeared in 1864; the fifth, of 1,000 pages, in

from crimes against the person to crimes against property is discussed briefly by Robert Darnton:

> Although Ferri's "law" may have been flogged to death, it has proved useful in comparing traditional and modern or rural and urban societies. The rate of violent crimes (murder and felonious assault, for example) tends to be much higher in archaic, agrarian villages, where communal norms regulate conduct, except in its most explosive, impetuous moments, whereas economic crime (theft and fraud) predominates in modern cities, where uprooted, money-oriented individuals struggle anonymously to strike it rich or simply to survive.
>
> This shift from passionate to commercial criminality seems to have occurred throughout the West during the early modern period . . . and so does the rise of the underworld. . . . (1990:265–66)

In the characteristic forms of medieval literature, people kill but they do not steal, except to deceive or to cause mischief. Once more we have come up against one of the boundary zones of the principle of relevance. Picaresque, rooted in the comic tradition of tricks and jokes, does not mix with death or brutal injury. High romance (exemplified by Cervantes' *Persiles y Sigismunda*) is of a different order; its subject is, as readers would agree, matters of life and death. The same may be said of the theater, where the milieu may be contemporary but the action often hinges on an archaic concept of honor.

The different literary representations of *la mala vida* were read by people who were in varying degrees threatened not only by its existence, its vitality, its lack of discipline and respect for boundaries, but the communitas that was generated within it. It was the destructive Other that threatened the survival of each class separately and of the whole body of society, as that body was symbolically conceived. The Russian formalists made us aware of the function of literature in "defamiliarizing" what is familiar or passes

---

1900. The American translation was made from the French of 1905, revised by the author.

unnoticed.[15] Among many other functions of literature is the opposite one, that of familiarizing, domesticating the dangerous, the outrageous, that which threatens us and is too monstrous to be ignored. So writers have created alternative worlds in which this monster, this irrational *vulgo*, this lawless mob, this mindless many-headed beast (to repeat some familiar phrases from the literature) may be symbolically brought under control. Alemán plays the game all ways; his monster is repugnant enough, but he gives it a biography, a human face, a conscience, and finally he redeems it. He moralizes it to the point where familiar and unfamiliar are interchangeable, where it can become us, and we become it. In *Lazarillo de Tormes*, a little work that continually springs new surprises, catching the reader in its steel traps of irony, there are no monsters. Nothing is outrageous. Nothing has to be moralized. Everything is "normal," that's the way the world is, and this is how you get along in it. But that, precisely, is what is so monstrous about the world the unknown author makes us see as our own. The reality that is so outrageous is that this monstrous world can be seen as normal, familiar, inviting no comment except that Lázaro deserves our respect for having played according to its rules. And our admiration for palming his story off as art. For Quevedo, the master of satiric overkill, nothing is normal, all is monstrous, there are no boundaries to divide us from that which we fear may destroy us. Then along come those bright, busy writers of fiction according to formula, stirring into their bland paste great gobs of facetious insouciance, a pinch of artificial indignation, and a drop of extract of morality. In their company are the commentators on the social scene, compilers of advice, warning against pickpockets and sighing for better days. Together they tell us that we can forget the old lesson that we must find, know, and stand in awe of our monsters if we are to know ourselves. The social world can be reduced to comedy and *costumbrismo* (literature of manners). The *literatura germanesca* may lean toward *costumbrismo*, but even at its most linguistically playful it cannot disguise the violence that it portrays, nor can it fail to let us see that its subversion of literary canons is a substitute for, or a displace-

15. See Viktor Shklovsky, "Art as Technique," in Lemon/Reis 1965:3–24.

ment of, social criticism. The *costumbrismo* that creeps into prose writing with Agustín de Rojas and other entertaining observers and proliferates in the fiction of the following decades becomes a snobbish concern with expensive furnishings, rich banquets, and so forth in the *novela cortesana*. Insofar as the upstart picaros and *pícaras* participate in this world, late picaresque fiction participates in the literature of self-flattery and self-congratulation. The threat of social transgression is no longer taken seriously.

Selected Bibliography

Primary texts are listed in the Abbreviations. All works not identified there are found in:

Valbuena Prat, Angel, ed. *La novela picaresca española*. 2d ed. Madrid: Aguilar, 1946.

Bibliographies

Laurenti, Joseph L. 1973. *Bibliografía de literatura picaresca/A Bibliography of Picaresque Literature*. Metuchen, N.J.: Scarecrow Press.
———. 1981. *Bibliografía de literatura picaresca: Suplemento/A Bibliography of Picaresque Literature: A Supplement*. New York: AMS.
Ricapito, Joseph V. 1980. *Bibliografía razonada y anotada de las obras maestras de la picaresca española*. Madrid: Castalia. A selective bibliography, valuable for its extensive summaries of the principal critical works up to about 1975.

Works Cited or Consulted

Achleitner, Alois. 1952. "Pasamonte." *AC* 2:365–67.
Actes: Picaresque espagnole. 1976. Actes de la Table Ronde Internationale du CNRS, Montpellier, November 1974. Etudes Sociocritiques. Montpellier: Université Paul Valéry.
Actes: Picaresque européenne. 1976. Actes du Colloque Internationale

du CERS, Montpellier, March 1976. Etudes Sociocritiques. Montpellier: Université Paul Valéry.

Alter, Robert. 1964. *Rogue's Progress: Studies in the Picaresque Novel.* Cambridge: Harvard University Press.

Approaches to Medieval Romance. YFS 51 (1974).

Archer, Robert. 1985. "The Fictional Context of *Lazarillo de Tormes.*" *MLR* 80:340–50.

Arias, Joan. 1977. *Guzmán de Alfarache: The Unrepentant Narrator.* London: Támesis.

Attridge, Derek. 1988. *Peculiar Language: Literature as Difference from the Renaissance to James Joyce.* Ithaca: Cornell University Press.

Aubrun, Charles V. 1979. "'La verdadera codicia de los bienes ajenos' (de Carlos García): Composición y compromiso político." In *Picaresca*, 619–30.

L'Autobiographie dans le monde hispanique. 1980. Actes du Colloque International de la Baume-lès-Aix, 11–13 May 1979. Aix: Université de Provence.

L'Autobiographie en Espagne. 1982. Actes du Colloque International de la Baume-lès-Aix, 23–25 May 1981. Aix: Université de Provence.

Avalle-Arce, Juan Bautista. 1972. "Lope y su *Peregrino.*" *MLN* 87:193–99.

Barthes, Roland. 1980. "L'Effet de réel." In *Littérature et réalité*, ed. Roland Barthes et al., 80–91. Paris: Seuil.

Bataillon, Marcel, 1954. *El sentido del "Lazarillo de Tormes."* Paris: Editions Espagnoles.

——. 1967. *Défense et illustration du sens littéral.* Cambridge: Modern Humanities Research Association.

——. 1969. *Pícaros y picaresca.* Madrid: Taurus.

——. 1973a. "Estebanillo González, bouffon pour rire." In *Studies in Spanish Literature of the Golden Age Presented to Edward M. Wilson*, ed. R. O. Jones. London: Tamesis.

——. 1973b. *Novedad y fecundidad del "Lazarillo."* 2d ed. Salamanca: Anaya.

——. 1973c. "Relaciones literarias." In *Suma cervantina*, ed. J. B. Avalle-Arce and E. C. Riley, 215–32. London: Tamesis, 1973.

Beer, Gillian. 1970. *The Romance.* London: Methuen.

Benassar, Bartolomé. 1969. *Recherches sur les grandes epidémies dans le nord de l'Espagne à la fin du XVE^e siècle.* Paris: Ecole Pratique des Hautes Etudes/S.E.V.P.E.N.

Berger, Peter L., and Thomas Luckmann. 1966. *The Social Construction of Reality.* New York: Doubleday.

Biraben, Jean Noël. 1975, 1976. *Les Hommes et la peste en France et dans les pays européens et mediterranéens.* 2 vols. Paris: La Haye.

Bjornson, Richard. 1977. *The Picaresque Hero in European Fiction.* Madison: University of Wisconsin Press.

Blackburn, Alexander, 1979. *The Myth of the Picaro: Continuity and Transformation of the Picaresque Novel.* Chapel Hill: University of North Carolina Press.

Blanco Aguinaga, Carlos. 1957. "Cervantes y la picaresca: Notas sobre dos tipos de realismo," *NRFH* 11:314–42.

Blecua, Alberto, 1971. "Libros de caballerías, latín macarrónico y novela picaresca: La adaptación castellana del *Baldus* (Sevilla, 1542)." *Boletín de la Real Academia de Buenas Letras de Barcelona* 34:147–239.

Bleiberg, Germán. 1966. "Mateo Alemán y los galeotes." *Revista de Occidente* n.s. 4, no. 39: 330–63.

———. 1967. "Nuevos datos biográficos de Mateo Alemán." In *Actas del Segundo Congreso Internacional de Hispanistas.* Nijmegen: Rijksuniversitet.

———. 1980. "El 'informe secreto' de Mateo Alemán sobre el trabajo forzoso en las minas de Almadén." *Estudios de Historia Social* 12: 357–443.

Booth, Wayne C. 1961. *The Rhetoric of Fiction.* Chicago: University of Chicago Press.

———. 1974. *A Rhetoric of Irony.* Chicago: University of Chicago Press.

Bourland, Caroline B. 1905. "Boccaccio and the *Decameron* in Castilian and Catalan Literature." *Revue Hispanique* 12:1–232.

———. 1927. *The Short Story in Spain in the Seventeenth Century.* Northampton, Mass.: Smith College.

Bouwsma, William J. 1979. "The Renaissance and the Drama of Western History." *American Historical Review* 84:1–15.

Bradley, Raymond, and Norman Swartz. 1979. *Possible Worlds: An Introduction to Logic and Its Philosophy.* Oxford: Basil Blackwell.

Brancaforte, Benito. 1980. *"Guzmán de Alfarache": ¿Conversión o proceso de degradación?* Madison, Wis.: Hispanic Seminary of Medieval Studies.

Brooks, Peter. 1984. *Reading for the Plot: Design and Intention in Narrative.* New York: Knopf.

Brown, Peter. 1967. *Augustine of Hippo.* Berkeley: University of California Press.

Brownstein, Leonard. 1974. *Salas Barbadillo and the New Novel of Rogues and Courtiers.* Madrid: Playor.

Carey, Douglas M. 1969. "Asides and Interiority in *Lazarillo de Tormes*: A Study in Psychological Realism." *Studies in Philology* 66:119–34.

———. 1979. "*Lazarillo de Tormes* and the Quest for Authority." *PMLA* 94:36–46.

Caro Baroja, Julio. 1969. *Ensayo sobre la literatura de cordel.* Madrid: Revista de Occidente.

Casalduero, Joaquín. 1962. *Sentido y forma de las "Novelas Ejemplares."* Rev. ed. Madrid: Gredos.

Casey, James. 1985. "Spain: A Failed Transition." In Clark 1985, 209–28.

Castro, Américo. 1925. *El pensamiento de Cervantes*. Madrid: Revista de Filología Española.

——. 1966. *Cervantes y los casticismos españoles*. Madrid: Alfaguara.

——. 1967. *Hacia Cervantes*. 3d ed. Madrid: Taurus.

Cavillac, Michel. 1980. "Mateo Alemán et la modernité." *BHi* 82:380–401.

——. 1983. *Gueux et marchands dans le "Guzmán de Alfarache" (1599–1604): Roman picaresque et mentalité bourgeoise dans l'Espagne du Siècle d'Or*. Bordeaux: Institut d'Etudes Ibériques et Ibéro-américaines de l'Université de Bordeaux.

——. 1990. "*Ozmín y Daraja* à l'épreuve de l'*Atalaya*." *BHi* 92:141–184.

Cavillac, Michel, and Cécile Cavillac. 1973. "A propos du *Buscón* et du *Guzmán de Alfarache*." *BHi* 75:114–31.

Chandler, Frank Wadleigh. 1899. *Romances of Roguery*. Pt. 1: *The Picaresque Novel in Spain*. New York: Macmillan. Rpt. New York: B. Franklin, 1961.

Chartier, Roger. 1982. *Figures de la gueuserie*. Bibliothèque Bleue. Paris: Montalba.

——. 1987. *The Cultural Uses of Print in Early Modern France*. Princeton: Princeton University Press. (Chap. 8, "The Literature of Roguery in the Bibliothèque Bleue," is a translation of the introductory essay in *Figures de la gueuserie*, above.)

Chatman, Seymour. 1978. *Story and Discourse*. Ithaca: Cornell University Press.

Chevalier, Maxime. 1968. *Sur le public du roman de chevalerie*. Talence: Institut d'Etudes Ibériques et Ibéro-americaines de l'Université de Bordeaux.

——. 1976. *Lectura y lectores en la España del siglo XVI y XVII*. Madrid: Turner.

——. 1980. "Cuento folklórico, cuentecillo tradicional, y literatura del Siglo de Oro." In *Actas del VI Congreso Internacional de Hispanistas celebrado en Toronto, 1977*, 5–11. Toronto: University of Toronto Press.

Clark, Peter, ed. 1985. *The European Crisis of the 1590s: Essays in Comparative History*. London: Allen & Unwin.

Cockburn, Claud. 1957. *In Time of Trouble: An Autobiography*. London: R. Hart-Davis.

Cohen, Ralph. 1986. "History and Genre." *NLH* 17:203–17.

Colie, Rosalie. 1973. *The Resources of Kind: Genre Theory in the Renaissance*. Berkeley: University of California Press.

Collard, Andrée. 1968. "The Unity of *Lazarillo de Tormes*." *MLN* 83: 262–67.

Courcelle, Pierre Paul. 1963. *Les "Confessions" de Saint Augustin dans la tradition littéraire: Antécédents et postérité*. Paris: Etudes Augustiniennes.

Cros, Edmond. 1965. "Deux épîtres inédites de Mateo Alemán." *BHi* 67:433–44.

———. 1967. *Protée et le gueux: Recherches sur les origines et la nature du récit picaresque dans "Guzmán de Alfarache."* Paris: Didier.

———. 1970. "La vie de Mateo Alemán: Quelques documents inédits, quelques suggestions." *BHi* 72:331–37.

———. 1971. *Mateo Alemán: Introducción a su vida y a su obra.* Salamanca: Anaya.

———. 1975. *L'Aristocrate et le carnaval des gueux: Etude sur le "Buscón" de Quevedo.* Etudes Sociocritiques. Montpellier: Université Paul Valéry.

Cruikshank, Don W. 1976. "Some Aspects of Spanish Book-Production in the Golden Age." *Library* 5th ser. 31:1–19.

———. 1978. "'Literature' and the Book Trade in Golden Age Spain." *MLR* 73:799–824.

Culler, Jonathan. 1981. *The Pursuit of Signs.* Ithaca: Cornell University Press.

———. 1982. *On Deconstruction: Theory and Criticism after Structuralism.* Ithaca: Cornell University Press.

Damiani, Bruno. 1977. *Francisco López de Ubeda.* Boston: Twayne.

Darnton, Robert. 1990. *The Kiss of Lamourette: Reflections in Cultural History.* New York: Norton.

Davies, C. S. L. 1985. "Popular Disorder." In Clark, 1985, 244–60.

De Haan, Fonger. 1903. *An Outline of the Novela Picaresca in Spain.* The Hague: Nijhoff.

Del Monte, Alberto. 1971. *Itinerario de la novela picaresca.* Barcelona: Lumen.

Delumeau, Jean. 1978. *La peur en occident (XIVe–XVIe siècles).* Paris: Fayard.

De Man, Paul. 1979. "Autobiography as De-facement." *MLN* 94:919–30.

Demerson, G., ed. 1984. *La Notion de genre à la Renaissance.* Geneva: Slatkine.

Deyermond, Alan D. 1975. *"Lazarillo de Tormes": A Critical Guide.* London: Grant & Cutler.

Díaz Migoyo, Gonzalo. 1978. *Estructura de la novela: Anatomía de "El Buscón."* Madrid: Fundamentos.

Dolezel, Lubomir. 1980. "Truth and Authenticity in Narrative." *Poetics Today* 1:7–25.

Domínguez Ortiz, Antonio. 1969. *Crisis y decadencia de la España de los Austrias.* Barcelona: Ariel.

Dubrow, Heather. 1982. *Genre.* London: Methuen.

Dunlop, John C. 1814. *History of Prose Fiction.* London: Longmans, Green.

Dunn, Peter N. 1950. "Individuo y sociedad en *La vida del Buscón.*" *BHi* 52:375–96.

——. 1952. *Castillo Solórzano and the Decline of the Spanish Novel*. Oxford: Basil Blackwell.

——. 1973. "Las novelas ejemplares." In *Suma Cervantina*, ed. J. B. Avalle-Arce and E. C. Riley. London: Tamesis.

——. 1979. *The Spanish Picaresque Novel*. Boston: Twayne.

——. 1982a. "Cervantes De/reconstructs the Picaresque." *Cervantes* 2:109–31.

——. 1982b. "Problems of a Model for the Picaresque and the case of Quevedo's *Buscón*." *BHS* 59:95–105.

——. 1985. "Cervantes and the Shape of Experience." *Cervantes* 5:149–61.

——. 1988. "*Lazarillo de Tormes*: The Case of the Purloined Letter." *REH* 22:1–14.

——. 1989. "Reading the Text of *Lazarillo de Tormes*." In *Studies in Honor of Bruce W. Wardropper*, ed. Dian Fox, Harry Sieber, and Robert ter Horst, 91–104. Newark, Del.: Juan de la Cuesta, 1989.

——. 1990 [1992]. "The Spanish Picaresque Novel as a Problem of Genre." *Dispositio* 15:1–15.

Durand, Frank. 1968. "The Author and Lázaro: Levels of Comic Meaning." *BHS* 45:89–101.

Eco, Umberto. 1979. *The Role of the Reader*. Bloomington: Indiana University Press.

Egido, Aurora. 1978. "Retablo carnavalesco del Buscón don Pablos (Artículo-reseña)." *HR* 46:173–97.

Eisenberg, Daniel. 1979. "Does the Picaresque Novel Exist?" *KRQ* 26:203–19.

Eisenstein, Elizabeth. 1979. *The Printing Press as an Agent of Change*. Cambridge: Cambridge University Press.

Elliott, John H. 1963. *Imperial Spain, 1469–1716*. London: Edward Arnold.

Elliott, Robert C. 1960. *The Power of Satire*. Princeton: Princeton University Press.

Erlich, Victor. 1981. *Russian Formalism: History-Doctrine*. 3d ed. New Haven: Yale University Press.

Fèbvre, Lucien, and Henri-Jean Martin. 1971. *L'Apparition du livre*. Paris: Albin Michel. Published in English as *The Coming of the Book: The Impact of Printing, 1450–1800*, trans. David Gerard. London: NLB, 1976.

Fernández Alvarez, Manuel. 1970. *La sociedad española del Renacimiento*. Salamanca: Anaya.

Fernández de Peñalosa, Luis F. 1949. "Juan Bravo y la familia Coronel." *Estudios Segovianos* 1:73–109.

Forcione, Alban K. 1970. *Cervantes, Aristotle, and the "Persiles."* Princeton: Princeton University Press.

Foucault, Michel. 1970. *The Order of Things*. New York: Random House.

Foulché-Delbosc, Raymond. 1918. "Bibliographie de Mateo Alemán, 1598–1615." *RH* 42:481–556.

Fowler, Alastair. 1971. "The Life and Death of Literary Forms." *NLH* 2:199–216.

——. 1982. *Kinds of Literature: An Introduction to the Theory of Genres and Modes*. Cambridge: Harvard University Press.

Francis, Alan. 1978. *Picaresca, decadencia, historia: Aproximación a una realidad histórico-literaria*. Madrid: Gredos.

Friedman, Edward H. 1987. *The Antiheroine's Voice: Narrative Discourse and Transformations of the Picaresque*. Columbia: University of Missouri Press.

——. 1988. "The Picaresque as Autobiography: Story and History." In Spadaccini/Talens, 119–27.

Friedman, Norman. 1955. "Point of View in Fiction: The Development of a Critical Concept." *PMLA* 70:1160–84.

Frohock, W. M. 1967. "The Idea of Picaresque." *Yearbook of Comparative and General Literature* 16:43–52.

——. 1969. "The Failing Center: Recent Fiction and the Picaresque Tradition." *Novel* 3:62–69.

——. 1971. "The *Buscón* and Current Criticism. In *Homenaje a William L. Fichter*, ed. A. David Kossoff and José Amor y Vázquez. Madrid: Castalia.

Frye, Northrop. 1957. *Anatomy of Criticism*. Princeton: Princeton University Press.

——. 1976. *The Secular Scripture: A Study of the Structure of Romance*. Cambridge: Harvard University Press.

Gaède, Edouard. 1983. "Conscience de soi et forme narrative: Réflexions sur le roman picaresque." In *Genèse de la conscience moderne: Etudes sur le développement de la conscience de soi dans les littératures du monde occidental*, ed. Robert Ellrodt, 119–72. Paris: Presses Universitaires de France.

García de Enterría, María Cruz. 1973. *Sociedad y poesía de cordel en el barroco*. Madrid: Taurus.

——. 1983. *Literaturas marginadas*. Madrid: Playor.

Genette, Gérard. 1980. *Narrative Discourse: An Essay in Method*. Ithaca: Cornell University Press.

Gennep, Arnold van. 1960. *The Rites of Passage*. London: Routledge & Kegan Paul. Trans. of *Les Rites de passage*. Paris: Nourry, 1909.

Gilbert, Allan H. 1940. *Literary Criticism: Plato to Dryden*. New York: American Book Co. Rpt. Detroit: Wayne State University Press, 1962.

Gilman, Stephen. 1966. "The Death of Lazarillo de Tormes." *PMLA* 81:149–66.

Gilson, Etienne. 1960. *The Christian Philosophy of St. Augustine*. New York: Random House.

Selected Bibliography

Girard, René. 1965. *Desire, Deceit, and the Novel*. Baltimore: Johns Hopkins University Press.

Glowinski, Michal. 1977. "On the First-Person Novel." *NLH* 9:103–14.

Gómez-Moriana, Antonio. 1983. "Intertextualidad, interdiscursividad y parodia: Sobre los orígenes de la forma narrativa en la novela picaresca." *Dispositio* 8:123–44.

González-Echevarría, Roberto. 1980. "The Life and Adventures of Cipión: Cervantes and the Picaresque." *Diacritics* 10:15–26. Rpt. in *Cervantes*, ed. Harold Bloom. Modern Critical Views. New York: Chelsea House, 1987.

Green, Otis H. 1966. *Spain and the Western Tradition: The Castilian Mind in Literature from "El Cid" to Calderón*. Vol. 4. Madison: University of Wisconsin Press.

Guillén, Claudio, 1957. "La disposición temporal del *Lazarillo de Tormes*." *HR* 25:264–79.

———. 1960. "Los pleitos extremeños de Mateo Alemán, I. El Juez, 'Dios de la tierra.'" *Archivo Hispalense* 32:387–407.

———. 1963. "Un padrón de conversos sevillanos (1510)." *BHi* 65:49–98.

———. 1971. *Literature as System*. Princeton: Princeton University Press.

———. 1982. "Quevedo y los géneros literarios." In *Quevedo in Perspective*. Proceedings of the Boston Quevedo Symposium, October 1980. Newark, Del.: Juan de la Cuesta.

Hägg, Tomas. 1988. *The Novel in Antiquity*. Oxford: Basil Blackwell.

Hale, J. R. 1971. *Renaissance Europe: Individual and Society, 1480–1520*. New York: Harper; London: Collins.

Haley, George. 1959. *Vicente Espinel and "Marcos de Obregón": A Life and Its Literary Representation*. Providence, R.I.: Brown University Press.

Hallam, Henry. 1837. *Introduction to the Literature of Europe in the Fifteenth, Sixteenth, and Seventeenth Centuries*. 4 vols. London: John Murray.

Hanrahan, Thomas, S.J. 1967. *La mujer en la novela picaresca española*. 2 vols. Madrid: Porrúa Turanzas.

Herrero, Javier. 1979. "Renaissance Poverty and Lazarillo's Family: The Birth of the Picaresque Genre." *PMLA* 94:876–86.

Hirsch, E. D., Jr. 1967. *Validity in Interpretation*. New Haven: Yale University Press.

Hitchcock, Richard. 1971. "Lazarillo and Vuestra Merced." *MLN* 86:264–66.

Howarth, William L. 1974. "Some Principles of Autobiography." *NLH* 5:363–81.

Hunter, J. Paul. 1988. "'News and New Things': Contemporaneity and the Early English Novel." *CI* 14:493–515.

Hutcheon, Linda. 1980. *Narcissistic Narrative: The Metafictional Paradox*. Waterloo, Ont.: Wilfrid Laurier University Press.

———. 1985. *A Theory of Parody*. London and New York: Methuen.

Ife, Barry W. 1985. *Reading and Fiction in Golden-Age Spain: A Platonist Critique and Some Picaresque Replies*. Cambridge: Cambridge University Press.

Iffland, James. 1978, 1982. *Quevedo and the Grotesque*. 2 vols. London: Tamesis.

Innocent, III, Pope. See Segni, Lotario dei.

Iser, Wolfgang. 1974. *The Implied Reader*. Baltimore: Johns Hopkins University Press.

——. 1980. *The Act of Reading: A Theory of Aesthetic Response*. Baltimore: Johns Hopkins University Press.

Jameson, Fredric. 1981. *The Political Unconscious: Narrative as a Socially Symbolic Act*. Ithaca: Cornell University Press.

Jauss, Hans Robert. 1982. *Toward an Aesthetic of Reception*. Minneapolis: University of Minnesota Press.

Johnson, Barbara. 1990. "Writing." In Lentricchia/McLaughlin, 39–49.

Johnson, Carroll B. 1974. "*El Buscón*: D. Pablos, D. Diego y D. Francisco," *Hispanófila*, no. 51, 1–26.

——. 1978. *Inside Guzmán de Alfarache*." Berkeley: University of California Press.

Joly, Monique. 1986. *La Bourle et son interprétation: Recherches sur le passage de la facétie au roman (Espagne, XVIe–XVIIe siècles)*. Toulouse: France-Ibérie Recherche.

Jones, Harold G. 1979. "La vida de Lazarillo de Tormes." In *Picaresca*, 449–58.

Jones, Royston O. 1971. *The Golden Age: Prose and Poetry*. Vol 4 of *A Literary History of Spain*, ed. R. O. Jones. London: Benn; New York: Harper & Row.

Kagan, Richard L. 1974. *Students and Society in Early Modern Spain*. Baltimore: Johns Hopkins University Press.

——. 1978. "The Decline of Spain: A Historical Myth?" *P&P*, no. 81, 24–50.

——. 1981. "Rejoinder. The Decline of Spain: A Historical Myth?" *P&P*, no. 91, 181–85.

Kristeller, Paul O. 1956. *Studies in Renaissance Thought and Letters*. Rome: Storia e Letteratura.

Krömer, Wolfram. 1984. "Lenguaje y retórica de los representantes de las clases sociales en la novela picaresca española." In *Estudios de literatura española y francesa, siglos XVI y XVII: Homenaje a Horst Baader*, ed. Fraucke Gewecke, 131–39. Editionen de Iberoamericana, no. 31. Frankfurt am Main: Vervuert.

Lázaro Carreter, Fernando. 1961. "Originalidad del *Buscón*." In *Studia Philologica: Homenaje a Dámaso Alonso*, 2:319–38. Madrid: Gredos.

——. 1972. *"Lazarillo de Tormes" en la picaresca*. Barcelona: Ariel.

Lemon, Lee T., and Marion J. Reis, eds. and trans. 1965. *Russian Formalist Criticism: Four Essays*. Lincoln: University of Nebraska Press.

Lentricchia, Frank, and Thomas McLaughlin, eds. 1990. *Critical Terms for Literary Study.* Chicago: University of Chicago Press.

Levisi, Margarita. 1988. "Golden Age Autobiography: The Soldiers." In Spadaccini/Talens, 97–117.

Lewalski, Barbara Kiefer, ed. 1986. *Renaissance Genres: Essays on Theory, History, and Interpretation.* Cambridge: Harvard University Press.

Lida, Raimundo. 1972. "Pablos de Segovia y su agudeza." In *Homenaje a Joaquín Casalduero,* 285–98. Madrid: Gredos.

Lida de Malkiel, María Rosa. 1964. "Función del cuento popular en el *Lazarillo de Tormes.*" In *Actas del Primer Congreso Internacional de Hispanistas,* 349–59. Oxford: Dolphin.

Lomax, Derek. 1973. "On Re-reading the *Lazarillo de Tormes.*" In *Studia Iberica: Festschrift für Hans Flasche,* ed. Karl-Hermann Körner and Klaus Rühl, 371–81. Bern: Francke.

Lotman, Jurij M. 1979a. "The Origin of Plot in the Light of Typology." *Poetics Today: Theory and Analysis of Literature and Communication* (Tel Aviv) 1:161–84.

Lotman, Jurij M., and Escuela de Tartu. 1979b. *Semiótica de la cultura.* Madrid: Cátedra.

McGrady, Donald. 1968. *Mateo Alemán.* New York: Twayne.

Maitre, Doreen. 1983. *Literature and Possible Worlds.* London: Middlesex Polytechnic Press.

Maravall, José Antonio. 1975. *La cultura del barroco: Análisis de una estructura histórica.* Barcelona: Ariel.

——. 1976. "La aspiración social de 'medro' en la novela picaresca." *CH,* no. 312, 590–625.

——. 1977. "Relaciones de dependencia e integración social: Criados, graciosos y pícaros." *Ideologies and Literature* 1, no. 4: 3–32.

——. 1986. *La literatura picaresca desde la historia social (siglos XVI y XVII).* Madrid: Taurus.

Márquez-Villanueva, Francisco. 1975. *Personajes y temas del "Quijote."* Madrid: Taurus.

Martin, Henri-Jean. 1969. *Livre, pouvoirs et société à Paris au XVIIe siècle (1598–1701).* 2 vols. Geneva: Droz.

——. 1977. "Pour une histoire de la lecture." *Revue française d'histoire du livre* n.s. 16:583–610.

Martz, Linda. 1983. *Poverty and Welfare in Habsburg Spain.* Cambridge: Cambridge University Press.

May, Terence E. 1950. "Good and Evil in the *Buscón*: A Survey." *MLR* 45:319–35.

——. 1969. "A Narrative Conceit in *La vida del Buscón.*" *MLR* 44:327–33.

Miller, Stuart. 1967. *The Picaresque Novel.* Cleveland: Case Western Reserve University Press.

Molho, Maurice. 1972. *Introducción al pensamiento picaresco.* Salamanca: Anaya.

——. 1977. "Cinco lecciones sore el *Buscón.*" In *Semántica y poética*, 89–131. Barcelona: Crítica.

Moreno Báez, Enrique. 1948. *Lección y sentido del "Guzmán de Alfarache."* *RFE*, anejo 40.

Morris, C. B. 1965. *The Unity and Structure of Quevedo's "Buscón": "Desgracias encadenadas."* University of Hull Occasional Papers in Modern Languages.

Muecke, D. C. 1969a. *The Compass of Irony.* London: Methuen.

——. 1969b. *Irony and the Ironic.* Rev. ed. London: Methuen.

Nelson, William. 1973. *Fact or Fiction? The Dilemma of the Renaissance Storyteller.* Cambridge: Harvard University Press.

Norval, M. N. 1974. "Original Sin and the 'Conversion' in the *Guzmán de Alfarache*," *BHS* 51:346–64.

Oakley, Robert J. 1972. The Problematic Unity of *Guzmán de Alfarache.*" In *Hispanic Studies in Honour of Joseph Manson*, ed. Dorothy M. Atkinson and Anthony H. Clarke, 185–206. Oxford: Dolphin.

Ong, Walter J. 1975. "The Writer's Audience Is Always a Fiction." *PMLA* 90:9–22. Rpt. in *Interfaces of the Word: Studies in the Evolution of Consciousness and Culture*, 53–81. Ithaca: Cornell University Press, 1982.

——. 1982. *Orality and Literacy: The Technologizing of the Word.* London: Methuen.

O'Reilly, Terence P. 1986. "Discontinuity in *Lazarillo de Tormes*: The Problem of Tratado Five." *JHP* 10:141–49.

Pacheco-Ransanz, Arsenio. 1986. "Varia fortuna de la novela corta en el siglo XVII." *RCEH* 10:407–21.

Palomo, María del Pilar. 1976. *La novela cortesana (forma y estructura).* Barcelona: Planeta.

Parker, Alexander A. 1947. "The Psychology of the Picaro in *El Buscón.*" *MRL* 42:58–69.

——. 1967. *Literature and the Delinquent: The Picaresque Novel in Spain and Europe, 1599–1753.* Edinburgh: University of Edinburgh Press.

Parker, Patricia, and David Quint, eds. 1986. *Literary Theory/Renaissance Texts.* Baltimore: Johns Hopkins University Press.

Paulson, Ronald. 1967. *The Fictions of Satire.* Baltimore: Johns Hopkins University Press.

Pavel, Thomas G. 1975. "'Possible Worlds' in Literary Semantics." *JAAC* 34:165–76.

——. 1981. "Ontological Issues in Poetics: Speech Acts and Fictional Worlds." *JAAC* 40:167–78.

——. 1986. *Fictional Worlds.* Cambridge: Harvard University Press.

Perry, Ben Edwin. 1967. *The Ancient Romances.* Berkeley: University of California Press.

Peyton, Myron A. 1973. *Alonso Jerónimo de Salas Barbadillo.* New York: Twayne.

Pike, Ruth. 1966. *Enterprise and Adventure: The Genoese in Seville and the Opening of the New World*. Ithaca: Cornell University Press.

——. 1972. *Aristocrats and Traders: Sevillian Society in the Sixteenth Century*. Ithaca: Cornell University Press.

Plantinga, Alvin. 1974. *The Nature of Necessity*. Oxford: Clarendon.

Poggio Bracciolini, Giovanni Francesco. 1964. *De miseria humanae conditionis*. In *Opera omnia*, ed. Riccardo Fubini, vol. 1. Torino: Bottega di Erasmo.

Pollard, Arthur. 1970. *Satire*. London: Methuen.

Pope, Randolph. 1974. *La autobiografía española hasta Torres Villarroel*. Frankfurt: Peter Lang.

Pratt, Mary Louise. 1977. *Toward a Speech Act Theory of Literary Discourse*. Bloomington: Indiana University Press.

Prince, Gerald. 1982. *Narratology: The Form and Functioning of Narrative*. Janua Linguarum, Series Maior 108. Berlin: Mouton.

Pring-Mill, Robert, 1962. "Sententiousness in *Fuente Ovejuna*." *Tulane Drama Review* 7:5–37.

Propp, Vladimir. 1968. *Morphology of the Folktale*. 2d ed. Austin: University of Texas Press, for American Folklore Society.

Quinones, Ricardo J. 1972. *The Renaissance Discovery of Time*. Cambridge: Harvard University Press.

Quint, David. 1983. *Origin and Originality in Renaissance Literature: Versions of the Source*. New Haven: Yale University Press.

Reardon, Bryan P. 1969. "The Greek Novel." *Phoenix* 23:291–309.

——, ed. 1989. *Collected Ancient Greek Novels*. Berkeley: University of California Press.

Redondo, Agustín. 1977. "Del personaje de don Diego Coronel a una neuva interpretación de *El Buscón*." In *Actas del Quinto Congreso Internacional de Hispanistas*, 699–711. Bordeaux: Université de Bordeaux.

Reed, Helen H. 1984. *The Reader in the Picaresque Novel*. London: Tamesis.

Reed, Walter L. 1981. *An Exemplary History of the Novel: The Quixotic versus the Picaresque*. Chicago: University of Chicago Press.

Reiss, Timothy J. 1986. "Montaigne and the Subject of Polity." In Parker/Quint, 115–49.

Rico, Francisco, 1966. "Problemas del *Lazarillo*." *BRAE* 46:277–96.

——. 1970. *El pequeño mundo del hombre*. Madrid: Castalia.

——. 1984. *La novela picaresca y el punto de vista*. Rev. ed. Barcelona: Seix Barral, 1970. Published in English as *The Spanish Picaresque Novel and the Point of View*, trans. Charles Davis. Cambridge: Cambridge University Press, 1984.

Riffaterre, Michael, 1990. *Fictional Worlds*. Baltimore: Johns Hopkins University Press.

Riggan, William. 1981. *Picaros, Madmen, Naifs, and Clowns*. Norman: University of Oklahoma Press.

Riley, E.C. 1964. *Cervantes's Theory of the Novel*. Rev. ed. London: Oxford University Press.

——. 1976. "Cervantes and the Cynics." *BHS* 53:188–99.

Rodríguez-Luis, Julio. 1979. *"Pícaras*: The Modal Approach to the Picaresque." *CL* 31:32–46.

Rodríguez Matos, Carlos A. 1985. *El narrador pícaro: Guzmán de Alfarache*. Madison, Wis.: Hispanic Seminary of Medieval Studies.

Rodríguez Pérez, Osvaldo. 1983. *La novela picaresca como transformación textual*. Estudios filológicos, no. 11. Valdivia: Universidad Austral de Chile.

Rosenblatt, Louise. 1978. *The Reader, the Text, the Poem: The Transactional Theory of the Literary Work*. Carbondale: Southern Illinois University Press.

Rowland, David. 1586/1924. *The Pleasaunt Historie of Lazarillo de Tormes, Drawen out of Spanish by David Rowland of Anglesey*. Ed. J. E. V. Crofts. Oxford: Basil Blackwell.

Russell, Peter E. 1953. "English Seventeenth Century Interpretation of Spanish Literature." *Atlante* 1:65–77.

Sánchez y Escribano, F. 1951. *Cosas y casos de los albores del siglo XVII español*. New York: Hispanic Institute.

San Miguel, Angel. 1971. *Sentido y estructura del "Guzmán de Alfarache" de Mateo Alemán*. Madrid: Gredos.

——. 1974. *"Tercera parte del 'Guzmán de Alfarache':* La promesa de Alemán y su cumplimiento por el portugués Machado de Silva." *Iberoromania* 1:95–120.

Scholes, Robert, and Robert Kellogg. 1966. *The Nature of Narrative*. New York: Oxford University Press.

Schwartz-Lerner, Lía. 1989. "Mulier . . . milvinum genus: La construcción de personajes femeninos en la sátira y la ficción áureas." In *Homenaje al Professor Antonio Vilanova*, 2 vols., ed. María Cristina Carbonell and Adolfo Sotelo Vázquez, 1:629–47. Barcelona: Universidad de Barcelona, Departamento de Filología Española.

Scobie, Alexander. 1969. *Aspects of the Ancient Romance and Its Heritage*. Beitrage zur Klassischen Philologie, no. 30. Meisenheim am Glan: Hein.

Segni, Lotario dei (later Pope Innocent III). 1969. *On the Misery of the Human Condition*. Trans. Margaret M. Dietz. Ed. Donald R. Howard. Indianapolis: Bobbs-Merrill. Latin text, *De miseria humane conditionis*, ed. Michele Maccarrone. Lugano: Thesaurus Mundi, 1955.

Senabre, Ricardo. 1979. "El doctor Carlos García y la picaresca." In *Picaresca*, 631–46.

Serrano Poncela, Segundo. 1959. *"¿El buscón*—Parodia picaresca?" *Insula* 12, no. 154: 10–11. Rpt. in *Del Romancero a Machado*. Caracas: Facultad de Letras, 1962.

Seznec, Jean. 1961. *The Survival of the Ancient Gods*. New York: Harper Torchbooks.

Shipley, George A. 1982. "The Critic as Witness for the Prosecution: Making the Case against Lázaro de Tormes." *PMLA* 97:179–94.

———. 1983. "The Critic as Witness for the Prosecution: Resting the Case against Lázaro de Tormes." In *Creation and Recreation: Experiments in Literary Form in Early Modern Spain,* ed. Ronald E. Surtz and Nora Weinerth. Newark, Del.: Juan de le Cuesta.

———. 1986. "Lazarillo de Tormes Was Not a Hardworking, Clean-Living Water Carrier." In *Hispanic Studies in Honor of Alan D. Deyermond: A North American Tribute,* ed. John S. Miletich, 247–55. Madison, Wis.: Hispanic Seminary of Medieval Studies.

Sieber, Harry. 1968. "Apostrophes in the *Buscón*: An Approach to Quevedo's Narrative Technique." *MLN* 83:178–211.

———. 1977. *The Picaresque.* London: Methuen.

———. 1978. *Language and Society in "La Vida de Lazarillo de Tormes."* Baltimore: Johns Hopkins University Press.

Simonde de Sismondi, Jean-Charles-Léonard, 1813. *De la littérature du midi de l'Europe.* 4 vols. Paris: Crapelet, 1813.

Smith, Barbara Herrnstein. 1978. *On the Margins of Discourse.* Chicago: University of Chicago Press.

Smith, Hilary D. 1978. *Preaching in the Spanish Golden Age: A Study of Some Preachers of the Reign of Philip III.* Oxford: Oxford University Press.

Smith, Paul Julian. 1987. "The Rhetoric of Representation in Writers and Critics of Picaresque Narrative: *Lazarillo de Tormes, Guzmán de Alfarache, El Buscón*." *MLR* 82:88–108.

———. 1988. *Writing in the Margin: Spanish Literature of the Golden Age.* Oxford: Clarendon.

Sobejano, Gonzalo. 1967. "De la intención y valor del *Guzmán de Alfarache*." In *Forma literaria y sensibilidad social,* 9–66. Madrid: Gredos.

———. 1975. "El *coloquio de los perros* en la picaresca y otros apuntes." *HR* 43:25–41.

———. 1977. "De Alemán a Cervantes: Monólogo y diálogo." In *Homenaje al Profesor Muñoz Cortés.* Murcia, Universidad de Murcia.

Soons, C. Alan. 1961. "El paradigma y el carácter de *Guzmán de Alfararche*." *Hispanófila,* no. 12, 25–31.

———. 1976. *Haz y envés del cuento risible en el Siglo de Oro.* London: Tamesis.

———. 1978. *Alonso de Castillo Solórzano.* Boston: Twayne.

Souden, David. 1985. "Demographic Crisis and Europe in the 1590s." In Clark, 1985, 231–43.

Spacks, Patricia Meyer. 1976. *Imagining a Self: Autobiography and Novel in Eighteenth-Century England.* Cambridge: Harvard University Press.

Spaduccini, Nicholas, and Jenaro Talens, eds. 1988. *Autobiography in Early Modern Spain.* Minneapolis: Prisma Institute.

Spingarn, Joel. 1899. *A History of Literary Criticism in the Renaissance.* New York: Columbia University Press.

Spitzer, Leo. 1927. "Zur Kunst Quevedos in seinem *Buscón.*" *Archivum Romanicum* 11:511–80. Published in French as *L'Art de Quevedo dans le "Buscón."* Travaux de l'Institut d'Etudes Ibéro et Latinoaméricaines de l'Université de Strasbourg. Paris: Ediciones Hispano-Americanas, 1972.

Starobinski, Jean. 1980. "The Style of Autobiography." In *Autobiography: Essays Theoretical and Critical,* ed. James Olney, 115–22. Princeton: Princeton University Press.

Suleiman, Susan R., and Inge Crosman, eds. 1980. *The Reader in the Text.* Princeton: Princeton University Press.

Tarr, F. Courtney. 1927. "Literary and Artistic Unity in *Lazarillo de Tormes.*" *PMLA* 42:404–21.

Thompson, I. A. A. 1979. "The Purchase of Nobility in Castile, 1552–1700." *JEEH* 8:313–60.

Thompson, Stith. 1957. *Motif Index of Folk Literature.* Bloomington: Indiana University Press.

Ticknor, George. 1849. *The History of Spanish Literature.* New York: Harper.

Tierno Galván, Enrique. 1974. *Sobre la novela picaresca y otros escritos.* Madrid: Tecnos.

Todorov, Tzvetan. 1976. "The Origin of Genres." *NLH* 8:159–70.

Tompkins, Jane P., ed. 1980. *Reader-Response Criticism: From Formalism to Post-structuralism.* Baltimore: Johns Hopkins University Press.

Torrente Ballester, Gonzalo. 1979. "Lectura otoñal de *El diablo cojuelo.*" *BRAE* 59:433–40.

Trinkaus, Charles E. 1940. *Adversity's Noblemen: The Italian Humanists on Happiness.* New York: Columbia University Press.

Truman, R. W. 1968. "Parody and Irony in the Self-portrayal of Lázaro de Tormes." *MLR* 63:600–605.

——. 1969. "*Lázaro de Tormes* and the *homo novus* tradition." *MLR* 64:62–67.

Turner, Victor. 1969. *The Ritual Process: Structure and Antistructure.* Ithaca: Cornell University Press.

——. 1974. *Dramas, Fields, and Metaphors; Symbolic Action in Human Society.* Ithaca, N.Y.: Cornell University Press.

Waley, Pamela. 1956. "The Unity of the *Casamiento engañoso* and the *Coloquio de los perros.*" *BHS* 34:201–12.

Wardropper, Bruce W. 1961. "El trastorno de la moral en el *Lazarillo.*" *NRFH* 15:441–47.

——. 1977. "The Strange Case of Lázaro González Pérez." *MLN* 92:202–12.

Watt, Ian. 1962. *The Rise of the Novel.* Berkeley: University of California Press.

Selected Bibliography

Weimann, Robert. 1976. *Structure and Society in Literary History*. Charlottesville: University Press of Virginia.

Weinberg, Bernard. 1961. *A History of Literary Criticism in the Italian Renaissance*. Chicago: University of Chicago Press.

Weinstein, Arnold. 1981. *Fictions of the Self: 1550–1800*. Princeton: Princeton University Press.

Welles, Marcia. 1986. "The *Pícara*: Towards Female Autonomy, or the Vanity of Virtue." *KRQ* 33:63–70.

Whinnom, Keith. 1967. *Spanish Literary Historiography: Three Forms of Distortion*. An Inaugural Lecture delivered in the University of Exeter on 8 December 1967. Exeter: University of Exeter Press.

———. 1980. "The Problem of the Best Seller in Spanish Golden Age Literature." *BHS* 57:189–98.

White, Hayden. 1970. "Literary History: The Point of It All." *NLH* 2: 173–85.

———. 1978. *Tropics of Discourse*. Baltimore: Johns Hopkins University Press.

———. 1987. *The Content of the Form: Narrative Discourse and Historical Representation*. Baltimore: Johns Hopkins University Press.

Wicks, Ulrich. 1972. "Picaro, Picaresque: The Picaresque in Literary Scholarship." *Genre* 5:153–216.

———. 1974. "The Nature of Picaresque Narrative: A Modal Approach." *PMLA* 89:165–81.

———. 1978. "The Romance of the Picaresque." *Genre* 11:29–44.

Willis, Raymond, S. 1959. "Lazarillo and the Pardoner: The Artistic Necessity of the Fifth *Tractado*." *HR* 27:267–79.

Wiltrout, Ann. 1978. "Ginés de Pasamonte: The Pícaro and his Art." *AC* 17:11–17.

Woodward, L. J. 1965. "Author-Reader Relationship in the *Lazarillo de Tormes*." *Forum for Modern Language Studies* 1:43–53.

Yates, Frances A. 1966. *The Art of Memory*. London: Routledge.

Zahareas, Anthony. 1988. "The Historical Function of Picaresque Autobiographies: Toward a History of Social Offenders." In Spadaccini/Talens, 129–62.

Zimmermann, T. C. Price. 1971. "Confession and Autobiography in the Early Renaissance." in *Renaissance Studies in Honor of Hans Baron*, ed. Anthony Molho and John A. Tedeschi, 119–40. De Kalb: Northern Illinois University Press.

Index

Index

Bernanos, Georges, 135
Bernard de Morval, 151
Bernard of Clairvaux, 151–52, 192
Bernardino, Saint, 167
Bjornson, Richard, 131, 264, 265, 279, 281
Blanco Aguinaga, Carlos, 14, 56, 208–12, 293
Blecua, Alberto, 36
Bleiberg, Germán, 69, 138
Boccaccio, Giovanni, 31, 102, 119, 129
Bonaventure, Saint, 195
Booth, Wayne C., 204
Borges, Jorge Luis, 45
Bourland, Caroline B., 31
Bouwsma, William J., 124
Bradley, Raymond, 115
Brancaforte, Benito, 140, 180
Brecht, Bertolt, 135
Brooks, Peter, 116
Brown, Peter, 181

Cadiz, 207
Calderón, Rodrigo, 234
Calderón de la Barca, Pedro, 143, 173, 283
Camerino, José, 103, 304
Carr, E. H., 26
Casalduero, Joaquín, 219, 225
Casey, James, 119
Castelvetro, Ludovico, 18
Castiglione, Baldassare, 32, 104
Castillo Solórzano, Alonso de, 102, 103, 106, 107, 244–48, 259, 265, 285, 286, 297, 302; *La garduña de Sevilla*, 245–47, 293; *Las harpías en Madrid*, 248; *La niña de los embustes, Teresa de Manzanares*, 245, 250
Castro, Américo, 14, 59, 145, 159, 203, 211
Cavillac, Cécile, 74
Cavillac, Michel, 55, 56, 60, 62–63, 74, 75, 122, 133–38, 140, 142, 144, 145, 166, 178, 289, 304–5
Cervantes, Miguel de, 13, 65, 173, 203–31, 259; *El amante liberal*, 222; *El casamiento engañoso y coloquio de los perros*, 46, 212, 229–31, 291; *El celoso extremeño*, 75; *Don Quixote*, 14, 48, 63, 68, 95, 100, 119, 146, 164, 166, 171, 220, 229, 234–35, 253, 266, 292–93, 310; *La española inglesa*, 222; *La fuerza de la sangre*,

209; *La gitanilla*, 209, 222, 268; *La ilustre fregona*, 209, 241, 307; *Novelas ejemplares*, 100, 182; *Persiles y Sigismunda*, 72, 100, 102, 119, 229; *Rinconete y Cortadillo*, 100, 126, 212, 221–28, 268, 271; *El viaje del Parnaso*, 205–8
Céspedes y Meneses, Gonzalo de, 63, 101–2, 108–10, 119, 182, 259
Chandler, Frank W., 7, 25, 73, 125–26, 153, 258, 279
Charles V, Holy Roman emperor (Charles I, king of Spain), 127
Chartier, Roger, 272, 305–6
Chatman, Seymour, 204
Chaucer, Geoffrey, 119, 151
Chevalier, Maxime, 14n, 15, 30–32, 35–36, 50, 99, 165, 304
Cicero, 76, 174, 182
Clark, Peter, 119
Cockburn, Claud, 225
Cohen, Ralph, 19, 20
Colie, Rosalie, 22, 49, 63, 129
Colloquy, 274, 281, 288–89
Comedia de capa y espada (Cloak-and-sword drama), 100
Comedy, 129
Commedia dell'arte, 134
Confession, 166–68, 176–80, 231
Contreras, Jerónimo de, 94
Conversos, 149
Copernicus, 283
Coronel family, 75, 79, 157–59
Correas, Gonzalo, 31
Cortázar, Julio, 73
Counterreformation, 87, 135
Covarrubias, Sebastián de, 32
Croce, Benedetto, 17
Cros, Edmond, 33, 55, 60, 62, 73, 75, 132, 136, 138, 143, 144, 175, 191, 219
Culler, Johnathan, 16–17

Dante Alighieri, 151
Darnton, Robert, 312
Davis, Natalie Z., xi
Decorum, 16
Defoe, Daniel, 6
De Haan, Fonger, 6,
Della Porta, Giambattista, 129
Del Monte, Alberto, 258, 279
Delumeau, Jean, 171–72
De Man, Paul, 89
Demerson, George, 19

Index

Hardy, Thomas, 90
Heliodorus, 65
Hemingway, Ernest, 49, 291
Hernadi, Paul, 18
Herrero, Javier, 39, 131–32
Herrero García, Miguel, 57
Herrick, Marvin T., 98
Hirsch, E. D., 4
History, 124
Hitchcock, Richard, 43
Homer, 52, 63, 189; *Odyssey*, 65–66, 92, 140, 263
Honor/*honra*, 33, 119–20, 172–73, 245, 289, 312
Horace, 76, 98, 147, 197
Hugh of St. Victor, 191
Hume, David, 37

Ife, Barry, 110, 176, 180
Isabella, queen of Castile, 158, 159
Isaiah, 167
Iser, Wolfgang, 38, 41, 116, 177
Interiority, 162–200

James, Henry, 90, 204
Jameson, Fredric, 28
Jauralde Pou, Pablo, 248
Jauss, Hans Robert, 4, 10, 16, 27, 49, 167
Jeremiah, 50
Jests, 83, 130, 246–48
Job, 150
Johnson, Barbara, 236
Johnson, Carroll B., 158, 180, 181, 184
Jones, Harold, 41
Jones, Royston O., 243
Juan Manuel, 119, 266

Koestler, Arthur, 135
Kristeller, Paul O., 150
Krömer, Wolfgang, 126, 127
Kuhn, Thomas S., 27

Ladurie, Emmanuel Le Roy, 306
Laguna, Andrés, 31, 275, 288
Lakoff, George, 176
Language, 219–21, 224–28
Lazarillo de Tormes, 5–15, 25, 29–46, 48–57, 65, 74, 119, 120, 125–34, 169–75, 188, 212, 219, 240–41, 266, 278, 295–300, 313
Lázaro Carreter, Fernando, x, 9–10, 15, 30, 48, 50, 72–75, 78, 79, 82, 86

Lea, Henry C., 168, 190
León, Fray Luis de, 140, 147, 153
León, Padre Pedro de, 168
Le Sage, Alain René, 258
Levisi, Margarita, 94
Lewalski, Barbara, 64
Lida, Raimundo, 73, 79, 86
Liñán y Verdugo, Antonio: *Guía y avisos*, 274–78
Literatura marginada (*pliegos de cordel, poesía germanesca, romances de ciegos*, etc.), 78, 85, 88, 98, 302–3, 307, 313
Locke, John, 37
Lomax, Derek, 128
López de Ubeda, Francisco: *La pícara Justina*, 13, 47, 74, 95, 106, 108, 198, 205, 232–37, 265, 280, 296
López de Vega, Antonio, 129
López Pinciano, 32, 63, 128–29, 187–89, 288
Lorenzo Palmireno, Juan, 31
Lotman, Jurij, 67
Louis XIII, king of France, 273
Lovejoy, Arthur O., 152
Low life, 15, 85–87, 127, 291–314
Lozana andaluza (Francisco Delicado), 234
Lubbock, Percy, 204
Lucas Hidalgo, Gaspar, 31, 103, 288
Lucian, 281
Luckmann, Thomas, 187, 250
Lugo y Dávila, Francisco, 103, 106
Luján de Sayavedra, Mateo [pseud.]. *See* Martí, Juan
Luna, Juan de, 265

Mabbe, James, 57, 63
Machado de Silva, Félix: *Tercera parte de Guzmán de Alfarache*, 69–72
Madrid, 186, 280–81
Maitre, Doreen, 116
Mal Lara, Juan de, 31
Malraux, André, 135
Map, Walter, 141
Maravall, José Antonio, 244, 289, 295, 300–302, 307
Márquez-Villanueva, Francisco, 296
Martí, Juan: *Segunda parte de Guzmán de Alfarache*, 13, 47, 61, 74, 82, 85, 108, 121, 252–58, 265
Martin, Henri-Jean, 182, 191
Martínez de Toledo, Alfonso (Arcipreste de Talavera), 243
Martz, Linda, 131, 139, 143

334

Index

Spanish Picaresque Fiction

A New Literary History

PETER N. DUNN

"A very important book, gracefully and clearly written. Dunn is one Hispanist whose every published word I have found it rewarding to read, and with this book he joins the finest thinkers in the field. Contextualizing the picaresque within the larger literary horizons of the period, Dunn has produced a fascinating case study of the way in which genres come into being and flourish within a culture, and of the inevitable tension between critics in search of orderly patterns and writers in search of expressive possibilities. The chapter on rogue females is the best I know on the subject."

—Mary M. Gaylord, Harvard University

"Spanish picaresque fiction has been studied frequently in the twentieth century as a major stage in the evolution of the modern European novel, but never before by a scholar so thoroughly familiar with all the primary texts. Dunn's clarity of mind, straightforward style, and firm philosophical grasp on literature as a whole allows him to explain the Spanish picaresque in a more broadly humanistic way than ever before."

—Elias L. Rivers, SUNY at Stony Brook

Exiled to the margins of society and surviving by his wits in the course of his wanderings, the pícaro marks a sharp contrast to the high-born characters on whom previous Spanish literature had focused. In this illuminating book, Peter N. Dunn offers a fresh view of the gam-

Library of Congress Cataloging-in-Publication Data

Dunn, Peter N.
    Spanish picaresque fiction : a new literary history / Peter N. Dunn.
        p.   cm.
    Includes bibliographical references and index.
    ISBN 0-8014-2800-9
    1. Picaresque literature, Spanish—History and criticism.   2. Spanish
fiction—Classical period, 1500–1700—History and criticism.   I. Title.
PQ6147.P5D82   1993
863.009'351—dc20   92-36854